The Heydays Of
Selly Oak Park
1896–1911

*For my Children and Grandchildren,
and to the memory of my Great Grandfather,
the Park Keeper, Josiah Thomas Horton.*

The Heydays Of
Selly Oak Park
1896–1911

Compiled by
KEN PUGH

HiP
HISTORY INTO PRINT

First published by
History Into Print, 56 Alcester Road,
Studley, Warwickshire B80 7LG in 2010
www.history-into-print.com

© Ken Pugh 2010

All rights reserved.

ISBN: 978-1-85858-336-5

The moral right of the author has been asserted.

A Cataloguing in Publication Record
for this title is available from the British Library.

Typeset in New Baskerville
Printed in Great Britain by
Information Press Ltd.

CONTENTS

	Introduction	vi
	Selly Oak Park – A Timeline Summary	viii
1.	Before Selly Oak Park	1
2.	Preparations for Selly Oak Park	8
3.	Selly Oak Park – the Detail	17
4.	1899	18
5.	1900	73
6.	1901	97
7.	1902	107
8.	1903	121
9.	1904	132
10.	1905	140
11.	1906	147
12.	1907	156
13.	1908	168
14.	1909	185
15.	1910	194
16.	1911	205
17.	Other Commentaries & References	230
18.	The Oak Tree of Selly Oak memorialised in Selly Oak Park	233
	Appendix I – The Gibbins Family, Donors of Selly Oak Park	235
	Appendix II – The Park Keeper, Josiah Thomas Horton (1863-1940)	246

INTRODUCTION

My great-grandfather, Josiah Thomas Horton (who died in 1940 before I was born), was the first Park Keeper at Selly Oak Park, and he and his family (including my grandfather when he was in his youth) lived in the Park Lodge in Gibbins Road, Selly Oak from the Park's opening in 1899 until he retired in about 1929.

My mother and grandfather often spoke of "The Park", but in my early years I took little notice, and my curiosity was not stirred again until I embarked on my family history quest in 2001. Indeed, whilst I knew where the Park was, and had travelled along Harborne Lane frequently, I had never ventured into Gibbins Road. My first visit to the Park was not made until 2007!

As I gathered information about my great-grandfather I was intrigued by his role as Park Keeper. I wanted to know more about the Park, but initially found information quite scant – especially as I was living in Aberdeen and did not have ready access to local records. Following our relocation to the West Midlands in 2008 I began to search with more vigour. This volume records my findings about Selly Oak Park, and is offered to any who may be interested.

Though not immediately accessible, the number of accounts of different events at, and aspects of, the Park, at different times, has astounded me. This book deals with the the Park in its heydays up until 1911 whilst it was in the hands of Kings Norton and Northfield Urban District Council. At the end of 1911 the Park passed into the care of Birmingham City Council – but that is another story.

Selly Oak Park: Early 1900s. Nb. Near centre – a figure sitting on a bench (Photograph reproduced from family records).

Much of the information presented is material in the public domain, albeit not in normally published form, and it is merely reproduced here verbatim to bring relevant items into one place, sequentially, to provide a coherent history, and in passing throw some light on life in the Selly Oak community around 1900. Where possible I have acknowledged all sources of material. I believe this to be an accurate account, but apologise for any inadvertent errors, omissions or misrepresentations, and for any offence that may be caused by the contents.

I have produced a timeline summary of the history of the park as the first few pages of this book, with subsequent sections providing the underlying detail culled from various sources.

My search has been greatly facilitated by:

- the staff of the Archive and Heritage Section of the Birmingham Central Library, who have been very patient in response to my frequent requests and enquiries; and given permission to use information from their records;
- several others, including Martin Robson Riley, Mrs Beatrice Painter, and the late James Hyland, who have shared their research and information with me;
- the Library of Haverford College, Pennsylvania, US, for permission to use photographs from the Jones-Cadbury Collection in their Quaker Collection;
- the "Friends of Selly Oak Park", for their support and enthusiasm;
- my wife, Susan, who understands the importance of anyone "playing in the Park"; and let me do so.

To them all I am very grateful. Thank you.

Finally I hope, reader, that you will spend some time and enjoy your walk in this literary Park as much as I have mine.

Ken Pugh, Solihull, January 2010

Selly Oak Park: August 2007 (Ken Pugh).

SELLY OAK PARK – A TIMELINE SUMMARY

This section contains a summary of key events at the Park. Subsequent sections contain the more extensive detail upon which it is founded – information from Council minutes, newspaper reports, etc.

1896
Selly Oak, part of the parish of Northfield, was becoming a progressively more populated area, as industry from Birmingham migrated to find room for massive expansion. Members of the Parish Council began to recognise a need for open spaces for recreational purposes and proposals were made to satisfy that need.

1898
Members of the Gibbins family – Mrs Emma Joel Gibbins (nee Cadbury) with her four sons, William, Thomas (who was Chairman of the Kings Norton and Northfield Urban District Council at the time), John and Benjamin, of 10 Carpenter Road[1], Edgbaston, who were the proprietors of the Birmingham Battery & Metal Company, a company that had expanded from Digbeth to the site which is now the Battery Retail Park in Selly Oak – espoused the pursuit of open spaces for the recreation of their workers and others in the Selly Oak neighbourhood. They prepared 11 acres, 2 roods, 5 perches of land, having a frontage of 271 yards in Old Lane, Selly Oak as a park. The area allocated was formerly part of Weoley Park Farm. The plot was fenced and flower borders, with trees incorporated, were created around the perimeter; walkways were also laid out. Planning permission for a Park Keeper's lodge, closets and a shelter was sought and granted, and the buildings duly erected. Josiah Thomas Horton, gardener, of Tennal Road, Harborne, transferred from Queen's Park, Harborne (a new park recently opened by the Birmingham City Council), to assist with the laying-out of the new park.

1899
The prepared land was gifted formally to the recently formed Kings Norton & Northfield Urban District Council by the Gibbins family. Amongst the conditions attached to the gift were – that no intoxicating liquor should be sold or used in the park; it should not be open for playing games on Sundays; and its gates

---

[1] The house at this location has been removed to make way for more modern expansion / development; but adjacent properties still retain their historical character and give some idea of what the Gibbins' home was like.

should not be closed for more than two consecutive days for the holding of any event, such as a flower show, for which it may be let, freely or with charge, as the Council may determine. There was a motion to name the park "Gibbins Park", but the donors requested that its name not include theirs. Consequently the land was designated "Selly Oak Park"[2], and Old Lane was renamed Gibbins Road[3] in recognition of the gift.

Early in the year, after competition, Josiah Thomas Horton was appointed to the post of Park Keeper / Superintendent[4], with coat and cap provided, and residence at the Lodge. He was appointed on a month's notice; his salary was 24/- per week.

The formal opening of the Park occurred at 3pm on Easter Monday, 3rd April, when a large crowd witnessed the 88 year old Mrs Gibbins open the gates with a silver key and listened to speeches by the donors and local dignitaries, all of which was reported in the local press. The donors were presented with a resolution of the District Council, engrossed on vellum, recording their gratitude. Entertainments followed the opening ceremony.

The Park was overseen and administered by the Baths, Parks and Cemeteries Committee of the Kings Norton and Northfield Urban District Council. They set about drafting bye laws and insuring the buildings in the park. Policing arrangements were made, though for legal reasons it had not been possible to swear in the Park Keeper as a Special Constable as the Committee wished, instead the local Watch Committee provided the necessary cover. Further developments and provisions were made; the drainage of the land was attended to, and a set of swings – one for boys, and another for girls – and gymnastic equipment was purchased and erected.

There was early demand for use of the park by various organisations. Five major users in this first year were:

i) the (Oddfellows and Foresters) Amalgamated Juvenile Fete Committee for an event on 3rd June;
ii) the annual Selly Oak and Bournbrook Children's Fete on 3rd July – an event which had been held in the district since the Parish church had been dedicated 35 years earlier, and would be held in the park for many years;
iii) the annual Selly Oak Horticultural Show on 5th August;
iv) the Order of Rechabites for an unspecified event on 19th August; and
v) a special event, with sports, on 26th August, staged by and for the Selly Oak Victoria Brass Band who had given a programme of music on Wednesday evenings during June, July and August – and who would be another regular user of the park in subsequent years.

---

[2] There is a district in Birmingham adjacent to Selly Oak which is called Selly Park. Care has to be taken not to confuse Selly Oak Park, i.e. the park in Selly Oak, with the district of Selly Park!
[3] According to a report in the South Birmingham Chronicle of an Urban District Council meeting, street name plates were not adopted in the District until 1905.
[4] The title of Superintendent was used more as his duties increased and he was called into a supervisory and reporting role.

According to the extensive and detailed press reports all the events, except one, were very successful and well subscribed, often thousands attending. The Selly Oak Horticultural Show, usually very popular and successful, "reached the lowest water mark" this year. A post mortem on the event, in committee and in the press, ascribed the Show's lack of success to the absence of a beer tent! A beer tent had not been allowed under the terms of use of the park – in accordance with the conditions of its gift by the Gibbins family. The contention was so bitter that the show did not return to the park for several years.

This was not the only bone of contention. Soon after the first bookings of the Park were made, the Council agreed operational conditions upon which the Park could be used by the different organisations. There was an upswell of opinion – again expressed in the various organising committees and the press – that the Council were being too draconian in demanding that the secretary of the organisation using the Park be responsible personally for any damage done during use and that he agree to repay the full cost of repair; and in giving the Surveyor and Park Keeper "absolute power and control in all respects in the matter". It appears that the conditions were eventually upheld, at least in spirit, if not letter.

So it was a very eventful first year in the life of the park. It was the Urban District Council's first park; and, whilst they were on a learning curve, it became a model and base for their subsequent parks and recreation grounds.

1900

The bye-laws were finally agreed and displayed publicly. A 14' x 6' propagating frame was requested and provided to generate and maintain plant stocks. The area around the new swings and the main drive was asphalted. Seasonal assistance was provided for the Park Keeper, and some of the trees were relocated and more added.

The Selly Oak Victoria Brass Band gave another series of Wednesday evening concerts during June, July and August, and held their own fete and sports day on 25th August. The annual Children's Fete was held on 30th July; it was reported to be the largest held up to that time, close on 2,500 children being entertained to tea. A minor accident was reported, when on 11th July a girl was struck on the face by a swing and knocked down. A similar accident had occurred on Whit Monday, a day on which the Park Keeper estimated between 10,000 and 12,000 people (i.e. half the population of the district) had used the park.

1901

More asphalting was undertaken, this time the road to the shelter. Action had to be taken to prevent people cutting turf from the flower borders for their caged birds, and boys raiding bird's nests. In the autumn the Committee visited the park and decided that the outside woodwork should be painted. The Park Keeper, who early in the year had been provided with a "proper uniform", was granted 8 days leave in the autumn, and nearer the end of the year his duties were extended to attend to the trees in the village, for which he was given temporary assistance. A glacier stone found in Frederick Road during the construction of part of the Birmingham Water Scheme was placed in the park.

Selly Oak Victoria Brass Band gave another series of concerts during the period mid May to August, this year on either Wednesday or Saturday evenings, but there is no reference to their annual fete and sports day in the park. Postponed by one day because of heavy rain, the annual Children's Fete was held on Tuesday 27th August – they catered for 3,200 children!

1902

The outside painting identified at the end of the last year was completed, as was the asphalting. It was proposed to purchase a span roof greenhouse for the park.

Undoubtedly the great event of the year in the Park was the festivities (including a bonfire) on 26th June to mark the Coronation of King Edward VII. The (Foresters and Oddfellows) Juvenile Fete was held on 23rd August. I assume the Selly Oak Victoria Brass Band delivered its usual summer programme of music. Whilst no report of this has been found, there was a request from the band for a contribution towards music, to which the Baths, Parks, and Cemeteries Committee was not able to accede. There is also a reference to a request for permission to be granted for the sale of refreshments on a Wednesday evening – presumably to coincide with the band concerts. The request was granted to the applicant provided the Park Keeper was unable to provide the service; it transpired that he was able to provide the refreshments.

1903

Five years after the park was opened, this was a busy year of maintenance. There were repairs to the Lodge, including painting, papering and whitewashing; the roof of the Lodge and Shelter were repaired; tree guards and swings were varnished; the iron fencing was painted; the footway along the park frontage was widened and the fence raised to allow asphalting. There was a proposal to install a gas supply to the Lodge. Trees up the centre drive of the park which were not flourishing were removed and new ones of a more hardy variety were substituted. The Park Keeper was supplied with a new uniform and cap.

The annual Selly Oak and Bournbrook Children's Fete, which for the first time included a musical competition, was held on Tuesday 28th July, the booked day before having been rained off. The Selly Oak Victoria Brass Band again gave their weekly concerts, and held their annual sports in the Park on a fine 29th August when between 700 and 800 people attended. Finally it was reported that visitors to the park during the summer had been more numerous than in previous years, more especially on Wednesday evenings when the weekly concerts given by the band took place. The press reported: "Selly Oak Park is becoming more popular than it was. As the village expands there will be no dearth of visitors to the park, but at present its patronage is checked by the distance that has to be travelled to get to it".

1904
Maintenance continued. Following an inspection by the Committee, there was a large programme of painting – the iron fence fronting the Park, the seats, the shelter, the ironwork of the swings and gymnastic equipment all receiving attention. The park staff was instructed to paint the tree guards. The overhanging eaves of the Shelter roof were repaired. Sand was obtained for the floor of the swings. Shrubs in the borders were thinned out and replanted, with the excess (we subsequently learn that it was 270 plants) being sent for use at Lodge Hill Cemetery; additional labour (2 men) being provided for this task. Three double back seats were ordered for the shelter. Mr. William Gibbins provided 18 lime and 18 elm trees which were planted in place of horse chestnuts up the centre drive of the park. Consideration was given to the provision of cricket pitches and a bowling green. The Park Keeper's wages were increased to 27/- per week, and his assistant's wages were reviewed.

The Church Lads' Brigade was granted permission to drill once or twice a week in the park. The Victoria Brass Band gave its usual programme of music during June, July and August. The Selly Oak and Bournbrook Children's Fete, now called the Festival and under a new arranging committee, was again rained off but then held successfully the next day, on Thursday, 1st September, with the associated sports being held on the following Saturday afternoon. Approx 3,500 (one report stated 3,400, another 3,600) children were looked after by 200 helpers. The engine attached to a roundabout at the Festival damaged the asphalt drive, but the drive was soon repaired.

1905
The Lodge was painted; there were alterations to the shelter and the double back seats arrived and were installed. The plans for a bowling green were ditched – it would have to wait another 6 years. Surplus shrubs and trees were removed to other recreation grounds. A cricket pitch – only to be used by children of school age – came into use in the middle of the year. Later in the year, football for those less than 14 years old was allowed in the park; and boys of the Selly Oak School were allowed to play football in the park on Saturday mornings under the supervision of the Park Keeper. The Park Keeper was provided with new work wear.

There were the usual uses of the park – the Victoria Brass Band held its summer concerts; and the Selly Oak and Bournbrook Children's Festival, with 3,600 attending, was held on Wednesday, 26th August. The Band had asked for assistance with their expenses; the Council were unable to accede to their request, but allowed pledges of voluntary contributions to be received at the entrance to the park.

(Mrs. Emma Joel Gibbins, aged 94 years, died on 26th April 1905)

1906
Early in the year the park was reported to be in very good order. The trees in Northfield were formally declared a responsibility of the Park Keeper, who was

also being more frequently referred to as the Superintendent. Several proposals were tabled: i) the erection of a 25' x 12' greenhouse (to provide for 4,000 – 5,000 plants) and potting shed; ii) standards and wire for the protection of beds; iii) bulbs; and iv) the planting of trees for the protection of the shelter from wind and rain. A gas supply was laid to the Lodge, some internal cleaning and redecoration was approved, and a proposal to enlarge the pantry was considered. An application for increased wages for the Park Keeper's assistant came under review. In the autumn the flower beds were reported to be "looking exceedingly well".

There were the usual uses of the park. The Selly Oak and Bournbrook Children's festival was held in glorious weather on 18th July; it was bigger than ever (4,000 attending) and declared the most successful to date; the Park Keeper and his assistants were later singled out and rewarded for their work. The following Wednesday evening, during one of the weekly Victoria Brass Band concerts, the Raddle Barn maypole dancers, who had performed impressively at the Children's festival, gave a repeat performance to the delight of everyone. On 1st September the Royal Staffordshire Blues Band gave afternoon and evening performances to great acclaim; the event was organised by the Progressive Association Education Committee with public subscriptions gathered by the chairman of the Baths and Parks Committee who was not wearing his committee hat for this project which had been initiated earlier in the year.

1907
The enlargement of the pantry in the Lodge became a reality. Three cricket pitches were allocated for the various schools belonging to the Selly Oak Wesleyan Sunday School. A sub-committee visited the park with a view to providing tennis courts in the park. Meanwhile the Park Keeper's remit was slowly expanding – he had been involved in planting at Bournbrook and Muntz Recreation Grounds and various libraries in the district, and was instructed to plant a privet hedge at Northfield Library. The Superintendent / Park Keeper laid proposals regarding staffing, and their remuneration, for the various parks and recreation grounds before the Committee, and after Committee review in conjunction with him a scheme for the rearrangement of staff was prepared. Staffing numbers were considered sufficient for the winter months but would need to be reviewed the following summer.

The Selly Oak and Bournbrook Children's Festival was held on Wednesday, 17th July, again 4,000 children attending a very successful event. After the 1899 fiasco, the Selly Oak Horticultural Society had held its annual show elsewhere, often finding itself in competition with the Bournbrook Society. As time passed there were suggestions for an amalgamation which finally came about in 1907 with an application, which was granted, for the use of the park by the Selly Oak, Bournbrook and District Horticultural Society for their annual exhibition on Saturday, 27th July. It turned out to be blighted by inclement weather. Several applications from Pierrot troupes to give entertainments in the parks were received and granted (at their own expense).

1908
The big development in the park during 1908 was the provision of a bandstand. It was eventually supplied and fixed by the St. Pancras Iron Works Co. Ltd., London for £94 6s. 8d., on a concrete base that was constructed departmentally for £20. The Committee agreed that tennis courts should be prepared. A 22" lawn mower was purchased from Parker, Winder and Achurch, Ltd for £7 17s. 3d., and old machines were repaired. There is a record that a Mr. John Bowen started work at the Park as a labourer in July.

After newspaper advertisements inviting offers from bands and concert parties to play in the various parks, arrangements were made by the Urban District Council for entertainments to be given on each Saturday evening during July, and on several of them in August, and these were advertised by poster and newspaper advertisements. It was reported later in the year that 23 entertainments had been given in the various parks and recreation grounds of the District Council during July, August and September, 14 of them by bands who had been paid £1 per band. On 15th July the annual Selly Oak and Bournbrook Children's Festival was held; the Selly Oak Victoria Brass Band, accompanied by the Harborne Industrial Boys' Band, played its usual part. The seventh annual charity sports in aid of the Selly Oak and Bournbrook District Nurses Fund were held in the park on 18th July; an impressive feature of this was a competition in which eight local fire brigades competed for cups and medals.

(Mr. Thomas Gibbins died on 23rd May 1908.)

1909
The 1907 proposals were realised when two tennis courts were opened in the spring – their use was charged at eight pence per hour per court. A peacock was gifted to the park by Mr. C. Cartwright of Chapel Lane, Selly Oak.

Once more the Parks Committee advertised for voluntary offers from bands and concert parties to give entertainments in the parks, and with the responses they organised a summer programme. The band members were paid one shilling and six pence and the band master five shillings per performance – maximum of 25 band members. Entertaining groups / bands could take the hire money for seats around the bandstand when performances were given, and they were allowed to make collections to defray their own expenses. During the year Selly Oak Park hosted 11 band performances, and 7 other entertainments (– only half the number that were held in the new King's Heath Park which was in its ascendancy). The annual Selly Oak and Bournbrook Children's Festival (attendance now up to 5,000) was another outstanding success on 14th July. Three days later (17th July) there was another children's party in the park, this time organised by the Selly Oak and Bournbrook branch of the Ten Acres and Stirchley Co-operative Society, with about 1,000 children attending. At the end of September the annual charity sports in aid of the Selly Oak and Bournbrook District Nurses' Fund was held in the Park, the fire brigade competition again being the principal feature. Comment was made in the autumn that the measure of the appreciation of the local people for their park was evident in the extensive use being made of it. Conscious of this the local authority allocated additional funds for the Park, and in so doing also found work there for the unemployed.

1910

An iron fence enclosure, 3' 6" high, was constructed around the bandstand and initially 8 dozen chairs were provided; another 8 dozen were purchased later in the year. Back in 1906 there had been a proposal to plant trees to protect the shelter from wind and rain, but now a wind screen was specified, planned and constructed. The opportunity was taken to include the Lodge in the tender for painting the new wind screen. It was agreed to provide swings, a "giant stride" and a see-saw for the park. In view of the number of parks and recreation grounds under the supervision of the Park Keeper, he was provided with a cycle ("costing no more than £10") to enable him to move between, and supervise, them.

As last year, press notices were placed seeking offers from bands and concert parties to play in the Park. During the year Selly Oak Park hosted 10 band performances, and 15 other entertainments – running third to the number at the newer King's Heath and Cotteridge Parks. There was also a press notice inviting offers from refreshment caterers and others for the right to sell refreshments in the Park. The Ten Acres and Stirchley Co-operative Society used the park for a Children's summer party on 16th July when about 1200 children participated. After a stuttering start with the committee debating "To be or not to be", the annual Selly Oak and Bournbrook Children's Festival was not organised this year.

1911

The construction of a bowling green was approved. Permission was granted for adults to play cricket and football in the park from the time of opening until 8.30 am. The Park Keeper / Superintendent's salary was increased to take account of the fact that several of the other parks and recreation grounds in the District were under his control, as well as the grounds at several libraries, and trees in certain of the streets. The increase was from 28 to 30 shillings per week then rising by annual increments of one shilling per week to 32 shillings per week.

Press notices were placed seeking offers from bands and concert parties to play in the Park. Permission was given for; i) the concluding band concert and sports day associated with the Shopping Week Festival which was held on Wednesday, 17th May, several thousand people congregating to see the various events and enjoy an evening in the Park; ii) the Selly Oak and Bournbrook Children's Festival to be held on Coronation Day in June; and iii) the Ten Acres and Stirchley Co-operative Society's children's party on a Saturday in July. A serious accident occurred during the Coronation Day festivities; a young member of the Church Lads' Brigade was badly injured when firing a royal salute in the park, and his hand had to be amputated. There was considerable concern for the wellbeing of the boy and a major fund-raising effort, sponsored by the local press, was made on his behalf with contributions arriving from many quarters including one from

HM, The Queen. (As a result of the fund, the lad was eventually apprenticed in photography, and then set up in his own business.)

In November 1911 the Kings Norton and Northfield Urban District Council ceased to exist, and under the terms of the Birmingham Extension Order 1911 the district and all its facilities was transferred to the jurisdiction and care of the Birmingham City Council. The Birmingham News, in its 11 November edition, observed:

> The urban district of Kings Norton and Northfield, which ceased to exist at midnight on Wednesday, has a worthy record in the sphere of local government activities. ....
>
> The provision of parks, baths and washhouses next became a burning question, but this took far longer to settle. A magnificent impulse was given to the movement, however, by private generosity, the Gibbins family making a gift to the community of a fine park at Selly Park (sic). ....
>
> So far as the District Council was concerned a period of remarkable activity was ushered in about seven ago and since then parks and open spaces and allotments have been provided in all directions, until today there is no district around Birmingham and probably few in the country better furnished in this respect than Kings Norton and Northfield. ....

And so ended the heydays of Selly Oak Park when it had been in the vanguard.

Chapter 1

BEFORE SELLY OAK PARK

According to 1885 and 1890 Maps of Staffordshire (http://www.old-maps.co.uk/IndexMapPage2.aspx) the area subsequently occupied by Selly Oak Park seems to have been part of Weoley Park Farm.

Prior to his removal to Ceredigion, Martin Robson Riley lived in Lepid Grove adjacent to Selly Oak Park. Martin has researched the area of Weoley Park Farm in great detail and has kindly written the following very well referenced piece for me:

A Brief History of Weoley Park Farm – by Martin Robson Riley

The area that became Selly Oak Park was originally part of the agricultural land associated with Weoley Park Farm, the Farmhouse of which formerly stood on what is now the site of Lepid Grove, off Corisande Road. The name Weoley Park itself refers to the ancient medieval deer park, which at one time might possibly have stretched from today's Harborne Lane as far west as Shenley Lane, and was bounded by the Bourn Brook on its northern edge and the route of the Bristol Road to the south[5]. Although the parkland appears to have been largely turned over to farming by the 17th century, the earliest reference so far discovered to Weoley Park Farm itself relates to a ground plan for the Farmhouse dating from 1734[6]. At this point the Farm seems to have been called Lodge Farm, a name obviously connected with nearby Lodge Hill, the site of the modern cemetery and the land for which also once formed part of the Farm's estate.

In the early 19th century the Jervoise family, who were then Lords of the Manor of Northfield and Weoley, were forced to auction off much of their holding of manorial land after a case at the Court of Chancery in London[7]. Eventually, in 1824, Joseph Weatherby Phipson bought Lodge Farm, together with other property and land. A few years later, however, Phipson was declared bankrupt, and the Farm and its land, as well as the manorial title, were acquired by Joseph Frederick Ledsam of Chad Hill, Edgbaston, in 1835[8]. It is important to note here that the Ledsam family's right to the title of Lord of the Manor of Northfield and

---

[5] See conjectural map showing possible extent of Weoley Park in R. P. Hastings, et al., *Discovering Northfield*, Northfield Society Occasional Paper No. 18 (2nd ed. 1987), p. 4.
[6] 'Ground plan of Lodge farm house at Weoley Park', Hampshire Record Office, ref. 44M69/P4/4.
[7] Several advertisements appeared in the *Times* newspaper for three property sales which took place on 18-19 September 1820, 27 June 1821 and 12 August 1824, all of which included Lodge Farm.
[8] "May 12 [1835], Bought Northfield Manor and Estates for £27,000 and 16th Weoley Castle for £9,000 inclusive of Timber, Railway etc.", 'The Diary of Joseph Frederick Ledsam' (1860), p. 15.

Weoley, as well as ownership of much of the old manorial land, only begins with Joseph Frederick and not with a Daniel Ledsam (who may well have been his uncle), nor with the oft-quoted but incorrect date of 1809[9].

Shortly after acquiring the Farm, J. F. Ledsam appears to have changed its name from Lodge Farm to Weoley Park Farm, a name it retained in one form or another from then until its demolition in 1959. As well as being known as Lodge Farm or Weoley Park Farm, at times the property was often simply called 'Weoley Park' or even 'Park Farm', though later it also had the street address of 64 Gibbins Road and, later still, of 208 Corisande Road. Some maps occasionally incorrectly show it as 'Selly Park' or 'Selley Park', as on a map of 1834[10]. In the early 20th century a Selly Park Farm did stand near the junction of Weoley Park Road and Shenley Fields Road, and indeed this same building is now number 98 Weoley Park Road, but this is not the farm marked on these maps, which was definitely Weoley Park Farm.

One of the earliest known tenants of Lodge Farm was Charles Carpenter, who was farming there in 1824 and whose lease had begun in 1805[11]. After buying the Farm in 1835 J. F. Ledsam let it out to a Charles William Firchild, who is recorded as living there in the 1841 census[12]. Firchild, however, appears to have got into debt, and his tenancy was taken over by Messrs Waddell and Bretherton in 1842[13]. Interestingly, Waddell and Bretherton are for some reason listed as the occupiers in the Tithe Apportionment, which was supposedly compiled a few years earlier in 1838[14]. By 1851 the tenant of the Farm was Bartholomew Bretherton[15]; and later a William Randel was farming there from around 1878 until the mid 1880s. In 1890 James Goddington Ledsam, who was the landowner and seems to have acted as Lord of the Manor of Northfield and

---

[9] The erroneous date of 1809 which has been unfortunately frequently quoted and re-quoted in relation to the Ledsam's purchase of the Lordship of the Manor of Northfield and Weoley, as well as Daniel Ledsam's supposed involvement in this, appears to derive from a mistake in Ralph H. Hall's *Weoley Castle and its Families*, Northfield Society Occasional Paper No. 12 (1981), p. 11, which in turn seems to be based on an incorrect assumption made by Frank S. Pearson in his 'The Manor of Northfield and Weoley', *Transactions of the Birmingham Archaeological Society*, p. 57, wherein he claims a Daniel Ledsam bought the estate in the "19th century". For a more accurate assessment of the situation see Susan Tungate's 'The Transfer of the Demesne Land and the Lordship of the Manor of Northfield and Weoley', Final Assignment for a Certificate in Higher Education on Research in Local history (1999).

[10] Ordnance Survey, 1:64460, First Series, Worcestershire Sheet 62.

[11] *Particulars and Conditions of Sale of [...] The Manor of Northfield & Weoley* (1824) p. 5, Birmingham City Archives, ref. DRO 14/217/7.

[12] 1841 Census returns for 'Weoley Park', ref. HO107/1197/20, f. 7, p. 5.

[13] "Mar. 4 [1842], Waddell & Bretherton accepted as tenants of Weoley Park in room of Firchild who sold up under execution by the Sheriff, leaving a large debt to me, which I shall lose through my forbearance, trusting his promises.", 'The Diary of Joseph Frederick Ledsam' (1860), p. 21.

[14] For further details of the Tithe Survey see Ken Avery's *The Tithe Apportionment for Northfield 1838*, Frankley Society Occasional Paper No. 3; in particular p. 38 for entries relating to Lodge/Weoley Park Farm.

[15] 1851 Census returns for 'Weoley park', ref. HO107/2049, f. 71, p. 14.

1. Before Selly Oak Park

Weoley for the children and heirs of his brother Joseph Ledsam as they were still minors, was living at Weoley Park and resided in the house until about 1903[16]. From around 1909 Arthur Percy Marsh was the tenant farmer, who was then followed by the Lyde family in 1915 and who remained there until 1922[17].

Gradually some of the Farm's land was sold off by J. G. Ledsam, such as that for creating Lodge Hill Cemetery which was opened in 1895[18]. At some point land was also sold to the Gibbins family, proprietors of the Birmingham Battery & Metal Co. Ltd, whom as we will see gifted it to the King's Norton and Northfield Urban District Council for the creation of Selly Oak Park in 1899[19], with a subsequent donation being made in 1913. In 1919 Ledsam sold what was left of the Weoley Park Farm estate to the Gibbins family, though possession was not obtained until the expiration of the Lydes' lease as tenant farmers in 1922. At this time a further donation of land was made to Birmingham Corporation (the area having been absorbed into the City in 1911) as yet another extension to Selly Oak Park, and the remaining farm land passed from the Gibbins family to the Birmingham Battery, who set aside nine acres as a sports ground for their works[20].

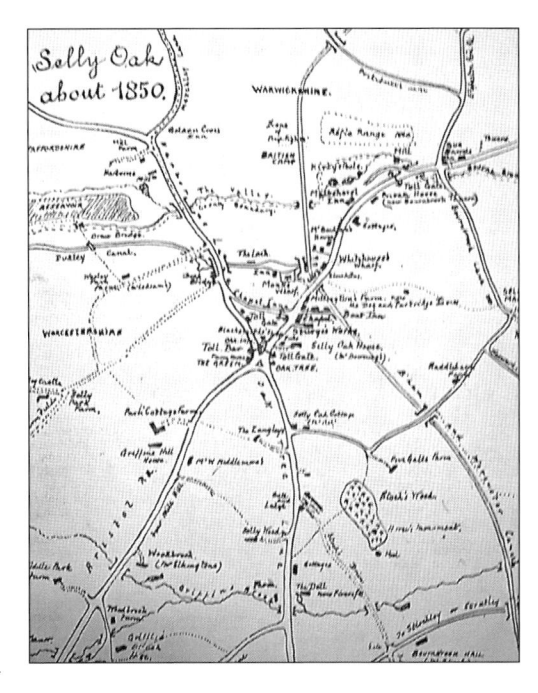

Selly Oak 1850 – Showing the area around Weoley Park Farm before Selly Oak Park was established. From: F.W. Leonard (1933), The Story of Selly Oak, Birmingham – written on behalf of St. Mary's Parochial Church Council.

In 1934 the Birmingham Battery sold the last acres of the Weoley Park Farm estate for building purposes and the Farmhouse, together with a portion of the land, was bought by a builder called Douglas Dyas James; though the House itself

---

[16] *Kelly's Directory of Birmingham*, 1903.
[17] *Kelly's Directory of Birmingham*, 1922.
[18] See Joseph McKenna's *In the Midst of Life: A History of the Burial Grounds of Birmingham* (1992), p. 26.
[19] The initial gift of land to create Selly Oak Park comprised most of a field formerly known as Gorsty Leasow; 'gorsty' being an archaic variant of gorsy (i.e. abounding in, or covered with, gorse), whilst 'leasow' has the meaning of pasture or meadow-land. In this instance the field was probably used for grazing cattle. See *The Oxford English Dictionary*, (2nd ed. 1989), Volume VI, p. 696 & Volume VIII, p. 772.
[20] See Arthur Rowntree's *The Birmingham Battery and Metal Company: One Hundred Years 1836-1936*, p. 93.

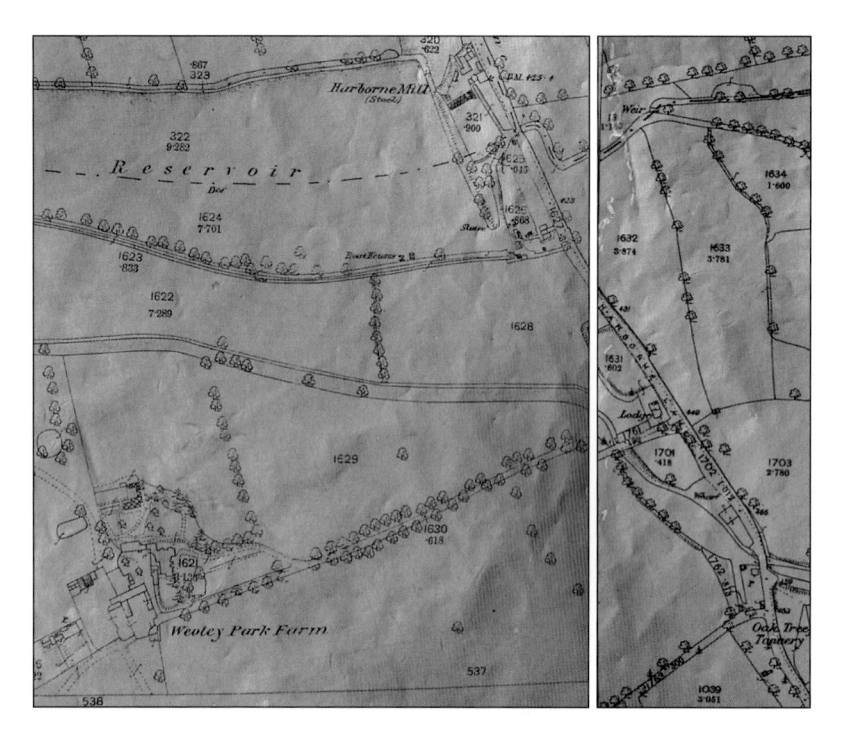

Maps showing part of the area that would be occupied by Selly Oak Park. Photographs of 25" OS maps. Left: Staffordshire (1885), surveyed in 1883 Right: Worcestershire (1890), surveyed in 1886.

had been leased only a few months previously, in 1933, by Sealey Patrick Dobbs[21]. Dobbs went on to buy the Farmhouse from James in 1935 and the Dobbs family lived there right up until 1945, after which the House was auctioned, when it was described as "formerly the Old Manor House of Weoley Park"[22] with claims that parts of the building dated back to the 16th century. In 1946 the Farmhouse was bought by a building partnership, but the partnership was dissolved only a year later when Edward Albert Holmes, one of the partners, became the sole owner. Holmes finally sold the House to the Colmore Development Company Limited in 1959, and it was this company which demolished it to build sixteen new houses on the site in what became Lepid Grove and the adjacent parts of Woolacombe Lodge and Corisande Roads.

---

[21] Property Deeds relating to house in Lepid Grove, 1934-1987.
[22] Unfortunately there is little evidence to support a claim that the Farm was ever used as a Manor House, other than its occupancy by J. G. Ledsam when he acted as the surrogate Lord of the Manor during the minority of his brother's children.

1. Before Selly Oak Park

There is another abstract of title to Weoley Park Farm which has recently become available in the Archive and Heritage Section of the Birmingham Central Library[23]. This confirms Martin Robson Riley's account of people and dates.

F.W. Leonard (1933)[24] reproduced a map of 1850 and described an imaginary journey along Harborne Lane and Oak Tree Lane, Selly Oak. He writes of Weoley Park Farm too:

> *"As we continue the journey from the reservoir towards Selly Oak, no houses would be met with until we come to the old Dock bridge, replaced recently by a modern bridge near the entrance to Gibbins Road. A drive on the right from the Harborne Lane over the canal leads to Weoley Park Farm, which was the residence of J.T. Ledsam, Esq., Lord of the Manor. At the Dock bridge a boat building industry was carried on by a member of the Monk family. Just past the Dock bridge a long fordraught ran across the fields to Selly Park Farm. This fordraught is now Gibbins Road, and Selly Park Farm is at the end of Weoley Park Road, adjacent to the entrance to Lodge Hill cemetery."*

It would appear that whilst this general description is correct, by comparison with the previous accounts the reference to a J. T. Ledsam may not be.

Martin Robson-Riley[25] wrote a short article on Weoley Park Farm for the Brummagem Magazine, Issue No. 60, March 2006, p8. It is reproduced here by kind permission of the Editor, Prof Carl Chinn.

BRUMMAGEM — Weoley Park Farm

I thought I'd just send you these pictures in the hope that you'll put them in your Brummagem Magazine, together with an appeal for information. The photos were taken sometime in the late 1930s by Mrs Joyce Dobbs, and have been kindly passed to me by her daughter Mrs Beatrice Painter. They are quite rare and show the old Weoley Park Farm, an important and historic farm which formerly stood at the back of Selly Oak Park. The main picture shows the front of the farmhouse, which looked out into the Park, whilst another shows the farm buildings from a distance and was taken looking along the lane running from Gibbins Road. There are also two pictures of the farm's ancient barn, one showing it from the outside, with its large sloping roof, and the other giving a glimpse inside.

A ground plan for the Farm survives from 1734, when it was called Lodge Farm (a name connected with nearby Lodge Hill, the site of today's cemetery). The façade of the farmhouse was probably Victorian, but other parts were believed to have dated back to Tudor times. Interestingly when the house was auctioned in 1946 it was claimed it was 'formerly the Old Manor House of Weoley Park'. The farm was finally demolished around 1959 and a small cul-de-sac, called Lepid Grove, built on the site.

I am keen to hear from anyone who recalls this farmhouse, or who might have other old photographs of the area. There is a gully-way at the back of Selly Oak Park which ran past the house into Corisande Road, so people may well remember having walked past it. I have also heard that nurses used to board there at one time, so maybe someone might have memories of this or even of when the Farm was still working. Any information, no matter how small, would be most gratefully received as I believe there is still much to be discovered about the farm. I may be contacted at: 6 Lepid Grove, Selly Oak, BIRMINGHAM, B29 6RU.

Martin Robson-Riley

---

23 Archive Accession No. 2003/35; Collection Ref: MS 2500.
24 The Story of Selly Oak, Birmingham – written on behalf of St. Mary's Parochial Church Council. Birmingham Central Library Ref: 1046067 SELLY OAK.
25 Martin Robson Riley no longer lives at the address shown in the reproduced article.

THE HEYDAYS OF SELLY OAK PARK

Martin Robson-Riley also obtained plans for Weoley Park Farm – i) a ground plan of 1734 (the copyright for which is retained by Hampshire Record Office; ii) conveyance plans dated 1935, and iii) other items from Mrs. Beatrice Painter.

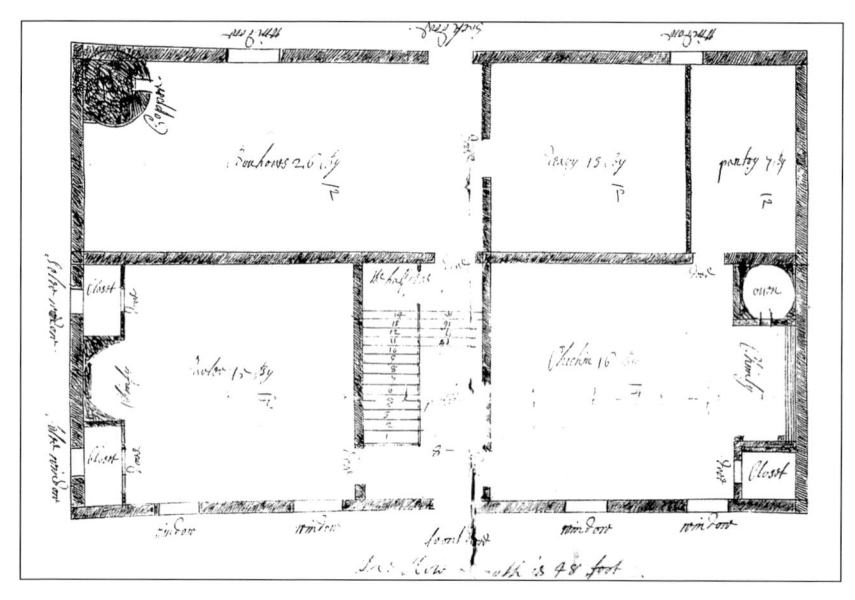

The Ground plan of Weoley Park Farm, 1734.

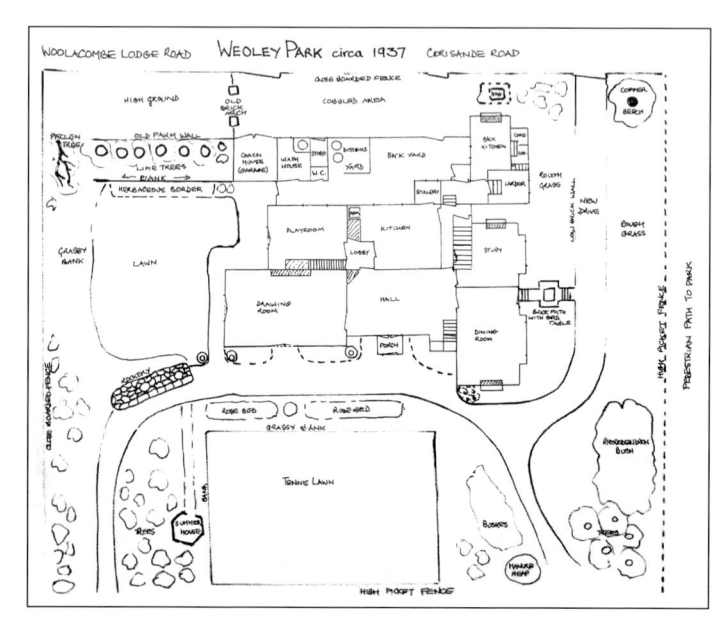

A sketch plan of Weoley Park, circa 1937.

1. Before Selly Oak Park

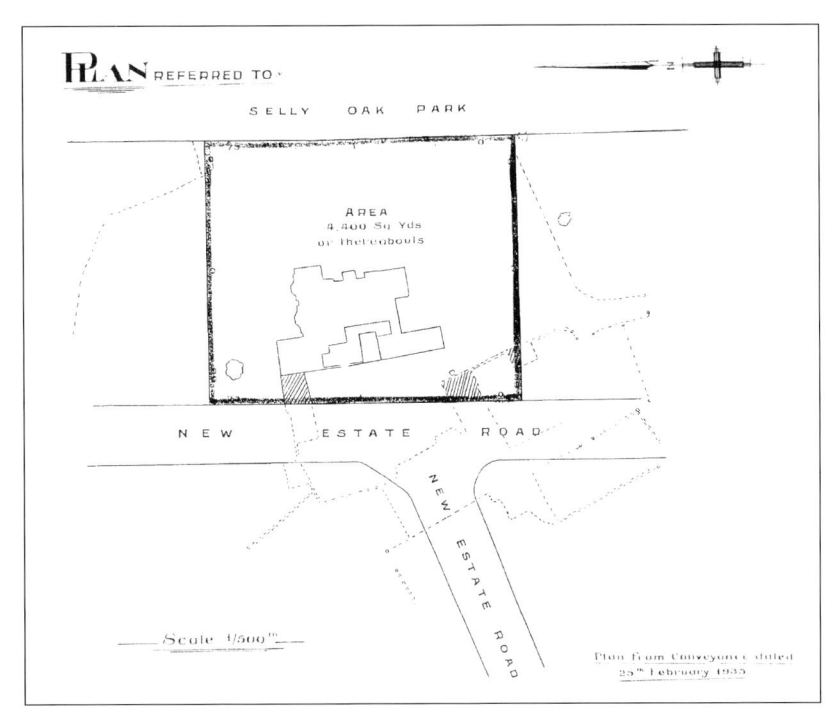

Conveyance Plans of Weoley Park Farm, February 1935.

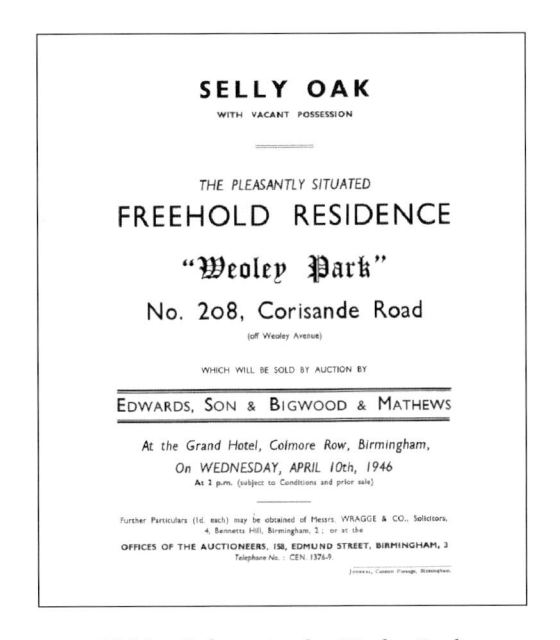

1946 – Sale notice for Weoley Park.

Chapter 2

PREPARATIONS FOR SELLY OAK PARK

The Gibbins family, having associated with the proposals to provide a recreation ground for Selly Oak, set about building a Park Keeper's lodge, closets and a shelter for the park. The building plans, as submitted to Kings Norton planning authority are still available[26] (albeit in frail condition, and thus not forced flat for photography), and photographs of them are reproduced on the following pages. (There was also a plan for the development and sewering of Gibbins Road, ref 3204, but this is no longer available.)

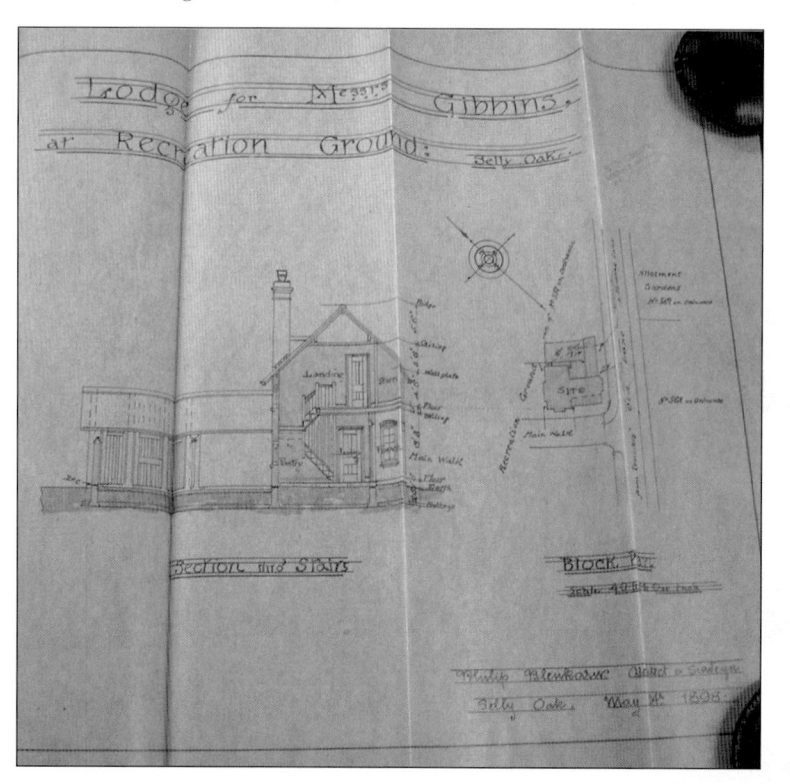

The Lodge: plans drawn by Philip Blenkarn,
Architect and Surveyor, of Selly Oak, in May 1898. Ground plan and section.

---

[26] In the Archive Section of Birmingham Central Library: Refs 3324, 3333 and 3334.

2. Preparations for Selly Oak Park

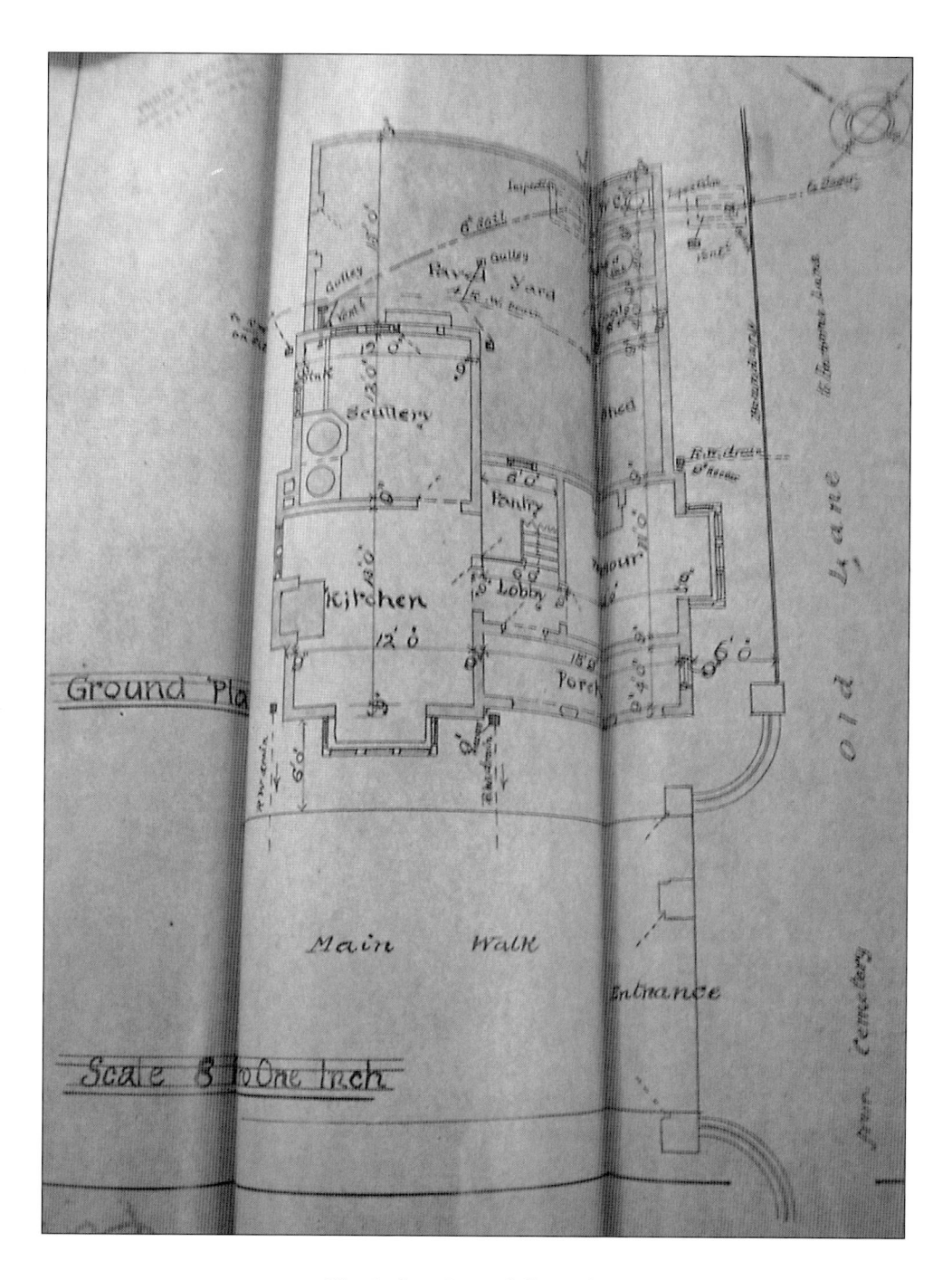

The Lodge: Ground floor Plan.

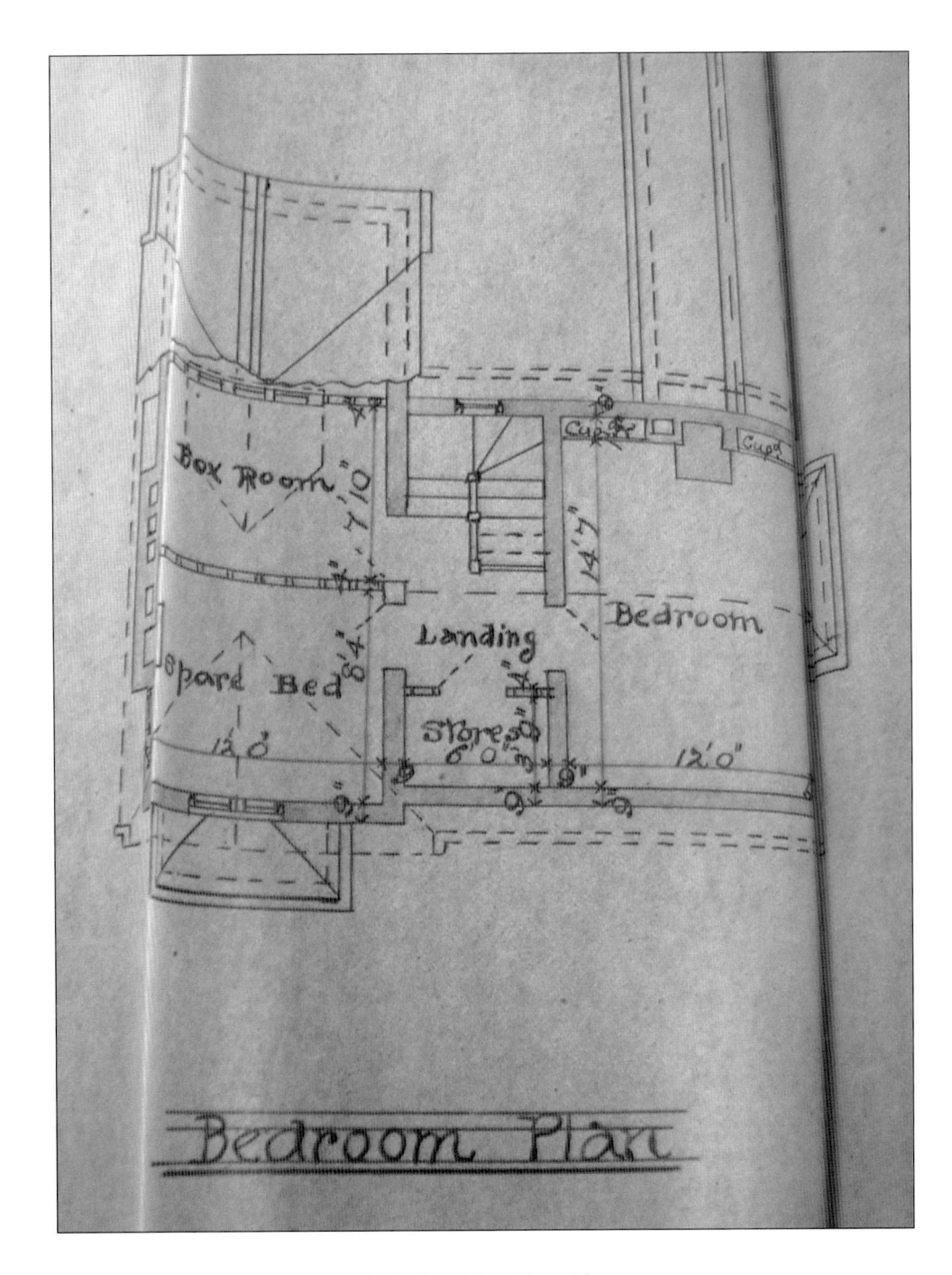

The Lodge: First Floor Plan.

2. Preparations for Selly Oak Park

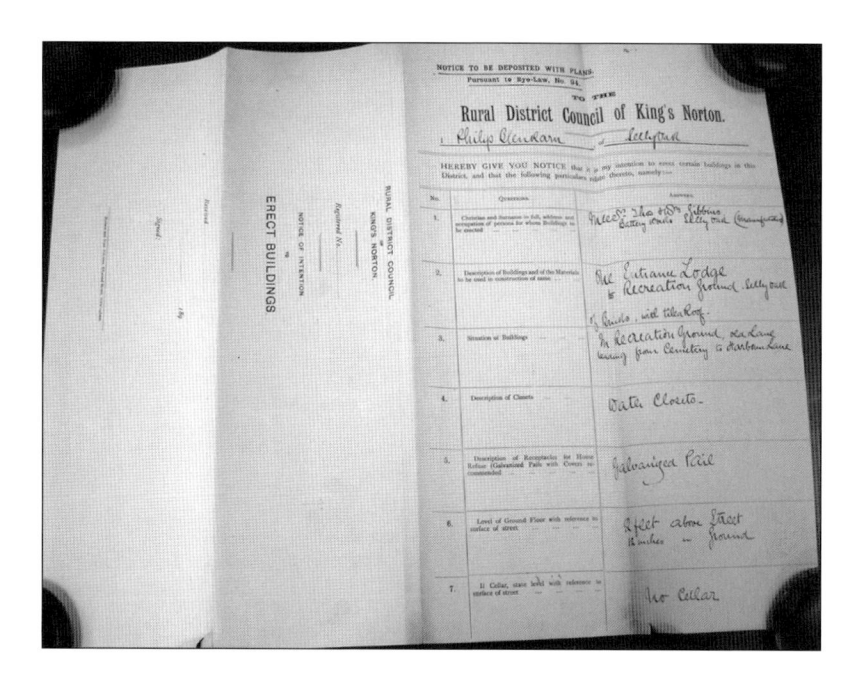

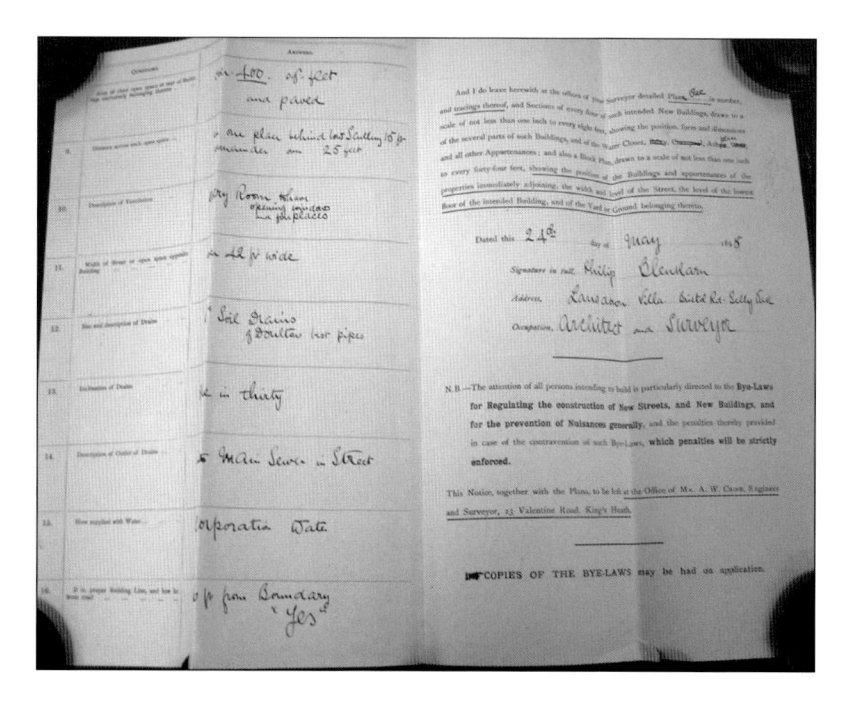

The Lodge: Schedule that accompanied the Plans.

The Heydays Of Selly Oak Park

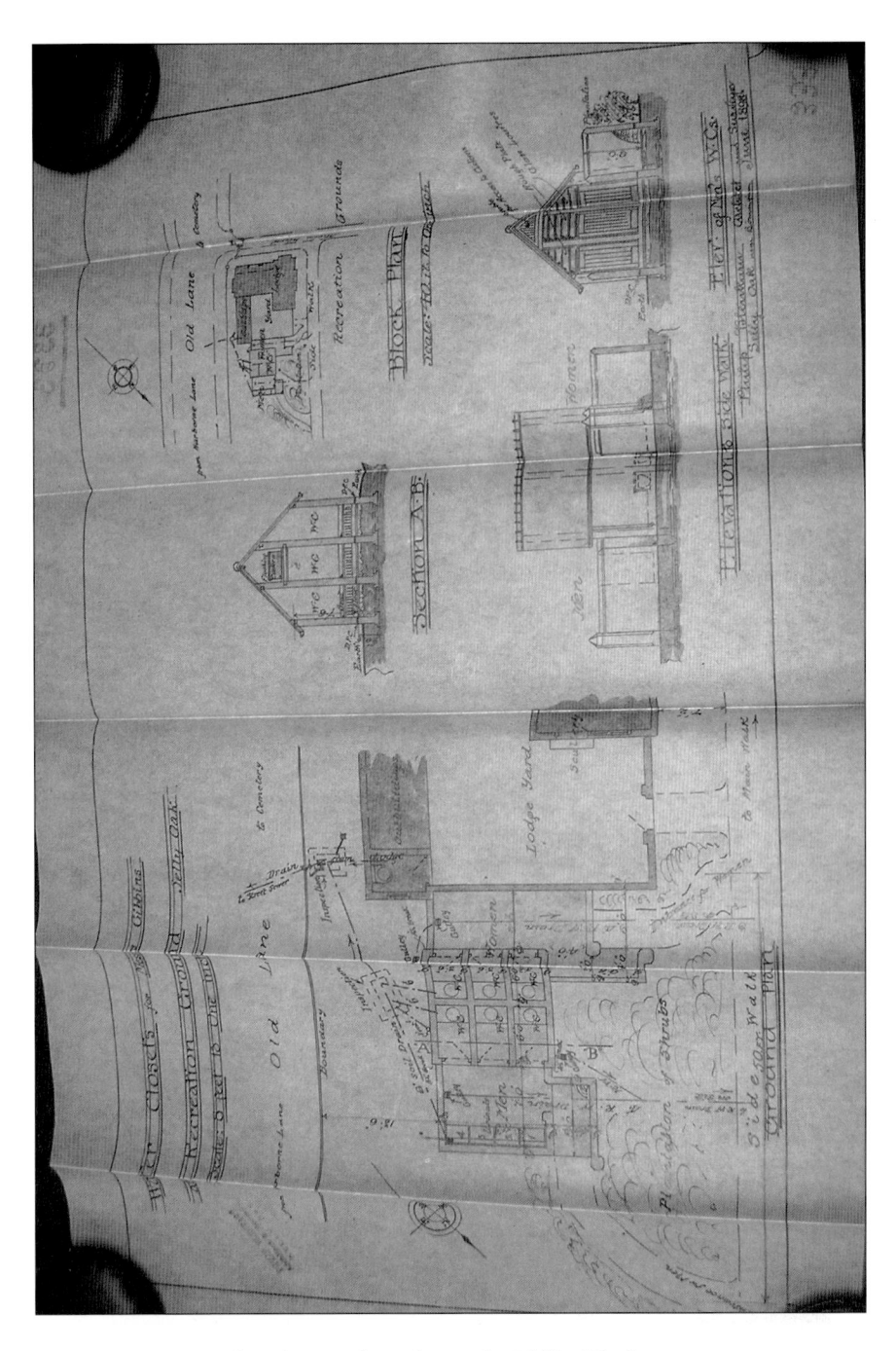

*The Closets: plans drawn by Philip Blenkarn,
Architect and Surveyor, of Selly Oak, in June 1898.*

2. Preparations for Selly Oak Park

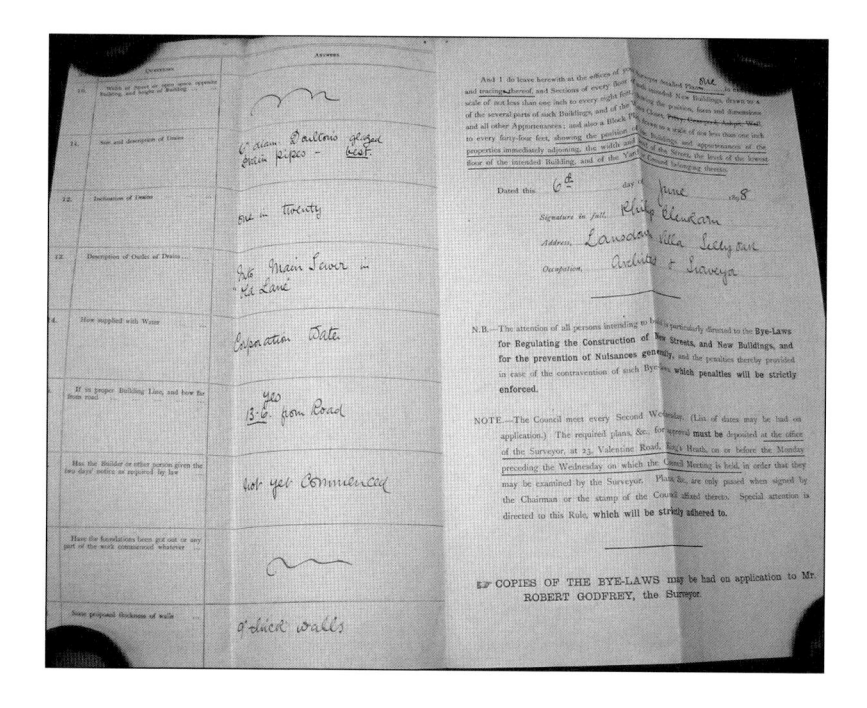

Closets: Schedule that accompanied the Plans

The Heydays Of Selly Oak Park

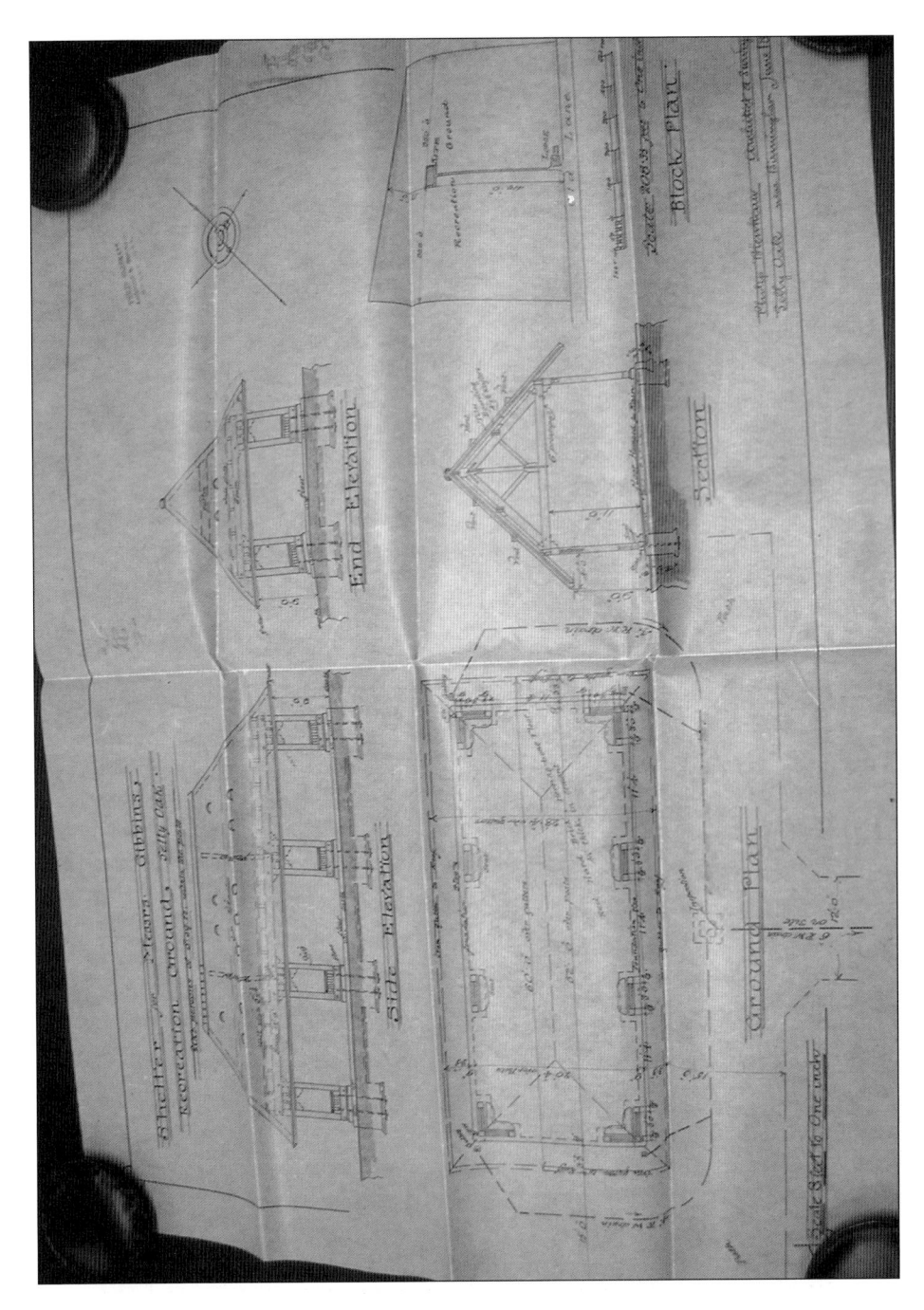

*The Shelter – plans drawn by Philip Blenkarn,
Architect and Surveyor, of Selly Oak, in June 1898:*

2. Preparations for Selly Oak Park

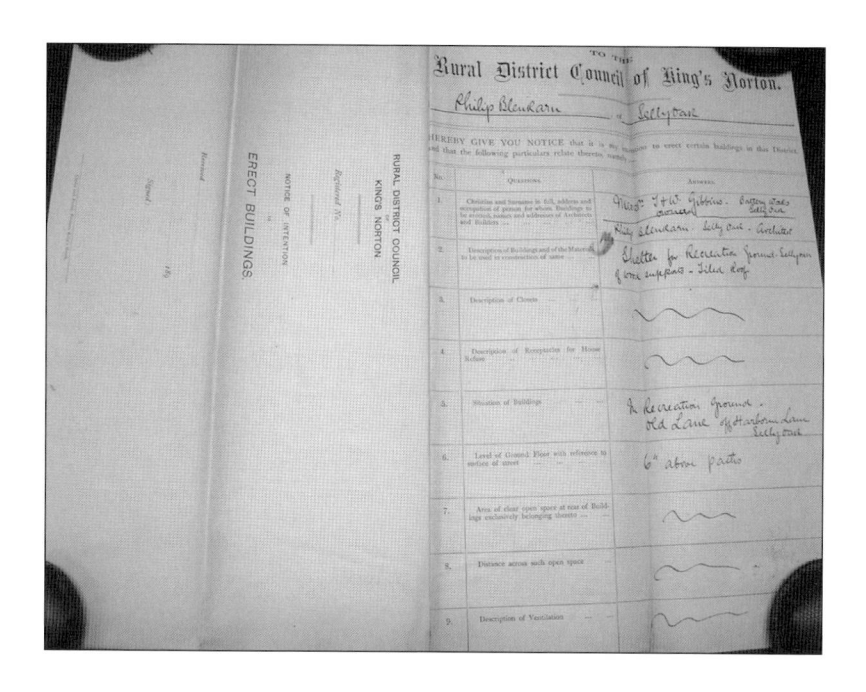

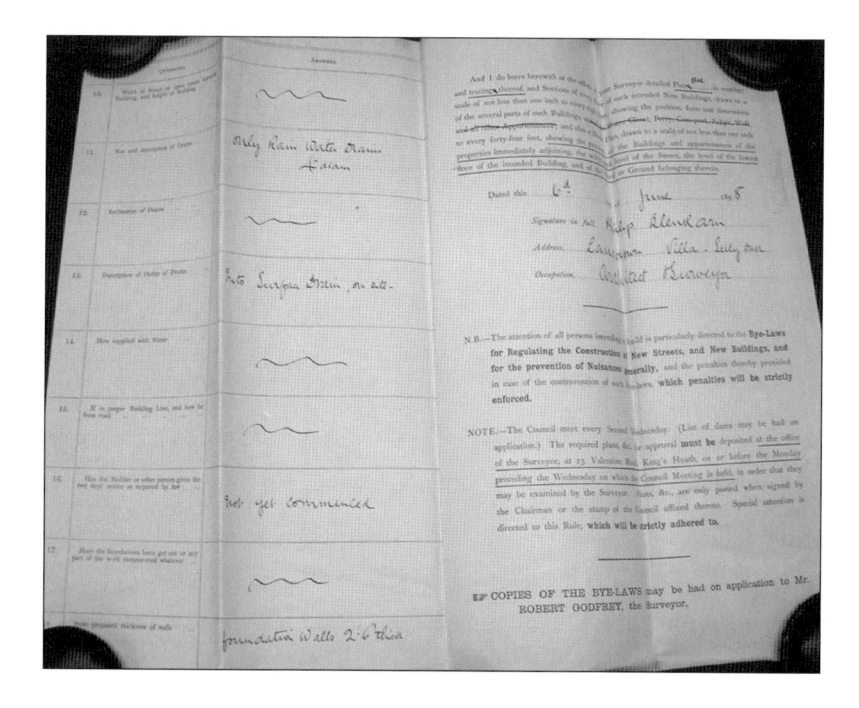

Shelter: Schedules that accompanied the Plans.

Shelter – Building certificates, show that the building work in preparation for the Park was well under way in August 1898.

Whilst these preparations were underway, Birmingham City Council was laying out ground in Harborne for what would be Queen's Park, which was formally opened on 5th October 1898, the sixtieth anniversary of Queen Victoria's coronation. We learn, from speeches made at the opening of Selly Oak Park, that there was good cooperation between the Birmingham Parks administration and Kings Norton Parish Council's park aspirants. And so it was that Josiah Thomas Horton, a gardener who had started work at Queens Park Harborne on 2nd January 1898, was transferred on 4th March 1898 to lay out Selly Oak Park for Kings Norton and Northfield Urban District Council[27].

---

27 Information gleaned from later employment records of the Birmingham City Council Parks Department – see Appendix II.

Chapter 3

SELLY OAK PARK
– THE DETAIL

The history of Selly Oak Park can be traced through extracts from the minute books of:

- Kings Norton & Northfield Urban District Council (**KN&N UDC**) (1898 to 1911)[28];
- their Baths, Parks and Cemeteries Committee[29];

and various articles, notices, etc in the press; all of which are held in the Archive and Heritage Section of the Birmingham Central Library.

Records of the same event or administrative decision occur in different places. Where the individual records, especially the newspaper articles, supply different (complementary) information, convey a different perspective, or are written in a different style, then the individual records are reproduced. When there is nothing to be gained from repetition, only one account (the fullest) is reproduced, and an indication of the other occurrences is given.

Kings Norton & Northfield Urban District Council set up a Cemeteries Committee in 1898. The Cemeteries Committee initially had a Baths & Parks Sub-Committee. In May 1898 the sub-committee ceased to exist and the Cemeteries Committee became a Baths, Parks and Cemeteries Committee.

---

[28] Kings Norton & Northfield Urban District Council Minutes – Archive reference BCK/AA 1/1/21 .. 33; also reference L30.4.
[29] Kings Norton & Northfield Urban District Council, Baths, Parks & Cemeteries Committee Minutes – Archive reference for volumes 1 to 3 is BCK/AK 1/1/1 .. 2 .. 3

Chapter 4

1899

1st February 1899 – Minute of KN&N UDC

Recreation Ground Selly Oak

The Clerk presented and read Deed of Gift by Mrs Emma Joel Gibbins[30], William Gibbins, Thomas Gibbins, John Gibbins and Benjamin Gibbins of a piece of land 11 acres 2 roods 5 perches in extent situate in Old Lane Selly Oak for the purposes of a Recreation Ground.

Moved Mr Brown, seconded Mr J R Bayliss, and unanimously resolved, that this Council do gratefully accept the gift by Mrs Gibbins and her sons William, Thomas, John and Benjamin of a piece of land eleven acres two roods and 5 perches in extent situate in Old Lane Selly Oak for the purposes of a Recreation Ground and do hereby record their thanks, as representing the public, to the donors for their generous gift, and that the Common Seal of the Council be and is hereby authorised to be affixed to the Deed of Gift.

It was further resolved that the foregoing resolution be engrossed on Vellum and presented to the donors on the occasion of the opening ceremony.

Resolved also that the Baths and Parks Sub-Committee be requested to take into consideration all matters connected with the Recreation Ground Selly Oak and to report thereon.

2nd February 1899 – The Birmingham Daily Post[31]
2nd February 1899 – The Birmingham Daily Mail[32]

KINGS NORTON DISTRICT COUNCIL
A GENEROUS GIFT

A meeting of the Kings Norton District Council was held yesterday, at the offices, Newhall Street, Birmingham; Mr. T. Gibbins presiding. ....etc.

---

[30] She was the mother of Councillor Thomas Gibbins who himself was sometime Chairman of the District Council. Emma Joel Gibbins (1811-1905) was from the Cadbury family and married Thomas Gibbins Snr: (1796-1863): see –
www.haverford.edu/library/special/aids/jonescadbury/page4.html. Appendix I at the end of this History provides more information about the Gibbins family.

[31] Microfilm Collection, Local History Section, Birmingham Central Library.

[32] Microfilm Collection, Local History Section, Birmingham Central Library.

4. 1899

Before the conclusion of the business the Clerk (Mr. E. Docker) read a deed of gift by which Mrs. Emma Joel Gibbins, Messrs W. Gibbins, T. Gibbins, J. Gibbins and B. Gibbins, have conveyed to the Council, for ever, a park, eleven acres in extent in Old Lane, Selly Oak.

Mr. J. W. B. BROWN said that the reading of the document was an unexpected pleasure. It conveyed to the Council a very valuable park for the use of the inhabitants of Selly Oak, and that gift came to them through the instrumentality and liberality of the chairman, his mother, and brothers. (Applause.) He was sure the Council would receive the gift, and convey their hearty thanks to the donors. (Hear, hear.) He moved that the best thanks of the Council be given to the donors, and that the resolution should be expressed on vellum. (Applause.)

This was seconded by Mr. BAYLISS supported by Mr. A. JONES, and carried by acclamation.

The CHAIRMAN expressed his pleasure that the gift had met with the approval of the Council.

4th February 1899 – The Birmingham News[33]

The Weoley Park Recreation Ground Handed over to the Public for Ever

At the meeting of the Kings Norton Urban District Council on Wednesday, Mr. Edwin Docker (clerk) announced that he had received a deed of gift, by which Mrs. Emma Joel Gibbins and Messrs. William, Thomas, John, and Benjamin Gibbins, made over to the Council, as trustees of the public, a piece of land at Selly Oak, 11 acres in extent, and having a frontage of 271 yards in Old Lane (Harborne Lane), to be used as a public park and recreation ground. The only restrictions were that intoxicating liquors should not be sold on it, that it should not be open for playing games on Sunday, and that its gate should not be closed to the public for more than two consecutive days by reason of the holding of any event thereon, such as a flower show, for which it may be let, however, either free or at a charge, as the Council might order.

Mr. Brown expressed the pleasure of himself and his colleagues in receiving the gift, which, he added, had been secured through the instrumentality and generosity of the chairman. He moved that the offer be most gratefully accepted and that the thanks of the Council be presented to the donors for their generosity.

Mr. T. R. Bayliss seconded the motion, which was carried with a hearty round of applause.

The formal opening of the park was left to the consideration of the Baths and Parks Committee.

Mr. Frank Smith, as a member of the late Northfield Parish Council, spoke of the gentlemanly manner in which the donors had consulted the wishes of the people in every respect, in the manner of the laying out and arranging of the park.

---

[33] Microfilm Collection, Local History Section, Birmingham Central Library. A weekly newspaper, published on Saturday.

The Heydays Of Selly Oak Park

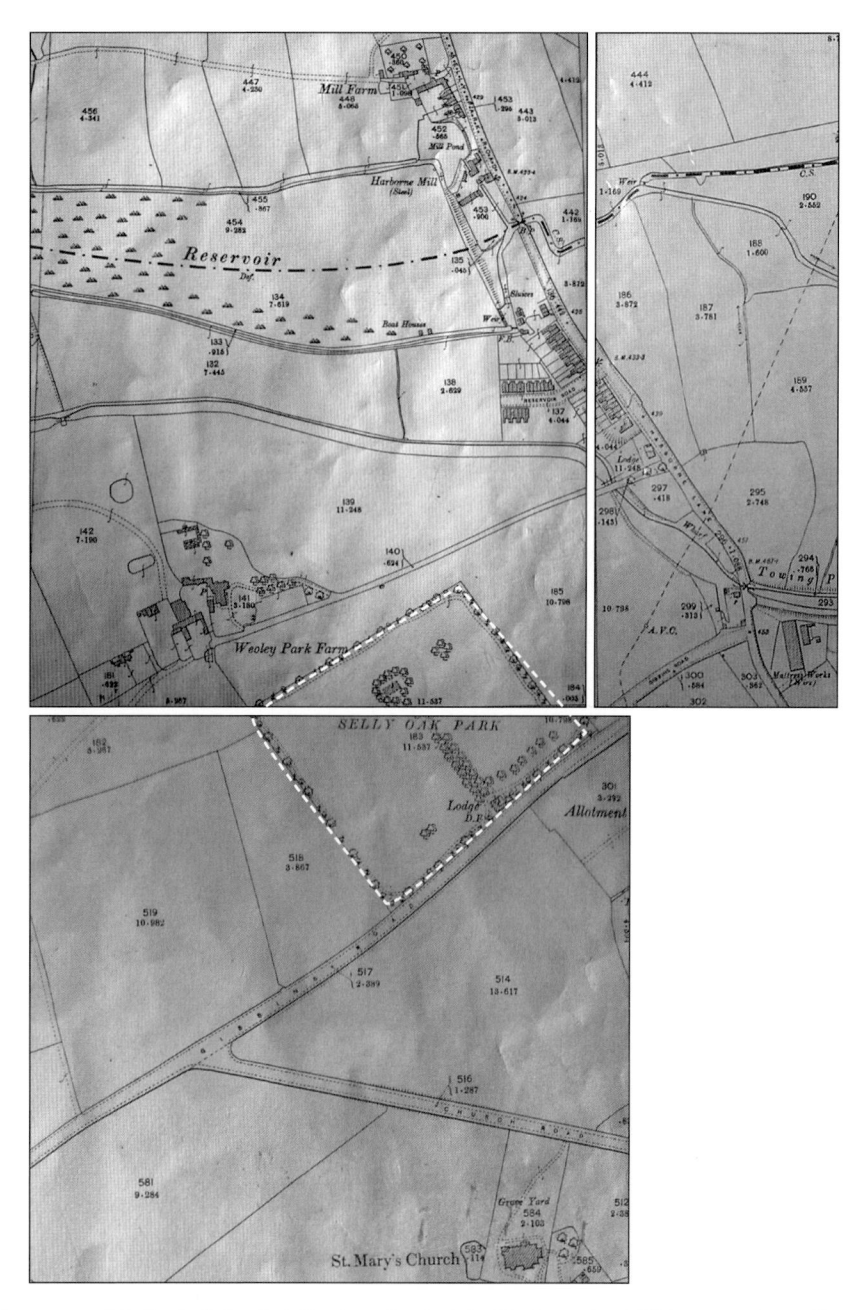

The extent of Selly Oak Park following the 1899 gift from the Gibbins Family. Collage of photographs of 25" OS maps. Worcestershire (1904), Surveyed in 1882, Revised 1901 Worcestershire (1904), Surveyed in 1882, Revised 1902-3. Worcestershire (1904), Surveyed in 1886, Revised 1901-2. Compare with 1885/1890 maps earlier in this History.

4. 1899

An early photograph of Gibbins Road, Selly Oak, reproduced from an original in Archive & Heritage Section, Birmingham Central Library (WK/S4/79).

From "Records of the Gibbins Family", 1911, ed. Emma Gibbins. Copy in Archive and Heritage Section, Birmingham Central Library. Ref: 546025 IIR73.

The Heydays Of Selly Oak Park

25th February 1899 – The Birmingham News

Park for Selly Oak
To be Opened at Easter

The Kings Norton Urban District Council have decided to call the new park for Selly Oak the "Gibbins Park" – out of courtesy to the family who have so munificently placed an extensive site of over eleven acres at the disposal and for the pleasure of the local public for ever.

The opening will take place on Easter Monday.

1st March 1899 – Minute of KN&N UDC

<u>Selly Oak Park</u>

It appeared from a report of the Parks Sub-Committee that they were arranging for the formal opening ceremony on Easter Monday, April 3rd, and also recommended that the park should be designated as "Gibbins Park".

A letter was read from Mr Wm Gibbins stating that the donors would prefer that the Park should be given an impersonal name and suggested that "Selly Oak Park" or "Selly Oak Recreation Ground" should be the designation.

It was moved Mr Oswald, seconded Mr Whitelock, and resolved, that the Ground situate at Old Lane purchased, laid out and presented to the Council by Mrs Gibbins and her Sons be designated as Selly Oak Park.

It was further resolved that the lane known as Old Lane Selly Oak leading from Harborne Lane and Lodge Hill Cemetery be and is hereby designated as Gibbins Road and that the Surveyor provide and fix a name plate subject to the approval of the owners.

4th March 1899 – The Birmingham News

Opening of Selly Oak Recreation Ground
Old Lane Rechristened

In our last issue we announced that the Kings Norton Urban District Council had decided to perpetuate the name of the generous donors of the recreation ground at Selly Oak by naming it Gibbins Park, but at the Council meeting on Wednesday a letter was read from Mr. William Gibbins stating that it would be more pleasing to the donors of the ground if an impersonal name were found for the recreation ground, instead of the name it was proposed to give it. "Selly Oak Recreation Ground" or "Selly Oak Park", names which had already been given to the ground by the populace were suggested.

Mr. J. R. Oswald, in accordance with the request, moved that it should be known as "Selly Oak Park", and this was agreed to.

4. 1899

Arising out of a suggestion of Mr. Oswald's it was decided to re-christen Old Lane, upon which the park abuts, and this will in future be known as Gibbins Road. At least, humorously added Mr. Oswald, they can't prevent us perpetuating their name in this way.

11th March 1899 – The Birmingham News

Local & District News
Selly Oak

<u>Selly Oak Flower Show</u> – The committee of the Selly Oak and District Cottage Garden Horticultural Association have made an alteration in the date of the holding of this year's show, which, instead of being a fortnight after the August bank Holiday, as it was last year, will, on this occasion be held on the Saturday before bank Holiday, i.e. on August 5. Providing the weather is at all reasonable, we think the popularity, and therefore the wisdom, of the change will be shown by the presence of a considerably larger number of visitors than was present at last year's show – record though the attendance then was. We would commend intending exhibitors to closely study the schedule of prizes, as a number of alterations of, and additions to those of 1898 have been made. They would do well, too, to read through the rules, as several revisions have been made in this direction. The exhibition takes place at the Selly Oak Recreation Ground, and the general public will be admitted at two o'clock in the afternoon. The Secretary (Mr. James Henry Walton) will be pleased to give any information about the show, and communications should be addressed to him, care of Mrs. Lilley, Oak Tree Lane, Selly Oak.

29th March 1899 – Minute of KN&N UDC

<u>Selly Oak Park</u>

On the motion of Mr Gibbins, seconded Mr Oswald, it was resolved, that the following report of the Public Works Committee be approved and adopted and that as therein recommended Mr Josiah T. Horton[34] be appointed as Park Keeper at Selly Oak Park at a weekly wage of 24s/- with residence at the Lodge and that he be provided with a Coat and Cap, the engagement to be subject to one month's notice.

(The above named report)

Arrangements have been made for the opening ceremony to take place on Easter Monday, April 3rd, at 3 o'clock p.m., and public notice of the day and hour has

---

[34] Appendix II at the end of this volume records a family history of Josiah Thomas Horton. Photographs are in the plates.

been posted throughout the district and advertised. The Chairman and members of the late Northfield Parish Council, the Representatives of Friendly Societies, and Bands of Hopes (sic), in the Parish of Northfield, have been invited to attend the ceremony, and to cooperate in rendering the function successful. Mr Oswald (Chairman of the Sub-Committee) has been asked on behalf of the Council to express, at such ceremony, the grateful thanks of the Council and of the public to Mrs Gibbins and her sons for their generous gift.

Arrangements have been made for the presentation to the Donors of an Engrossment on Vellum of the Resolution of the Council accepting the gift, and also of a Silver Key.

The Sub-Committee have considered 33 applications and interviewed selected candidates for the appointment of Park Keeper, and upon their report it is now recommended that Mr Josiah Thomas Horton, of Tennal Road, Harborne, be appointed as Park Keeper at Selly Oak Park, at a weekly wage of 24/-, with a residence at the Lodge, and that he be provided with a coat and cap, the engagement to be subject to one month's notice.

25th March 1899 – The Birmingham News

Public Announcement
Kings Norton and Northfield Urban District Council
Opening of Selly Oak Park

NOTICE IS HEREBY GIVEN that on MONDAY, 3rd day of APRIL, 1899, at Three o'clock in the afternoon, the NEW PARK, which is to be designated SELLY OAK PARK, will be formally DECLARED OPEN, and handed over to the keeping of the Urban District Council by or on behalf of the Donors, Mrs. Gibbins and Sons.

The attendance of the Public at the Ceremony is cordially invited.
Dated this 16th of March, 1899.
By Order,
EDWIN DOCKER.
Clerk of the Council.

1st April 1899 – Daily Argus[35]

The Opening of Selly Oak Park

Selly Oak Park is to be opened at three o'clock on Monday by Mr. Gibbins. The park having been formally transferred to the District Council in trust for the public, a vote of thanks to the donors will be moved by Councillor Oswald, who will ask the donor's acceptance of an engrossment on vellum of the resolution passed

---

[35] Microfilm Collection, Local History Section, Birmingham Central Library.

by the Council accepting the gift. The vote will be seconded by Mr Simeon Hill (Chairman of the late Northfield Parish Council), and on behalf of the Foresters (Court Royal Oak), supported by Mr W. Haddon, on behalf of the Oddfellows (Selly Oak Pride), and acknowledged by Mr John Gibbins. Afterwards a squad of boys and girls from Shenley Fields Cottage Homes will give an exhibition of dumb-bell drill. The Selly Oak Victoria Brass Band will lead the procession to the park gates. For the present the park will be open from 8 a.m. to 7 p.m.

4th April 1899 – The Birmingham Daily Mail

A BREATHING-PLACE FOR SELLY OAK

The industrial expansion of Birmingham during the last quarter of a century has been so enormous that many of the suburban fringes of the city, which a few years ago were entirely rural in character, are now thickly-populated districts and the centre of large manufacturing concerns. Among the neighbourhoods which have so changed, and in a marked degree, are Bournbrook and Selly Oak. A quarter of a century ago the provision of a public park or recreation ground in this locality would have been considered superfluous, the whole district being scarcely anything but green fields and country lanes. The industrial progress of Birmingham, however, seems to have hopped over Edgbaston and started a new and rapidly-expanding colony of manufactures and toilers at Bournbrook and Selly Oak. And this being so, the late Northfield Parish Council prudently initiated a movement some three years ago for the acquirement of a park or recreation ground before the whole of the available land in the district was taken up for other purposes. The movement obtained the cordial sympathy of Mrs. Emma Joel Gibbins and her four sons, Messrs. William, Thomas, John and Benjamin Gibbins, who are connected with one of the largest and most important works in the district, with the result that eventually Mrs. Gibbins and her sons resolved to undertake the provision of a park at their own cost. The members of the Parish Council selected a site some 11½ acres in extent, situated a short distance from the main Bristol Road, near Selly Oak Church, and in the direction of Harborne. The situation is high and bracing, and in every respect will form an admirable breathing-space for the inhabitants of the district, and an excellent playground for the children. The laying-out of the ground has been conducted on simple lines, and includes the planting of a large number of trees and shrubs, a flower border extending round the full space enclosed, and the provision of a keeper's lodge at the entrance, and a commodious shelter in the park. The ceremony of formally opening the park and the handing over of the gift to the custody of the King's Norton and Northfield Urban District Council were performed yesterday afternoon, in the presence of a large concourse of residents, who will doubtless long bear in grateful remembrance the generosity of the donors. The opening was fittingly performed by Mrs. Gibbins, the gates being unlocked with a silver key, presented on behalf of the District Council by Mr. J. R. Oswald. Very few people heard the brief simple words in which the lady declared the park open to the public, but the swinging back of the gates was the signal for a hearty cheer from the assembled throng, who at once made their way to the greensward. The remainder of the proceeding was conducted in the vicinity of the shelter. Here Mr. William Gibbins, in the name and on behalf of the donors, formally transferred the park to the keeping of the Council in trust for the use of the public for ever. Mr. Gibbins remarked that, on behalf of his mother, his brothers, and himself, he had to offer the park to the Council for the use of the rapidly-growing neighbourhood. (Cheers.) When the scheme was first proposed it had their hearty support, and they felt that they would like to assist in the movement. The work of laying-out the park had been carried out most satisfactorily and they were there that day to complete the scheme by handing over the ground. (Cheers.) He associated with the progress and development of the scheme the members and officials of the late Parish Council and expressed indebtedness to Councillor Johnson (chairman of the Baths and Parks Committee of the Birmingham Corporation), Alderman White, Mr. Hearn, Mr J. G. Ledsam, and Mr. J. T. Middlemore, J.P. for assistance rendered. It was the hope of his mother, his brothers, and himself that the park might be a source of pleasure and benefit to the inhabitants of the district. (Cheers.) Mr. T. Gibbins, as chairman of the Urban District Council, accepted the park and the conditions accompanying the gift on behalf of that body.

Mr Oswald moved a vote of thanks to the donors, and requested their acceptance of a resolution engrossed on vellum recording the thanks of the Council for the generosity of Mrs. Gibbins and her sons. The motion was seconded by Mr. S. Hill and supported by Mr. W. Haddon.

At the request of the Chairman, Alderman White made a brief speech in which he reminded the assembly that fifty years ago Birmingham was without a public park, or recreation ground, and now it had several beautiful parks and breathing-spaces for the public. He knew of no more generous or valuable gift to a thickly-populated district than a park, or recreation ground, and he felt sure the gift of Mrs. Gibbins and her sons would prove a blessing to the district. (Cheers.)

Mr. H. W. Elliot also spoke of the generosity of the donors. The resolution was carried by acclamation, and Mr. John Gibbins acknowledged the resolution. Among those present at the opening in addition to the names mentioned were Messrs. J. W. B. Brown, G. P. Underhill, F. Smith, G. Talliss, T. E. Bladon, J. J. Bryden, W. J. May, J. Norris (members of the Urban District Council), Edwin Docker (clerk), Alderman White, Alderman Clayton, Councillor Johnson, J. C. Aster, J. S. Kemp, Pumphrey, &c. After the speech making a squad of boys and girls from Shenley Fields Cottage Homes gave an exhibition of dumb-bell drill, and the Selly Oak and Stirchley brass bands played selections of music.

4th April 1899 – Daily Argus

Birmingham Day by Day

Selly Oak spent Bank Holiday in opening its new park. Very fortunate it has been in getting one. Other places have been obliged to plan and scheme and discuss for years before their hopes have been crowned with accomplishment. But it was only about three years ago that Northfield Parish Council began to think about the acquirement of a park before its available land in the district was taken up for works and dwellings. To their help came Mrs E. J. Gibbins and her four sons. They undertook the provision of a park at their own cost, and that park, well situated and arranged, was handed over to the people yesterday afternoon. Mrs Gibbins and her sons were heartily thanked for their generosity and were presented with a resolution of the District Council, engrossed on vellum, recording their gratitude.

8th April, 1899 – The South Birmingham Chronicle[36]

OPENING OF SELLY OAK PARK
A Noble Gift
Presentation to the Donors

Easter Monday was a great day in the history of Selly Oak and Bournbrook, and much enthusiasm was displayed by the inhabitants. The occasion was the opening ceremony of the park, which has been presented by Mrs. Gibbins and her four sons. Long before the hour stated in the programme for the opening ceremony, considerable excitement manifested itself in the district, and the flags and bunting which adorned the main street, betokened the fact that some event out of the ordinary was about to take place. About two o'clock a procession of the various friendly societies – Oddfellows, Foresters, Rechabites – headed by the fire brigade, under the charge of Captain Crump and Lieutenant Green, and the Selly Oak Victoria Band, under the conductorship of Mr. White, paraded the village, and proceeded in the direction of the new park, followed by immense crowds of people. At the park gates and in Gibbins Road thousands of people had assembled, including Messrs. William and John Gibbins, Councillors Thos. Gibbins, J.R. Oswald, G. P. Underhill, Frank Smith, T. E. Bladon, George Talliss, J. Norris (members of the District Council), Alderman Clayton and Alderman White, Councillor Johnson (Chairman of the Birmingham Baths and Parks Committee), Messrs. J. A. Tuckley, S. Hill, J. C. Aston, W. Haddon, W. Holmes, W. Hall (members of the late Northfield Parish Council), H. W. Elliott, C. Smith, W. Morgan, W. Jones, A. Gittins, W, Burdett, R. Roberts, W. Humphreys, J. Whitehouse (clerk to the late Parish Council), H. Bracey, A. G. Wilson, Edwin Docker (clerk to the District Council), W. Bayliss, J. A. Harrison, S. Hopkins, J. Hodson, etc.

Shortly before three o'clock Mrs. Gibbins arrived in her carriage, and was loudly applauded. Councillor J. R. Oswald, on behalf of the Council, presented to Mrs. Gibbins a silver key with which she unlocked the entrance gates amid enthusiastic applause. Mrs Gibbins then declared the park open and the large crowd which had assembled proceeded to the shelter.

---

[36] Microfilm Collection, Local History Section, Birmingham Central Library. A weekly newspaper published on Saturday.

Mr. Edwin Docker announced letters of apology from Rev. Father O'Rourke, Messrs. J. W. Willson, M.P., Neville Chamberlain, Austen Chamberlain, George Cadbury, T. R. Bayliss, C.C., W. A. Baldwin, and others.

Mr William Gibbins then said it was with great pleasure, on behalf of his mother, brothers, and himself, that he handed over that ground to the Kings Norton and Northfield Urban District Council, for the use of the inhabitants of the rapidly growing neighbourhood which they controlled. When the scheme was first proposed, they felt that they would like to assist with it. They communicated with the then Parish Council and offered to undertake the scheme, and they were present that day to complete the work and hand over the park to the District Council. (Applause). He pointed out the extent of the land, explaining that beds and walks had been laid all round, and a good space of grass was still left for play. The beds were planted with shrubs and trees, and he hoped flowering plants would shortly be added. It was to be regretted that there were no trees on the land; but the donors had planted a great many, and hoped that the needful want would be amply supplied. They had also built a Park Keeper's lodge and a large shelter in case of rain, which would not only be a shelter but a place in which the children could play in showery weather. He associated with the work the names of Mr. S. Hill, members of the Parish Council, and the Parish Council clerk (Mr. J. Whitehouse) who were most earnest in the work. They found the land, and the donors only came in to complete the scheme. They were also indebted to the Baths and Parks Committee of the Birmingham City Council, and Alderman White, for allowing Mr Hearne (baths and parks superintendent), to superintend the laying out of the land. Mr. Gibbins also spoke of the assistance of Mr. J. G. Ledsam and Mr. J. T. Middlemore, M.P., in joining to make a good road to the park in place of the old lane. He hoped that the park might be a source of health and recreation to all who visited it. (Applause).

Councillor Thomas Gibbins (chairman of the District Council) then accepted the gift on behalf of the Kings Norton and Northfield Urban District Council. He also accepted the conditions which accompanied the gift, which were that the Council retain the land as a recreation ground for the use of the inhabitants of Selly Oak, Bournbrook, Northfield, and neighbourhood, for ever– (applause) – that it should be open on week days and Sundays during such hours as the council should fix, and subject to such regulations as the council should from time to time make, and that no intoxicating drinks should be sold on the ground. (Hear, hear). Power was also given to the Council, under certain restrictions, to let or lend the land for the holding of flower shows and for other similar purposes. (Applause). These conditions were made with a view that the ground continue to be used for the purpose for which it was intended as embodied in the deed. The deed was dated 1st February, 1899 and was signed by Mrs. Gibbins and her four sons, and sealed by the Kings Norton and Northfield Urban District Council as directed by the minute of the Council. He had great pleasure on behalf of the Council to confirm what Mrs. Gibbins said in opening the gates that the "park was now open". Before he concluded he would like to add a word on his own account, and say how pleased he was that Selly Oak and neighbourhood had a park, and it had been a great pleasure to him personally to join in providing it. (Loud applause).

Councillor J. R. Oswald then moved a vote of thanks to the donors and said he had been honoured by the members of the Council, requesting him to present Mr. John Gibbins, on behalf of his mother and brothers, a copy of the resolution passed by the Council, engrossed on vellum as follows:- "Unanimously resolved that this Council accept the gift of Mrs. Gibbins and her sons, William, Thomas, John, and Benjamin, of a piece of land 11 acres, 2 roods, and 3 perches, in Old Lane, Selly Oak, for the purpose of a recreation ground, and hereby record their thanks to the donors and that the common seal of the Council is hereby affixed to the gift." On the opposite side the names of the members of the Council were added. He asked the older folk to assist in preventing damage to the grounds, shrubs, etc. He knew that thousands in the locality were very grateful for their great generosity, and there were thousands yet to come who would more appreciate the gift, as through the extensive building operations the time would come when these breathing places would be wanted more than at present. Personally, he was grateful to the Gibbins family, and he was sure everyone there would go away with kind feelings towards the good lady and her sons. (Applause).

Mr. S. Hill, as Chairman of the late Parish Council, and on behalf of the Foresters (Court Royal Oak), seconded the motion, and said it was in May, 1896, that he moved a resolution, which was seconded by Mr. William Holmes, that the Parish Council appoint a committee to look after the provision of a recreation ground for the village and district. From the time that resolution was passed by the unanimous vote of the Council the Parish Council had never lost sight of the work they undertook. Of course a great deal of work was done before Mrs. Gibbins and her sons took it up, and he might say the bulk of the work fell on Mr. Jacob Whitehouse, himself, and the members of the Parish Council. At the parish meeting which was held a good substantial majority voted in favour of their work, but, nevertheless, a poll was demanded and an enquiry was held, when Mr. Willis Bund – who only came on great occasions – came down. Owing to the hour at which the enquiry took place, they began to fear for their scheme. However, Mr. Willis Bund, to his honour, agreed to postpone his enquiry to a more suitable date, at any time they might think fit. But before that adjourned meeting took place, he came into possession of a letter, and that letter came from the offices of the Battery Company – (applause) – and in it stated that Mrs. Gibbins and her sons had decided to purchase the land and make it a suitable recreation ground for that district. Although the forces were in battle array at the enquiry, as soon as the letter was read, friends and foes vied as to who should be loudest in praise. To friends and foes it was no longer a bare garden, but a garden of Eden, and not too far off. (Applause). And here they were that day with the whole thing complete, made for the village for all time. He represented not only the Parish Council, but also the large body of Foresters, who wished him, on their behalf, to express their heartiest thanks to Messrs. Gibbins. (Applause).

Mr. W. Haddon, who represented the Oddfellows (Selly Oak Pride), and was also a member of the late Parish Council, supported the motion, remarking that most of the best things had already been said. The provision of that park was a great gratification to the inhabitants of Selly Oak, for, as they knew, the gentlemen responsible for the ratepayers' money were loth (sic) to spend the ratepayers' money on parks, baths, etc. Mrs. Gibbins and her sons, however came forward, and they were now in a position to vie with other parts of the district. (Applause). In his subsequent remarks Mr. Haddon said that for the children's school treat he could see in his mind's eye how that land would assist the committee, for he believed that Messrs. Gibbins had provided boilers and all the necessary arrangements for tea, so that they would be able to conduct the arrangements without unnecessary expense. He concluded by remarking how grateful they must all feel to the donors of the park. (Loud applause).

Alderman White expressed pleasure at being present, and to find himself in the company of so many of his old and valued friends with Mrs. Gibbins and her sons. When he first came there on a dull wintry afternoon some eighteen months ago, he felt how much the Messrs. Gibbins had in store for them in connection with the gift they contemplated offering to the district of Selly Oak, and that day they had the pleasure of making that offering one of the best gifts that could be given to a population like that residing in Selly Oak and neighbourhood. (Applause).

Mr. H. W. Elliott said he had been asked to say a few words and gladly did so. He thought they should all be prepared from the bottom of their hearts to thank the donors of such a gift as that presented that day. (Applause).

Mr. John Gibbins returned thanks on behalf of his mother, brothers, and himself. He might say that all the work in connection with that park had been to them a source of pleasure and satisfaction, and their hope was that it would be a great enjoyment to those who lived around. (Applause). To the children they knew it was most beneficial to have a good place to play in, and there would be abundance of fresh air and green grass within easy reach of their homes. (Applause).

Afterwards, on the suggestion of Mr. J. R. Oswald, hearty cheers were given for Mrs. Gibbins and the Messrs. Gibbins.

The proceedings were enlivened by the Selly Oak Victoria and the Stirchley Brass Band, who rendered selections at intervals.

8th April 1899 – The Birmingham News

Notes of the Week

Monday was a proud day for Selly Oak, witnessing, as it did, the formal handing over to the district and public opening of the new park, the noble gift of the Gibbins family. Favoured by glorious weather, the opening ceremony was a signal success, the function attracting probably the largest gathering ever seen in the district. The speeches were graceful and to the point, and the speakers vied with each other in praise of the generous impulse which led to a gift so rich in the promise of lasting benefit to the community. It would be impossible to speak too

4. 1899

highly of the consideration for the well-being of the district which has been throughout the inspiring motive of the donors of the park. Selly Oak is literally growing by leaps and bounds, and in a few years' time no doubt the speculative builder will have practically obliterated its rurality (sic). But whatever the development of the district there will always now remain the consolation that an open space has been preserved for all time. The lapse of years indeed will only help to emphasise and enhance the value of the gift, and the people of Selly Oak cannot better demonstrate their appreciation of the generosity of the Gibbins family than by making it their business to see that the park is in no way abused.

Local & District News
Selly Oak

<u>Selly Oak Park: The Opening Ceremony</u> – The people of Selly Oak have long looked forward to the day when they should be in possession of a public park and recreation ground of their own, and on Monday they had the pleasure of being present at a ceremony which realised their best hopes in this respect. This ceremony consisted of the formal opening and the hand over to the local governing authority as the people's trustees of what for some months previously had been popularly christened as Selly Oak Park – a handsomely proportioned and conveniently situated piece of land, laid out with shrubs and trees without stint of money or care, and presented to the district by Mrs. Gibbins and her sons. Those to whom the gift was made showed their deep sense of appreciation of the generous feeling which prompted the donors to make it by being present practically *en masse* at Monday's function. Acting on the suggestion of the District Council, the local friendly and temperance societies arranged to be present in an official capacity, and at about an hour before the time fixed for the opening ceremony the members, attired in regalia, assembled at the schools in Dawlish Road, where a procession was marshalled. The Selly Oak Fire Brigade also identified themselves with this demonstration, Captain Crump, Lieutenant Green, and Firemen Belcher, Stanley, Pickering, Lewis, Taylor, Withy, Perkins, and Stanworthy being present with the steamer and manual, with which the procession was headed. The Oddfellows and Foresters, headed by the Selly Oak Brass Band (conducted by Mr. A. White), followed immediately behind the brigade, and were accompanied, the former by the Noble Grand (Bro. C. Chapman), the Vice-Grand (Bro. C. Adams), the Secretary (Bro. William Humphries), and the Secretary of the Juvenile Branch (Bro. T. Wheatley); and the latter by the Chief Ranger (Bro. A. Wheeler), the Sub-Chief Ranger (Bro. F. J. Smith), the Secretary (Bro. William Pritchard), and the Juvenile Branch Secretary (Bro. J. Eaton). The rear was brought up by a strong contingent of Rechabites, headed by the Stirchley Brass Band (conducted by Mr. Ernest Quinton), and accompanied by the District Chief Ruler (Bro. H. Bracey). The parade proceeded via the High Street, which was thickly lined with spectators, to the park gates, and when the carriage containing the venerable lady who was to unlock the gates

rolled up, it was flanked on either side with a crowd which would number probably not less than 6,000. A silver key, recording on one side the occasion of its use, and bearing on the other a reproduction of the District Council's seal, had been made with which to unlock the gate, and this Councillor J. R. Oswald, who, as chairman of the Baths and Parks Committee of the Council, had charge of the ceremony, presented on behalf of the Council to Mrs. Gibbins, as she was lead to the gate, leaning on the arm of her son William. Having unlocked the gate, Mrs Gibbins declared the park to be open for the use of the public for ever, a declaration which was greeted by the crowd with ringing cheers. The key, enclosed in a morocco case, was presented to Mrs. Gibbins as a memento of the occasion. Upon the lid of the case was a silver plate, which bore the following inscription: "Presented to Mrs. Emma Joel Gibbins and her sons, donors of the Selly Oak Park, on the occasion of the opening ceremony, April 3rd, 1899. Mr. Edwin Boden Corah, Mr. Thomas Richard Bayliss, J.P., Mr. William Ward, Mr. John Robert Oswald, Mr. Frank Smith, Mr. William Henry Whitelock, Mr. John Norris, Mr. George Talliss, Mr. William Arthur Baldwin, Mr. Aaron Jones, Mr. George Pope Underhill, Mr. James William Bray Brown, Mr. James Johnstone Bryden, Mr. Edward Holmes, Mr. John Walter May, Mr. Thomas Edward Bladon, Mr. Edward Davison, members of the Council; Edwin Docker, clerk; Richard James Curtis, assistant clerk; Ambrose Wooten Cross, surveyor and engineer". Immediately upon the opening of the gates the company proceeded to the shelter in the centre of the park, where the remaining part of the function took place. On the shelter and amongst the surrounding crowd were, in addition to the donors of the park (Mrs. Gibbins, Mr. Thomas Gibbins, Mr. William Gibbins, and Mr. John Gibbins), Alderman White, Alderman Clayton, and Dr. S. E. Johnston (Birmingham City Council); District Councillors J. R. Oswald, G. P Underhill, J. W. B. Brown, J. Norris, Geo. Talliss, F. Smith, J. J. Bryden, W. J. May, T. E. Blaydon, and W. Ward, with the clerk (Mr. Edwin Docker), and the assistant surveyor (Mr. Joe Webb); Messrs. Simeon Hill, J. C. Aston, W. Haddon, R. Roberts, W. Hall, W. Payne, and J. A. Tuckey (members of the late Northfield Parish Council), with the clerk to that authority (Mr. Jacob Whitehouse); the Rev. C. W. Barnard, Dr. Hollinshead, Messrs. H. W. Elliott, J. S. Keep, W. H. Wynn, G. G. Poppleton, Wm. Burdett, J. Hadley, Wm. Holmes, M. Fryer, J. Wasley, A. Gittins, R. Prescott, T. Mumford, and T. Cottle; Mesdames R. C. Gibbins, C. W. Barnard, H. W. Elliott, G. P. Underhill, J. Norris, G. G. Poppleton, W. H. Wynn, T. E. Bladon, F. Hollinshead, J. H. Lloyd, M. Pryor, and J. R. Oswald, and Miss Keep. Law and order was represented at the ceremony by Inspector Holmes, Police-sergeants Rudnick and Caudle; and Police-constables Stanley, Young, Powell, Gall, Clarke, Nash, and Jennings. Between thirty and forty letters of apology for non-attendance were received, amongst the writers being Mr. J. H. Wilson, M.P., Mr. Austen Chamberlain, M.P., Mr. Neville Chamberlain, Mr. and Mrs. Walter Chamberlain, Sir Henry and Lady Wiggin, Mr. George Cadbury, Mr. and Mrs. T. R. Bayliss, Mr. J. G. Ledsam, Mr. and Mrs. W. A. Baldwin, Mr. and Mrs. Kendrick, Mr. and Mrs. Mapplebeck, Mr. R. Lloyd Gibbins, Mr. A. H.

Wiggin, the Misses Cadbury, and Mr. Edward Holmes. Proceedings were commenced by Mr. Oswald calling upon Mr. William Gibbins, who in response came forward and said: Ladies and gentlemen, it is with great pleasure that I, on behalf of my mother, my brothers and myself hand over this ground to the Kings Norton and Northfield Urban District Council for the use of the inhabitants of this rapidly growing neighbourhood. When the scheme for a recreation ground was first proposed it had our hearty sympathy, and we felt we should like to assist in it. On communicating with the Parish Council we offered to undertake to buy the ground, and we are here to-day to complete the work, and hand it over to the District Council. (Applause.) The land enclosed within the fences is 11½ acres in extent, and, as you will see, there are flower beds, and a walk laid out all round it. But a good piece of grass is still left for playing upon. The beds are planted with shrubs and trees, and I hope flowers and plants will also be added. We regret that there were no trees on the land, but we have planted a good many, and in a few year's time they will, I hope supply the deficiency. We have built a Park Keeper's lodge and this shelter, which can be used in case of sudden rain, and will also make a nice place for the children to play in the showery weather. I think we ought to associate with this work the names of Mr. Simeon Hill and the other members of the late Parish Council, as well as its clerk (Mr. Jacob Whitehouse). They were most earnest about it; they found the land, and we only came in and completed the scheme. We are also much indebted to the Baths and Parks Committee of the City Council, and our friend Alderman White, for having allowed Mr. Hearne to superintend the laying out of the land. With the large experience he has had, I do not think we could have found a more able man for this purpose. I should also mention the kindness and courtesy of Mr. J. G. Ledsam and Mr. J. T. Middlemore, M.P., who joined with us in making the good road which has taken the place of the old narrow lane. This has enabled the park to be properly completed, which it could not be, so long as the old lane remained. I will only add that I hope this park may be a source of enjoyment and recreation to all who use it, whether old or young, and that they may gain health and happiness from it. (Applause.) The deeds of the land were handed to Mr. Thomas Gibbins, who said: Ladies and gentlemen, as chairman of the District Council, I have been deputed on its behalf to accept the land and buildings transferred to the Council by this deed, and also to accept the conditions that accompany the gift. The conditions are: That the Council shall maintain this ground as a recreation ground for the use of the inhabitants of Selly Oak, Bournbrook, and neighbourhood, for ever – (hear, hear); – that it shall be open on week-days and on Sundays during such hours as the Council shall fix, and subject to such regulations as the Council shall from time to time make; that no intoxicating drinks shall be sold on the ground – (hear, hear); – and that the Council shall have power, under certain restrictions, at their discretion to lend or let the ground for the holding thereon a flower show or for similar purposes. These conditions were made with the view of securing that the ground should continue to be used for the purposes for which it is intended by the donors, and, as I say, are embodied in this deed, which is dated February 1st, 1899, signed by Mrs. Gibbins and her four sons, and sealed by the Kings Norton and Northfield Urban District Council, as directed by a minute of the Council. I have great pleasure, on behalf of the Council, in accepting the gift, and confirming Mrs. Gibbins' words in opening the park, namely, that it is a park open to the use of the public for ever. Before I retire, I should like to add a word on my own account, and say how pleased I am that Selly Oak and neighbourhood have a park. It has been a great pleasure to me, personally, to join in its provision. (Hear, hear, and applause.)

Councillor Oswald, stepping forward, then said, I have been honoured by the members of the Council by their requesting me to present to Mr. John Gibbins a copy of the resolution of thanks for the gift passed by the Council, engrossed on vellum. The wording of the resolution is as follows: "Unanimously resolved, that this Council do gratefully accept the gift of Mrs. Emma J. Gibbins and her sons William, Thomas, John, and Benjamin, of a piece of land, 11 acres, 2 roods, 5 perches in extent, situate in Old Lane, Selly Oak, for the purpose of a recreation ground, and do hereby record their thanks, as representing the public, to the donors for their generous gift; and that the common seal of this Council be and is hereby authorised to be affixed to the deed of gift". On the other side, proceeded Mr. Oswald, holding up the engrossment, is recorded the names of the members of the Council, and, as you will see, the whole is a most handsome production on the part of the artist. In making the presentation, I have but a few words to say. As chairman of the committee that will now have charge of these grounds, however, I make this request to each and all. Our young people have not that care and thought that older people possess, or are supposed to possess, and I ask everyone present, if ever they see any destruction being carried out by the youngsters, that they will mildly, but firmly, warn them of the injury they are doing, and of the consequences to which they are rendering themselves liable. There are thousands of people in this locality who will ever be grateful for the gift; there are thousands still to come who will more thoroughly appreciate it than we do to-day, inasmuch as the builder, that useful, yet at the same time destructive agent – so far as rural scenery is concerned – may in the course of time surround this breathing place with bricks and mortar, and thus render it all the more valuable. This contingency only accentuates the necessity of public bodies taking time by the forelock, and providing such breathing spaces as this, which ensure health – without which you cannot have happiness – and thereby cement that vigour in youth which in after life may be so greatly useful. Personally, let me say I am grateful to the Gibbins family for the part they have played in this good work, and although in their presence we do not care to say overmuch, I am sure everyone here present will go away with warm feelings toward that good lady and her sons, and they can take it from me that all persons in this locality thank them from the bottom of their hearts for their generosity. (Applause.) I now ask to second this resolution Mr. Simeon Hill, chairman of the late Parish Council, who, as has been said by Mr. Gibbins, took an exceptionally prominent part in the infant stage of this project, which the Gibbins family have so handsomely completed.

4. 1899

In response to this request Mr. Hill came forward, and said: Ladies and gentlemen, a gentleman in my company was asked yesterday whether he thought there would be many people present at the opening ceremony of the park, and he expressed his belief that everybody and his wife would be there, and he was right, for I verily believe that everybody in this district, including his wife, is here. And it is quite right that they should be, for the occasion is one which I suppose we shall never live to see repeated. The cheer with which you greeted me I take to be a recognition of the part that the late Parish Council took in connection with this recreation ground – (Hear, hear.); and although it is no part of my business here today to speak of the work of that Council, I may be permitted to say a word or two in reference to that part that the Council took in connection with this ground. In May of 1896 I moved, and Mr. William Holmes seconded, a resolution appointing a committee whose duty it should be to look after a ground to be used as a recreation ground for this village and the surrounding district. The resolution was unanimously passed, and from that time the Parish Council never lost sight of the work they undertook. A great deal of work of an onerous character was done previously to the Messrs. Gibbins taking the matter up, and I may say that the bulk of that work devolved upon Mr. Jacob Whitehouse and myself. We were splendidly backed up by nearly every member of the Council, who never lost sight of the site we had undertaken to obtain, clearly perceiving the benefit that would be conferred upon the village if it could be secured. I well remember the meeting of parishioners convened to give their opinion upon the work we had undertaken on their behalf, and I remember that a good, sound, substantial majority voted in favour of its sanction. Notwithstanding this, however, a poll was demanded, and again the people asserted their demand for a recreation ground for this district. After that it was arranged that a Local Government Board inquiry should be held, and Mr. Willis Bund, whom he had noticed only came into the district on great occasions, – (laughter) – came down from Worcester. The inquiry was held, and there was some opposition to and severe criticism against the scheme, for which, however, it was probably all the better. But it made us fear for its safety – we thought our little boat may be capsized, and so began to make provision for a final onslaught. To commence with, we objected to the inquiry being held in the middle of the day, as being unsuitable to the working men – (applause); and as a result got it postponed. The postponed inquiry was held at Bournbrook Institute, and a great number of both friends and foes was present. At that inquiry was read a letter, of which I had previously come into possession, such as had never previously been read at any meeting in Selly Oak, and probably will never be read again. That letter came from the Battery Company, and in it was stated that Mrs. Gibbins and her sons had determined to purchase the land, lay it out, and provide all things necessary to make it suitable for a recreation ground, and present it to the people of the district. (Applause.) This was the culmination point, and although the forces were drawn up in battle array, no sooner was that letter read than friends and foes vied with each other as to who could speak the loudest in praise of the land and the donors, and everything connected with it. (Laughter.) Objections vanished, the ground had undergone a change; it was no longer a bare garden, it was no longer too far off, it immediately became a Garden of Eden, most suitable for the purpose, and within a comfortable distance of the village. (Laughter.) Here we are today with the whole thing completed, and the park made over to this village for all time. Shall we ever forget such a gift as this? (No, no.) The recreation ground will be one of the chief memories of the generosity of this family; we need no monument to immortalise what can never die. I have only to say that I represent not only the late Parish Council, but also a body of Foresters, numbering between 400 and 500, who are here today – as they were represented by their delegates at the inquiry to which I have referred. I am glad to say that I am informed that everyone of these wishes to give his heartiest thanks to the Messrs. Gibbins for their noble and generous gift. They say that it is unanimous because they are informed that but one opposed it, and he has left the Court. (Laughter.) I second the resolution.

Mr. W. Haddon (representing the Oddfellows) supported the proposition. He said: I think most of the best things have been said, and that there is little I can add. Still, as representing the Oddfellows, it is a great pleasure to me to give expression to their thanks to the Messrs. Gibbins for their great gift, and to the esteem in which they are held by them. Our governing authority are very careful how they spend the ratepayers' money in the provision of recreation grounds, baths, etc, which I claim to be for the public good, but the Messrs. Gibbins very generously came forward, and placed the district upon a footing with other surrounding districts by presenting to it this handsome park. It is a great addition to the assets of the ratepayers of Northfield, and the benefits which it will confer are not merely confined to the present, but will be enjoyed in increasing measure by our children, as the park is gradually surrounded, as it in time will be, with bricks and mortar. It is a gift for ever; it will remain for others' enjoyment and appreciation after we are gone. I can foresee many ways in which the park will benefit the district in a secondary but important sense. The Children's Trust, for instance, will be able to be held here, and thanks to the thoughtfulness which has led the Messrs. Gibbins to provide a boiler and all the necessary conveniences for the provision of tea, the committee will be able to conduct their arrangements at the least possible expense. (Hear, hear.) Gentlemen, I think that most has been said that can be said. I am here to represent the Oddfellows, and I wish it to be handed down how grateful the working men of this district are to the Messrs. Gibbins for the great gift they have bestowed upon Selly Oak and her children for ever. (Applause.)

In supporting the resolution, Alderman White said: It gives me great pleasure to be here to-day for several reasons. It is a great pleasure to find myself in the company of so many of my old and valued friends – Mrs. Gibbins and her sons. When I came here on a dull winter afternoon some eighteen months ago, with Mr. William Gibbins, I felt how much pleasure was in store for him and for his brothers in connection with the gift which they contemplated offering to the district of Selly Oak – one of the very best gifts, be it said, that could be made to a population like that residing in Selly Oak and neighbourhood. (Hear, hear.) I have had the pleasure of taking part in the opening of most of the parks possessed by the city of Birmingham, as being a member of the Baths and Parks Committee, the present chairman of which (Councillor S. E. Johnston) it is my pleasure to be accompanied with this afternoon. Let me say, ladies and gentlemen, in connection with this park, how sincerely I hope that the best use will be made of this charming piece of ground – that everyone who comes here to enjoy the air and the sunshine and the leafage of the trees will do his best to preserve order, to prevent mischief, or anything that may from any point of view be a detriment to these beautiful grounds, or in any way appear to disparage the noble gift. I have always felt that there is no gift which can be bestowed upon the population of a district such as this which is more valuable than a piece of ground like this, in the form of a park. May you who listen to these imperfect words of mine, and your children's children, long enjoy it, and may they hand down to remotest generations the names of the kind and noble donors. (Applause.)

Mr. H. W. Elliott also supported the resolution. I have been asked (he said) to say a few words, and, although quite unprepared, gladly do it. It needs no preparation to say from our hearts how grateful we are for the thoughtfulness and the kind and gracious generosity of the Messrs. Gibbins, and especially of the venerable lady who joins with them in this noble gift. I trust that the recipients of the gift, so well worthy of those who have given it, will show their appreciation of it by welcoming it and endeavouring, to the best of their ability, to keep it in the same splendid order in which it is to-day. I think each one of us should be guardians and custodians of the park, and take care that no mischievously inclined little boys and girls shall do any damage to the shrubs and trees which now so greatly beautify this splendid grounds, and which, as time goes on, will continue to add to its beauty. We must not forget that it is not only a gift to us, but to future ages, whose children will be able to assemble here and think of how much good has been done by those who preceded them. As one of the oldest inhabitants of the neighbourhood – perhaps the oldest – and as one of those who, with Messrs. Gibbins, have been the means of providing the need for such a park as this, I say, and say it advisedly, that no more acceptable or welcome gift could possibly have been given to the inhabitants of Selly Oak than this, the opening of which we commemorate today, and in my own name, and in the name, I am sure, of everyone present, I thank the venerable lady, Mrs. Gibbins, and I thank each one of her noble sons for her splendid gift to us, the inhabitants of Selly Oak. (Applause.)

The resolution was carried with great enthusiasm.

Mr. John Gibbins, in replying to the resolution, said: I have to thank you on behalf of my mother, my brothers, and myself for the kind way in which you have referred to this gift, and also for the very handsome copy of the resolution of the Council which you have given us. I may say that all the work in connection with the park – its laying out, etc. – has been to us a source of very much pleasure and satisfaction. Our hope is that it will be a great enjoyment to those who live around. To the children we all know it is most beneficial to have a good place to play in, and I think that here will be found abundance of fresh air and green grass within easy reach of their homes. (Hear, hear.)

The conclusion of this most pleasing function was three mighty cheers, making the welkin ring again, for the donors, with an extra, and special cheer, for Mrs. Gibbins. Later in the afternoon a squad of children from the Shenley Fields Cottage Homes gave an exhibition of dumb-bell exercises.

19th May 1899 – KN&N UDC Baths, Parks and Cemeteries Committee

<u>Lettings</u> The Clerk reported that the Committee of Amalgamated Juvenile Fete had now selected June 3rd as the date they desired to use the Park.

Resolved that the use of the Park on Monday July 3rd be granted to the Selly Oak and Bournbrook Children's Fete Committee[37] subject to conditions to be imposed.

Resolved that the following conditions[38] be attached to the letting of the Park on June 3rd, July 3rd and August 5th

1. That no alcoholic refreshments be taken on the ground or permitted to be offered for sale.
2. That permission be given for the erection of tents, swing boats, refreshment stalls (temperance), ice cream and sweet stalls, and variety entertainments (such as Punch and Judy shows), and also on July 3rd for the erection and use of a steam roundabout.
3. That no coconut-throwing be permitted in the Park.
4. That all erections be made in such positions and in such manner as the Park Keeper may approve.
5. That the Secretary of the Committees applying give their own personal undertaking to repay the full cost of restoring any damage done or arising out of the use of the Park, and the fixing of any erections in the Park or removal of the same.
6. That the Surveyor and Park Keeper have absolute power and control in all respects in the matter.
7. That the applicants be given to understand that upon what is done on these occasions will very much depend the decisions of the Committee on future applications.

---

[37] This fete was originally a celebration of the opening of the parish church. There is an item in the 15th September 1900 edition of the Birmingham News in the section "Selly Oak and District Notes" – "On Wednesday afternoon the children attending Selly Oak and Bournbrook day schools were given a holiday, in celebration of the dedication, 35 years ago, of the parish church. Years ago it was the custom to hold a treat for the children on this day, and it was from this that the children's fete sprang."

[38] These conditions were printed verbatim in the South Birmingham Chronicle, and in The Birmingham News, on Saturday, May 27th, 1899.

8. That the Surveyor be consulted before the steam roundabout is taken into the Park, and all his requirements and conditions as to fixing and removing same strictly complied with, but this provision is not to be taken as relieving the aforesaid Secretaries of liability for any damage that may be done.
9. That at first ringing of the Park bell all proceedings must terminate, and the Park be cleared of the public by the second ringing.
10. That the Council accept no liability or responsibility with respect to any interference with or damage that may be done to the private road known as Gibbins Road.

Insurance against fire Resolved a Policy of Insurance against Fire be taken out in the Royal Insurance Company:

For the Lodge	£350
For the Shelter	£150

Bye Laws The Committee considered suggested Bye Laws and approved the same and it was resolved to recommend that such Bye Laws be made and adopted by the Council and that notice be given as required by Statute of intention to apply for confirmation of the same by the Local Government Board.

Park Keeper Resolved to recommend that application be made to the Justices to swear in Park Keeper Mr Josiah Thomas Horton as a Special Constable.

Music in the Park Resolved that the application of the Selly Oak Victoria Brass Band for permission to play in the Park every Wednesday during the months of June, July and August be acceded to and the Band given the sole use of the Park for an open air concert at the end of the season but that if any weekly collection is made this privilege be withdrawn.

The Surveyor was instructed to cause a platform 18" high to be erected for the use of the Band.

20th May 1899 – The Birmingham News

Local & District News
Selly Oak

Selly Oak and Bournbrook Children's Fete – .... the committee finally settled upon Monday as the day upon which the fete should be held, and after some further discussion fixed the date for July 3rd. The secretary was instructed to make application to the Kings Norton and Northfield District Council for the use of the park on that date. ....

The Heydays Of Selly Oak Park

3rd June 1899 – The Birmingham News

The Use of Selly Oak Park

The beneficent intentions of the donors of Selly Oak Park seem in danger of being defeated to some extent by the over-anxiety of its custodians to prevent its misuse or abuse. When the park was handed over to the district it was recognised as an inestimable boon, not merely because it secured an open space for ever in a neighbourhood which is becoming more and more congested every year, but because it provided a much needed recreation ground for the children. The donors, while wisely stipulating as one of the conditions of the gift that no intoxicating drinks should be sold on the ground, generously made provision for the use of the park for flower shows or for similar purposes, under certain restrictions, which were left at the discretion of the Kings Norton and Northfield Urban Council, in whom the park was vested as the people's representatives. Everybody will sympathise with the desire of the Council to take all possible precautions for the protection and preservation of so valuable a possession, but the conditions upon which it is proposed to grant the use of the park to the Selly Oak and Bournbrook Children's Fete Committee for the holding of this year's fete seem more exacting than the circumstances demand.

 Not only is it proposed to give the surveyor and Park Keeper absolute control over the arrangements of the event in the park, but the secretary of the committee is to be made personally responsible for any damage that may be done, and, furthermore, it is laid down that "upon what is done on these occasions will very much depend the decisions of the committee in future applications". Compliance with the same conditions is insisted upon also in the case of the Selly Oak Foresters' and Oddfellows' annual fete and the Selly Oak flower show. But, as will be seen, there is a very great difference in the character of these events, for while in the case of the Foresters' fete and flower show certain specific objects or funds will be benefited, the children's event is a public event, promoted simply and solely for the enjoyment of the children. The former affairs, too, are in the nature of business speculations, while the latter is purely philanthropic, and on this ground, the committee think, is deserving of superior consideration. Undoubtedly, as Mr. Cole pointed out at the meeting of the Children's Fete Committee on Monday, some conditions are necessary, if only to create a sense of responsibility on the part of those hiring it, for the protection of the park, but, as Mr. S. Hill suggested, liability should be made contingent upon the damage done being manifestly the result of the negligence of the committee to take reasonable measures to secure the grounds from wanton injury.

 Selly Oak people are naturally proud of their park, and we venture to think it would be far from the wish of its donors that such unnecessarily stringent conditions as those described should be attached to its use for philanthropic public purposes. It is to be hoped the Council will see their way to effect some slight modification in such cases on the lines we have suggested. All reasonable requirements would be satisfied if it were simply stipulated that the Children's Fete Committee should make good any damage resulting from negligence, without rendering them liable to be called upon to repair the damage to turf, paths, etc., which must inevitably result from the use of the park for any public event. A moral obligation rests upon all who use the park to see that it is not abused, and while many are no doubt indifferent to all sense of obligation, moral or otherwise, it is only fair to give those who interest themselves in the promotion of such events as the children's fete, credit for a full appreciation of their responsibility for the protection of the public property.

Letters to the Editor
The Use of Selly Oak Park

Sir, – the conditions upon which the District Council offer the use of Selly Oak park to the Selly Oak and Bournbrook Children's Fete Committee afford a fine example of a riotously mad red tapeism (sic). A Whitehall official in his most frenzied moment could hardly have done better. The document only lacks a little medieval English to make it a perfect specimen of its genus, and the individual directly responsible for it deserves immortality. The officialism (sic) which characterises the government of the park is entirely alienating the local public from its use, and thus depriving the gift of all its intended beneficence. Last Saturday, though beautifully fine, scarcely saw a score of children in the park. Local folk are asking what the donors think of this. It surely does not meet with their approbation. –

Yours truly,   "VILLAGER"

Bournbrook, May 29th, 1899

Local & District News
Selly Oak

<u>Children's Fete Committee – An animated meeting</u> – The first meeting of the newly constituted Children's Fete Committee was held at Bournbrook Institute on Monday evening, Mr. T. A. Cole presiding. The hon. secretary (Mr. A. Gittins) announced that Mr. W. Holmes had reconsidered his determination to retire from office, and had consented to accept the position of treasurer to which he was elected at the public meeting held three weeks ago. Mr. W. Haddon, too, has consented to act on the committee.

Arising out of the minutes was the consideration of the conditions upon which the District Council intimate their willingness to permit the park to be used for the holding therein of the fete, and upon the subject a rigorous discussion turned. The principal clauses of the conditions are those which stipulate that the secretary shall make himself personally liable for any damage which may be done by reason of the fete being held at the park, and that the surveyor to the Council and the Park Keeper have absolute control of the arrangements of the event so far as they relate to its use.

The Secretary expressed the opinion that the conditions were harsh. It was impossible, he said, that some damage should not be done at an event which would draw together some six or seven thousand people, and seeing that the occasion was a public one in its broadest sense, and would not result in the financial benefit of any section of the community – no entrance or other charge whatever being associated with it – he did not think any responsibility for damage should be cast upon the committee or any of its members. Any liability incurred should be upon the public who used the park, and defrayed out of the rates. In addition to the Council throwing the whole of the responsibility upon the committee, they proposed to deprive them of any control over the event, and, further, added insult to injury by putting them upon their good behaviour in giving them to understand that upon what was done on that occasion very much depended the Council's decision in regard to future applications. The conditions were known in the village before the Baths and Parks Committee of the Council had seen them, and to his mind they savoured very much of a "one man" arrangement. In any case, he considered the Council had acted in a spirit of meanness in sanctioning them. He did not feel at all disposed, as secretary, to accept the responsibility which they implied.

Mr. J. H., Walton thought Mr. Gittins was taking too serious a view of the matter, and expressed the opinion that the conditions were only such as the Council ought to make in self-protection.

Mr. Cole said that the committee had never yet had a ground where they had not been responsible for any damage incurred, and he thought the Council were quite right in making such a stipulation. Some such rules were needed to create a sense of responsibility, and this would go far to act as a protective agent by making the members of the committee or society using it, for the time being, policemen over what went on in the park.

Mr. S. Hill, while thinking some conditions necessary, said that in those drawn up there seemed to have been an over-haste in trying to make officialism (sic) felt, and he thought the act of the committee in forbidding the playing of cricket and rounders, etc., in the park, by the children, supported his view. True, it was said that the order was meant to apply to adults only, but the Park Keeper did not interpret it in that sense, and it was not till himself and several others made representations to members of the committee that more specific instructions were given to that official. The conditions under discussion were stringent, and could be legally enforced, and he for one did not care to make himself responsible under them. He thought the conditions should have made liability contingent upon lack of reasonable care, or negligence, rather than upon actual damage. The park belonged to the public, and was given for their use generally, as well as specifically for such functions as that for which the committee sought it, and the rates was consequently the proper source from which to defray the cost of putting right any damage done.

Mr. Cole and Mr. Frank Smith offered to solve the point by personally undertaking the liability for any damage done, but, while thanking them for their generosity, the committee declined upon principle to take advantage of it.

4. 1899

Eventually on the motion of Mr. Hill, seconded by Mr. Sheasby, the secretary was instructed to ascertain whether the Council intended the conditions to be interpreted according to their letter, and if so, to endeavour to secure some modification to them.

The Secretary announced that he had opened an account on behalf of the committee at Lloyd's Bank, in the names of the chairman, treasurer, and himself, and that there stood to the credit of the account a sum of £5.

It was decided that collecting cards be placed in every shop in the village, and Councillor Frank Smith and Mr. S. Hill were entrusted with the responsibility of distributing the cards and collecting the moneys so obtained.

The collectors for the house to house collection were also appointed.

As Monday evening is found to be a generally inconvenient night for the members of the committee, it was unanimously decided to hold the future meetings on Thursday evenings, at 8.30 o'clock as hitherto.

The next meeting is on Thursday next.

7th June 1899 – Minute of KN&N UDC

The report of this Committee (i.e. the Baths Parks & Cemeteries Committee[39]) having been printed was taken as read and ordered to be entered on the Minutes as follows:-

Lettings
That the use of the Park has been granted on the dates and for the purposes named, subject to the following conditions:-

> June 3rd – "Oddfellows and Foresters' Juvenile Fete"
> July 3rd – "Children's Fete"
> August 5th – "Annual Show of Horticultural Society"

(There then follows the conditions as listed in the minute of the Committee on 19 May 1899 – see above)

Rules and Regulations

That by virtue of the powers enabling them in this behalf, this Council hereby makes the following Bye Laws with respect to the Park or recreation ground belonging to them, and known as "Selly Oak Park" and hereby authorises and instructs the Baths, Parks and Cemeteries Committee to take all necessary steps in the name and on behalf of this Council, and under the Common Seal for the confirmation of such Bye Laws, and when the said Bye Laws have been duly confirmed, for giving effect thereto.

---

[39] This meeting was reported in the South Birmingham Chronicle, Saturday, June 10th, 1899.

(There then follows a list of the Bye Laws which were subsequently adjusted and are reproduced below in the minute dated 3 January 1900 – where the adjustments have been indicated.)

Music in the Park
That the application of the Selly Oak Victoria Brass band for permission to play in the park every Wednesday during the months of June, July and August be acceded to, and a platform erected for the use of such band, who be granted the sole use of the park for an open-air concert upon some evening at the end of the season subject to their not making any weekly collection.

Park Keeper
That application be made to the Justices or Chief Constable of the County to swear in the Park Keeper (Mr. Horton) as a "Special Constable"

10th June 1899 – The Birmingham News

Selly Oak and Bournbrook Children's Fete Committee

A meeting of this committee was held at the Institute on Thursday evening, Mr. T. A. Cole presiding.

The Chairman read a letter which he had received from Mr. J. R. Oswald, denying the accuracy of the statement made by Mr. Gittins at the preceding meeting, that the conditions upon which the District Council would grant the use of Selly Oak Park for functions of a public character were known before they had been submitted to the Baths, Parks, and Cemeteries Committee for approval.

An offer was announced from a local troupe of minstrels – the Minnesota – of an entertainment on the day of the fete free of charge, and this was referred to the Sports and Fields Sub-Committee along with an application from Mr. Dowell to be given the order for providing the Punch and Judy Show, as at last year's fete.

Quite a long list of new committee men were enrolled, the proposals being as follows: Messrs. E. Morris, G. Ollis, Pember, Jacob Whitehouse, J.G. Purser, T. W. Lawrence, H. Humphries, A. Honeybourne, and F. Spurrier.

The sub-committees for making all the necessary arrangements for the fete were then appointed, power being given to each to add to their number. Sports and Fields: Mr. J. Draper (chairman), Messrs. Jordan, Sheasby, Greswolde, James, Darby, Halward, and Ollis; Catering: Mr. Humphries (chairman), Messrs. Hall, F. Smith, and R. Roberts; Procession: Mr. W. Holmes (chairman), Messrs. Gilbert, Castagni, Hill, Morris, Haddon, and F. Goode.

It was decided to have the steam roundabout again, and also to permit villagers to have stalls in the ground at so much per yard of the frontage occupied by their booths.

Mr. E. Morris announced his intention of offering a special prize of a guinea for the competition, and also to give half a guinea to the funds of the fete. A subscription of 10s. was also announced from Mr. B. Connop, of the High Street.

4. 1899

Local & District News
Selly Oak

<u>Selly Oak Victoria Band</u> – The programme to be given by the band in the park, on Wednesday next, commencing at seven o'clock, is as follows:-

    March..........................."High School Cadets".........................(Sousa)
    Overture......................."Cross of Honour"..........................(Bleger)
    Valse..................................."Promenade"............................(Cannon)
    Fantasia........................"Beauties of Ireland"......................(Newton)
    Cornet Solo...................."Two Brass Men" ....(Laing)
    (Soloist: Mr. R. White)
    Selection ...."Gondoliers" ....(Sullivan)
    Caprice........................"La Garde Montante" ....(Wely)
    Galop................................."Ormonde"............................(Seaman)
    God save the Queen

<u>Music at Selly Oak Park</u> – The Selly Oak Victoria Brass Band recently offered to give a weekly selection of music in the park, and the Baths, Parks, and Cemeteries Committee of the District Council giving the necessary permission, the band gave their first programme last Wednesday evening, in the presence of a good number of visitors. Weather permitting, the band will play every Wednesday evening throughout the summer months, and the programme to be given will appear at the head of our Selly Oak news in the preceding Saturday's issue, as next Wednesday's programme this week. In consideration of the band making no collection, the Council have granted them the sole use of the park for an open air concert upon some evening at the end of the season, when of course a charge for admission will be made. The money so obtained will be used for the purchase of music, which is always a very appreciable item in any band's accounts, and it is to be hoped that the concert, whenever it is, will be favoured with fine weather, and that the villagers will show their appreciation of the band's generous offer by being present in very large numbers. The step is one which will do more perhaps than anything else could have been done to accustom the local public to the regular use of the park, and in this way will make it a thoroughly popular place of resort on an evening. The Baths, Parks, and Cemeteries Committee of the District are to be thanked, too, for the readiness with which they took up the band's offer and acquiesced in their stipulation for a suitable stand. As those who have visited the park lately will know, this is already erected, and it certainly forms a very good pedestal for the purpose, and one from which the band can shed their dulcet strains upon the admiring music-loving throng without being prodded and pin-pricked by small boys inquisitive to know if it is possible for a bandsman to produce anything else but music, and also as the where he keeps his stock of wind.

<u>The Park Keeper a "Special Constable"</u> – At the monthly meeting of the District Council, on Wednesday, authorisation was given for an application to the justices

or Chief Constable of the county to swear in Mr. Horton, the Park Keeper, as a "special constable".

Juvenile Foresters and Oddfellows Annual Fete – For the past six years or more the annual fete of the juvenile Foresters and Oddfellows has been held on a Whit Monday, but owing to the weather the success of the event has on almost every occasion been more or less marred, and it is doubtful if it has ever been what might truly be termed a complete success, while last year it was – financially, of course – a complete failure. As a result the amalgamated committee of the two Orders, by which the arrangements of the fete are made and carried out, decided to abandon Whit-Monday as the day for holding the event, and selected June 3rd, i.e. last Saturday. The complete justification of the step was shown in the fact that Whit-Monday was again a shockingly wet day, and would certainly have resulted in a repetition of last year's failure had it been chosen, while Saturday was beautifully fine, and resulted in the fete being far the most all-round success that has yet been achieved. Henceforward it is not likely that the claims of the so called popular Bank Holiday as a fitting day for the event will be even considered. The procession started from St. Mary's Schools shortly after one o'clock, and before reaching the park, where the fete was held, paraded Oak Tree Lane, Katie Road, Lottie Road, Elliott Road, High Street, Hubert Road, Exeter Road, Dawlish Road, High Street, Frederick Road, and Gibbins Road, in which the park is situate. The secretaries of the respective Orders, Messrs. T. Wheatley (Oddfellows) and J. Eaton (Foresters), headed the procession on horseback. Following was the Selly Oak Victoria Brass Band, under the conductorship of Mr. H. White, and behind the band came a number of competitors for prizes offered by the committee for decorated mail-carts, vehicles, and ponies, and also for the best fancy costume worn by a rider of the ponies. The entries included the following:- Horses (the owner's name only being given): Messrs. W. Hughes, T. Hunt, Dugmore, Cullimore, and Halward, and Mrs. Hinton. Vehicles: T. Meere (only competitor). Mail-cart: Duckworth (only competitor). Bicycles: Rogers, Cooper, Garratt, Oswald. Costumes: Messrs. Hughes, Hunt, Moore, and Dugmore. Special mention must be awarded to the only competitor in the vehicle section (T. Meere), his vehicle being very tastefully decorated with lilac, laburnum, and May-blossom, while the mail-cart of Master Duckworth, the only entry in its class also, is worthy of the highest praise. This was a representation of Dick Whittington and his cat, the bundle, milestone and cat of this well-known old story being excellently imitated. The prize-winners were as follows:- Ponies, Messrs. Dugmore, Cullimore, and Hughes; vehicles, Mr. Meere; costume, Messrs. Dugmore, Moore, and Hughes; mail-cart, Master Duckworth; bicycles, Messrs. Rogers and Garratt; and consolation prizes to Messrs. Williams and Hooper. The bicycle competition, in which only two prizes were offered, in the belief that it would not secure many entries, turned out to be the best of the lot. The boys who rode the ponies entered for competition were dressed by the committee, to whom the highest credit is due for the evident pains which they took in this, as indeed in every, direction. At the park the attractions included a couple of demonstrations by the Selly Oak Fire Brigade, variety entertainments by Feeney and Farrell (Irish comedians), Sam Hall (song and dance artiste), Dan Lasset (comic vocalist), and J. Powell (comedian and dancer), a very largely patronised punch and judy show, six mutoscope machines[40], for peering into which at a penny ahead there was a great demand; swing boats and dancing. The juvenile members, to the number of 285, were given a free tea in the shelter, in addition to receiving on entering the park a bun and a medal commemorative of the event. In addition to the children, there were fully 1,500 persons present at the fete.

17th June 1899 – The Birmingham News

Selly Oak and Bournbrook Children's Fete

The interest felt in the Selly Oak and Bournbrook Children's fete was well shown in the large and representative attendance present at the weekly meeting of the committee on Thursday evening. Amongst the company were Councillor J. R. Oswald, Messrs. J. Draper, T. W. Lawrence, S. Hill, E. Morris, Wm. Holmes, T. Hall, R. Roberts, F. Spurrier, W. Humphreys, J. Gough, Gilbert, James, Ollis, J. H. Walton, Perkins, Goode, A. White, and A. Gittins (hon. sec.). In the unavoidable absence of Mr. T. A. Cole (chairman of the committee), Mr. J. Draper was elected to preside.

The secretary read a letter from a roundabout proprietor, offering to provide a roundabout from two o'clock till the time of the closing of the park on the the day of the fete for £20, on condition that he was permitted to bring it into the park on the day preceding, and remove it on the day following the fete. As, however, a roundabout was provided last year for £7, and this year other offers, in one case of £5 and in a second of £8, have been received, the committee declined the offer with thanks.

Mr. Oswald took advantage of the opportunity to explain that the clause in the conditions upon which the Council granted the use of the park, stipulating that the arrangements should meet with the approval of the surveyor and Park Keeper, was introduced so that it could be ensured that the provision against damage to the turf by the heavy roundabout machinery would be taken in case the ground was soft through wet.

It was decided that the Selly Oak Victoria Brass Band should be engaged, and the Procession Sub-committee were empowered to draw up a prize list for decorated vehicles, mail-carts, bicycles, etc., providing for the expenditure of £5 in prizes.

It was further decided to have a Punch and Judy Show, a form of amusement which proved immensely popular last year.

On the suggestion of Mr. Oswald, it was decided that an appeal should be made to gentlemen in the district, through the medium of a circular, in which the history

---

[40] Later to be known as "What the Butler Saw" machines.

of the fete and the great interest which the local public evinced in it should be detailed.

The procession is to start from the day schools in Tiverton Road, and proceed straight to the park, via Dawlish Road.

Mr. Humphreys suggested the organisation of a sports programme on the field in the place of the "rough and ready" and by no means altogether satisfactory method which obtained last year; and the suggestion, which met with general approval, was referred to the Sports and Field Committee for consideration.

Mr. Oswald stated that the committee would be allowed to enclose the shelter with boards, canvas, or such like, if desired, so as to provide a place for cutting up provisions, etc.

Various amounts were handed in by the collectors, bringing up the funds to a total at present of £12. Last year, as the residents will have seen from the balance sheets, which have been freely distributed, £65 was spent, and as at least as large a sum is required this year, it is to be hoped a liberal response will be made to the invitation of the collectors (who will call at every house in the village) to subscribe.

17th June 1899 – The Birmingham News

Local & District News
Selly Oak

<u>Selly Oak Victoria Band</u> – The following is the programme to be given in the park by the band on Wednesday evening, commencing at seven o'clock:-

March	"Palmer House"	Pettec
Overture	"Tancredi"	Rossini
Cornet Solo	"Queen of the Earth"	Ciro Pinsuti
	(Soloist: T. Hems)	
Valse	"Albion"	H. Sibold
Selection	"Haddon Hall"	A. Sullivan
Intermezzo	"Honoria"	Thos. Bidgood
Fantasia	"Songs of Yore" (Arranged by E. Newton)	
Galop	"Express"	T. Dawson

God Save the Queen
Conductor ………….. H. White

24th June 1899 – The South Birmingham Chronicle:

THE BAND – Selly Oak Band was favoured with fine weather again on Wednesday, and there was consequently a good attendance of the public at the weekly voluntary entertainment. Next Wednesday the band will render the following programme:- March, "Collingwood", by Pettel; selection, "Geisha" (S. Jones); overture, "Under the British Colour", (H. King); cornet solo, "Lizzy Polka", (J. Hartman), soloist, J.

Ketteridge; valse, "Morning Glories", (W. Rimmer); selection, "Dandy Fifth", (C.C. Corri); barn dance, "Washington Post", (Theo. Bonheur); galop, "Express", (J. Dawson). – Conductor, H. White.

24th June 1899 – The Birmingham News

Selly Oak and Bournbrook Children's Fete Committee

Mr. T. A. Cole presided at the weekly meeting of this committee held at Bournbrook Institute on Thursday evening, and amongst those present were Councillor J. R. Oswald, Messrs. J. G. Purser, J. Draper, W. Holmes, E. Morris, W. Humphries, T. W. Lawrence, T. Hall, R. Roberts, S. Hill, J. Gough, James, White, Roy, Felton, Gilbert, Perkins, H. G. Humphries, Spurrier, Goode, Honeybourne, Sheppard, Smith, Taylor, Jordan, Hollies, and the secretary (Mr. A. Gittins).

It was decided that no children over twelve years of age should be admitted unless attending school, and that the general public should not be admitted to the Park on the day of the fete until 5 o'clock. Each member of the committee is to wear a rosette of a peculiar make, which will render any attempt at imitation easily detected, and no person not displaying one of these will be permitted to pass the constable who will be on duty at the Park gates until the time specified for the admission of the general public. An offer by the Birmingham Mutoscope Company for the exhibition of a number of mutoscope machines was accepted. The procession was fixed to start at 1.15 p.m. prompt.

The secretary was instructed to write to the Clerk of the District Council asking for the use of the Park on the following day should the day upon which it is intended to hold the fete prove wet.

Local & District News
Selly Oak

<u>Music in the Park</u> – The following is the programme to be given by the Selly Oak Victoria Brass Band in the Park on Wednesday next:- (and then follows the same list as in The South Birmingham Chronicle – see immediately above).

27th June 1899 – KN&N UDC Baths, Parks and Cemeteries Committee

A letter was read form the Honorary Secretary of the Amalgamated Juvenile Fete Committee expressing thanks for the use of the Park on 3rd June 1899 and testifying to the hearty support and co-operation received from the Park Keeper.

<u>Music in the Park</u> The Honorary Secretary of the Woodgate Brass Band wrote offering their services to give a programme of music in the Park some Saturday evening and the Clerk was directed to thank him for the offer and to state that the same shall be considered at the next meeting.

The Heydays Of Selly Oak Park

<u>Application for use of the Park</u> Resolved that the Selly Oak Victoria Band be granted the use of the Park on Saturday August the 26th 1899 and permitted to make a collection, the letting to be subject to the usual conditions.

Resolved that if suitable arrangements can be made by Councillor Talliss, the application from the Order of Rechabites for the use of a portion of the Park on Saturday the 19th August be granted on the usual conditions.

<u>Drainage</u> – resolved that the Surveyor do what is necessary for the drainage of the Park.

<u>Swings at the Park</u> Resolved to recommend that a set of swings [similar to those erected in Queens Park Harborne] be purchased and erected in Selly Oak Park, at a total estimated cost of £100.

1st July 1899 – The South Birmingham Chronicle:

THE CHILDREN'S FETE – The committee met on Thursday evening at the Institute to make final arrangements for this fete, which takes place on Monday next. Mr. T.A. Cole presided, and amongst others present were Messrs. J. Whitehouse, W. Holmes, J. Draper, Lawrence, Jordan, Sheasby, Griswold, F.C. James, S. Hill, W. Perkins, Shepherd, Gilbert, Goode, T. Hall, R. Roberts, W. Humphreys, C.H. Smith, T. Smith, Taylor, Brittain, Honeybourne, Morris, J. Gough, G. Hollies, J.H. Walton and A. Gittins (honorary secretary). The catering committee recommended the expenditure of about £37 on the tea, which they said would run about 4½d. per head. The recommendation was agreed to. The Sports Committee reported that they proposed giving 320 prizes, and they had arranged for a large number of races for both the boys and girls. They also proposed to purchase 60lbs. of sweets to be given away in one-ounce packets to the smaller children. The report was adopted. The Procession Committee recommended that Mr. Holmes should lead the procession on horseback, and this was agreed to. Should the weather be unfavourable on Monday, the committee have been granted the use of the park for the following day. Up to ten o'clock on Thursday evening the secretary had received subscriptions amounting to nearly £49.

THE FLOWER SHOW – The arrangements for the Selly Oak Flower Show to be held on Saturday, August 5th, are progressing. The committee have secured the bee tent once again, and the Rev. E. Davenport, the County Council bee expert, will attend and give lectures. The Selly Oak Brass band has been engaged for the occasion, and a sports sub-committee have been appointed to draw up a programme of sports. The collectors are now paying their annual visit to the residents, and we hope the subscriptions will be liberal.

4. 1899

1st July 1899 – The Birmingham News

Selly Oak and Bournbrook Children's Fete

Monday's Arrangements

All that is now required for the success of the Children's Fete at Selly Oak on Monday is good weather. For the past seven or eight weeks a large committee, and one thoroughly representative of the village, has been engaged in the making of the arrangements, which are extensive and varied in character. The children for whom the fete is intended have of course been first and mainly catered for, but their parents, who will be admitted to the park after five o'clock in the evening, have not been wholly overlooked, and they will find not a few things provided to attract their attention and excite their interest. In every direction possible the committee have carefully taken note of and profited by the experience of past events, and if things do not go off on Monday as smoothly as the working of an automaton, no charge of lack of care and forethought can be laid against the committee, who, if they cannot command, have certainly merited a completely successful issue of their labours. The committee earnestly solicit the cooperation of the public in the carrying out of the arrangements by maintaining order and avoiding in any way impeding the movements of the various officers. The procession will start from the schools in Dawlish Road promptly at 1.15, and will be headed by Mr. William Holmes, on horseback. Tea will be served to children in sections, commencing at four o'clock, and till the whole have had tea the public will not be permitted to enter the park. After tea the children's sports programme will be gone through, and for this 320 prizes have been provided.

The final meeting of the General Committee was held at Bournbrook Institute on Thursday evening, Mr. T. A. Cole in the chair. Amongst those present were Messrs. Holmes, Draper, Whitehouse, Lawrence, Hill, Roberts, Hall, Norris, Brittain, Hinton, Jordan, Greswolde, James, Walton, Perkins, Humphries, Sheppard, Gilbert, Goode, Haynes, Honeybourne, and A. Gittins (secretary). It was reported that the funds had reached the sum of £49. The Catering Committee were authorised to expend £37 in provisions for the children's tea. In the event of any indications of bad weather, the committee will meet at St. Mary's Schools, at 8.45 a.m. on Monday morning to decide whether the fete shall be held or postponed to the following day.

Local & District News
Selly Oak

<u>Music in the Park</u> – Owing to the violent thunderstorm which broke out on Wednesday evening, the Selly Oak Victoria Brass Band were unable to give their usual weekly programme of music in the park. The programme arranged, which is as follows, will, weather permitting, be given next Wednesday evening:

March	"Collingwood"	Pettel
Selection	"Geisha"	S. Jones
Overture	"Under the British Colours"	H. King
Cornet solo	"Lizzy Folk"	J. Hartman
Valse	"Morning Glories"	W. Himmer
Selection	"Dandy Fifth"	C. C. Corri
Barn dance	"Washington Post"	Theo Bonheur
Gallop	"Express"	J. Dawson

"God save the Queen"
Conductor .... H. White

5th July 1899 – Minute of KN&N UDC

The report of this Committee (the Baths Parks & Cemeteries Committee) having been printed was taken as read and ordered to be entered on the Minutes as follows:-

This committee beg to recommend:

That in future it be the duty of this Committee to take charge of and to maintain such trees planted on public highways and village greens and open spaces as the Council have undertaken or may undertake the care of, together with the guards and fences.

That the use of Selly Oak Park be granted to the Selly Oak Victoria Band on Saturday, the 26th August, and permission given for a collection to be made, such use being subject to the usual conditions.

That the use of a portion of the Park on the usual conditions be granted to the Order of Rechabites for Saturday, the 19th August, subject to suitable arrangements being made by Councillor Talliss.

That a set of swings (similar to those erected in Queen's Park, Harborne) be purchased and erected at Selly Oak Park at a total estimated cost of £100.

Moved Mr Oswald, seconded Mr Holmes, that the proceedings of the Baths, Parks and Cemeteries Committee as set forth in their minutes be and are confirmed and adopted.

An amendment, moved by Mr Jones, seconded by Mr Brown, that the Committee's recommendation as to swings be not approved but that a swing at a cost of £3 be purchased from Messrs Glover and Sons as a trial, was lost the voting thereon being, For 4, Against 13.

A further amendment, moved Mr Underhill, seconded Mr Brown, that that part of the Committee's Report relating to trees on highways except in Village

4. 1899

Greens and open spaces be referred back for further consideration was declared to be carried, the voting thereon being, For 10, Against 6, Neutral 1.

The motion for the adoption of the Report as amended was then put and carried.

8th July 1899 – The South Birmingham Chronicle

The Baths, Parks and Cemeteries Committee of the District Council recommended on Wednesday that in future it be the duty of this Committee to take charge of and maintain such trees planted on public highways and village greens and open spaces as the Council have undertaken or may undertake the care of, together with the guards and fences. Councillor Oswald spoke of the present discreditable condition of some of the trees in the district, and said it was the intention of the Committee to make this a part of the duty of the gardeners. Mr. Underhill did not like the trees being taken off the Public Works Committee, and in spite of the suggestion that gardeners were better able to look after the trees than roadmen he moved that the first part of the recommendation be referred to the Public Works Committee, and his amendment was carried.

The Selly Oak Band have fixed August 26th as the date for the evening concert in the Park when a collection will be made. The Council have granted the necessary permission, and we hope the public will show their appreciation of the services of the band by a bumper attendance and a record collection.

A tedious, and in our opinion, frivolous discussion ensued over the recommendation of the Parks Committee that a set of swings (similar to those erected in Queen's Park, Harborne) be purchased and erected at Selly Oak Park at a total estimated cost of £100. Fortunately, the recommendation was ultimately agreed to.

THE BAND – The Selly Oak Band will play the following programme of music in Selly Oak Park next Wednesday evening: March, "Barnforth", Major Hitchen; selection, "L'Emotion", Bousquier; Fantasia on American airs, "Welcome Bro. Jonathan", W. Stewart; selection, "H.M.S. Pinafore", A. Sullivan; valse, "The longest reign", Marquis de Leuville; trombone solo, "Death of Nelson", Braham; selection, "Belle of New York", G. Kerker; galop, "On the track", R. Smith; "God save the Queen". Conductor – H. White.

8th July 1899 – The Birmingham News

Local & District News
Selly Oak

<u>Music in the Park</u> – The following is the programme to be given by the band at the park on Wednesday evening next: (and there follows the same list as immediately above).

The band has been granted the use of the park on Saturday, August 26th, for the holding of a concert at which a collection will be made to enable them to purchase music.

<u>The Children's Fete</u> – This annual event, the most widely interesting, if not the most important, in the local calendar, took place on Monday, and was in every sense a distinct success. The whole of the arrangements of the event had been carefully thought out by the committee, and the only thing needed to carry them out successfully was a freedom from rain, a condition for the existence of which the weather of the several preceding days and its general appearance on Monday morning, boded ill. Fortunately, however, the wind veered round to a dry quarter, and though the day was dull and cold, and far from being an ideal one for the occasion, there was no wet. The main street and the several side streets in which the procession was made up were gaily decorated with flags, bannerettes, and bunting, and gave a cheery and festive aspect to the village. The effectiveness of the procession from a spectacular point of view was aimed at by the offering, as in past years, of prizes for decorated vehicles, mailcarts, and bicycles, and for novelties of any description. Altogether there were twenty three entries, nine entering for the novelty, eight for the cycle, five for the mailcart, and one for the vehicle competition. This number was smaller than that of last year, and the procession, though attractive and interesting, was generally voted to be below last year's. The first prize for the best decorated mailcart was won by Mrs. Hitch, and Mrs. Horton was a good second. The third prize was awarded to Masters Jacobs and Frank Oswald for an exhibit, which was entered as a novelty, however, but which got associated with the mailcart entries, and was therefore regarded as one of them by the judges, who were total strangers to the village. In the cycle competition the first prize was won by Mrs. Smith, the second by Miss Marion Clarke, and the third by Arthur V. Steed. The first prize for the best novelty was taken by Mr. C. R. Clarke, with a mechanical arrangement mounted in a trap and set in motion by the revolution of the wheels. The chief part of the mechanism was a windmill pattern wheel moving in an horizontal plane, and in addition there was a representation of a something climbing a greasy pole, a feat which was never accomplished, insomuch as it slipped down to the original point of starting every time it got within a few inches of the top. The second prize was award to Mr. T. F. Bostock for a Maypole, with ten prettily dressed girls holding the various coloured ribbons. This was a very tasteful and effective exhibit, and in the opinion of many should have had the first prize. The third prize in this section was taken by a troupe of fifteen minstrels in mock costume, entered as "Muldoon's Kitchen Band". In the section for vehicles there was some misunderstanding, due, we believe, to a difference of opinion as to the date when two vehicles were entered for competition, and as a result only the second prize was definitely awarded, and this went to Mr. Jordan. The awarding of the first and third prizes is to be settled shortly by the committee. The children and the competitors in the procession met in the side streets at the bottom end of the village, and at about two o'clock, the

procession was marshalled and commenced to move. Altogether there were about 2,500 children in the procession, and many of the smallest of these were conveyed in vehicles lent by, among others, the Cycle Components Manufacturing Company, Mrs. Kirby, Messrs. C. W. Pember, G. Halward, T. Baldwin, T. Bradshaw, F. Tucker, Hartwell, G. Wilde, A. Monk, D. A. Clark, J. Whitehouse, Honeybourne, W. Hunt, C. A. Lucas, W. Lilley, T. Meere, Monk Bros., Whitehouse and Pearce, J. Slater, G. Foster, and Quinton's Bread Co. The procession, which was nearly a mile in length, slowly wound its way, headed by Mr. W. Holmes on horseback, and provided with music by the Selly Oak Victoria Brass Band, to the park, where the children speedily scattered themselves about, and took advantage of the many forms of amusement provided for them. An important place amongst these was occupied by the steam roundabout, on which every child was given a free ride. In another part of the grounds Professor Myrth's punch and judy show attracted a large amount of patronage, while later on a large and varied sports programme, comprising, flat, sack, three-legged, and candle and match races for boys, and flat, egg and spoon, skipping rope, and hoop races for girls, was gone through, and no fewer than 328 prizes, consisting of workboxes and baskets, pocket knives, skipping ropes, hoops, cricket bats and balls, wickets, etc. were awarded. The sack race proved exceedingly amusing, and though not altogether free from risk, was gone through without a hitch. Another very popular amusement, and a source of considerable revenue to the committee's funds, was that of kicking, or trying to kick, a football through a large circular hole in a piece of boarding. Each one attempting the feat paid a penny for the privilege, and was awarded a threepenny coconut if successful. Several very good nigger entertainments were given by Muldoon's Kitchen Band, and still further entertainment was provided by the Welsh Choir, who gave a number of contributions. A series of interesting pictures in half a dozen mutoscopes, sent by the Birmingham Mutoscope Company, and these, too, came in for a large share of general patronage, while the same remark applies to the phonograph brought to the fete by Mr. Green, of Harborne. Between four and five o'clock the children assembled in sections on the ground near to the lodge for tea, and for half an hour, or thereabouts, a band of 150 persons were busily engaged in supplying them with bread and butter, cake and tea. In this way 100 quartern loaves, 50lbs, of butter, over 1,000lbs, of cake, and 100 gallons of tea (requiring 24lbs. of tea, 2cwts. of sugar, and 20 gallons of milk) were consumed. After tea the infants were each given an ounce packet of sweets, and this way three quarters of an hundredweight of confectionery was distributed. Utensils for the tea were kindly lent by Mr. George Cadbury, Mr. W. Morgan (master of the Workhouse), Mr. A. Gittins, and Mr. J. Smith. After tea the gates were thrown open to the general public, who flocked in in very large numbers. As the afternoon wore on the band gave selections of dance music, of which eager advantage was taken by all who could find dancing room on the wooden floor of the shelter and by not a few who did not mind the rougher surface of the turf. One of the final acts was the sending up of a number of balloons by Mr. J. Deaman and Mr. A. Gittins – a delicate operation, rendered none the easier by the large number who found an absorbing interest in watching the process of getting the balloons inflated. The Selly Oak Ambulance Corps, under the direction of Mr. George Perkins, attended the event, and rendered their service in one or two slight accidents which occurred. At about nine o'clock the park was cleared, the assembled company, numbering certainly not less than 6,000, and estimated by many at 10,000, following the band in disorderly array into the village, and completely blocking up the road and footpath for a long stretch. As the children passed St. Mary's Schools buns were distributed to as many as possible. The day's proceedings, which throughout had gone off with as much smoothness as so large an undertaking could be expected to, terminated with the playing of the National Anthem outside Bournbrook Institute, and in half an hour later the street was clear, and the children's fete of 1899 a thing of the past – a memory exceedingly pleasant to all who had assisted to carry it out, as it was, no doubt, to those who had participated in it. The committee was as follows[41]: Messrs. T. A. Cole (chairman), W. Humphries (chairman of the Catering Sub-committee), J. Draper (chairman of the Sports and Fields Sub-committee), W. Holmes (chairman of the Procession Sub-committee and treasurer of the fund), Alfred Gittins (hon. secretary), J. R. Oswald, J. G. Purser, S. Hill, R. Roberts, Frank Smith, J. Gough, J. Baldwin, J. Castagni, G. Corthall, J. Felton, C. A. Gilbert, T. Greswolde, T. Hall, F. C. James, G. Perkins, Hadden, F. Tucker, J. H. Walton, T. Smith, J. Wheelwright, C. L. Cullimore, D. Roy, H. White, J. Quinton, G. Sheasby, A. Halward, F. Goode, T. Bostock, F. Jordan, A. Darby, J. Deaman, W. Pomford, A. Hudson, W. Hudson, Edwin Morris, W. Clarke, F. Spurrier, A. Honeybourne, G. Hollins, T. W. Lawrence, C. W. Pember, Jacob Whitehouse, F. Taylor, and S. H. Brittain. Of the foregoing names all, with the exception of a dozen at most, gave energetic assistance to the work. The committee desire to express their deep thanks to the large band of helpers and to those who took charge of the collecting boxes, which proved a source of substantial assistance to the funds.

<u>Swings for the Park</u> – A set of swings similar to those erected in Queen's Park, Harborne, is to be purchased and erected at Selly Oak Park at an estimated cost of £100. The proposal was recommended to the District Council by their Baths, Parks and Cemeteries Committee, and elicited quite a long debate before it was finally adopted. Councillor Underhill thought £100 a large sum for a set of swings, which he had been told could be obtained for £35, and while not wanting to rob the children of them, he wanted to know what the Council was going to get for their money before voting for the proposition. Mr. Aaron Jones said the best swing on the market at the present time, and one used by royalty, could be obtained from a Warwick firm for £3, and he moved as an amendment to the committee's recommendation that one should be obtained on approval. Mr. J. W. R. Brown seconded this, but it was lost, and the recommendation agreed to. The Surveyor

---

[41] This list is not complete, and may be disorganised – the page on the microfilm had a crease which distorted the text through this list.

stated that the set comprised nine swings, with a gymnastic apparatus in the centre. The pillars, etc., were of cast iron, and the contraption generally, such as would stand the wear and tear of years. The swings themselves cost about £70, and the balance was for concrete to erect them in, but the estimate was a very liberal one, and probably when the work came to be done it would be effected for £85 or thereabouts.

15th July 1899 – The South Birmingham Chronicle, and
15th July 1899 – The Birmingham News

THE BAND – Next Wednesday the Selly Oak Band will give the following programme of music in the Selly Oak Park: March, "Suzerain", (G. Wallace); selection, "Gondoliers", (A. Sullivan); selection, "Patience", (A. Sullivan); overture, "La Couronne D'or" (A. Hermann); valse, "Belle Amie", (Josef Meissier); cornet solo, "Mona" (soloist, A. Robinson) (S. Adams); slow march, "Sadawa", (H. Millars); gallop, "An Indian Ride" (descriptive), (Paul de Loetx). Last Wednesday there was a good attendance of the public.

22nd July 1899 – The Birmingham News, and
22nd July 1899 – The South Birmingham Chronicle

Local & District news
Selly Oak

<u>Music in the Park</u> – The band's programme, to be given in the park on Wednesday, will be as follows:

March	"Liberty Belle"	Sousa
Selection	"Pirates of Penzance"	A. Sullivan
Fantasia	"Rose De Amour"	Bleger
Overture	"Poet and Peasant"	Suppé
Slow march	"Honour to the brave"	G.H. Hallett
Selection	"Primrose"	E. Brepsant
Muzurka	"L'Auvergnale"	Louis Ganne
Gallop	"Indian Ride"	Paul de Lock
	Conductor .... H. White	

The band will bring their series of concerts in the park to a termination on August 26th, when a grand fete will be held. A variety of sports, including six-a-side football matches, with handsome medals for prizes, will be included in the fete programme. Clubs desirous of entering for the football competition or anyone wishing to obtain further information of the fete, can do so by applying to Mr. J. T. Browell, secretary, 120, Maryvale Road, Row Heath, or to Mr. T. Hems, Providence Buildings, Lottie Road, Selly Oak. If any gentleman of the district felt disposed to recognise the service of the band in the park for the past three months by the offering of prizes for competition the bandmaster (Mr. H. White), 78, Lottie Road, Selly Oak, would be very glad to receive them.

29th July 1899 – The South Birmingham Chronicle, and
29th July 1899 – The Birmingham News

THE BAND – Owing to the unpropitious state of the weather on Wednesday evening, the Selly Oak Band could not give a performance in the Park. The programme for next week will be: – March, "Liberty Belle, Sousa; selection, "Pirates of Penzance", A. Sullivan; fantasia, "Rose D'Amour", Bleger; overture, "Poet and Peasant", Suppe; slow march, "Honour to the brave", G.H. Hallett; selection, "Primrose", E. Brepsant; mazurka, "L'Auvergnale", Louis Ganne; gallop, "Indian Ride", Paul de Laetx.

5th August 1899 – The South Birmingham Chronicle, and
5th August 1899 – The Birmingham News

THE BAND – The Selly Oak Band will play the following programme of music in the Park next Wednesday:- March, "Belle of New York", (G. Rirker); selection, "H.M.S. Pinafore", (Sullivan); fantasia, "Welcome Brother Jonathan", (W. Stewart); valse, "Mimosa", (T. Bidgood); overture, "Poet and Peasant", (Suppé); mazurka, "L. Auvergnate", Louis Ganne; slow march, "Sadowa", (H. Millars); gallop, "Express", (J. Dawson). Splendid attractions are being arranged for the fete on the 26th inst. Applications for stalls, etc, are to be made to T. Hems, Providence Villas, Lottie Road, Selly Oak, or J. T. Browell, hon. Secretary, Lauriston, Maryvale Road, Bournville.

12th August 1899 – The South Birmingham Chronicle:

SELLY OAK FLOWER SHOW

The Selly Oak Horticultural Society reached the lowest water mark on Saturday. The annual show which was held in the Selly Oak Park was unsuccessful whichever way one likes to look at it. The amount taken at the gate was very much below the average, only reaching £11 4s. 6d., the staging was bad, and the programme of sports provided was almost a farce. The only two redeeming features were the excellent catering by Mr. Nephti Phillips, of Stirchley, and the performances of the Selly Oak band, under the able conductorship of Mr. H. White. We endeavour in another column[42] to give the reasons for the non success of the show. Touching the exhibits themselves, the entries were numerous, but in few classes was there anything approaching keenness of competition. The quality of the exhibits was, if anything, a little under the average, and compared somewhat badly with the

---

[42] The anticipated article came in the next edition of the newspaper, one week later.

preceding year, which was, however, an exceptional one from all points of view. The gentlemen's gardeners' classes were well represented, the first prize being taken by Mr. A. H. Wiggin's gardener (F. Deddicot), and the second by Mrs. Deakin's gardener (H. Oakley). A silver medal offered for the best exhibit by a cottager, amongst the winners of the first prizes for trays of vegetables, was easily taken by W. Caesley. The classes for table decoration, in which there were sections for ladies, for parlour maids, and for cottager's wives, produced a keen competition, and some very pretty and effective exhibits. The judges were: Messrs. Newall, Jones, Thormloe and Thompson. Mr. R. Sydenham should have been the fourth judge, but the staging was completed so much later than was expected that he was obliged to forego the enjoyment. The County Council's bee-tent, under the superintendence of the Rev. E. Davenport, proved a very strong attraction.

The winners of the sports prizes are as follows:- (and there follows a list)

The following is a complete list of prizewinners:- (and there follows a much longer list).

12th August 1899 – The Birmingham News

The Flower Shows
Selly Oak

The annual show of the Selly Oak Cottage Garden Association was held at Selly Oak Park on Saturday last. From a variety of causes the show was not the general success which it has been on past occasions, and when compared with the record achievement of last year it showed up rather badly. The show has depended for its success in the past as much on its recommendations as to time, place, and circumstances, as to the efforts of the committee, which, owing to its composition, are not so effective as they might be, and it was not altogether a matter of surprise therefore to find that the experimental changes of date and locale, with the all important restriction which the latter involved, adversely affected the exhibition, and rendered it less successful than it might have been. The number of entries, nearly 550, gave promise of a phenomenally large display, but as probably fully forty percent of these failed to be staged, the anticipation was not realised. The staging of such as were brought to the field left much to be desired, partly as a result of the fact that many exhibitors failed to bring their produce in time, and partly as a consequence of many members of the committee being unable to find time to devote to the work, as well as to arrange their own exhibits, or protect them from injury through the many disturbances in position occasioned by the late comers. As to the exhibits themselves they were of mediocre quality, neither surpassing nor being conspicuously under the average of merit. In the principal division, viz. the cottager's, there were, as usual, a good show of vegetables, but the entries for plants, flowers, and fruit were small and indifferent in quality. A silver medal offered to the cottager exhibiting the best tray of vegetables in the show was won by W. Casely, with a very meritorious exhibit. The majority of special prizes for which, for which amateurs were allowed in most instances to compete, were taken, but in the division for amateurs only nine out of 22 prizes offered were able to be awarded. Nor was the patronage of the gentlemen's gardeners' division at all satisfactory, and for the three substantial prizes for groups there were but two entries. All but two of the 28 prizes taken out of the 46 offered in this division fell to Mr. A. H. Wiggin's gardener (F. Dedicott) and Mrs. Deaken's gardener (H. Oakley). The show of honey was small, but of better quality than last year, albeit this is not due to the beekeepers, but the season, which is more favourable for the production of good honey by the bees than was last. In the straining and preparation of honey for exhibition, a matter which the keeper does control, however, much care and attention might easily have been taken, and the weakness in this respect would have disqualified some exhibits had the competition been at all keen. The prettiest tent of the lot was that which covered the charming exhibits of the ladies in the table centre competitions. The judges were Messrs. George Newell, G. Thorniloe, R. Jones, and A. Thompson, and, en passant, it is worthy of mention that there were few, if any, cavillers at their awards. The means extraneous to the show itself whereby it was sought to attract and amuse the public included a sports programme and athletic displays by the Selly Oak Wesleyan Gymnasium. Much interest was shown in the practical demonstrations of bee keeping, by the Worcestershire County Council's expert (the Rev. J. Davenport). The attendance was below the average, and compared with last year's record gate showed a falling off of 40 per cent, or more. The secretary (Mr. J. H. Walton) upon whom the bulk of the work fell, was ably assisted by Mr. J. Darby, Mr. F. Overthrow, and A. N. Other. The prizes are distributed by the President (Mr. A. H. Wiggin), at St. Mary's schools, next Thursday, at 8 o'clock.

(There then follows an extensive list of all prizewinners.)

19th August 1899 – The South Birmingham Chronicle

THE FLOWER SHOW – A meeting of the committee of the Selly Oak Horticultural Society was held on Wednesday evening, when the treasurer reported that he had received from the secretary in all £78 8s. Of that sum he had paid £15 13s. 6d., which left a balance of £62 14s. 6d. The prize money to be paid was a little over £50, and the outstanding debts amounted to about £19, so that the balance from last year of £10 19s. would have to be very largely drawn upon. On the following evening in St. Mary's Schools, Selly Oak, Mr. A. H. Wiggin (president of the Society) distributed the prizes to the successful exhibitors. In opening the proceedings, the president said he was sorry on that the first occasion he had had the honour of being the president of the Selly Oak show, to hear that it had not been so successful as it had always been in the past. No doubt there were several causes which mitigated against the show this year. He was told that it was not up to the mark either in the quality of the exhibits or in the attendance. With regard to the quality of the exhibits they must put that down to the dry weather. He was also informed that the high wind on the day of the show rather told against the staging and the showing of the plants to the best advantage. As to the attendance well, he supposed it could only be put down to the statement that the Park was not a suitable place. In his own mind he could not agree with that. He was sadly afraid that the absence of intoxicating liquors had something to do with the matter. He was by no means narrow-minded, but he thought it was a very sad thing that in a large place like Selly Oak, people could not go to look at flowers for themselves. If the show was looked upon as an opportunity for an afternoon drinking, the sooner the show ended the better. Speaking of the prizes offered to gentleman's gardeners, Mr. Wiggins suggested, as there was so little competition, that in future the gentlemen of the district should be asked to lend plants, etc., not for competition. He was sure his gardener would have been better pleased to have taken less prizes if there had been more competition. He was afraid they could not get much competition in Selly Oak, and for that reason he threw out the suggestion of approaching the gentlemen to lend plants, etc. He now proceeded to distribute the prizes. The children were the first recipients, and he congratulated them upon the large number of awards they had won, the money totalling to £1 7s. The other winners, together with the amounts they received, are as follows: – J. Beacham, £2 17s.; W.H. Goodwin, £2 7s., and 3lbs. tea; F.C. James, £1 19s. 6d., and 3lbs. tea and a pork pie; J. Deaman, 18s. and a tobacco pipe; A. Wise, 15s. 6d.; C. Bragg, 13s. 6d. and a ham, and 6s. worth of goods; E. Mapplebeck (gardener – Lawie), 8s. 6d.; J.G. Ledsam (gardener – Pagett), 7s. 6d.; Mrs. Deakin (gardener H. Oakley), £3 16s. 6d.; A.H. Wiggin (gardener J. Dedicott), £6 0s. 6d.; J. Connop, senr., £1; J. Rhodes, 10s. 6d.; W. Boylin, £4 11s., and a peck of flour, a cake, a white skirt, and a spade; E. Baldwin, £2 3s. and a saw; H. Crook, £1 14s.; S. Moss, 3s.; J. Draper, 8s. 6d.; J.E. Poyner, £2 4s. 6d., and 1lb. of tea and a pair of trousers; J. Hull, 4s 6d.; J. Davis, £1 19s. and a box of cigars, three garden syringes, and a leg of mutton; E.J. Price, 8s. 6d.; W. Caesley, £1 1s. and a silver medal; J. Gunning, £1 3s. and 8lbs. of beef and a ham; H. Archer, 14s.; R. Jones, £1 8s. 6d.; J. Bate, £2 0s. 6d., a leg of pork and a peck loaf; R. Williams, £1 3s.; J.R. Hunt, £1 11s. 6d., a fork, 7lbs. of jam, an Oxford shirt, and braces; J. Jobson, 8s.; A.F. Williams, 17s. 6d.; Mrs. J. Davis, 5s. 6d.; Miss G. Hollinshead, 10s.; Mrs. Peacocke, 7s. 6d.; Mrs. S. James, 5s.; Miss A. Taylor, 10s.; Miss A. Shaw, 7s 6d.; Miss S.M. Eyles, 5s.; Mrs. F. Hopkins, 10s.; Mrs. Dedicott, 7s. 6d.; and Miss Hunt, 5s. – Upon the motion of Mr. J.E. Poyner, seconded by Mr. J. Beacham, a hearty vote of thanks was accorded the president for so kindly distributing the prizes, and the proceedings concluded.

WHY SELLY OAK FLOWER SHOW WAS UNSUCCESSFUL

Extreme pressure on our space alone prevented us from dealing with the question last week. It is a matter which demands very serious attention. Selly Oak Flower Show is one of the most popular institutions in the district, and the news that this year's efforts had proved disastrous in spite of the favourableness of the weather –

an all important factor – came as a great surprise and disappointment to the people generally. We do not think that any place has given more generous support to the local horticultural society than has Selly Oak. In foul weather as well as fair the residents have stuck loyally to the working committee. We are afraid, however, their patience came to an end last Saturday week. The blame for the non-success of the show attaches solely in our opinion to those of the committee who so blindly favoured the use of the park, and those who pandered to the teetotallers. An account of the way in which the park came to be chosen may perhaps be interesting. Immediately upon the present working committee coming into office a few of the members interested themselves in endeavouring to get the show held in Bournbrook[43] for once in a while. They approached Mr. E. A. Olivieri, and he very generously offered the use of a field in every way suitable for the purpose. He further did not object to the presence of a beer tent. The offer was brought before the committee and their next meeting, and was very gratefully accepted. Unfortunately, however, some of the members living Selly Oak way could not see their way to allow Bournbrook to have the privilege even for one year. Further, they had the opinion that the park was the proper place in which to hold it. Accordingly at the next meeting a motion to rescind the resolution accepting Mr. Olivieri's offer was brought forward and carried by the votes of one or two who had been specially whipped up for the occasion. The fact that no intoxicating drinks could be consumed in the park was fully recognised, and was not by any means the least factor in determining the vote of those in favour of the park as against Mr. Olivieri's field. A greater mistake, or one more fatal to the success of the show, could not have been made. In pandering to the teetotallers, the committee lost their very best supporters, the working men of the district. The working man is as fond of freedom as anyone, and if he finds any attempt being made to take away one of the few privileges – however small a one it may be – he kicks, and no one can kick harder or to greater effect. Saturday week was an ideal day for a flower show, and although the park was rather an out-of-the-way place in which to hold it, still we confidently believe an excellent attendance would have been assured even there if only a beer tent had been erected. That it would have been an even greater success on Mr. Olivieri's land is evidenced by the fact that at a Catholic Fete which was recently held there over £1000 was taken in gate money. While we believe the exclusion of beer was the principal cause of the non-success of Saturday week, we also believe there were other causes which, although of minor importance, all helped to bring about the disaster. Reforms of a very drastic nature will have to be made if the society is to live many more years. We do not on

---

[43] Whilst it is not the subject of this history, it is clear from newspaper reports that the following year separate Flower Shows were held in each of Bournbrook (with Selly Park) and Selly Oak (where the Show was staged in a field in Oak Tree Lane, not in the Park). Both were very successful events, unlike the 1899 flop in Selly Oak Park for the want of a beer tent. Suggestions were made for subsequent combined events, but the organising committees could not find a way to reconcile their differences and prejudices for a number of years. During those years they did not use the Park.

the present occasion intend to point out any of the reforms needed; that may very well be left until the annual meeting is about to be held. We hope then that the residents of the district will turn up in full force and see that the strongest possible committee is appointed in order that next year's show may prove so successful as to entirely blot from remembrance this year's disaster. The new committee will need every encouragement for the fight will be an uphill one. Still, with the encouragement we are sure they will receive, and hard work, they will be successful. In reply to the remarks made by the President of the society on Thursday night it will be just as well if we point out that the advocates of a beer tent are not necessarily advocates of drunkenness. They also have faith in the people – the great majority of them – not abusing any privilege which is granted them, whereas those who voted for the exclusion of beer, evidently have no such faith. We firmly believe that the show this year being run on teetotal lines caused twice as much intoxicating drinks to be consumed than there would otherwise have been.

19th August 1899 – The Birmingham News

Selly Oak Flower Show
Distribution of Prizes

The prizes won at Selly Oak Flower Show were distributed by the President, (Mr. A. H. Wiggin) at St. Mary's Schools, Selly Oak, on Thursday evening. In a short speech delivered previously to the performance of this little duty Mr. Wiggin had some remarks to make with regard to the show. He regretted that it had not been so successful as its predecessors, and proceeded to deal with the cause assigned for the fact. The deterioration in the quality and reduction in the number of exhibits was, he thought, no doubt due to the drought. The shrinkage in the number who visited the show he had heard attributed to the unsuitability of the park, but he was informed that the real reason was to be found in the fact that the refreshments did not include intoxicating liquors, which the committee were debarred from providing by the conditions upon which the use of the park was granted. He was not a bigoted person, and liked a glass of ale or wine, but he thought it a very sad thing that in a place like Selly Oak the people could not be got to visit a flower show because they could not satisfy their thirst with alcoholic drinks. The Association was not formed to provide an opportunity, once a year, for an afternoon's drinking, and he would prefer to see it come to an end rather than it should be so. Speaking with regard to the poorly represented gentlemen's gardener's division at the show, and the majority of prizes in which were taken by his own and Mrs. Deakin's gardener, Mr. Wiggin said both himself and his gardener would have felt greater satisfaction to have taken fewer prizes in the face of keener competition. There was nothing particularly meritorious in taking first and second prizes where there were only two exhibits. There were not many people who kept gardeners who exhibited at the show, and he suggested to the committee that they should reconsider the advisability of having a gentlemen's gardener's division. He thought the money could be far better spent in the interests of horticulture in Selly Oak in other directions. The place of the division in the show might be occupied by non-competitive exhibits by local gentlemen, whom he suggested should be approached to either lend plants or allow their gardeners to set up groups, etc. The spirit of emulation amongst the gardeners to which the adoption of such a course would give rise would be sufficient to prompt them to do as well, if not better, than they did for the sake of the prizes they now got. He thought, however, they should be repaid for their time and trouble by the making of a small grant to them.

Mr. Wiggin then proceeded to hand away the prize money, starting with the children, amongst whom £1 7s. 0d. was distributed. He was pleased to see so many prizes awarded to them, and hoped that in the obtaining and preparation of their exhibits they did not receive too much assistance from their parents. (Laughter.) The picking of the wild flowers was a health giving occupation, as well as being highly instructive. The prizes for the table decorations (amounting to £3 7s. 0d.) were next presented, and were followed with the distribution of the general prizes, the recipients of which were as follows: – F. Dedicott, £6 0s. 6d.; W. Boylin, £4 11s. 0d., a peck of flour, a cake, a white shirt, and a spade; H. Oakley, £3 16s. 6d.; J. Beacham, £2 17s. 0d.; W. H. Goodwin, £2 7s. 0d., and 3lbs. tea; E. R. Baldwin, £2 3s. 0d., and a saw; J. E. Poyner, £2 4s. 6d., 1lb. of tea and a pair of trousers; J. Bate, £2 0s. 6d., a leg of pork and a peck loaf; F. C. James, £1 19s. 6d., 3lbs. tea and a pork pie; J. Davis, £1 19s. 0d., a box of cigars, three garden syringes, a leg of mutton, and a spade; H. Crook, £1 14s. 0d.; J. R. Hunt, £1 11s. 6d., a fork, 7lbs. of jam, an Oxford shirt, and a pair of braces; R. Jones, £1 8s. 6d.; J. Gunning, £1 3s. 0d., a ham, and 8lbs. of beef; R. Williams, £1 3s. 0d.; J. Connop, senr., and Mrs. Connop, £1; J. Deaman, 18s., and a tobacco pipe; A. F. Williams, 17s. 6d.; A. Wise, 15s. 6d.; H. Archer, 14s.; C. Bragg, 13s. 6d., a ham, and 6s. worth of goods; J. Rhodes, 10s. 6d.; J. Lawie, 8s. 6d.; J. Draper, 8s. 6d.; E. J. Price, 8s. 6d.; T. Johnson, 8s.; J. Pagett, 7s. 6d.; Mrs. J. Davis, 5s. 6d.; J. Hull, 4s. 6d.; and H. Moss, 3s.

On the motion of Mr. J. H. Poyner, seconded by Mr. J. Beacham, a hearty vote of thanks was accorded the chairman for presiding. The proposer, in submitting the motion, voiced the general appreciation which all present felt at the interest which Mr. Wiggin had shown in the above.

26th August 1899 – The South Birmingham Chronicle

WHY SELLY OAK FLOWER SHOW WAS UNSUCCESSFUL

To the Editor "South Birmingham Chronicle",

Dear Sir, – Having read your leader last week "Why Selly Oak Flower Show was unsuccessful", I would like to thank those members of the committee, through your columns, who so nobly stood by the temperance cause in this matter; and if, as you say, the show was a failure through having no beer tent, then I say thank

God it was a failure. And if flower shows can only be supported through the sale of such drinkables, then the sooner they die a peaceful death the better. I believe that the Bournville Flower Show was a success, although held in a comparatively secluded place, and I doubt whether that was made to pay on the profits of beer. Trusting for an insertion, I remain,
A GOOD TEMPLAR OF SELLY OAK

To the Editor "South Birmingham Chronicle",

Dear Sir, – Allow me to thank you for your outspoken remarks last week on the cause of the non-success of the Selly Oak Flower Show. The absence of a beer tent did not in itself cause the small attendance, but because of the fact that the committee had chosen the park in order that they might curry favour with the fanatical teetotallers. Any deliberate attempt to take away the freedom of the people is sure to be resented. Why should the moderate drinker of beer be deprived of drinking his glass of ale any more than the teetotaller his glass of so-called non-alcoholic stout and ale, or his cup of tea or coffee? A man who abuses his privileges should certainly have them taken from him. In my opinion the teetotaller who attends a tea meeting and drinks more than is good for him of the tea provided for him is worse than the man who drinks too much beer, because the one is supposed not to get his wits impaired, however much tea he may drink, whilst the other man, after a certain glass does not know how much or how little he is imbibing. I am in favour of temperance in all things, but this much-desired end will never be reached as long as we have committees appointed like that of the Selly Oak Horticultural Society.
Yours truly,
TEMPERANCE

2nd September 1899 – The South Birmingham Chronicle

SELLY OAK VICTORIA BRASS BAND
GRAND FETE IN SELLY OAK PARK

There was a large gathering in Selly Oak Park last Saturday, the 26th, to witness the sports in connection with the Victoria Brass Band. The weather was perfect and great credit is due to the committee for the excellent manner in which they managed every event in its turn, everything being admirable. The sports were worthy of a much larger attendance, and those who were present had a real treat. The band discoursed some excellent music, which was well received, and, judging from the quality of the music and the care in rendering it, there is no doubt we expect to have very shortly one of the best brass bands in the Midlands. The following is the programme: – 2 to 2.30, selections by the band; 2.30, boys' race; 2.45, football contest; 3.0, J. Pashley (humorist); 3.30, wheelbarrow race; 3.45, Feeney and Farrell (duettists, &c.); 4.0, egg and spoon race (ladies); 4.15, high jump; 4.45 120 yards scratch race (cricketers); 5.0, long jump; 5.15, J.W. Pashley; 5.30, ham cutting competition; 5.45, Feeny and Farrell; greasy pole climbing, dancing.

The boys' race was greatly enjoyed by the young people, while the football contests were entered into with as much vigour and excitement by the players as if they were real League matches. Mr. J.W. Pashley (humorist) was well received and kept everybody amused. The Wheelbarrow Race, as was expected, caused great fun. Feeny and Farrell (duettists, &c.) gave great satisfaction. The Egg and Spoon Race by ladies was watched with keen interest by the fair sex, and amused the general spectators. The High Jump was very well performed, and Mr. H. Broad carried off the first prize after a smart jump of 5ft. 2in., the next best being Mr. Collett, who won the second prize with 4ft. 10in. The Long Jump was also a good performance. Mr. H. Broad also managed to carry off the first prize (two bottles of champagne). Not being teetotallers, they evidently considered the prizes worth jumping for, the other performance of jumping on the empty bottles, after the contents were disposed of, was not witnessed by the general spectators. 120 Yards Scratch Race (Cricketers) was quite an exciting event, and greatly interested lovers of the game. The Ham Cutting Competition created roars of laughter. The Greasy Pole Climbing caused great merriment as the competitors struggled frantically to reach the top, but failed in the attempt, eventually had to be given up as a failure. The prize of a leg of mutton, which was a prize from Mr. B. Connop, had to be decided upon later. From beginning to end there was not a dull moment. The refreshment arrangements were most satisfactory. After the programme of sports was exhausted, dancing was carried on in the park, and lasted until dusk. The following is a list of prizewinners:- Boys' race: 1st prize, won by Master Priest, 5s; 2nd, David Hale, 2s.6d. High Jump: 1st prize, 5ft. 2in., H. Broad, two bottles of champagne; 2nd, 4ft. 10in., Mr. Collett, one bottle of champagne. Long Jump: 1st prize, H. Broad, two bottles of champagne; 2nd, W.S. Jones, one bottle of champagne. The champagne was given by Mr. Olivieri. Scratch Race (Cricketers): 1st prize, won by W. Jones, cricket bat; 2nd, T. Hewitt, cricket ball (given by Mr. Ralph Docker). Wheelbarrow Race: 1st prize, won by T. Cutter, joint of beef; 2nd, W. Lowe, goods value 3s. 6d. (given by Mr. Benbow). Egg and Spoon Race (Ladies): 1st prize, Miss Such, pair of boots, value 10s. 6d. (given by E. Jenks); 2nd, Miss Lowe, umbrella (given by Mr. Benbow). Ham-Cutting Competition: 1st prize divided between H. Broad and C. Horton (ham given by C.W. Pember). Football Contest (6 medals awarded): Components, 3 goals; 3 points; Selly Oak Albion, 1 goal, 1 point; Tube Mill, 2 goals, 5 points. Second round, Stirchley, 2 goals, 2 points; Cycle Components, 1 goal, 1 point; Tube Mill, a bye. Final, Stirchley, 2 points; Tube Mill, 1 point.

THE NEW SWINGS AT SELLY OAK PARK

On Saturday last, 26th ult., an interesting ceremony took place in Selly Oak Park. Several hundreds of people had assembled there to witness the opening of the new swings. The Baths and Parks Committee have spent nearly £100 in providing swings, parallel bars, and gymnasium. There is a set of swings for boys, and another for girls. Councillor J.R. Oswald (chairman of the Baths and Parks Committee) in a short but interesting speech, dealt with the importance of outdoor amusements and exercise for children. He pointed out that the swings in the park would keep the children away from the streets, that the fresh air and exercise indulged in would greatly improve the health of the children, and he hoped that district would take full advantage of the splendid facilities now placed at its disposal. Mr. Thomas Gibbins, after a few remarks, formally declared the swings public property. Mr. Andrew Crump proposed a vote of thanks to the Chairman, which was seconded by Mr. Smith.

2nd September 1899 – The Birmingham News

Notes of the Week

If the action of the Kings Norton and Northfield Urban Council with regard to the baths question at Selly Oak has not afforded much satisfaction to the residents of the district, at least they are entitled to thanks for their efforts to popularise the park. The Council have recently had a set of swings and gymnastic appliances erected in the park, and these were formally devoted to use on Saturday. There is no direction in which the Council could render greater service to the rising generation than in encouraging the love of gymnastics. The importance of healthy outdoor exercise is happily being recognised by local authorities throughout the country, and in many towns similar provision has been made to that at Selly Oak. But it is one thing to provide the means of physical development, and another for them to be utilised. It remains to be seen whether the latest gift of the Urban Council to Selly Oak will be as much appreciated as it deserves to be.

Local & District News
Selly Oak

The Band Fete – On Saturday last a fete promoted by the Selly Oak Victoria Brass Band was held in the park, the use of which was granted them by the District Council out of consideration of the free weekly musical programmes which they have given in the park during the past several months. This year the band has to provide new uniforms for its members owing to the operation of the Uniforms Act, under which they are prevented from wearing their present military uniforms after the present year, and the proceeds of Saturday's event were devoted to the fund opened for that object. The organisation of the affair and the carrying out of the day's arrangements was undertaken by a committee consisting of Messrs. H. White (bandmaster), J. T. Browell (secretary), T. Hems, P. Hopkins, W. Baldwin, and T. Hyman, and the well-directed energy which they bestowed upon their work was crowned, deservedly, with a successful issue. The basis of the day's entertainment consisted of an attractive programme of sports, which produced a fairly good number of competitors, and was witnessed by large crowds of spectators. Several of the events, such as the six-a-side football contest, and the ham-cutting and greasy pole climbing competitions, excited special interest, while the last-named created no little amusement. The pole had been "greased" with liberal hands with soft soap, and a leg of mutton was offered by Mr. J. Connop to the one who could shin up its slippery surface and gain the top. Two competitors – a man and a boy – assayed the feat, and the former, who tried first, sought to achieve success by the use of sand, with a large quantity of which he had filled his shirt round the waist. But the sand was no match for the soap, and although he tried four or five times he never got more than halfway up the pole. He deserved a prize, however, for his pertinacity, and for the fun his efforts provoked. It is safe to say that no one worked so hard to entertain the crowd, or did so more effectively, than the one who fought against soap to win mutton. The second competitor, the boy, was content with a couple of unsuccessful attempts. For the ham-cutting competition, three entered, and two – Messrs. Horton and Broad – succeeded in severing the string twice, and as it was growing late agreed to divide the ham, which was given by Mr. C. W. Pember. For the football contest, for which six silver medals were offered, six teams entered, and in the first round "Stirchley" defeated the "Dog and Partridge" team, the Cycle Components defeated "Sheasby's six", and the Tube Mill Rovers defeated the Selly Oak Albion. The Tube Mill Rovers won the bye in the next round, and the other two teams taking the field, the Cycle Components were beaten, and the Tube Mill Rovers opposed Stirchley for the prizes, which were won by the latter team, who beat the Rovers by two points to one. The members of the winning team were Messrs. F. Humphries, M. Pittaway, H. Shaw, A. Dance, W. Bullock, and J. Mason. The prize-winners in the other events were as follows:- High Jump (prizes, two bottles and one bottle of champagne, given by Mr. E. A. Olivieri): 1, Broad (5ft. 2in.); 2, Collett (4ft. 10in.). This made the sixth high jump competition which Broad has won this season. Long Jump (prizes, same as in previous competition, and by the same donor): 1, Broad; 2, Collett. Wheel-barrow Race (prizes, a joint of beef by Mr. J. Whitehouse, and 3s. 6d. worth of goods by Mr. Benbow): 1, T. Cutler; 2. W. Lowe. Egg and Spoon Race, ladies (prizes, 10s. 6d. pair of boots by Mr. E. Jenks, and a 4s. 6d. umbrella by Mr. Benbow): 1, Miss Such; 2. Miss Lowe. 120 Yards Race, boys under 14 (first prize, value 5s. by the Band; and 2s. 6d. worth of goods by Mr. Benbow): 1, Priest; 2, Hale. 120 Yards Scratch Race for cricketers of the district (prizes, a cricket bat and cricket ball given by Mr. R. Docker): 1, W. Jones; 2, T. Hewitt. The programme also included a race for men over 45 years of age, for which Mr. C. Harbun offered a 12s. 6d. box of cigars, and Mr. J. A. Thomas 7s. 6d. worth of goods, but as there were only two competitors, and one of these (Mr. J. Langford) fell ill since entering and was unable to appear, the race was abandoned. The sports were supplemented by humorous entertainments by Mr. J. W. Pashley, the well known whistler, mimetic and sketch artiste; Feeney and Farrell, comic singers and dancers; and Harry Wiley. All these gave two turns from the bandstand, and secured a large and attentive circle of listeners. The band itself gave numerous selections, and as the evening wore on, gave dance music for the benefit of a numerous company, who found in the wooden block floor of the shelter a by no means bad dancing ground. The catering was done by Mr. Nephi Phillips, of

Breedon Cross, who brought with him a choice variety of confections, as well as a plentiful supply of more substantial edibles, and an ample supply and extensive range of temperance beverages. Thus he was able to find something to meet all tastes, and so gave general satisfaction. As the expenses were very small, a good sum should be realised for the object for which the fete was held. To the committee its success, and the entire absence of any hitch in the arrangements, must be very gratifying, and should be an encouragement to them to further effort in the uphill fight which the band has before it of raising the large sum required to provide the new uniforms. During the afternoon a pleasing little ceremony, to which further reference is made below, was performed by Mr. W. W. Gibbins, who set in motion for the first time a handsome set of swings, which have been erected at considerable cost by the District Council.

Swings and Gymnastic Apparatus at the Park – No better means of making the park popular with the children, for whom it was chiefly intended, could have been devised than that which the District Council adopted a couple of months ago, when after a little demur they sanctioned a proposal initiated and ably pleaded for by Councillor J. R. Oswald for the erection therein of a set of swings and gymnastic appliances. The provision of such things for a public place is a vastly different matter to providing them for a home, as will be readily understood when it is stated that they entailed an expenditure of £120 – a fact which explained the hesitancy of the Council, whose finances are not at present in so rosy a condition as to lead them to give over eager countenance to any expenditure that can be avoided. The swings are of iron throughout, and the framework is supported on concrete beds. There are three divisions, each of the two outer being for boys and girls respectively. The central division is fitted with a couple of pairs of rings and a trapeze. The other gymnastic apparatus consists of parallel bars and a compound horizontal bar. For a considerable distance around the swings the earth has been removed to a depth of a foot or so, and filled in with sand, so as to provide a soft and yielding surface in case of falls. The area within which a child might be struck by a swing in use is marked off by a wooden rectangular border, another excellent precaution, and it is proposed, later on, to make this more conspicuous by laying down a wooden block pavement of a few feet in width outside the border. The first use of the swing – on Saturday afternoon last – was marked by a little ceremony, which was very fittingly conducted by a representative of the Gibbins family, in Mr. Waterhouse Gibbins. In introducing Mr. Gibbins, Mr. Oswald tendered his thanks to the members of the Council for the support they had given to the proposal for the provision of the swings and gymnastic appliances, which he said had cost £73, and inclusive of the expense of installation would cost close upon £120. He appealed to the local public to aid the Park Keeper to protect them from injury and misuse. Mr. Gibbins expressed his pleasure at the very substantial character of the swings, which he said showed that the Council had not undertaken their provision in a begrudging spirit. The gymnastic apparatus excited his warm approval as he was a great believer in getting fresh air with exercise, and this was not got with an indoor gymnasium. The importance of healthful invigorating recreation for the children needed no demonstration. They were the mothers and fathers of the morrow, and upon them the stability of the race depended. Selecting a boy and a girl from amongst the surrounding company, and, setting each on a swing, Mr. Gibbins set the swings in motion, and declared them open for use. A vote of thanks was accorded Mr. Gibbins on the proposition of Mr Andrew Crump, and the proceedings terminated with a rush on the part of the youngsters for the swings, which were kept merrily on the go till fastened up by the Park Keeper at dusk.

9th September 1899 – The South Birmingham Chronicle

SELLY OAK FLOWER SHOW

To the Editor of the "Chronicle",

Dear Sir, – It is hardly fair to lay the blame on to what your correspondents call the teetotal section of the community.

Although I am not a teetotaller, yet I must agree with your correspondent who says that it is a pity that a flower show cannot be made a success without catering to the boozing section.

And yet, in common fairness to all, I am decidedly against holding such a show on any piece of ground where the rules forbid you to do this, that, or the other. If English men or women uphold their right of freedom and speech they would always do as they have done on this occasion, that is, stay away from anywhere were the giver of owner endeavours to dictate to them, forcing them to bow to his opinions, whether they wish to or not. Since this show I believe there has also been another failure, that of our local band, so perhaps after all the people of Selly Oak and Bournbrook are showing their appreciation of the Park in their own way after all, and the section who so loudly blew their own trumpets when they defeated (in their own blind way) the motion for a park where it would have done good, perhaps will take a back seat and give somebody else a chance who does know what the people want. If the secretary and committee take the matter in the right light it won't hurt them.

I am

A WELL WISHER

23rd September 1899 – The South Birmingham Chronicle

VICTORIA BRASS BAND, SELLY OAK

A supper in connection with the Victoria Brass Band was held on the evening of Wednesday, at the Plough and Harrow Hotel, Selly Oak. There was a very large gathering of members of the band and friends, the room being packed. In addition to the band, the following gentlemen were present:- Messrs. Harbun, Ben Connop, Junks, Pratt, Neale, Pember, T.C. Menzies, Horton, Jones, Overthrow, and others. Letters of apology were received from Messrs. R. Docker, Olivieri, and others.

After an excellent supper, the arrangement of which was carried out in admirable manner by Mr. Scullimore, a very good programme of music was carried out. Mr. Scullimore took the chair, and in a brief but interesting speech pointed out that this was the first supper which had been held in connection with the band. He explained that the band had been formed for the purpose of providing music to the people of Selly Oak and district. They had very kindly offered their services to play in the park during the summer months. The band was composed of working men, and he considered that their offer to supply music to the people was almost equivalent to the gift of the park.

Mr. Bromwell, the secretary, read the report of the sports which took place in the park last month, and pointed out that although they had raised about £10, they still required about another £40 in order to provide uniforms for the men. He explained that they would require to discontinue the wearing of their present uniforms as an Act of Parliament passed in 1893 allowed them six years to discontinue wearing them. The Act prevented civilians wearing uniforms that are worn by the various regiments of the British Army.

Mr. White, in a short speech, said that the object of having the supper was to bring together in a social manner those who had already subscribed, and to ascertain the best means to adopt to raise the necessary funds to provide uniforms for the men. They were anxious to make the band a credit to Selly Oak.

A vote of thanks was passed to the gentlemen who had kindly given prizes to the sports. The motion was unanimously carried, amid cheers.

An excellent programme of music followed the business of the evening. The band played selections which were well received.; Mr. T. C. Menzies contributed to the comic element; Mr. Scullimore's rendering of the "Four Jolly Smiths" was very good indeed; Mr. Hems sang with taste and feeling, his song, which brought hearty applause; then followed a trombone solo by Mr. Ryman, and songs from Mr. Harbun, Mrs. A. Robinson, and Mr. A. Gray.

Altogether a very pleasant and enjoyable evening was spent, and a vote of thanks to the chairman brought the meeting to a close.

4th October 1899 – KN&N UDC Minute, and reported in the press on
14th October 1899 – The Birmingham News

The report of this Committee (i.e. the Baths Parks & Cemeteries Committee[44]) having been printed was taken as read and ordered to be entered on the Minutes as follows:-

This Committee beg to report:-

Your Committee, having been informed by Colonel Carmichael, Chief Constable of the County of Worcester, that there are legal difficulties in the way

---

[44] Its minute shows that this Committee met on 15th September 1899.

of granting the application that the Park Keeper should be sworn in as a special constable, have desired the Chief Constable to give directions to have the Park systematically patrolled by the Police.

1st November 1899 – Minute of KN&N UDC

The report of this Committee (the Public Works Committee) having been printed was taken as read and ordered to be entered on the Minutes as follows:-

This Committee have considered and approved the following report of the Works Sub-Committee, and now recommend the same for adoption by the Council:-

That subject to the owners asphalting the footway on the north side, this Council do adopt and declare Gibbins Road at Selly Oak as a highway in future repairable by the Council.

Moved Mr Gibbins, seconded Mr Underhill, resolved that the proceedings of the Public Works Committee as set forth in their Minutes be and are hereby approved and adopted as the acts and proceedings of this Council.

24th November 1899 – Minute of KN&N UDC

The Committee considered a letter from the Local Government Board upon the proposed Bye Laws and gave the Clerk instructions for replying thereto.

<u>Open Spaces, Village Greens</u>:
The Surveyor submitted a list of above as follows:-

From which
Selly Oak Park, 11ac., 2rds., 5 p. Freehold

6th December 1899 – Minute of KN&N UDC

The report of this Committee (the Public Works Committee) having been printed was taken as read and ordered to be entered on the Minutes as follows:-

This Committee have considered and approved the following report of the Works Sub-Committee, and now recommend the same for adoption by the Council:-

Your Sub-Committee beg to recommend:-

<u>Gibbins Road, Selly Oak</u>
That the agents for the owners have declined to agree to the condition laid down by minute No. 168, as to the adoption of Gibbin's (sic) Road as a highway.

Chapter 5

1900

3rd January 1900 – Minute of KN&N UDC

<u>Bye Laws, Selly Oak Park</u>

Moved Mr Oswald; seconded Mr Danson, and resolved that by virtue of the provisions of the powers enabling them in this behalf, this Council hereby makes the following Bye Laws with respect to the Park or recreation ground belonging to them, and known as "Selly Oak Park" and hereby authorises and instructs the Baths, Parks and Cemeteries Committee to take all necessary steps in the name and on behalf of this Council, and under the Common Seal for the confirmation of such Bye Laws, and when the said Bye Laws have been duly confirmed, for giving effect thereto.

BYE-LAWS

Made by the Urban District Council of King's Norton and Northfield with respect to the Park or Recreation Ground known as Selly Oak Park belonging to them.

---

1. Throughout these Bye-Laws the expression "The Council" means the Urban District Council of King's Norton and Northfield, and the expression "the park" means the park, or recreation ground, belonging to the Council, known as Selly Oak Park, and situate and being in the road designated and known as Gibbins Road, Selly Oak, in the parish of Northfield.

2. A person other than officer of the Council, or a person or a servant of a person employed by the Council, on or about any work in connection with the laying-out, planting, improvement, or maintenance of the park, shall not on any day enter the park before the time appointed for the opening thereof, or enter the park or remain therein after the time appointed for the closing thereof.

3. A person shall not wilfully or improperly remove or displace any board, plate, or tablet, or any support, fastening, or fitting of any board, plate, or tablet used or constructed, or adapted to be used for the exhibition of any Bye-law or notice and fixed or set up by the Council in any part of the park, or in or upon

any building or structure therein, or at or near any one of the appointed means of entrance to or egress from the park, or in or on any wall or fence enclosing the park.

4. A person shall not wilfully, carelessly, or negligently deface or carelessly, or negligently injure any part of any wall or fence in or enclosing the park, or any part of any building, barrier, or railing, or of any fixed or moveable seat, or of any other structure or erection in the park.

5. A person shall not wilfully, carelessly, or negligently remove or displace any barrier, railing, or post, or any fixed or moveable seat, or any part of any building, structure, or erection, or any monument, work of art, ornament, or decoration, or any implement, utensil, apparatus, appliance, or article provided for use or used or adapted to be used in the laying-out, planting, improvement, or maintenance of the park, or in the care or cultivation of any tree, sapling, shrub, underwood, gorse, furze, fern, herb, or plant in the park.

6. A person other than an officer of the Council, or a person or a servant of a person employed by the Council in or about any work in connection with the laying-out, planting, improvement, or maintenance of the park, shall not at any time ride, drive, or bring, or cause or suffer to be ridden, driven, or brought into the park any beast of draught, or burden, or any carriage, velocipede, bicycle, or vehicle, other than a wheeled chair drawn or propelled by hand and used solely for the conveyance of a child or children or an invalid (Nb originally omitted "or an invalid", and included "and no person shall cause or suffer any carriage to halt or loiter so as to impede the passage along such drives")

[A paragraph "A groom or horse-breaker shall not exercise or train any horse in any part of the park." was deleted.]

7. A person who shall wheel, or bring, or cause to be wheeled or brought into the park a wheeled chair drawn or propelled by hand, or a perambulator or chaise drawn or propelled by hand, shall not wheel or station such chair, perambulator, or chaise or cause or suffer such chair, perambulator, or chaise to be wheeled or stationed over or upon any part of a flower bed or lawn, or over or upon any shrub, underwood, gorse, furze, fern, or plant, or any ground in course of preparation or cultivation as a flower bed or lawn, or for the reception or growth of any shrub, underwood, gorse, furze, fern, or plant.

Where by a notice or notices affixed or set up in some conspicuous position at or near to each of the several entrances to the park, the Council may from time to time prohibit the use by any such wheeled chair, perambulator, or chaise or such part or parts of the park as shall be defined or described in such notice or notices, a person shall not at any time while such notice or notices shall continue so affixed or set up, wheel or station any such chair, perambulator, or chaise, or cause or suffer any such chair, perambulator, or chaise to be wheeled or stationed over or upon such part or parts of the park.

8. A person other than an officer of the Council or a person acting in pursuance of their directions in that behalf, shall not affix or post any bill, placard, advertisement, or notice to or upon any wall or fence in or enclosing the park, or to or upon any tree, or to or upon any part of any building, barrier, or railing, or of any fixed or moveable seat, or of any other structure or erection in the park.

9. A person other than an officer of the Council, or a person or servant of a person employed by the Council in or about any work in connection with the laying-out, planting, improvement, or maintenance of the park shall not at any time in any part of the park remove or disturb any part of the soil of any flower bed, or any soil under or about any tree, sapling, shrub, underwood, gorze (sic), furze, fern, or plant, or any soil in course of preparation or cultivation as a flower bed, or for the reception or growth of any shrub, underwood, gorse, furze, fern or plant.

10. A person other than an officer of the Council, or a person or servant of a person employed by the Council in or about any work in connection with the laying-out, planting, improvement, or maintenance of the park shall not at any time in any part of the park walk or run over, or stand, sit, or lie upon any part of any flower bed, or any shrub, underwood, gorse, furze, fern, or plant, or any ground in course of preparation or cultivation as a flower bed, or for the reception or growth of any shrub, underwood, gorse, furze, fern, or plant.

11. A person other than an officer of the Council, or a person or servant of a person employed by the Council in or about any work in connection with the laying-out, planting, improvement, or maintenance of the park shall not at any time in any part of the park, cut or displace any turf, or uproot and displace any gorse, furze, fern or plant.

12. A person shall not at any time, in any part of the park, pluck any bud, blossom, flower, or leaf of any tree, sapling, shrub, underwood, gorse, furze, fern or plant.

13. A person shall not wilfully, carelessly, or negligently soil or defile any part of any wall or fence in or enclosing the park, or any part of any building, barrier, or railing, or of any fixed or moveable seat, or of any monument, work of art, ornament, or decoration, or of any other structure or erection in the park, or wilfully, carelessly, or negligently throw or deposit any filth, rubbish, or refuse, or cause, or suffer any filth, rubbish, or refuse to fall or to be thrown or deposited upon any part of the park.

[A paragraph "A person other than an officer of the Council, or a person acting in pursuance of the direction of the Council, shall not discharge any fire-arm or wantonly throw or discharge any stone or other missile, make or light any fire, or throw or set fire to any fireworks in the park" was replaced with:]

A person shall not in the park, except as hereinafter provided, set fire to or let off any squib, rocket, or any other description of fireworks or discharge any firearm.

Provided:-

(a) That this bye-law shall not be deemed to prohibit the setting fire to or letting off any squib, rocket or any other description of fireworks or the discharge of any firearm on any day when in pursuance of any Statutory provision in that behalf the Council may close the park to the public, and where upon an application to the Council for permission to set fire to or let off any squib, rocket, or any other description of fireworks or to discharge any firearm upon such occasion as shall be specified in such application, the Council may grant such permission subject to compliance with such conditions as they may prescribe.

(b) That this bye-law shall not be deemed to apply to any case where an offence is committed against Section 80 of the Explosives Act, 1875.

A person other than an officer of the Council, or a person acting in pursuance of the direction of the Council, shall not make or light any fire in the park.

A person shall not in the park throw or discharge any stone or other missile to the damage or danger of any person.

A person shall not climb any wall or any fence in or enclosing the park, or any tree, or any barrier, railing, or post in the park

14. A person shall not in any part of the park wilfully displace or disturb, injure or destroy any bird's nest, or wilfully take, injure, or destroy any bird's eggs.

15. A person shall not, in any part of the park, take, injure, or destroy any bird, or spread or use any net, or set or use any snare or other engine, instrument, or means for the taking, injury, or destruction of any bird.

16. A person shall not cause or suffer any dog belonging to him or in his charge to enter or remain in the park, unless such dog be, and continue to be, under proper control, and be effectually restrained from causing annoyance to any person.

5. 1900

17. A person shall not play or take part in any game of football, quoits, bowls, bandy, rounders, hockey, golf, or cricket, or any other game which by reason of the rules or manner of playing, or for the prevention of damage, danger, or discomfort to any person in the park, may necessitate at any time during the continuance of the game the exclusive use by the player or players of any space in the park, except in such parts of the park and at such times and subject to such regulations as may from time to time be prescribed by a notice or notices affixed or set up by the Council in a conspicuous position within the park.

18. A person other than an Officer of the Council, or a person or a servant of a person employed by the Council in or about any work in connection with the laying-out, planting, improvement, or maintenance of the park shall not, except as hereinafter provided, erect any post, rail, fence, pole, tent, booth, stand, building, or other structure in any part of the park.

Provided that the foregoing prohibition shall not apply in any case where upon an application to the Council for permission to erect any post, rail, fence, pole, tent, booth, stand, building, or other structure in the park upon such occasion and for such purpose as shall be specified in such application the Council may grant, subject to compliance with such conditions as they may prescribe, permission to any person to erect such post, rail, fence, pole, tent, booth, building, or other structure.

19. A person shall not in any part of the park beat, shake, sweep, brush, or cleanse any carpet, drugget, rug, or mat, or any other fabric retaining dust or dirt.

20. A person shall not in any part of the park hang, spread, or deposit any linen or other fabric for the purpose of drying or bleaching.

21. A person shall not preach or deliver any public address in any part of the park, nor shall any person or persons assemble in the park for the purpose of holding or taking part in any religious, political, or party meeting [there was deleted "or any meeting which, in the judgement of the Council is not proper to be held therein, and which shall be prohibited by any notice or notices affixed or set up in a conspicuous position in the park"].

22. A person shall not, in any part of the park, sell or offer, or expose for sale, or let to hire, or offer or expose for letting to hire, any commodity or article, unless in pursuance of an agreement with the Council or otherwise in the exercise of any lawful right or privilege, such person may be duly authorised to sell or let to hire in the park such commodity or article.

23. A person who is in a state of intoxication shall not enter or remain in the park.

24. No person shall behave in an indecent manner in the park, or to the annoyance of any person use indecent, or obscene language, in the park.

   A person shall not frequent or use the park for the purpose of betting or wagering or of agreeing to make any bet or wager. (Nb. This paragraph had not appeared in early drafts of the bye laws.)

25. A person shall not smoke tobacco in any building in the park.

26. A person shall not, on any day, play any musical instrument or sing in the park, except in any case where, upon an application made to the Council for their permission to play any musical instrument or instruments, or to sing in the park on such occasion, or on such days and at such hours as shall be specified in such application, the Council may grant to such person, or to any body of persons including such person, permission to play any musical instrument or instruments, or to sing in such park, subject to such conditions as the Council may prescribe.

27. A man, or a boy above eight years old resorting to the park shall not intrude on or use any closet or building therein which shall be set apart for the use of any woman, girl or child under eight years old.

   A woman or girl resorting to the park shall not intrude on or use any closet or building therein which shall be set apart for the use of any man, or boy above eight years old.

28. A person shall not, in any part of the park, wilfully obstruct, disturb, interrupt, or annoy any other person in proper use of the park, or wilfully obstruct, disturb, or interrupt any officer of the Council in the proper execution of his duty, or any person or servant of any person employed by the Council in the proper execution of any work in connection with the laying-out, planting, improvement, or maintenance of the park.

29. Every person who shall offend against any of the foregoing Bye-laws shall be liable, for every such offence, to a penalty of five pounds.

   Provided nevertheless that the Justices or Court before whom any complaint may be made, or any proceedings may be taken in respect of any such offence may, if they think fit, adjudge the payment as a penalty of any sum less than the full amount of the penalty imposed by this Bye-law.

30. Every person who shall be guilty of a breach of any Bye-law relative to the park may be removed therefrom by any servant of the Council, or by any constable, in any one of several cases hereinafter specified, that is to say:-

5. 1900

(i) Where the infraction of the Bye-law is committed within the view of such servant or constable, and the name and residence of the person infringing the Bye-law are unknown to and cannot be readily ascertained by such servant or constable.

(ii) Where the breach of the Bye-law is committed within view of such servant or constable, and from the nature of such breach, or from any other fact of which such servant or constable may have knowledge, or of which he may be credibly informed, there may be reasonable ground for belief that the continuance in the park of the person breaking the Bye-law may result in another breach of a Bye-law, or that the removal of such person from the park is otherwise necessary as a security for the proper sue and regulation thereof.

30th January 1900 – KN&N UDC Baths, Parks and Cemeteries Committee

Resolved that a synopsis of the Bye Laws when approved be drawn up and posted in a conspicuous position near to the Entrance gate.

22nd March 1900 – KN&N UDC Baths, Parks and Cemeteries Committee, and reported on 7th April 1900 – The Birmingham News

The Clerk reported he had objected to the assessment of the rates of the Park and Lodge and had returned the demand notes received and now understood the assessment was discharged.

Propagating frame Resolved that a propagating frame be provided at an estimated cost of £9 (14ft x 6ft including brickwork).

Swings Resolved that the space about two yards wide round the public swings be paved with asphalt at an estimated cost of £10. 16. 0.

Asphalting Main drive An estimate for laying the main drive with asphalt at an estimated cost of £74. 14. 0. was considered and the matter was referred to a sub-committee consisting of Messrs. Talliss, Ward and the Chairman to consider and report.

9th May 1900 – KN&N UDC Baths, Parks and Cemeteries Committee

Asphalting main Drive Resolved the Sub-Committee appointed at last meeting be continued with same power as before.

Extra Assistance Resolved that the services of two men be engaged to assist the Park Keeper for a fortnight.

The Heydays Of Selly Oak Park

2nd June 1900 – The Birmingham News

Local & District News
Selly Oak

<u>Gibbins Road</u> – The District Council have decided to undertake the work of paving with asphalt the footway on the park side of Gibbins Road, Selly Oak, the work to be executed by the Council's employees within four months from completion of agreement at the cost of the owners of the frontages, the estimated cost being first deposited. Upon execution of the agreement referred to, Gibbins Road is to be declared a highway repairable in future by the Council.

Selly Oak & District Notes

The Selly Oak Victoria Brass Band commence to play next week in the Park, as they did last year.

Weather permitting they will play every Wednesday evening during June, July, and August.

At the meeting of the District Council on Wednesday, an expenditure of £9 was sanctioned for the provision of seats on the bandstand.

9th June 1900 – The Birmingham News

Selly Oak & District Notes

There was an extraordinarily large number of children at Selly Oak Park on Whit Monday, the attendance establishing a record which it will be difficult to beat.

The Park Keeper estimates the number as between 10,000 and 12,000, and to him at least Monday was not a day of relaxation and rest.

One child received a nasty blow in the face from a returning swing, and this circumstance seems to point to the necessity of surrounding the swings with a suitable barrier. Such a provision would be inexpensive, and besides obviating a present source of danger, would immensely lighten the task of the Park Keeper.

16th June 1900 – The South Birmingham Chronicle:

THE BAND – The Selly Oak Victoria Military Band re-commenced playing in the Park last Wednesday week. There was a large attendance. They will continue to play every Wednesday evening as last year.

30th June 1900 – The South Birmingham Chronicle:

CHILDREN'S FETE – A general committee meeting was held at the Institute, Bournbrook, on Thursday evening, Mr. T.A. Cole presiding. The minutes of the last meeting were read and adopted. The secretary reported that he had seen Dr. Hollinshead, who said that although there was no increase in the illness prevalent among the children there was no decrease. The schools are closed for three weeks. Mr. Gittins said that he had made inquiries, and he thought that the best time for holding the fete would be July 30, upon which date they would be allowed to use the Park. This was agreed to, on the understanding that if the illness increases it would again be postponed. It was moved by Mr. S. Hill, and seconded by Mr. Holmes, that they should appoint Mr. R. Roberts as a vice-chairman. This was unanimously agreed to. Mr. Hill read the minutes of the last meeting of the Procession Committee which were confirmed, with the exception of the one referring to the second band which it was decided at a former meeting should be engaged. They had, the secretary explained, received three applications, viz., one from the Stirchley Band, another from Bartley Green, and the third from Mr. White, of the Selly Oak Victoria Band. The Procession Committee decided that, as Mr. White's band had been engaged to head the procession, he should not, as Mr. White had suggested, have the order for the second band. Mr. White said he would like to ask why they wanted to go out of Selly Oak for the band. He would get a second band together, and if there was any complaint they need not engage him again. After further discussion the matter dropped. The Field and Sports Committee presented their report, and it was decided to have the usual attractions, such as Punch and Judy, steam horses, etc., and it was also decided to give prizes of 15s., 10s. and 5s. respectively for the best decorated houses or premises in the village on the day of the fete. The question of "dressing up" and walking in the procession came in for some discussion, and it was decided that nothing of an objectionable nature should be allowed to take part in it.

14th July 1900 – The South Birmingham Chronicle:

ACCIDENT AT THE PARK – An accident occurred on Wednesday evening to a girl named Kate Saneebury, 6, Grove Avenue, Katie Road, Selly Oak, who was struck on the face by a swing and knocked down. P.c. Paxton rendered first aid, and then took the girl home to her parents. Dr. Hollinshead was sent for, but her injuries only proved to be of a slight character.

28th July 1900 – The South Birmingham Chronicle:

THE CHILDREN'S FETE

Selly Oak is justly proud of its Children's Fete. There is indeed no local event which is more popular, or creates a greater amount of enthusiasm both among parents and children. Young and old, men and women, all seem to vie with each other in making this annual fete a success, and no effort is spared to see that each year it beats the preceding one, and everybody seems determined that it shall do so. The original promoters have, indeed, every reason to congratulate themselves in having started in our midst the Children's Fete, which has become a feature in Selly Oak life. "Children's Day" is now a recognised one in the calendar of the year of our district, and, as the summer comes round, everyone looks forward to it as the event of the season. We are sure that those who originated this undertaking some years since could never have dreamt that out of a very modest beginning so large and important a concern could have grown, and that there is no question that their most sanguine hopes have been more than realised. There is something generous and something noble in the way this fete is arranged. Children of all creeds, of all denominations, are welcome, and are treated alike, no matter what school they attend; then, again, the committee comprises men of all stations of life, men belonging to different sects and religions all working together and pulling together for one common object – that of brightening up and cheering up the life of the children one day in the year, who in their turn brighten up and cheer all the year round the life of those homes which are blest with them. It is, indeed, a great and noble work to contribute to the merriment of our children, a great number of whom have little pleasure or comforts in their homes; and the self-sacrificing work of those who are responsible for the arrangements and carry out the details of this undertaking are entitled to our gratitude and support. We have every reason to believe that the fete which is to be held on Monday will not only be worthy of its predecessors, but will to some extent beat all former ones. Everything indicates this. This determination with which the committee have worked, the amicable manner in which they have pulled together, the new element introduced, the experience gained from former fetes, the apparently settled state of the weather – which to all indications will be fine on Monday – and, last, but not least, the increased interest which everyone seems to take both in Selly Oak and Bournbrook in the coming event, all augur well, and go to prove that the children will have a grand day on Monday, and the parents will be as happy and as merry as the children themselves.

SELLY OAK AND BOURNBROOK CHILDREN'S FETE

The final meeting for this year of the general committee in connection with the above fete took place on Thursday evening in the Friends' Institute, Bournbrook. Mr. T.A. Cole occupied the chair, and there were also present Messrs. S. Hill, secretary, W. Holmes, treasurer, R. Roberts, vice-chairman, W. Humphries, Gough, Jordan, James, Draper, White, Hall, Shephard, etc.

The balance-sheet for the year 1899 showed the receipts to be £82 9s. 10½d., and the expenditure £72 12s. 9d., leaving a balance in hand of £9 17s. 1½d.

The minutes of the last meeting were read and passed for discussion. The first minute was with reference to who should supply the cake. Mr. Humphries said that the Catering Committee held a meeting last Tuesday to consider the tenders, and after tasting and smelling, etc., (laughter), they decided that Mr. Roy should supply the cake. Mr. Roy's price was 37s. per cent, or about 4d. per pound. Mr. Caleb Watts's offer to supply stakes at 9d. each was accepted. Mr. Cole said that he would supply a second platform.

5. 1900

It was decided to wear a piece of black ribbon in the centre of the rosettes worn by the committee as a token of regret for the late Mr. Halward, and it was also decided to send a letter of condolence to Mr. Halward's widow. Mr. White was entrusted with supplying of two bands, and Mr. Shephard's tender to supply the steam horses for £10 was accepted. The minutes were confirmed and signed.

Procession Committee
Mr Holmes said that the committee would like all tradesmen with vehicles to join in the procession, and assemble at the schools at 12.30 on Monday next. Last year, continued Mr. Holmes, they appointed judges who lived out of the district to award the prizes, and he thought that was the best, because they did not know who the competitors were, except by their numbers. He knew three or four gentlemen whose only acquaintance in Selly Oak was by driving through it, and he would like to propose those as judges. The band would assemble at 1.15, and he wanted as many of those who could to get off for the day, as it was a big order to get all the children loaded up. The judging would take place at 12.30 by the schools. In reply to a question as to how the judging would take place, Mr. Holmes said that he would engage carts (sic) at his own expense from Palfreys's, and they would be numbered 1, 2, 3, 4, etc. He thought that would be the best way, and as each vehicle drew up he would give them their number.

Catering Committee
Mr. Humphries said that he would like to ask helpers if they would lend clothes baskets or hampers with their names on. He also said that if they could not hire enough jugs they would have to buy some, as for the last two years the tea had been spoilt for want of jugs. With reference to the tenders for milk they had received some at 8d. and 10d. per gallon, but they did not know whether that was morning or afternoon milk. What they wanted was milk which had been obtained about an hour before tea. They also wanted about twenty urns if possible. He wished to draw attention to the fact that the treat is for the children who live in Selly Oak and Bournbrook, and are of school age. In previous years the treat had been taken advantage of by boys and girls over 13 years of age and who had left school. A great difficulty had been found in discriminating in these cases. A strong effort is to be made this year to put a stop to this. He thought that children who had left school should be debarred from having a ticket. (Hear, hear). Any boy or girl who lives in Selly Oak or Bournbrook and attends school anywhere can come, but those who have left, if they are 11 or 12, or whatever age, they cannot be admitted.

Mr. Cole: Can they come if they are 16 or 18, and yet attend school?

Mr. Humphries: Yes, because if so they will be mentally deficient. (Laughter). Mr. Humphries suggested that when the band play "Soldiers of the Queen" the children should take it as a signal for teatime.

Mr. Draper said that he had seen Dr. Hollinshead about the balloons, and he had given him a prescription. It was decided to ask Mr. Birt, the chemist, to let them off. In reply to a request from the committee Mrs. Holmes and Mrs. Humphries had consented to distribute the prizes.

A committee was formed to purchase the prizes for the races and sports. It was stated that last year £4 had been spent on them, and it was agreed to spend the same this year.

Mr. Gilbert suggested that they should have a torch-light procession as they left the Park, and intimated his willingness to supply forty torches if the funds would not meet the additional expense.

It was decided to allow Mr. Baker to take photographs of the committee and the procession during the day, provided he did so on his own responsibility, and not with the intention of getting the committee-men to buy them afterwards.

The meeting then concluded.

A committee meeting was held yesterday (Friday), when other arrangements of a minor character were made.

28th July 1900 – The Birmingham News

Selly Oak and Bournbrook Children's Fete
Arrangements for Monday

The final meeting of the general committee of the Selly Oak and Bournbrook Children's Fete was held on Thursday evening. Amongst a large attendance were:- Messrs. W. Holmes, W. Humphreys, S. Hill, J. Gough, J.A. Sheppard, W. Perkins, J. Hall, S.H. Brittain, F.C. James, J. Draper, R. Roberts, T. Breeze, W. Gilbert, Edwards, Davis, Greswolde, Tranter, Taylor, J.A. Jones, G. Sheasby, Overton, and Knowles.

The reports of the various sub-committees were received, and their recommendations approved. The catering sub-committee reported that they had accepted the tender of Mr. D. Roy at just under 4d. per lb. for the cake. The whole of the local bakers had been invited to submit samples of a cake which they were prepared to supply at a cost not exceeding 3d. per lb., but Mr. Roy was the only one to respond to the invitation. He submitted three samples of cake, one of which he was prepared to supply at 2½d. per lb., a second at 3d. per lb., and a third at approximately 4d. per lb. After examining and tasting all three, the sub-committee unanimously decided to accept the highest priced tender, and they asked the committee to approve of their actions in placing the order. This was done by a unanimous vote.

Mr. S. Hill stated that Mr. T. Gibbins, of the Birmingham Battery Co., told him, in reply to a request for a subscription, that he would willingly subscribe if the committee would alter the day of the fete from Monday till Saturday. Mr. Gibbins was informed that that would be impossible for this year at any rate. Authority was given to the sports sub-committee to spend between £4 and £5 on the provision of prizes for the children, and to purchase 80lbs. weight of sweets.

The component parts of the procession assemble in the Heeley, Exeter, Hubert and Dartmouth Roads not later than 12.30 o'clock on Monday, and the procession, led by Mr. W. Holmes on horseback, and headed by the Selly Oak Band, will start from the neighbourhood of the day school in Tiverton Road, at 1.15 p.m. prompt. The entries for competition will be judged en route to the park by gentlemen from Birmingham so that whatever competitors may think of the judges' decisions they will at any rate be unable to impute partiality to them. No vehicle will be admitted to the park, nor will the public be able to gain entrance thereto until after 5 o'clock, when the children will have had tea. It is hoped that this fact will be borne in mind, and the gatekeeper not importuned to give admittance. On leaving the park the procession will be headed by a company of torch bearers. The committee appeal to the local public to do nothing to hinder them in their arduous task of controlling the event.

4th August 1900 – The South Birmingham Chronicle

VILLAGE CHIMES

There is no doubt about it that from every point of view the Children's Fete was a great success on Monday, and the Committee and those responsible for the arrangements and carrying out of them are to be congratulated and deserve the best thanks of the community at large. The weather was ideal from the fact that it was not too hot, a gentle breeze was blowing the whole of the day, and the atmosphere was clear and bright. The Park was crowded to excess, and all kinds of amusements both for young and old were provided and well patronised. A large number of prominent residents visited the Park in the afternoon and evening, and we were pleased to see that everything passed off without a single hitch. Our band, as usual, went through their programme in an admirable manner, and kept everybody merry and in a good humour during the whole of the day.

The procession in connection with the children's fete on Monday was larger than any of its predecessors. For the first time in the history of the fete, the start was made from the Bournbrook Schools, and, after parading the village, proceeded to the Park. Mr. W. Holmes acted as Marshal, and assisted by the committee, succeeded in keeping admirable order amongst the youngsters.

As usual, the streets were thickly lined by the villagers, who showed their appreciation of the procession by giving hearty cheers as some comic character came into view. En route a collection in aid of the funds was made by grotesquely-dressed committee-men, and no doubt by this means the finances were considerably augmented.

Although at the expense of ourselves, we did not fail to be amused at a joke we overheard at the children's fete, the author being a would-be comedian. The humorous individual posed as a clown, and of another gentleman of similar occupation, he asked: "Have you seen any advertisement in the Crocodile – no, I mean 'Chronicle'"? The sally managed to raise a laugh, but we should be glad if the "joker" would forward a cheque in payment for the advertisement – or shall we render the account again?

The police arrangements at the fete on Monday were carried out, as usual, in a very creditable manner, under the superintendence of Sergeant Rudnick and two other police officers. We think that the fact that everything went off satisfactorily, and that there were no accidents, is due in a great measure to their vigilance and tact in keeping order.

SELLY OAK AND BOURNBROOK CHILDREN'S FETE
A Magnificent Pageant

The annual children's fete took place on Monday, and was, as usual, the occasion for a general village merry-making. The street decorations, for which, this year, a prize was offered by the committee, were a considerable improvement on former years, and High Street was simply one blaze of many coloured flags, tastefully interspersed with appropriate messages, such as "Success to the Children's Fete", "God bless the children", etc. It would be invidious on our part to endeavour to describe in detail the charming manner in which the decorations were made, but it is a very tangible proof of the popularity of the fete, and the judges' task in awarding the prize must have been a difficult one, although we can heartily congratulate the winner on his well-deserved success. The procession, and indeed a more glorious pageant we do not recollect in local history, was undoubtedly one of the principal features of the day's rejoicings. To this committee, whose hard work during recent weeks has culminated so satisfactorily, we extend our heartfelt congratulations on the result of their efforts to make "the children's day" one round of joy and pleasure to the thousands of little toddlers whose hearts throbbed with excited and joyous happiness on this their "gala" day. Starting from the Bournbrook Schools at about 1.30, the lengthy procession set out for the Park, marching to the strains of the Selly Oak Victoria Military Brass Band. Numerous decorated vehicles and grotesquely attired characters formed a principal feature of the pageant, and aroused the cheers, laughter, and enthusiasm of thousands of holiday-making on-lookers. Beside the adult portion of the procession there were about two thousand children, of all ages, who formed an exceedingly pretty spectacle as they marched light-heartedly along with their cups and cans. The procession was marshalled by Mr. William Holmes, who, we might mention, has been closely associated with this village fete since it was first inaugurated years ago. At the Park games and racing were indulged in, and a capital tea was served by many willing workers to the children, who all appeared to have remarkable keen appetites. After tea the general public were admitted to the Park, and the weather, which had been somewhat threatening in the morning, was now all that could be desired, and everyone gave way to merry-making and rejoicing. Among the gentlemen who took a prominent part in the arrangements were Messrs. W. Humphreys (school master), A. Gittins, W. Holmes, R. Roberts, S. Hill, Jordan, W. Haddon, Sheppard, G. Hollis, F. James, T.A. Cole, J. Hull, J. Gough, G. Draper, and several other members of the committee. During the afternoon air balloons were liberated, to the delight of the children, who watched their ascent with much glee, and followed their progress with their eyes, until they became a dot on the horizon, and then disappeared from sight. The gramophone tent was largely patronised, as also was the Punch and Judy show, and several other innocent amusements, besides the prime attraction – the steam-horses. The amusements also included an innovation in the shape of a football kicking apparatus, in connection with which a prize of a coconut was awarded to those competitors who sent the "leather" through a hole in a board, which was painted to represent the "gaping" mouth of Kruger.

During the day the Band[45] played selections, and towards evening a programme of dance music was provided for those young people who wished to "trip the light fantastic toe".

At the conclusion a torch-light procession was organised, which, headed by the band, paraded the village with very pretty effect.

Prizes were given for the best decorated mail carts, cycles, etc., and the winners were as follows: – Novelties: 1, Clark; 2, Bostock; 3, Hardy. Cycles: 1, ——; 2, Taylor; 3, Steeve. Budd was highly commended, and awarded a consolation prize. Mail-carts: 1, Kimberley; 2, Lee; 3, Hitch. House decoration: 1, Hopkins; 2, Perkins; 3, Cartwright. Decorated vehicles: 1, Hunebourne; 2, Draper; 3, Henshaw.

4th August 1900 – The Birmingham News

Local and District News
Selly Oak

The Children's Fete – Another Huge Success – With the close of Monday was added to the records of the past an event from every point of view as successful as any that has taken place in the village. July 30 was the local gala day, the day of the children's fete, when youth and age unite to realise the desire so eloquently expressed by the generosity of the villagers that the children shall spend a day full of happiness. Many hours of unstinted labour, given without desire of material recompense or even verbal recognition, had been spent by the large body of workers elected of the people, in the organisation of the event, with its thousand and one items requiring thought and attention, and nothing but good weather was needed to ensure its success. This, fortunately, and despite the gloomy portents and prophecies, was vouchsafed, and the whole of the day's proceedings were gone through without as much as a spot of rain to mar them. The procession was marshalled, as in previous years, in Tiverton and Dawlish Roads. Compared with last year a falling off in the number and variety of the competitive entries was noticeable, the whole of the exhibits numbering only sixteen, while there were, too, fewer instances of the attractiveness of the procession being added to by non-competitive effort. There was

---

[45] There is a picture of the Selly Oak Victoria Band in the 11th August 1900 edition of the South Birmingham Chronicle. Unfortunately the microfilm copy is of very poor quality and not suitable for reproduction here.

one phase of the of the diminution, however, which was altogether pleasing: there was a marked absence of the vulgar and questionable exhibitions from which the procession in the past has not been entirely free, and so far as our observation went there was nothing to which the most susceptible might take exception. The decoration of the main street was not quite so lavish as last year, but it was none the less effective, and imparted to it the air of festivity proper to the occasion. The committee had hoped that this feature of the event would have been more conspicuous than heretofore, and to stimulate the residents to a rivalry in the embellishment of their houses and shop fronts they had offered three prizes of 15s., 10s., and 5s. respectively for the best decorated fronts. The response was not very encouraging, only three entries, and but two of these from residents in the main street, being received. The first prize was awarded to Mrs. Hopkins (High Street, Selly Oak), for a very tasteful decoration, in which tri-coloured paper had been used with great effect stretching from the walls of the house to the garden front where ropes which had been covered with fancifully cut paper, while in front a framework in which were two hoops had been treated in like fashion. From the two sides hung festoons of ropes similarly adorned with paper, and suspended at odd intervals about the framework were Chinese lanterns, many of them of handsome proportions and designs, which when lit in the evening gave a charming appearance to the whole. The second prize was taken by Mrs. G. Perkins (Tiverton Road, Bournbrook), for a neat embellishment of the front of her house with flags and art muslin, while the third prize was taken by Mrs. Cartwright (High Street, Bournbrook), who had adorned her shop front with pictures of Generals made popular by the war. A picture of the Queen formed the centre of this decoration, and immediately underneath this was a bust of the cheery "B.P.". Effigies of John Chinaman and of Mr. Kruger were suspended in front of the design. There was another decorated shop front, not entered for competition, which also calls for notice. It was that of Mr. Benbow, who displayed a fine array of effigies during the day, and in the evening illuminated his shop front with fairy lamps, as well as tendering to the crowd in fireworks at the finish the parting salutation "Good night". Turning to the procession, which was headed by Mr. W. Holmes on horseback, the first call for notice after the band (the Selly Oak Victoria), was made by five mounted men in military uniform. Most conspicuous amongst these was Mr. T. Cooper (Dawlish Road). His cocked hat and plume showed him to be at least a General, and a closer inspection discovered him to be wearing the cross batons of a Field Marshal. To make assurance doubly sure he was asked "Who are you?" and the questioner went away amply satisfied with the laconic reply, "Lord Roberts". Behind his lordship were three humble artillerymen (Messrs Roy, T. Bradshaw, and S. Johnson), and a hussar (Mr. A. Roy). Mr. Roy is an old army man, and was wearing his long service and Afghan frontier medals. Next came a corps of stretcher-bearers (Selly Oak Ambulance Corps), and a group of children on horseback (Masters Gordon Hughes, Walter Cullimore, Walter Haines, and Arthur Monk, and Miss May Turrell). The most noticeable of the latter were Miss Turrell, who was dressed as a May Queen, and Master Hughes who looked very nice in a suit of green material with a tartan sash, and bestrode a very nicely decorated horse. Though not for competition, Mr. Hughes's turnout was one that impressed the judges so favourably that they decided to recommend it for a prize, which the committee will no doubt grant. The exhibits came next, with the children sandwiched in between, some in vehicles and others on foot. The neatness of the children's dresses reflects great credit upon the parents, who had evidently been animated by a commendable spirit of emulation to make their boys and girls appear in public as attractive as those of their neighbours, if not a little more so. The youngest of the children were stowed away in vehicles lent for that purpose by Messrs. J. Whitehouse, C.W. Pember, A. Chillingworth, and W. Hunt (each of whom sent two conveyances), and Mrs. Henshaw, Messrs. Clarke, H. Grigg, B. Connop, F. Monk, Whitehouse and Pearce, C. Halward, H. and F. Spurrier, Rainbow, T. Chapman, T. Meere, S. Chapman, George Wilde, E. Jackson, and W. Baldwin. In several instances the vehicles were nicely adorned. Messrs Whitehouse and Pearce and Mr. Chillingworth had decorated the harness of their horses with ball fringe, while greenery and coloured paper added to the appearance of the vehicles sent by Mrs. Henshaw, and Mr. T. Meere. Mr. Taylor, who had charge of Messrs. H. and F. Spurrier's conveyance, was attired in a fanciful garb of figured muslin. The best entries for the competition were seen in the novelty and mailcart sections. In the former four competed for the three prizes offered, and in the latter five. The first novelty prize was won by Mr. C. Clarke, with a ship mounted on a cart, the motion of the wheels of which formed the motive power of an ingenious mechanical device to make the ship roll and pitch. The man in charge of the exhibit had made himself a suit of clothes for the occasion out of an old blanket, and wore a vermilion stove-pipe hat. The second prize was awarded to Mr. T. F. Bostock, who had sought to illustrate "the old lady who lived in a shoe" and her place of abode. Miss Nellie Wheatley, adorned with a birch, personated the old lady, and sat very comfortably in a large cardboard shoe built upon a mailcart. Her family numbered eight – the Misses Wheatley (2), Haywood (2) Titley, and Thompson (3). The winners of the third prize essayed the ambitious task of representing the four principal characters in the well-known story "The basket of flowers". Alice Hickling stood for the Countess, Nellie Sheasby for the lady'smaid (sic), Lily Hickling for Mary, and Walter Harvey for James. The fourth entry was by a quintette (sic) styling themselves "Hardy and Co.", and was a rather mixed affair. Mr. A. Hardy was pushed along on an ancient tricycle, the wheels of which were "free" when pedalling forward as well as when putting back pressure on. Mr. A. Cull, armed with boxing gloves and a gun, and Mr. Bracey, attired in a soldier's tunic and carrying a matchet (sic), were the fighting men of the "Co.". The other two (Messrs. Parkes and Phillips) seemed to have no particular function. The judges had no difficulty in awarding the first prize in the mailcart section, Mrs. Kimberley's handsomely decked out vehicle being easily first. A bower had been made over the mailcart with asparagus and other greenery, in which were set sunflowers, cornflowers, sweet peas, marguerites, etc. The second prize went to Mrs. Lea, who had skilfully adorned her cart with coloured papers and Chinese lanterns; while Mrs. Hitch took the third prize for a mailcart decorated after the same fashion, but less profusely. A fourth consolation prize was awarded to Mrs.

Budd, whose twin babies, labelled "The babes in the wood", were exhibited in a mailcart decorated with flowers and greenery. For the vehicle competition there were three entries. Mr. A. Honeybourne won first prize with a floral decoration, and the second went to Mr. Draper. The third was awarded in error to a non-competitor, and the question as to who is to receive it will accordingly have to be decided by the committee. The third entry was a decorated vehicle by Mr. T, Genderton, in charge of someone capitally dressed to represent Mother Shipton. The show of decorated cycles was a poor one. The first prize went to Miss Marion Clark, who had a very neatly decorated machine; Master Taylor took the second with a horse-tricycle; and Master Steed took the third. One of the most interesting features in connection with the procession was the get up of several of those who had consented to collect from the general public en route to the park, in which the fete was held. First place must be given to Messrs. J. Sheppard and J. A. Jones, who, dressed in Japanese robes, were at once the most conspicuous and effective figures in the procession. They were very busy collecting, and many there were who gave their pence almost unconsciously, engrossed the while in their inspection of the novel and interesting attire of the canvassers. Amongst the ladies the most striking attire was that of Miss Meere, who was dressed as a daughter of the Sunny South, in a Turkey-red skirt and a black velvet corselet over a bodice of old gold coloured material. A neat little tambourine, gay with streamers, and speedily well stocked with pence, completed her get up. She was accompanied by Miss Lily Grove, who though not so picturesquely dressed, looked very becoming in a white skirt and gold coloured blouse, trimmed with satin, and a hat trimmed with poppies and cornflowers, and set at a saucy angle. Like her friend's, her tambourine was well filled with coppers. The progress of the procession to the park was witnessed by a large crowd, which lined both sides of the road several ranks deep. On arrival the various recreations and diversions arranged for the entertainment of the children were immediately commenced. The majority of the youngsters went straight for the steam roundabout, and the luckless committeemen who had volunteered "to do duty on the horses" were soon labouring hard in the cultivation of some fine stiff limbs and aching backs for the morrow. The Punch and Judy shows, given under the superintendence of Mr. J. Gough, drew large crowds; while the phonograph stand and the gramophone tent were well patronised throughout the afternoon. The goal shooting competition with the football, again in the charge of Messrs. F. C. James and G. Ollis, were met with a very large measure of support, and proved a source of considerable income to the committee. Mr. T. Breeze and his minstrels again gave their services, and delighted the youngsters with a couple of sketches. Shortly after four o'clock the massed bands played "Soldiers of the Queen", which was the signal for the assembly of the children for tea. Close upon 2,500 children attended the fete, and some idea of what was meant by the provision of tea for so large a number may be obtained when it is stated the committee purchased for their consumption 900lbs. of bread from Mr. A. E. Smith, 1,100lbs. of seed and fruit cake, and 2,500 large buns from Mr. D. Roy, 50lbs. of butter from Mr. C. W. Pember, 35lbs. of tea and 224lbs. lump sugar from Mr. Harry Curtis, and 30 gallons of milk from Mrs. W. Hunt. For several years past the feeling has been growing amongst some of the oldest members of the committee that too much was being paid for the provisions, and this opinion found expression this year in a motion submitted by Mr. W. Holmes, and carried nem. con. at the meeting of the committee on July 19th, "That orders for goods be given out by tender". This departure has given offence to the local bakers, to whom the view that the fete was organised for the benefit of the children, and not the tradesmen, seems to have come as a great surprise, and all but one (Mr. D. Roy) ignored the invitation to tender. The committee hold it to be their bounden duty, however, to spend the money entrusted to them, and given for the most part by people in poor circumstances, to the best possible advantage, and they feel sure they will obtain the verdict of public opinion in the course they have taken. This year it has resulted in a saving of close upon £10. The arrangement of the children for tea had been left in the hands of Mr. W. Humphreys, whose plan worked admirably, and enabled the children to be served with a minimum of trouble. In this connection acknowledgement must be made of the services of the large band of helpers, who spent several hours in the morning in cutting the bread and butter and cake, and in the afternoon made light labour of the work of serving the children. If there was a fault in regard to the tea, it was that the time allowed for it was a little too short. One or two of the sections got supplied a little quicker than the others, and having had enough the children commenced to wander about, a circumstance which suggested the propriety of saying grace, which in the interests of some of those who ate rapidly, or had not been fortunate in having their wants attended to, might well have been postponed for another ten minutes or a quarter of an hour. In catering for so large a number it was inevitable, if the risk of being short of provisions was to be guarded against, that there should be some surplus, or, as it is called, "waste". This year, however, it was smaller than usual, and what was not subsequently distributed amongst the children was sold to the public in pennyworths. After tea the programme of races arranged by the Sports Committee, which had been already entered upon, was resumed. The events consisted of flat races, ranging from 50 to 200 yards, sack, three-legged, egg and spoon races, and the prizes, upon which £4 16s. 0d. had been spent, were workboxes and lady's companions, school satchels, writing sets, pencil cases, helmets, pen knives, mouth organs, skipping ropes, boxes of paints, balls, hoops and sticks. Nineteen balloons, kindly provided, as in past years, by Dr. Hollinshead, were let up, and provided a source of unmeasured delight to the youngsters, who gathered in knots and followed their progress through the air until they were out of sight. Only one of the nineteen was spoilt – by catching fire. Eighty pounds weight of sweets were distributed in ounce packets, while each child received a bun from the supply referred to above on passing St. Mary's schools on the way home. Towards nine o'clock the bands played to the park gates, and preceded by a torchlight procession (a suggestion of Mr. C. A. Gilbert's) marched to the village, followed by such as had not already gone home. The forty or more lighted torches gave a very effective appearance to the parade of the High Street, and formed a fitting wind up to the fete. In conclusion a few appreciative words are due to the committee who have well earned the thanks of the community. First and foremost is the hon. secretary (Mr. Alfred Gittins), who, though his work was immensely lightened by the principle of procedure of sub-division of labour, which was adopted this year, still proved himself an invaluable and indispensable member. Next to him must be placed the chairmen and secretaries of the sub-committees (Messrs. Holmes, Draper, W. Humphreys, S. Hill, Knowles, and F. C. James), the energetic and untiring chairman of the general committee (Mr. T. A. Cole), and the treasurer (Mr. Wm. Holmes), who was actively identified with every phase of the event, and was foremost in the ranks of the volunteers to give a hand wherever it was required. Mr. S. Hill's service to the committee as secretary, during the absence of Mr. Gittins, and in taking charge of the collecting cards, from which over £20 was realised, is deserving of a special mention; while individual tribute must also be paid to Mr. F. C. James, Mr. Geo. Ollis, Mr. Sheppard, Mr. J. A. Jones and Mr. J. Gough. The full committee was as follows: Mr. T. A. Cole (chairman), Mr. R. Roberts (vice-chairman), Mr. W. Holmes (treasurer), Mr. A. Gittins (hon. secretary), Mr. S. Hill (deputy hon. secretary), the Revs. C. R. Sharpe, E. A. Whitfield and H. W. I. Ward; Messrs. W. Barker, T. Breeze, S. H. Brittain, G. Brown, W. Brown, E. Bush, C. Clarke, T. Cooper, R. Cowan, R. Davis, J. Deaman, J. Draper, H. Dunning, L. Freakley, W. Foster, C. A. Gilbert, T. Gillett, T. Goode, J. Gough, T. Greswolde, W. Haddon, T. Hall, W. Hamilton, H. and W. Humphreys, J. R. Hunt, F. C. James, J. A. Jones, J. Jordan, J. Knowles, T. W. Lawrence, W. McMaster, E. A. Olivieri, G. Ollis, J. R. Oswald, G. Perkins, J. Quinton, Frank Smith, Chas. H. Smith, T. Smith, G. Sheasby, J. Sheppard, T. Taylor, J. Tranter, Vickery, and J. Wheelwright.

Selly Oak & District Notes

The income of the Children's Fete up to date amounts to £75 16s. 4d. The hon. sec. would be glad to receive all sums due to and claims upon the committee as early as possible, so that the accounts may be closed.

Mr. George Ollis heads the list of amounts collected in the boxes with 26s. odd. Mr. J. Sheppard made a good second.

No less than 300 shots at a half penny a time were made at the football board.

The question is being asked as to what the bakers were on the committee for.[46]

One wrote on his collecting card "Where you get the cake, there you can go for the bread for money".

I understand that an effort will be made to hold the fete next year despite their opposition.

The committee have saved £10 by putting the provisions out to tender.

The bakers' subscriptions, which the committee have lost, amount to one guinea – or less.

---

[46] Mr. W. H. Tallis, Secretary of the Selly Oak and District Master Bakers' Association, wrote a response to this challenge, and also the statement about their subscriptions (see above), in a letter to the editor published the following week, 11th August 1900, and followed up in further correspondence in subsequent weeks.

5. 1900

11th August 1900 – The Birmingham News

Letters to the Editor
Selly Oak and Bournbrook Children's Fete,

Sir, – Will you allow me on behalf of the committee of the above to thank those ladies and gentlemen who so willingly gave us nearly £80 for the treat, and the ladies who so kindly assisted with the tea. Thanks are also due to the tradesmen who sent their vehicles, and to others who decorated their houses, thus adding so much to the enjoyment of the children. – Signed on behalf of the committee,

ALFRED GITTINS
Hon sec

147 Bournbrook.

25th August 1900 – The South Birmingham Chronicle

SELLY OAK VICTORIA BAND FETE – As will be seen from our advertising columns this fete takes place in the Selly Oak Park today (Saturday). A large and varied programme of sports has been arranged besides various other amusements, so that visitors will get a good return for their money. Refreshments will be provided on the ground, and in the evening the band will render a programme of dance music.

The advertisement:

SELLY OAK VICTORIA BRASS BAND

THE ANNUAL FETE
Will be held in the Park TODAY (SATURDAY),
August 25th
A large PROGRAMME OF SPORTS has been
arranged as follows:-
FOOTBALL CONTEST, BOYS' RACE
BICYCLE RACE, WHEELBARROW RACE,
SACK RACE, EGG AND SPOON RACE,
HIGH JUMP, LONG JUMP,
120 YARDS SCRATCH RACE, AND WALKING
MATCH,
Entries to each Event 6d. Ladies' Race free.
Gates open at Two o'clock
Admission, 6d.; Children half price
First-class REFRESHMENTS will be provided.
DANCING in the Evening.

The Heydays Of Selly Oak Park

1st September 1900 – The South Birmingham Chronicle

VILLAGE CHIMES

It was indeed hard lines that the Selly Oak Victoria Brass Band Fete on Saturday should have been spoiled by such unpropitious weather. What with the rain, the wind, and the cold, one could almost have fancied that it was the middle of March instead of the latter end of August.

The 300 or more people who did brave the elements to put in an appearance were well rewarded for their trouble, and the programme of sports and entertainments provided was much appreciated by all. The swing-boats, cocoa-nuts, and shooting gallery, were all largely patronised, and we think we shall not be far wrong in saying that those who "turned up" did not regret having paid their money, and to quote the coster, "tiken their chice".

The wheel-barrow race was the cause of considerable hilarity. The contestants in this decidedly novel feature had first to be blindfolded and then push a wheel-barrow a distance of 80 yards, the one arriving "home" first being the winner. Of course, not being able to see, they went "all over the shop", one running into the "lookers-on", while another ran into his neighbour, causing them both to fall over. Eventually the first prize fell to Sheasby and the second to Gunning.

DISTRICT NEWS
SELLY OAK AND BOURNBROOK

<u>Victoria Brass Band Fete</u> – The annual fete of the Selly Oak Victoria Brass band took place in the park on Saturday afternoon. The day was both cold and wet, and in consequence there was only a meagre attendance of visitors – scarcely 350 being present during the afternoon. There was no lack of entertainment for those who did put in an appearance, however, and the cocoa-nuts, shooting gallery, swing-boats, etc., all received their fair share of attention. A football match between teams selected from Bournbrook and Selly Oak, and resulting in a win for the former, was watched with keen interest by all those present, who did not fail to show their appreciation of any particular bit of smart play. A programme of sports was gone through with the following results:- 80 yards wheel-barrow race – 1st heat: 1. Thomas; 2. Sheasby. 2nd heat: 1. Gunning; 2. Phillips. Final: 1. Sheasby; 2. Gunning. 100 yards boy's race; 1. James; 2. Hall. High Jump: 1. A. Houit; 2. Price and Broad equal. Long jump: 1. Broad. One mile walking match: 1. Ray; 2. Brett. Slow bicycle ride (slowest wins): 1. A. Stokes; 2. Lewis. 120 yards flat race: 1. Mole; 2. Jones. – At intervals selections of music were played by the band, which, towards evening, rendered a programme of dance music for the convenience of those who wished to wind up the day's proceedings by "tripping the light fantastic".

<u>The Concerts in the Park</u> – We are requested to state that the concerts given in the Selly Oak Park on Wednesdays, by the band, have been discontinued for the season.

5. 1900

1st September 1900 – The Birmingham News

District News
Selly Oak

<u>Selly Oak Band Fete</u> – The Selly Oak Victoria Brass Band held their annual fete on Saturday last. As was the case last year, the event was held in Selly Oak Park. Financially its success was considerably affected by the weather, which understandably kept away many who would otherwise have gone. The chief interest in the event centred in a sports programme, the events of which were won as follows:-
Boys' race – 1. James; 2. Hale. Prizes, salts and pendants.
Football contest – Selly Oak. Prizes, medals.
Slow bicycle race – 1. Oakes; 2. Lewis. Prizes, set of carvers and walking stick.
Sack race – W. Clift.
Mile walk – 1. Gay; 2. Brett; 3. Davis. Prizes, timepiece and box of cigars.
Egg and spoon race (ladies) – 1. Miss Such; 2. Mrs. Hopkins. Prize, umbrella.
120 yards scratch race – 1. B. Jones. Prize, tobacco jar.
High jump – 1. B. Hoult; Price and Broad equal second. Prizes, salts and meerschaum pipe.
Wheelbarrow race – 1. Sheasby; 2. Gunning. Prizes, box of cigars and inkstand.
Long jump – 1. H. Broad. Prize, umbrella.
The band gave selections at intervals, and dancing numbers in the evening. Mr. Nephi Phillips did the catering.

12th September 1900 – KN&N UDC Baths, Parks and Cemeteries Committee, and reported on **6th October 1900 – The Birmingham News**

Selly Oak and District Notes

The main drive at Selly Oak Park is to be guttered and gullied.
The gravel has been stopping up the drains and causing no end of trouble.

10th November 1900 – The South Birmingham Chronicle

COUNCILLOR THOMAS GIBBINS, J.P.
(An image was reproduced in the paper; but it is
not suitable for copying from the microfilm)

It is with no small degree of pleasure that we give our readers this week the portrait of the much-respected and highly-esteemed Chairman of the Kings Norton and Northfield Urban District Council. We take the opportunity of doing so in view of the ceremony he performed on Tuesday at Lifford in connection with the extension of the drainage area, a report of which will be found in another column. As we have remarked before, the inclusion of the outer districts of Kings Norton and Northfield in the sewerage system of the Birmingham Tame and Rea Joint Drainage Board is undoubtedly one of the greatest improvements which has ever taken place in our district.

The subject of our sketch has been Chairman of our Urban Council since it came into existence, about two years ago, and has, during this time, won the esteem and respect, not only of every member of it, but of everyone connected with it, by his strict impartiality, absolute fairness, genial manner, and marked courtesy. As our readers are well aware, Mr. Gibbins is one of the proprietors of the Birmingham Battery Co., of which his father was one of the original founders, and with which he has been himself associated ever since he left school. He comes from an old and well-known family. His mother was a Miss Cadbury, and a prominent member of the Society of Friends, in which, although now something like 87 years of age, she still takes a keen interest. Mr. Gibbins was for some years a member of the Birmingham Board of Guardians, and is at the present moment a Guardian of the Poor for our district. Selly Oak owes to Mr. Gibbins's family its Park, which was presented to the inhabitants only a short time since. Not only was the land given, but the grounds laid out at their own expense. Mr. Gibbins is well known for his generosity towards our local public institutions, and for his charity to those in need of it. No one, we feel sure, ever appealed to him in vain for help, if the case had been a deserving one.

14th November 1900 – KN&N UDC Baths, Parks and Cemeteries Committee

Resolved that subject to Mr Gibbins approval, the chestnut trees in the Park be removed and placed in a more suitable position and that arrangements be made with the contractors (Messrs J Aird & Sons) to plant the displaced trees from the Main Bristol Road in the Park.

Chapter 6

1901

13th March 1901 – KN&N UDC Baths, Parks and Cemeteries Committee

The report of the Superintendent was read.
    Resolved to provide a proper uniform for the Park Keeper, the selection and cost left with the Chairman.

11th May 1901 – The South Birmingham Chronicle

A CRYING NEED

In another few days we hope we may be in a position to state authoritatively that Selly Oak is no mean village, no insignificant place, but a growing and thriving little town of 18,000 or 20,000 inhabitants. The returns of the census should not be long in being made public now, and the day close at hand when we should know what our village, which in 1891 consisted of seven or eight thousand inhabitants, has done in the way of growth in population during the last ten years.
    Many things have taken place during the last decade which have materially improved and developed Selly Oak. Ten years ago we had no Park. Today we have a splendid one; thanks to the munificence of the Gibbins family. ....
(The article then continues reviewing developments past, and anticipated, in Selly Oak.)

DISTRICT NEWS
SELLY OAK AND BOURNBROOK

<u>Music in the Park</u> – Through the kindness of the Selly Oak Victoria Military Band (conductor, Mr. H. White), the following arrangements (which are, however, subject to alteration) for playing in the Park have been made:- Wednesday, May 15th, 7 p.m. to 9 p.m.; Saturdays, May 25th and June 1st, 6.30 p.m. to 9 p.m.; Wednesdays, June 5th and 12th, 7 p.m. to 9 p.m.; Saturdays, 22nd and 29th, 6.30 p.m. to 9 p.m.; Wednesdays, July 3rd and 10th, 7 p.m. to 9 p.m.; Saturdays, July 20th and 27th, 6.30 p.m. to 9 p.m.; Wednesdays, July 31st and August 7th, 7 p.m. to 9 p.m.; Saturdays, August 17th, 24th and 31st, 6.30 p.m. to 9 p.m.

25th May 1901 – The South Birmingham Chronicle, and
25th May 1901 – The Birmingham News

CORRESPONDENCE
Selly Oak Park

To the Editor of "South Birmingham Chronicle"
Sir, – The keeper of the Selly Oak Park reports to me that a number of persons are in the habit of cutting turf from the borders for their caged birds, and also that boys have in many cases robbed or destroyed the bird nests.
May I appeal to your readers to help the Council in preventing either of the above things being done in the future, and so oblige, yours truly,
J.R. OSWALD,
Chairman of the Parks Committee.
60, Bournbrook Road, Selly Oak.

5th June 1901 – Minute of KN&N UDC, and reported on
8th June 1901 – The Birmingham News, and on
8th June 1901 – South Birmingham Chronicle

A printed report of this Committee (the Baths, Parks and Cemeteries Committee) was presented and taken as read and ordered to be entered on the Minutes as follows:-

This Committee beg to report:-

Selly Oak Park

Your Committee beg to report that a glacier stone found in Frederick Road, Selly Oak, where excavations are being made in connection with the Birmingham Water Scheme, has been very kindly presented and delivered to the park by Mr. R. W. Newman, the representative of Messrs. John Aird & Sons, to whom a vote of thanks has been accorded.

It was moved by Mr. Oswald, seconded Mr. Meakin, and resolved that the proceedings of the Baths, Parks and Cemeteries Committee be and are hereby confirmed and adopted as the acts and proceedings of this Council, except the part relating to the boring of a well at Selly Oak which was ordered to be deleted.

10th July 1901 – KN&N UDC Baths, Parks and Cemeteries Committee, which was reported on **31st July 1901 – Minute of KN&N UDC**, and on **3rd August 1901 – The South Birmingham Chronicle**

The Surveyor was instructed to submit an estimate of the cost for tar-paving the road to the Shelter.

6. 1901

<u>Selly Oak and Bournbrook Children's Fete</u>

Resolved: the Committee of the Selly Oak and Bournbrook Children's Fete be granted use of the Park on August 26th on the terms and conditions as heretofore.

3rd August 1901 – The Birmingham News

Selly Oak, Stirchley, Kings Norton & Northfield Notes

The District Council have granted the use of Selly Oak Park for the children's fete. Councillor Oswald gave the Council an invitation to come and see Selly Oak's annual entertainment to its children.

There have, by the way, been some complaints that children have not received their tickets for the fete.

The committee desire it to be known that they will see that every child entitled to a ticket shall have one.

17th August 1901 – The Birmingham News

Selly Oak, Stirchley, Kings Norton & Northfield Notes

There was a special meeting of the Selly Oak Children's Fete Committee on Thursday night, when the reports of the various sub-committees were handed in.

The procession committee reported that they had engaged the Selly Oak and Bournville Bands, while Mr. W. Holmes and Mr. J.W. Goode promised to pay all expenses for the engagement of the Marston Green Homes band. The offer was accepted with thanks.

The plan of arrangements for the park was submitted by the field and sports committee, and £6 was asked for to be spent in prizes for the children.

A circular has been issued to all the vehicle owners in the district asking for the use of their vehicles to convey the small children to the park on the day of the fete.

It is intended to start the procession at one o'clock prompt in order to enable the employees of the various works to witness its passage without losing time.

In former years this has been a source of considerable annoyance to the manufacturers in the neighbourhood, and every effort will be made on this occasion to prevent its necessity.

Steps have been taken to get the trams to cease running from Dawlish Road to the terminus between one and two o'clock to prevent the possibility of accident to the children or spectators.

A balance sheet of last year's fete has just been issued together with an appeal for help from the local gentry.

Funds are coming in fairly well, but owing to the large number of children to be provided for a more liberal response is needed.

On the day of the fete no one but the children and workers will be admitted to the park till 5 0'clock.

24th August 1901 – The South Birmingham Chronicle

Selly Oak and Bournbrook Children's Fete

The Selly Oak and Bournbrook Children's Fete takes place in the Selly Oak Park on Monday next. The holidays have, of course, seriously interfered with the work, but the committee are at present busily engaged getting everything into apple-pie order, and, from all accounts, the fete this year will eclipse anything previously held in our district.

The procession will start from the Dawlish Road Schools at one o'clock, and will proceed by way of High Street, Bournbrook, and High Street and Church Road, Selly Oak, to the Park. Prizes to the amount of £3 13s. 6d., will be given for the best decorated vehicle, mail cart, bicycle, and best novelty of any description in the procession, although the committee reserve the right to exclude anything they consider improper. Those entering for these prizes must give their names to the hon. Secretary (Mr. A. Gittins, 147, High Street, Bournbrook), in writing not later than Saturday, August 24th.

All the Park stalls will be let to villagers only at a charge of 2s., and if over two yards' frontage, 1s. per yard extra.

The procession will be of such a length that this year (it is estimated that there will be 3,000 children to cater for) three bands have been engaged, so that when one is out of earshot, another will strike up. At tea the youngsters will be able to gorge at their hearts' content, and, unlike Oliver Twist, will not need to ask for more, as, we are informed, nearly half-a-ton of cake and bread (not to speak of the tea) has been ordered.

In conclusion, we may say that the committee appeal to the inhabitants to do all they can by way of decorations, etc., to make the day enjoyable for the children. Owners of vehicles would also oblige by lending them to the committee for the use of the younger children.

31st August 1901 – The South Birmingham Chronicle

Selly Oak and Bournbrook Children's Fete

For weeks and months past the children of school age residing in Selly Oak and Bournbrook have been looking forward to August 26, the day fixed for the holding of the annual fete. The committee have been hard at work getting in subscriptions and making the necessary arrangements as to the engaging of bands, the provision of vehicles, the ordering of cake and bread sufficient to satisfy the cravings of 3,000 hungry mouths, and generally to get everything into that state of order known as apple-pie. Nothing that should have been done had been left undone, and all that

6. 1901

was needed to make the fete as successful as in previous years was a fine day. Whether the clerk of the weather was in a bad humour, or was simply possessed with a spirit of mischief we cannot say, but one thing is certain, and that is that Jupiter Pluvius, who had been "lying low" during the previous week, again showed his face, and what promised in the early morning to be fine turned out a wet and dreary day. The outlook at six o'clock of Monday morning was a most encouraging one, and not a drop of rain fell before eight o'clock. Then the sky grew overcast, and spots of rain began to fall. Even then hopes were entertained of its clearing off before the procession started, but this was not to be. At one o'clock the procession, headed by the Selly Oak Victoria Military Band, beguiled by a temporary lull in the storm, sallied forth. They had not proceeded very far, however, ere the rain again commenced to fall, and by the time they got into the high street (sic) it was coming down in the proverbial "cats and dogs". Although the youngsters were told to "run home", a great number remained in the procession, and marched on regardless of rain and slush, in the wake of the band. The little girls attired for the occasion in spotless white frocks, shoes, and stockings, were plastered with mud up to the knees, while their garments were soaked with the rain. What, however, cared they if on the morrow they were laid up with colds and chills? These thoughts, if they entered their heads at all, were paid no attention to. This was their annual treat, and, rain or no rain, they intended to enjoy themselves. One little toddler, trotting along the side his older brother, with his umbrella – almost as tall as himself – shut up, probably wet to the skin, cared as little for the tempest, as if it had been in the usual order of things in connection with the fete. The decorated cycles and vehicles, upon which so much care had been lavished on the preceding day, were treated mercilessly by the storm; and had they not been judged before starting, it was questionable whether any of them would have been deemed of sufficient merit to have taken a prize. Bespattered with mud, drenched with rain, they did, indeed, present a sorry spectacle, and must have been both an eye and a heart sore to their respective owners. The rain showed no sign of abating, however, and so the committee took the only course open to them, that was, to postpone the fete to the following day. This was intimated to the children by Mr. Wm. Holmes who, as usual, acted as marshal of the procession, and they then dispersed.

Although not exactly "king's weather" on Tuesday the climatic conditions were not so dispiriting as those of the previous day. The same order of things with regard to the fete were observed as on the Monday, and punctually at one o'clock the procession, this time headed by the Marston Green Cottage Homes Band, again set forth from the Dawlish Road Schools. The route taken was High Street, Bournbrook, High Street, Selly Oak, Church Road, Gibbins Road, to the Park. The procession was the longest that has ever been held, although, of course, the decorated vehicles were not as numerous owing to their having been deported by the rain on Monday. Flags and bunting flew from the houses all along the route traversed, and the footpaths were lined with the villagers, eagerly watching its progress. On arrival at the Park, games were indulged in until shortly before four o'clock, when the children sat down to tea. After this, races were indulged in, one of these, however, being attended with a slight accident. In the wheelbarrow race one of the competitors, a boy named Hawkins, fell and wrenched his neck, but all was soon put right by the Selly Oak Ambulance Corps, who were in attendance on the field. Each boy and girl had a ticket, enabling them to have a ride on the steam horses free of charge. The other amusements provided included the Punch and Judy, the "Tattoed (sic) Lady" show, etc., while in the evening fire balloons were sent up to the delight of the youngsters. At night the Marston Green Band's place was taken by the Selly Oak Victoria Military, who, at the conclusion of the proceedings, conducted the children down the village, to the stirring tune of the "British Grenadiers". Coloured fire burned from a number of houses as it did from some of the vehicles in the procession. The main street was packed with people, who were enjoying the proceedings quite as much as the children themselves.

Our report would be incomplete were we not to mention the names of Mr. A. Gittins, the hon. sec., and Mr. W. Humphries, the schoolmaster, with their staff of assistants, upon whom the bulk of the work devolved, and to whom the success of this year's fete is in a great measure due.

The prizes given for the best decorated vehicles, cycles, etc., were awarded as follows:- Best decorated vehicle: 1, No. 31; 2, No.25; 3, No. 27. Mail carts: 1, No. 33; 2, No. 22; 3, No. 20. Cycles: 1, No. 18; 2, No. 17; 3, No. 29. Best novelty: 1, No.2; 2, No. 12 and 3 (equal); 3, No. 1.

31st August 1901 – The Birmingham News

Selly Oak and Bournbrook Children's Fete

The Selly Oak and Bournbrook children's fete was sadly marred this year by the weather. For several years past the festival has been held under favourable atmospheric conditions, and it looked almost as if the event was honoured by the meteorological powers that be with a special dispensation. And the delightful weather that prevailed for nearly the whole of the previous fortnight gave colour to such a fancy. The clear blue sky and the brilliant sun seemed to spell out a preliminary welcome to the event and to give a promise of like favours on the day of its consummation. But alas! how rudely was such a fancy dispelled. Instead of a bright and cheery morning greeting, the weather clerk frowned upon the coming revel surlily, but in the vain hope that he would mend his mood, it was decided to proceed with the carnival. The decision was a luckless one. Instead of mending the Weather Clerk hourly grew more furious, and as if to punish the temerity that would dare to flaunt him, he assailed the revellers; when helplessly placed to resist or avoid his onslaught, with a storm of hurricane intensity. As Monday's procession moved up the main street it is true as a literal fact to say that the rain fell in sheets. Few if any who took part in it escaped a complete drenching, while the decorative components of the procession were in a few minutes reduced to limp and bespattered caricatures, shorn of nearly all effectiveness. It was a sorry sight, and sympathy will be freely extended to to those who for weeks previously had been

6. 1901

working hard and ungrudgingly in the heavy task of organising the event. The procession proceeded as far as Oak Tree Lane, when it dispersed, the festivities of the fete being postponed till the following day.

But a word of the procession. In preface to this it should be stated that at 11 o'clock on Monday morning the committee desired to postpone the fete in toto till the following day, but the fact that the competitors for the decoration prizes, as well as hundreds of children had already then assembled, forced them to sanction at least the holding of the parade and the awarding of the prizes. The procession was on all hands regarded as superior in its decorative aspect and scope to any that had yet been held. The inhabitants of the township entered with more than customary zeal into the competitions as was shown by the fact that the entries for them numbered 33, a figure which would probably have to be trebled the represent the actual number of individuals taking part in them. In three of the classes, those for the best decorated vehicles, mail carts and bicycles, there was but little scope from the restrictive terms of the competition for the display of striking originality, and the entries were consequently purely conventional. The fourth, however, provided plenty of opportunity for ingenuity and individuality of idea, and it was interesting to note the wide variety of ways in which these qualities shewed (sic) themselves. To give a detailed enumeration of the seventeen entries which this class obtained is beyond the scope of the space at our command, but amongst them it may be stated were an Indian chief in full war paint, an illustration of the death of Cock Robin, orientals, a lifeboat (we presume this was entered in this class), a bicycle which, since we are told there is nothing new under the sun, must be a facsimile of one our ancestral parent pedalled, a "golden wedding" pair, niggers, the first velocipede, "a gathering of fairies", a huntsman, a gipsy queen, etc. The prizes were awarded as follows: Vehicles, 31, 25 and 27; bicycles, 33, 22 and 20; mail carts, 1, 17 and 19; and novelties, 2, 12 and 13 (equals), and 1. We regret that we are able to indicate the winners only by their numbers. This is another consequence of the wet, which amongst its other achievements, completely destroyed the secretarial record. At the head of the procession was the familiar form of Mr. Wm. Holmes. He strenuously refused to fill this office at first, but he has done so much for the fete, and has led it to triumph on so many occasions – and he makes a fine leader withal – that the committee have come to regard him as having a prescriptive right to the position, and steadily scouted his suggestion that someone else should take it. Behind him was the Selly Oak Band; in the middle of the procession was the Bournville Brass Band, while a third band, present through the generosity of Mr. Holmes and Mr. J. W. Goode, brought up the rear in the Marston Green Cottage Home Band. Most of the local manufacturers and tradesmen lent vehicles for the conveyance of the younger children, and these being packed, there were many wee mites, picturesque as a whole from the wide variety of their spick and span frocks and smocks, whose bodies were chilled by Monday's downpour. As far as possible the committee prevented the older children from joining the procession, but they had come attired in their best, with their mugs round their necks and tea tickets duly pinned as per order on their breasts, to the children's fete, and it would have taken something more than the committeemen who could not show more than a mock sternness to those for whose pleasure they had been working, and a cataclysm of rain to have prevented them from participating in whatever was going forward.

Tuesday broke finer than its predecessor, but not so much as to lead to exuberant light-heartedness. Still, after a deluge, an occasional shower is not to be complained of. But very few of the committee could be absent from their ordinary avocations on a second day, however, and when the procession – a skeleton of the preceding day, and a miserable attenuated skeleton at that – started there were not more than three or four members to join it or direct the proceedings. Of course, the honorary secretary (Mr. Alfred Gittins) was there. In the matter of the children's fete, he is like the nimble mosquito, here, there and everywhere, and if there is anything going on that should not be his presence is generally as effective in putting matters to rights, as the visit of the busy little fly is stimulating. Apparently he has solved the problem of being in several places at one time, and on Tuesday he very much needed the possession of such a faculty. For with the Marston Green Band to lead them, no fewer than 3,200 children trudged blithely to the park, and were soon finding employment for all the hands who had to immediately take the deck. A hundred helpers, apart from the committee, which is nearly 60 members strong, and found other work to do, were required in the preparation of the tea, in which 1,050lbs. of cake, 3,000 buns, 254lbs. of sandwich loaves, 1 cwt. of butter, 35lbs. of tea, 2cwt. of sugar, and 26 gallons of milk were used. One half of the milk was the free gift of Mr. C. A. Lucas. Though everything was of the finest quality, the care exercised by the committee in purchasing and the fact that they were able to buy in large quantities, enabled them to provide the tea at a cost per head of 3d. The total bill amounts to just under £45. Those who have prepared tea on any scale for children know full well that there are others who can drink this beverage besides old women, and in the knowledge of their experiences the committee made 300 gallons, equivalent probably to 10,000 breakfast cupsful (sic), of tea. Mr. G. Cadbury's urns and teapots, the urns and copper cans which the master of the Workhouse was able to place at the committee's disposal, and Mr. Gittin's crocks, urns, jugs, tables and tablecloths came in very useful here, solving as they did the problem of how the tea was to be made without great expense in the provision of hired utensils. The amusements open to the children included the roundabout ride, sports, for a varied number of excellent prizes of the committee's provision, and Mr. Alexander's Punchinello, the order of which Mr. J. Gough again saw safely through. Promptly at 7.45 the roundabout was stopped, "God save the King" was played, and the band led the way out of the Park. The children, tired no doubt with their afternoon's play, readily followed, and after a little demonstration in the High Street, the children's fete of 1901 was a thing of the past – gone to join the long line of its predecessors in the ranks of which, despite all that Jupiter Pluvius did to wreck it, it will hold high and honourable position. Financially it is thought the committee will be able to induce both ends to meet. The disaster of Monday involved several expenses which would not otherwise have been incurred, but did not prejudicially affect the amount collected on the two days on the route so far as a comparison with last year goes at any rate. All who had anything to do with the festival will unite in their thanks to the hon. secretary for the predominating part he, as usual, played in it. The committee desire to thank all who rendered assistance, and the little unpretentious service rendered of an inability to greater things, is as much valued as more important assistance given of a larger capacity and greater opportunity. A special word of thanks is due to Mr. Connop, who collected no less than £5 12s., and secured a gift of 200 lbs. of cake for the fete. Unfortunately, however, the cake, which came through the donor from Edinboro' (sic) did not arrive in time, and when it was delivered on Thursday it had to be returned, as there was, of course, no use for it. The committee's thanks to others is only equalled by their own thankfulness that everything connected with the event passed off without the slightest accident to anyone. The committee, in which there was the usual 15 or 20 per cent. of non-workers or helpers, was as follows: T. A. Cole (chairman), R. Roberts (vice-chairman), W. Holmes (treasurer and chairman of the Procession Committee), Alfred Gittins (hon. secretary), J. Draper (chairman of the Field and Sports Committee), W. Humphreys (chairman of the Catering Committee), G. J. Purser, W. Parsons, jun., B. Connop, F. Jordan, A. White, L. Freakley, S. Hill, H. W. Stephens, W. Terry, J. Gough, D. Roy, W. Chambers, J. Deaman, A. T. Wilson, H. White, J. Quinton, W. Wheatley, T. Bostock, J. Nix, H. Crook, R. W. Chadney, J. R. Oswald, T. Cooper, G. Ikin, W. Moss, W. Hill, F. C. James, T. Hall, W. Haddon, C. A. Gilbert, E. Bush, J. A. Jones, T. Smith, T. Greswolde, J. Wheelwright, J. W. Goode, J. Shephard, G. Sheasby, J. M. Crow, J. W. Crow, S. H. Brittain, E. A. Olivieri, W. Whitehouse, J. Coley, A. Ford, F. Taylor, J. Griffiths, F. Goode, A. Gillott, and J. R. Hunt.

Selly Oak, Stirchley, Kings Norton & North Field Notes

The money paid in after the children's fete at Selly Oak by the various collectors had to be taken to the bank in a cart. It weighed three-quarters of a cwt.

Ben Connop and his money box are likely to become historic. Also Ben and his 200lb. of cake.

After this who will dare to say that Ben is not energetic on behalf of the fete, with which, by the way, his connection dates from, I believe, its origination.

The collectors' boxes turned out as follows: – J. Shephard, 10s. 2d.; J. A. Jones, 6s. 10½d.; E. Bostock, 13s. 6¼d.; J. W. Crow, £1 9s. 9½d.; C. A. Gilbert, 5s. 3½d.; and H. Jordan, 6s. 4½d.

A child took his boots off to run a race; those boots have not since been seen. The committee had a whip round to provide him with a new pair.

4th September 1901 – KN&N UDC Baths, Parks and Cemeteries Committee

<u>Painting</u> The Committee inspected the Park and decided that the outside woodwork should be painted. The minute was continued.

<u>Paving Drive</u> The Surveyor reported estimated cost of asphalting was £74.

Resolved to recommend the work be carried out.

<u>Trees</u> Resolved to instruct the Surveyor to supply the necessary poles to the Keeper.

2nd October 1901 – KN&N UDC Baths, Parks and Cemeteries Committee

<u>Park Keeper</u> Resolved Mr Josiah T Horton be granted 8 days leave of absence subject to such arrangements as the Chairman can make for the Cemetery Superintendent assisting in the duties during such absence.

2nd October 1901 – Minute of KN&N UDC, and reported on
5th October 1901 – The South Birmingham Chronicle, and again,
5th October 1901 – The Birmingham News

A printed report of this Committee (the Baths, Parks and Cemeteries Committee) was presented and taken as read and ordered to be entered on the Minutes as follows:-

> This Committee beg to report:-
>
> <u>Selly Oak Park</u>
>
> Your Committee recommend that the whole of the drive at the Park, Selly Oak, be asphalted at an estimated cost of £74, and the Surveyor instructed to have the work carried out departmentally.

It was moved by Mr. Oswald, seconded Mr. Talliss, and resolved that the proceedings of the Baths, Parks and Cemeteries Committee be and are hereby confirmed, and adopted as the acts and proceedings of the Council.

11th December 1901 – KN&N UDC Baths, Parks and Cemeteries Committee

The report of the Superintendent was presented and read and resolved the following instructions be given thereon.
    That the Superintendent be directed to carry out the work in connection with the flower borders, trees, walks, shrubs etc, as he may deem necessary and also prune the trees in the village (the Surveyor to provide a temporary man to assist in the work).
    That the Superintendent's suggestion to have a Shruberry (sic) Border round the Shelter be not approved.

<u>Painting outside woodwork</u> This minute was continued.

<u>Paving drive</u> This minute was continued.

Chapter 7

1902

12th March 1902 – KN&N UDC Baths, Parks and Cemeteries Committee

Outside painting, etc: Resolved to instruct the Surveyor to obtain an estimate for this work.

3rd May 1902 – The Birmingham News

Selly Oak, Stirchley, Kings Norton, & Northfield Notes

The arrangements for the celebration of the Coronation at Selly Oak are developing, and make it clear that they are made on a large and generous scale. The children are to be entertained on the first day, and their tea is to cost 4½d. per head, while the old folks are to be entertained on the Friday.

The streets are to be decorated, there is to be a great procession, and an all-the-day long programme of entertainment and recreation is arranged for the Park, in which a big and strong platform is to be erected.

17th May 1902 – The South Birmingham Chronicle

Village Chimes

The Selly Oak Coronation Committee have just issued the following circular:- "The Committee having charge of the above have pleasure in giving in rough outline the programme already agreed upon, and earnestly appeal to the inhabitants generally to render their financial help as will enable them to make Coronation Day one long to be remembered in the district."

A procession of children, friendly societies, and trades organisations. £25 given in prizes. A tea and bun for the children. Sports in the Park after tea. £10 in prizes voted. A grand display of fireworks in the Park at night. Fire balloons in the afternoon and evening. A dinner and a present to all people aged 60, and upwards. Selly Oak Victoria Brass Band. Maypole Dance by village children, and numerous other features. The Committee want fully £250 to carry out this scheme, and they confidently appeal to Selly Oak and Bournbrook to find it. Every little helps!

The Heydays Of Selly Oak Park

24th May 1902 – The Birmingham News

Local Coronation Items

In addition to the £10 contributed to the Selly Oak Coronation Fund by Messrs. Cadbury Bros., Ltd., Mr. George Cadbury has promised to give, privately, a box of chocolate to every child of school age in Selly Oak and Bournbrook, a quarter of a pound of tea to the old women, and two ounces of tobacco to the old men, who are to be entertained to dinner by the committee.

Mr. Edward Cadbury has given a donation £15 to the funds.

The box of chocolate which the youngsters are to receive is an artistic production.

It consists of a tablet of vanilla chocolate, wrapped in the familiar tin foil, bound with a white paper band bearing the Royal Crown in colours, and enclosed in a tin box measuring 3½ inches by 2 inches. The lid of the box bears a handsome portrait of the King and Queen in oval gold band frames, which slightly overlap after the present fashion of producing pair photographs in miniature. In the left hand upper corner is the King's initial ("E."), and in the other corner that of the Queen ("A."). Beneath the portraits and in the centre is the Royal crown, and on a green scroll is the inscription, "Coronation of King Edward VII, and Queen Alexandra, 26th June, 1902".

The Selly Oak Coronation Committee intend to ask the District Council's permission to plant a "Coronation" oak in Selly Oak Park.

The Selly Oak Committee have in hand, or have been promised, between £160 and £170 towards the £250 which they estimate they will require. It is the last £90, however, that will give trouble in raising, as the ready sources of support are represented in the amount which has been obtained, and for the rest probably something more than the mere asking for it will be required to raise it.

In addition to the £50 given the Stirchley Coronation Committee by Messrs. Cadbury, Mr. W.A. Cadbury has given £10.

The donations promised by Messrs. Cadbury Bros. Ltd., to the Coronation funds of Stirchley and Cotteridge (of £50), and of the Ten Acres and Selly Park, Selly Oak, Northfield and Kings Norton (of £10 each) were on condition that no intoxicants were provided at the various festivities, etc. All accepted the condition and have received their donations except Kings Norton, who will not accept contributions "unless given with no conditions whatever".

31st May 1902 – The Birmingham News

Kings Norton and Northfield District Council
Coronation of the King

The following recommendations by the General Purposes Committee were adopted: – (1) That the common seal of the Council be ordered to be affixed to a loyal and dutiful address to His Majesty King Edward the Seventh upon the occasion of the forthcoming Coronation, such address to be prepared by the Clerk and suitably engrossed. (2) That the Chairmen of Committees and Clerk and Surveyor be empowered to grant to the employees of the Council such leave of absence during the Coronation Celebrations as may be convenient to the respective departments.

Permission was given for the planting of "Coronation" oaks in Selly Oak Park, at Selly Park, and at Moseley, Mr. Olivieri and Mr. Holmes respectively bringing forward applications on behalf of the Coronation Committees of the two last named places. Sanction for the use of Selly Oak Park was also given to the Coronation Committee on June 26 and 27.

7th June 1902 – The Birmingham News

The Coronation Celebrations
What the Districts Intend Doing
Selly Oak

At Selly Oak a sum of £250 is being appealed for by the committee organising the celebrations, to enable them to carry out their programme. The main items of this, as of most others, are the entertainment of the children and the old people. Of the former, there are well over three thousand, who come within the limit of the committee's catering (all of school age being included), and to these a substantial tea and a bun are to be given. The old people number well over 200, and they are to be given a dinner and some form of present. An important item in the festivities will be the procession, in the organisation of which much trouble is being taken. From a spectacular point of view, it will rival, if not excel, that of the annual children's fete, which the Coronation celebration this year supplants. No less a sum than £25 is offered in prizes for the procession. After the tea to the children, which is given in the Park, there are to be sports, and £10 has been set aside for prizes for the competitors, while later on fire balloons will be liberated, with all their attendant pleasure and interest to the young. Then, too, there is the Maypole dance, which everyone who loves graceful movements and pretty effect will be well advised to make a point of seeing. The local band will provide the music, Mr. White conducting.

28th June 1902 – The South Birmingham Chronicle

OUR FESTIVITIES

Notwithstanding the unfortunate circumstances under which the country found itself placed in regard to the health of the King, the festivities arranged for the Coronation were pretty generally carried out in our district. With the first intimation of the King's serious illness[47], and the announcement of the postponement of the

---

[47] According to newspaper reports, on Monday before his scheduled coronation on the Thursday King Edward was hospitalised and operated upon to remove a "cyst" from his "intestines".

Coronation, the first conclusions were to cancel all festivities. But King Edward, ever thoughtful for his subjects, intimated his desire that the festivities arranged in the provinces should not be interfered with. As loyal subjects, all would have stopped their festivities, and even with the request from the King, it would have been more in keeping with the order of things if a greater portion – or even the whole – of the rejoicings had been postponed until the event which they were to celebrate had taken place. However, as most of the places desired to "coronate", the proceedings were generally most hearty, and the genial weather which prevailed made the day pleasant and one long to be remembered. In our own districts the proceedings were entirely cancelled at Kings Norton and Kings Heath, whilst there were slight modifications in some of the other programmes. In all, the proposed thanksgiving services were altered to intercessory ones. Selly Oak Ward was placed in an almost unique position, in that its festivities were not only in commemoration of the Coronation, but jointly so with the children's fete. There was a heartiness in all the proceedings from the time the children formed up in procession until the dying embers of the different bonfires proclaimed the end of the rejoicings. In the Selly Oak Park several thousands of people were assembled, and, the arrangements being well organised, passed off most satisfactorily. The second day was on a smaller scale, but general high holiday was kept. The old people had their dinner, and the poor had a supply of beef from the roasted ox at the Bournbrook. In Selly Park the people went very heartily to work, and the efforts of a most energetic committee were crowned with a complete success. Northfield went into holiday attire, and old and young were remembered. – the one with feasting, and the other with sporting; while Bartley Green and Woodgate, somewhat detached from the larger villages, decided to, if possible, outdo their larger neighbours. Certainly they meant to make more than their own proportion of noise and rejoicing. They succeeded, and that right well. Stirchley had a somewhat exciting time of vaccilation (sic). Up to the hour of procession it had been decided not to "process" or "festivate" (sic), but when the children were assembled and the banners were flying, it was too much for them, and so they decided to "go on". And who could blame them? All around was in joyous mood, it would have been hard on the Stirchley and Cotteridge children, especially if they had been denied what was being so freely given at Selly Oak and Selly Park, at Bournville, and at Northfield. It is pleasing to record that everything, everywhere passed off without a hitch, and that goodwill and good-fellowship were apparent on every hand. In conclusion, we cannot but express the hope that the illness which at so inopportune a moment robbed the festivities of much of their meaning, may speedily be passed, and our gracious King once again in and out amongst his beloved people.

CORONATION FESTIVITIES

Selly Oak and Bournbrook

There are two essentials for a successful outdoor affair – a good organising committee and good weather. In the possession of the former Selly Oak and

Bournbrook were fortunate, and in experiencing the latter the success was assured. The committee was large and representative, and was judiciously divided up, and no round men were put in square holes. Councillor Thomas Gibbins was the chairman of the General Committee, and Mr. T.A. Cole acted as vice; Councillor Olivieri held the purse strings and pulled in the "dimes", while the secretarial work of the General Committee was ably done by Councillor J.R. Oswald and Mr. A. Gittings, P.L.G. The different committees were composed as follows:- Procession Committee – Chairman, Mr. William Holmes; Secretary, Mr. H.W. Stephens. Catering Committee – Chairman, Mr. William Humphreys; secretary, Mr. F.C. James. Field and Sports Committee – Chairman, Mr. John Draper; secretary, Mr. S.W. Parsons. Fireworks and Balloons – Mr. J. Deaman and Mr. A. Gittings. Bonfire – Captain A. Crump. Old People's Dinner – Chairman, Mr. W. Humphreys; secretary Mr. F.C. James. Field-tent Catering Committee – Messrs. T.A. Cole, A. Gittings, J.R. Oswald, T. Smith, A. Crump and J.R. Hunt. The village people ably supported the committee in the way of decorations, and the whole of the route taken by the procession had a fine display of bunting in the way of flags, bannerettes, mottoes and festoons. The timetable for the Thursday monopolised the time from 11.30 in the forenoon until 9.30 in the evening, but long before 11.30 the whole village was "on the move", and the principal coigns of vantage from which to view the procession were early taken up. The marshalling of the children from the various schools, and also the many other items of the procession in the way of decorated cycles and turn-outs, the pantaloon and the jester, the little fairies and the big monstrosities, was a work calling for great tact and much patience. Commendably punctual to the time – noon – Mr. William Holmes, mounted on a "charger" led the way up Hubert Road, followed by one of the bands. It was a long time, however, before the procession was properly "on the move". The route lay by Hubert Road, Exeter Road and Dawlish Road, to High Street, Bournbrook, and on the High Street, Selly Oak thence to the Selly Oak Park by Frederick Road and Gibbins Road. The great heat told on many of the children, especially the young ones, who were not taken in conveyances, and by the time the top of the village was reached were hopelessly beat. The programme, on reaching the Park, was at once entered upon, and was of a very varied nature. Circling round the bandstand the children opened the proceedings with singing, first of all the "Old Hundred", followed by "Rule Britannia", and finishing with "God save the King". The item on the programme following this was eliminated, being the planting of an oak tree by Councillor Gibbins. This was to have been a Coronation oak, and thus very wisely the ceremony was postponed until a proper occasion. Races for the children of the various schools were then entered upon, and while these were in progress there was, in another part of the Park, an entertainment by Willie Hill's Minstrels, and later on Professor Barton's Punch and Judy show gave no end of amusement to the youngsters – and to the older ones, too. At four o'clock the timetable showed tea for the children, and the catering committee had its hands full for a long time until all the school children were served. A Maypole dance by children from St. Mary's School proved a great

attraction, and showed that Mr. Humphreys had spent much time in bringing on his pupils for this part of the programme. The members of the Selly Oak Ambulance Class then gave an interesting display in the different branches of the work. From this time, about seven o'clock there was a repetition of some of the former items. During the afternoon too, several balloons were sent off, and afforded delight to everyone. About ten o'clock a bonfire was lighted, and there was the usual fun around the fire, kept up in good spirit until very late. In the evening chocolate, the annual gift of Mr. G. Cadbury, and a bun were presented to the children in the Institute on presentation of their tickets. Prizes were offered for various decorated articles, the judging taking place immediately prior to the procession starting from Hubert Road. The awards were as follows:-
Decorated vehicle – 1, G. Chillingworth; 2, Albert Monk; 3, C. Tatton; 4, J. Quinton.
Decorated bicycle (lady's) – 1, Miss Bide; 2, Miss Elliott; 3, Miss M. Clarke.
Decorated bicycle (gent's) – 1, T.H. Lawrence; 2, John Lea; 3, — Taylor.
Special prize by Councillor Olivieri for best decorated bicycle – Miss Bide.
Special Prize by Selly Oak Cycle Club for decorated cycle – T.H. Lawrence.
Best novelty – 1, T. Monk; 2, B. Clarke; 3, W. Wassell and O.H. Stead; 4, Mr. Stych.
Mail Carts – 1, Mrs. Thompson; 2, Miss B. Lea; 3, W.E. Knibbs.
In the evening the illuminations in the village were exceedingly pretty and the greatest good humour prevailed. Some horseplay occurred at times, but everyone took it in good part. In addition to the bonfire at Selly Oak Park there was another at Selly Hill, to where the bugle band headed a procession about ten o'clock. The higher end of Bournbrook Road and the grounds at Selly Hill house were beautifully illuminated. From this position many of the bonfires in the surrounding districts could be seen, and fireworks were witnessed at every point of the compass. About twelve o'clock the company around the fires and amongst the illuminations at Selly Hill broke up. In the village the public houses closed at the usual hour.

The inmates of the Workhouse at Selly Oak, having been promised an extra diet, had that promise fulfilled, but the projected drive into the country was abandoned.

28th June 1902 – The Birmingham News

Coronation Festivities
Selly Oak

The celebrations at Selly Oak, which were to have marked the Coronation, and which will ever be associated with this historic event, assuming that in the providence of God, his majesty lives to be crowned, were carried out on a large and varied scale. The village is one which lends itself very readily to such a celebration, and with the prospective sum of £250 as the working basis of the festivities, the committee were able to arrange a programme which from every point of view would have done credit to a larger and more pretentious community. Upon the receipt of the news of the serious illness of the King, a gloom was cast over all, and grave misgivings filled the minds of the committee as to whether the celebrations should be held or not. They halted and hesitated, anxiously seeking a lead, but when this was forthcoming in the publication of the desire of the King himself, backed up by the way in which it had been interpreted by the Midland metropolis as well as by many of the smaller surrounding districts, they went straight ahead with the object (always providing that the King's condition did not become more alarming) of carrying out the programme in its entirety. The residents entered into all the arrangements with the greatest enthusiasm. Indeed, whilst both were useful, it is doubtful whether either the appeal of the committee or the spur offered by prizes for decorations were really needed to induce the villagers to give tangible expression of their feelings by the adornment of their premises. A good-humoured rivalry was shown by the tradespeople. The main street has never looked more distinctive or more attractive. It was literally "ablaze with colour". Nor were the bye-streets neglected. Many of them were gaily festooned from side to side, whilst the fronts of the houses were brightened by flags and bunting. Working-class householders co-operated in joint efforts, and in every respect did their best to make as brave a show as their better situated and better-to-do fellow townsfolk in the chief thoroughfare. It would take up far more space than we have at our disposal to describe the decorations in the side streets in anything like detail. Our remarks must, therefore, be principally confined to High Street. Even here we can do little more than attempt a generalisation. Where all was so good, it certainly seems invidious to pick out individual efforts for particular mention. Yet, at the risk of giving offence, we feel that many of the premises claim special reference. Amongst the more conspicuously embellished establishments in Bournbrook were those of Messrs. Ward, Harbun, Grigg, Fernhough, Seymor, Hodgetts, The Stafford and Northampton Boot Co., H. Parry, T.W. Lawrence, A. S. Smith, J. Peel, Chapman, Hughes, Phillips (an exceptionally fine display this one), Jones (corner stores), Barnacle, Pearce, Cartwright, and Mills (apparently a joint effort, and in any case, one of the most artistic of all the decorations), J. H. Daniels, Jones (17), and the Station Hotel, with its crown of fire set in a star, and flanked with the royal letters "E. R.". In Selly Oak we made a note of the fine displays of the following houses: Messrs. Leonard's, Turton's (an exceptionally interesting example of the art of decoration), The Prince of Wales Inn, Messrs Gough, Albert Cottage, Diamond Jubilee Stores, Messrs. D. Roy, Hopkins (an admirable display), and Deaman. In very many instances illuminations formed part of the decoration schemes. There were hundreds of Chinese lanterns and fairy lights, and some excellent set pieces, and when all were alight at night the village presented an appearance which, for picturesqueness, was unprecedented in its history. The committee offered four prizes, of the total value of £2 10s., for the decoration of the premises, and those who entered for this were as follows:-

Decorated Premises

Mrs. Brittain, Bournbrook; Mrs. Matty, Selly Oak; Mr. G. Barnacle, Bournbrook; Mr. W. Green, Selly Oak; Mr. A. Mills, Bournbrook; Mrs. Cartwright, Bournbrook;

Mr. A. Gittins, Bournbrook; Mr. J. Deaman, Selly Oak; Mrs. Banks, Selly Oak; Mrs. Green, Selly Oak; Mr. O. Reynolds, Bournbrook; Mr. H. Spurrier, Bournbrook; Mr. W. C. Baldwin, Bournbrook; Mr. A. E. Smith, Bournbrook; Mr. H. Parry, Bournbrook; Mr. J. Gough, Selly Oak; Mr. Phillips, Bournbrook; Mr. Hopkins, Selly Oak. The steward of this competition was Mr. Husselbee.

The day's festivities commenced early and took a varied form. A large procession, forming an outstanding feature of the committee's arrangements, commenced to assemble before eleven o'clock. The decorative entries for this ranged from the artistic to the grotesque. Some idea of the nature of it will be conveyed by an enumeration of those who entered for the prizes which were offered. But, first of all, it is as well, perhaps, to indicate the value of the prizes. For decorated vehicles, four prizes of the aggregate value of £2 10s. were offered, together with a silver medal for the first prize winner. Other awards were: Decorated mailcarts, four prizes, total value 25s. Decorated cycles, ladies' and gentlemen's, total value, one and a half guineas, together with a guinea offered by Councillor Olivieri as a special prize, and 10s 6d. by the Selly Oak Cycling Club as a special prize for the two best decorated bicycles or tricycles in the procession. Novelty, four prizes, valued at £2 12s. 6d. The entries were as follows:-

Decorated Vehicles

Mr. W. Hughes, Bournbrook; Mr. C. Potter, Bournbrook; Mr. A. Monk, Selly Oak; Mr. T. Halward, Selly Oak; Mr. C. Tatton, Bournbrook; Mr. W. E. Knibbs, Bournbrook; Mr. W. Chatham, Selly Oak; Mr. Nash, Bournbrook; Mr. Grigg, Bournbrook; Mrs. Meeres, Bournbrook; Mr. H. and F. Spurrier, Bournbrook; Mr. Chillingworth, Bournbrook; Mr. Monk, Selly Oak, Mr. T. Monk, Selly Oak; Mr. J. Quinton, Selly Oak; Mr. F. Wilson, Bournbrook; Mr. E. R. Fisher, Bournbrook.

Mailcarts

Mrs. W. B. Palmer, Bournbrook; Miss B. Lea, Bournbrook; Mrs. Thompson, Selly Oak; Miss A. Buggins, Bournbrook; Mrs. Chance, Bournbrook; Mrs. Silvester, Bournbrook.

Decorated Bicycles (Ladies)

Miss M. Clark, Bournbrook; Miss Ada Wells, Bournbrook; Miss F. Hedge, Bournbrook; Miss A. Williams, Bournbrook; Miss E. Maullin, Selly Oak; Mrs. Elliott, Bournbrook; Mrs. Taylor, Bournbrook.

Decorated Bicycles (Gentlemen)

Mr. J. H. Harris, Selly Oak; Mr. F. W. Deaman, Selly Oak; Mr. Herbert Griffith, Bournbrook; Mr. J. Lea, Bournbrook; Mr. E. Shaw, Bournbrook; Mr. T. H. Lawrence, Bournbrook; Mr. Price, Bournbrook; Mr. A. E. Smith, Bournbrook; Mr. G. Tye, Bournbrook.

Novelties

Mr. G. Morgan, Selly Oak; Mr. W. Begley, Bournbrook; Mr. Walker, Bournbrook; Mr. Reynolds, Selly Oak; Mrs. W. Hooper, Bournbrook; Mrs. Turrell, Bournbrook; Group of children from St. Edward's Catholic Church, Selly Hill; Mr. W. Wassall, Bournbrook; Mr. H. Stead, Bournbrook; Mrs. Matty and Mrs. Wareham, Selly Oak; Miss Landry, Selly Oak; Mr. Timerick, Bournbrook; Mr. T. Cooper,

7. 1902

Bournbrook; Miss Lilly Bromwich, Bournbrook; Mr. R. Morris, Bournbrook; Mr. A. Beaven, Bournbrook; Mr. F. Overthrow, Selly Oak; Mrs. Lewis, Selly Oak; Mr. F. Brook, Bournbrook; Mr. Archer, Bournbrook; Miss A. Sales, Bournbrook; Mr. T. Ieke, Bournbrook; Mr. J. Marshall, Bournbrook; Mr. F. Deaman, Selly Oak; Mr. F. Stock, Selly Oak; Miss M. Bullingham, Selly Oak; Miss L. Morgan, Selly Oak; Mr. Molesworth, Bournbrook; Mr. Watton, Bournbrook; Mr. W. J. Kerrod, Bournbrook; Mr. R. Stone, Bournbrook; Mr. G.A. Jones, Bournbrook; Mr. J. Shephard, Bournbrook; Mr. Styeh, Bournbrook; Mr. B. Clarke, Bournbrook; Mr. A. Mason; Bournbrook.

Messrs. J. M. Crow, J. W. Crow, R. Terry, P. Freakley, and A. Banner officiated as stewards.

The judges awarded the prizes as follows:-

Decorated Premises:- First. Mrs. Cartwright; 2nd. Mr. A. Mills; 3rd. Mr. Phillips; 4th. Mr. J. Deaman.

Decorated Vehicles:- First. Mr. G. Chillingworth; 2nd. Albert Monk; 3rd. Mr. C. Tatton; 4th. Mr. J. Quinton.

Decorated Bicycles (Ladies'):- First. Miss Bide; 2nd. Miss Collett; 3rd. Miss Clarke.

Decorated Bicycles (Gentlemen's):- First. Mr. T.H. Lawrence; 2nd. John Lea; 3rd. Mr. Taylor.

Decorated Bicycle (Councillor E. A. Olivieri's prize):- Miss Bide: (Selly Oak Cycle Club's prize):- Mr. T. H. Lawrence.

Best Novelty:- First. Mr. T. Monk; 2nd. Mr. B. Clarke; 3rd. Messrs. Wassall and O. H. Stead; 4th. Mr. Styeh.

Decorated Mail Cart:- First. Mrs. Thompson; 2nd. Miss B. Lea; 3rd. W. E. Knibbs.

In addition to the decorative components of the procession there were included in its long line the whole of the children of school age in the village, numbering at a moderate estimate, not less than 4,000. Many of the smaller children were provided with seats in vehicles lent by the tradesmen and local manufacturers, in pursuance of their normal practice. The vehicles were smart, clean, and nicely decorated. Mr. William Holmes headed the procession. Music was discoursed by the Selly Oak Brass Band, the band of the 1st V.B. Warwickshire Regiment, the Selly Oak Church Lads' Brigade Band, and the Selly Oak and Bournbrook Coronation Band. As the procession passed through the gaily decked out village, amid the brilliant climatic conditions of an ideal summer's day, it appeared to the writer, as he observed it from a coign of vantage near the canal bridge, striking in its variety, perfect in its ensemble, and exhilarating in its utter abandonment to the day's rejoicings. Selly Oak Park was the venue of the festive throng, and upon their arrival there the children massed round the bandstand under the direction of Mr. Humphreys, and their sweet trebles united in the joyous strains of the "Old Hundreth" (sic), "Rule Britannia" and "God save the King". This was to have been followed by the planting of the Coronation oak by Councillor Gibbins, one of the donors of the Park and Chairman of the Coronation Committee, but under the exceptional circumstances, the committee decided to defer this interesting little ceremony until the actual crowning of his Majesty. The afternoon's activities were entered upon without loss of time. A carefully organised and extensive programme of children's races had been drawn up, and the opening heats were immediately decided. In this manner the time slipped away rapidly until tea. For holiday makers to whom the children's races did not greatly appeal, rich entertainment was found in the melodies and drolleries of Mr. Willy Hill's Minstrels, in the delights of the Punch and Judy show by Professor Barton, with Mr. J. Gough, the champion in this district of this form of amusement, as supervisor of the whole proceedings. At 4 o'clock the children, as pre-arranged, commenced to assemble for tea which was substantial in kind, and of excellent quality, a proof of the capable manner in which the Catering Committee performed their duties. To satisfy the appetites of such a large family, sharpened as they were by much walking and running, was a vastly more serious matter than that which over-powered the old woman who lived in a shoe, as recorded in the annals of the nursery, but it was successfully grappled with. Hunger and thirst wholly disappeared as the rivers of tea and milk dried up and the mountains of cake and bread and butter crumbled steadily away. There was abundance and to spare of food and drink alike. Tea over, the day's amusements were resumed, the premier place being given to a May-pole dance by the children. Always attractive, the dance on this occasion appealed in an especial manner to the artistic feelings of the spectators. It was so entirely in keeping with the spirit of the whole proceedings. The eyes of the dancers twinkled with delight as they tripped gaily through the intricacies of the figures. Evidently they enjoyed the fun, at least as much as any of the bystanders. After this there was a further musical and vocal entertainment, a display by the members of the Selly Oak Ambulance Corps, a repetition of Professor Barton's Punchuinello (sic), with more music, and more Punch later on. The lighting of a bonfire fittingly brought to a close the festivities at the Park. In the village, however, ardent merriment prevailed throughout the long evening and into the "wee sma hours" of morning. Adorned in holiday attire the villagers sallied forth from their homes in Mafficking bent. And Maffick they did! No expedient for adding to the discordant noises that may be produced by a combination of the natural powers of the vocal organs with the weird effects of fearfully and wonderfully designed instruments of torture was neglected. The village rose to the occasion as one man. Every reveller revelled in his best style. There was an absence of restraint that enchanted everyone with nerves wiry enough to stand the strain. "All in a row", with arms linked, and chests thrown out, men and women, youths and maidens, walked up and down the High Street until well after midnight, singing that classic melody, that lyrical gem, "We'll all be merry on Coronation Day!" However, all things have an end. The secret of perpetual Mafficking has not yet been discovered any more than that of perpetual motion. The witching hour of midnight passed, the energies of the populace began to flag, and, slowly but surely, the streets emptied themselves, and Selly Oak became more like its former self. Altogether the day will live long in the recollections of those participating in the jubilations.

    Yesterday 350 old folk over 60 were entertained at Bournbrook Institute to a substantial dinner, and were afterwards presented with a half pound of tea (to the women) and two ounces of tobacco (to the men), the gifts of Mr. and Mrs. George Cadbury. Councillors Oswald and Olivieri were present and addressed a few words to them. The large number of poor who were not catered for by the Coronation Committee were provided for by the generosity of a number of Bournbrook gentlemen who subscribed towards the provision of an ox, costing £20, which was roasted outside the Bournbrook Hotel.

Councillor E. A. Olivieri provided a beautiful display of Chinese lanterns and other effective embellishments outside his residence, Selly Hill House. A May-pole had been erected in the roadway and the lanterns from the Orient stretched from the top of it to either side of the roadway in festoons. On a piece of ground close by a bonfire blazed merrily away, to the great satisfaction of a crowd of sightseers. The day did not pass without one or two accidents, though, fortunately, these were of a minor character. Mr. Andrews, of Hope Street, the operator of the Punch and Judy, was hurt by the giving way of the platform erected for the entertainments. He was not seriously hurt. Rather a severe shaking up, and bruised ankle of left leg. He was attended to by members of the Selly Oak Ambulance Corps, who took him on a stretcher to Dr. Longmore's. He was afterwards taken home on the stretcher by two members of the corps. A boy named Robert Lilley, of 26 Cleve Road, Selly Oak, who was on the platform at the time of the collapse, also sustained a bruise on his leg, and was treated by the Ambulance Corps, afterwards being taken home by them.

The Coronation Committee was composed of the following:- T. Gibbins (chairman), T. A. Cole (vice-chairman), E. A. Olivieri (treasurer), J. R. Oswald and A. Gittins (general secretaries), W. Holmes (Chairman of Procession Committee), J. Draper (Chairman of Fields and Sports Committee), W. Parsons (Secretary of the Fields and Sports Committee), W. Humphries (Chairman of the Catering Committee), E. C. James (sec. of the Catering Committee), G. J. Purser, B. Connop, F. Jordan, A. White, L. Freakley, S. Hill, W. Terry, J. Gough, D. Roy, W. Chambers, J. Deaman, T. T. Wilson, H. White, R. Roberts, W. Gee. J. Quinton, W. Wheatley, T. Cooper, G. Ikin, W. Hill, T. Hall, W. Haddon, T. Smith, T. Greswolde, J. Wheelwright, E. M. Sheppard, J. Sheppard, J. W. Goode, J. M. Crow, G. Sheasby, S. H. Brittain, W. Whitehouse, J. Coley, A. Ford, J. Taylor, – Griffiths, F. Goode, A. Gillott, E. Docker, the Rev C. R. Sharpe, A. H. Wiggin, T. Baldwin, W. Baldwin, R. C. Hinton, F. Smith, T. W. Lawrence, T. Lawrence, jnr., Andrew Crump, W. Green, W. Husselbee, J. Roddis, D. Roy, W. H. Moss, Doughy, H. Banner, jnr., and W. Cooper.

3rd July 1902 – KN&N UDC Baths, Parks and Cemeteries Committee (see also 9th July 1902 – Minute of KN&N UDC below)

A report of the Superintendent was presented and read. Resolved to approve same and that the Chairman be asked to report as to the frame mentioned therein to the next meeting.

5th July 1902 – The South Birmingham Chronicle:

On Thursday a meeting of the Coronation Committee was held at the Institute, Bournbrook, Mr. T. Gibbins presiding. The action of a certain member of the committee was severely criticised by some of his colleagues. It is alleged that the gentleman in question made himself much more officious than his official position warranted in the Park. There is no doubt that a considerable amount of feeling was displayed at the meeting, and, in fact, it ran very high, and some of the members of the committee were not at all particular in expressing their disapproval at the conduct of the gentleman in question. An attempt by one present to pour oil on troubled waters failed altogether, and rather seemed to increase the irritation of those who were already much irritated.

5th July 1902 – The Birmingham News

Selly Oak and Bournbrook

The Coronation May-pole Dance – The Coronation committee granted the sum of three pounds as prizes to children wearing the prettiest costumes in the may-pole dance. It was a most difficult task to make the awards (given below), as all really deserved a prize. It is to be hoped the committee will be able to do something to each of the sixty-four children, who after so many hours of practice were able to please so large a number of children and parents on Thursday and Friday last. It is proposed to have the may-pole dance several evenings in the park before the end of the season. Prizes:- Girls: 1st. prize, Nelly Sheppy, value 5s.: 2nd. prizes, Lily Ward, Ida Godfrey, Nellie Mason, Naomi Cotterell, Drusilla Woodward, 3s. each: 3rd. prizes, Ethel Whitehouse, Irene Hart, Nellie Waller, May Bunn, Augusta Smith, 2s. each. Boys: 1st. Prize, F. Meredith, value 5s.: 2nd. prizes, L. Roberts, 4s.: 3rd. prizes, C. Dugmore, S. Quinton, B. Haddon, E. Sheasby, C. Quinton, 3s. each: 4th. prizes, J. Kibble, A. Moore, H. Daniel, 2s. each.

9th July 1902 – Minute of KN&N UDC, and reported on
12th July 1902 – The South Birmingham Chronicle, and
12th July 1902 – The Birmingham News

Mr. Councillor Oswald presented the following report of the Baths, Parks and Cemeteries Committee (minute dated 3rd July 1902).

This Committee beg to report:-

Juvenile Fete at Selly Oak

(3) – Your Committee have granted the use of the park at Selly Oak, for the Selly Oak Juvenile Fete on 23rd August, 1902, subject to the usual conditions and restrictions being observed.

Selly Oak Victoria Brass Band

(4) – Your Committee have received an application from the Selly Oak Victoria Brass Band for a contribution towards the cost of the music, and have instructed the Clerk to reply the Council have no power to make such a contribution.

It was moved by Mr. Councillor Oswald, seconded Mr. Councillor Olivieri, and resolved (minute 780), that the proceedings of the Baths, Parks and Cemeteries Committee be approved and adopted.

17th July 1902 – KN&N UDC Baths, Parks and Cemeteries Committee

A letter was received from Mr G H Hansell of 61 Bristol Road Bournbrook asking whether the Council would grant him permission to sell refreshments in the Park on Wednesday evenings.
    Resolved that failing the Park Keeper being unable or unwilling to supply refreshments to visitors to the Park that Mr Hansell be allowed to do so.

16th August 1902 – The South Birmingham Chronicle

Local Chimes

(From a report on a "winding up" meeting of the Selly Oak Coronation Committee:)

Before the business of the meeting was over it was decided to send a letter of thanks to Mr. Horton, Park Keeper, for the trouble he took in connection with certain work on the occasion of the festivities. A similar letter was also ordered to be sent to Police-Inspector Hill, late of Selly Oak, for the very valuable assistance rendered by him.

30th August 1902 – The Birmingham News

Selly Oak and Bournbrook

Selly Oak Juvenile Foresters and Oddfellows Fete – The annual fete of the Selly Oak branch of Juvenile Foresters and Oddfellows took place on Saturday. The permission of the District Council having been obtained, the fete was held in the Selly Oak Park, proceedings commenced at 2 p.m, the children, numbering 250, assembling at Selly Oak Schools, and forming a procession, headed by the Selly Oak Victoria Band, and carrying numerous banners and flags, marched to the park, where a long programme of entertainments had been arranged by the committee. Among the attractions were punch and judy shows, swing boats, mutoscopes (sic), etc. Professor Alexander, conjuror and ventriloquist; Malone and

Conley, eccentric knockabouts; Baker and Brooks, negro comedians; Lerlax and Perpate, all gave performances during the afternoon. A programme of sports for the juveniles was also carried out. Great credit is due to Mr. J. C. Eaton (secretary of the Juvenile Foresters), Mr. Thomas Wheatley (secretary of the Juvenile Oddfellows), Mr. J. Alldrit (secretary for the combination), and Mr. A. Thompson (chairman of the committee), for the admirable way in which the arrangements were carried out.

10th September 1902 – KN&N UDC Baths, Parks and Cemeteries Committee

Refreshments to Visitors The Chairman reported that the Park Keeper was willing to supply refreshments to visitors to the Park and he had given him permission so to do.

Paving drive This minute was discharged the work having been completed.

Outside Painting It was reported this work had been carried out by Mr A Havell, in the sum of £5.10. 0. as per tender, accepted by the Chairman of the Committee. Minute was discharged.

Span Roof Greenhouse Resolved to approve the purchase of a span roof greenhouse for the sum of £9-15/-.

1st October 1902 – Minute of KN&N UDC, and reported on
4th October 1902 – The Birmingham News

Mr. Councillor Oswald presented the following report of the Baths Parks & Cemeteries Committee.

>   This Committee beg to report:-
>
> Selly Oak Park
>
>   That your Committee have purchased a Span-roof Greenhouse for the sum of £9 15s. for the Park, and ask that their action be approved.

It was moved by Mr. Councillor Oswald, seconded Mr. Councillor Smith, and resolved (minute 858), that the report of the Baths, Parks and Cemeteries Committee be approved and adopted.

Chapter 8

1903

28th February 1903 – South Birmingham Chronicle

WANTED, RECREATION GROUNDS

There are many questions being dealt with just now by our Urban District Council, and no one will deny that their hands are pretty full. What with schemes for Baths, Free Libraries, Destructors, Depots, Education, and other things, they have plenty of irons in the fire. Still, there are matters which are sufficiently urgent to need prompt and energetic action on the part of a governing body, whatever they may have already in hand, matters which, too long retarded or procrastinated, become of impossible realisation. We allude to the question of open spaces, or recreation grounds. We know we possess the Selly Oak park, and shall have, perhaps, for some time to come, a fair amount of fields which permit the children keeping off the streets, and afford them facilities for playing football in winter, cricket in summer, and engage in other sports and pastimes all the year round. The time is, however, nigh when the fields will, we fear, disappear altogether from our centres of population, and without wishing for one moment to be thought pessimistic, we are sure that we are not overstepping the mark in saying that in another ten years there will be very few vacant spaces of land in the Selly Oak, Bournbrook, Ten Acres, and Stirchley. Now, we say that it is the bounden duty of our representatives, particularly in the districts mentioned, to take time by the forelock, and endeavour to secure land at the earliest possible moment to render it possible for the school children of our district to have facilities afforded them for recreation for all time to come, and for young people generally, the opportunity of enjoying themselves to their hearts content away from the streets and in the more congested districts, and when their day's work is over. There is a great deal to be gained also from the provision of open spaces form (sic) an hygienic point of view; and whether you take the Metropolis or the rising cities in the provinces, large or small, we find ample provision is being made in this direction, and we feel that there is no reason why Kings Norton and Northfield should be behind other growing centres of population in this respect; and steps should be taken at the earliest possible moment, in fact before it becomes too late, to provide such open spaces. Much will be gained from a health point of view, both to adults and children living in congested areas, and we commend the idea very warmly to the members of our Council who represent such districts. We know that much has been done in the past to secure recreation grounds for Selly Oak, Bournbrook and other places, but the difficulties seemed so many and so unsurmountable (sic) then that those who tried gave up the task. We say, however, that if those who endeavoured to bring them about failed in times gone by, there is no reason why others now should not succeed, if they have another try. The same argument is applicable to Stirchley, as well as to Selly Oak and district, and we hope to hear before long that the members for both Wards have made it a part of their duty to secure what would be such a boon, not only to the present generation, but even more so to those that will follow it.

1st March 1903 – South Birmingham Chronicle

Selly Oak Then and Now
Reminiscences of the Past

Twenty years ago does not require much effort of memory, it seems but a flash, and yet a number of the residents of Selly Oak can throw their memories back twice, and in some instances even thrice that number of years. What a change has come over the scene since those days.

Streets, rows, groves, and terraces of houses where once the gentle stream murmured and rippled along the green meadows, and the gardens and orchards gave forth their rich harvest of flowers and fruits in due season. The meadows are but a memory, although we do get here and there the gleam of a garden. The old days were not troubled much by the noise of the builder's trowel or the hooters of the gigantic factories calling the toilers to their work. Only a little while since the stream of life flowed so placidly that even a straw thrown into it would sometimes cause a slight eddy, only, however, to flow on again as if nothing had happened. The old Parish Council that used to do so well for us has now given place to the new District Council. Where we were able to govern our local affairs in days gone by we now have to put up with the impudent attempts put forward by those venturesome gentlemen who try to interfere in those matters which concern them not. Our old leading lights who used to meet at "The Plough" or "The Oak" have now given place to the "Inkslingers" and "Innuendo murmurers" that have, unfortunately for the community at large, inflicted themselves on us in these later days.

The work that used to be done emanated from sound, solid, and sensible men, men who had brains, and men who used them. "Deeds not words" was evidently their motto in those days.

No pamphlet scatterers or health reform splutterers, no "Down with this" and no "Down with that" cries that are being uttered simply to pander to a certain class of people who wish for a certain amount of notoriety from their vapid and absolutely senseless arguments.

"Yes, that's all very well," says one of the smart ones, "but they had no park in those days".

"No," was the answer that very quickly came. "We have a park; that is about the sum total of our local attractions".

It is just possible that the time is coming when we may see a fair exchange for the days past recalling. When the working man of the district will say to our misrepresentatives "Get thee hence".

In place of the meadows and streams that were let him have his baths. Let him have his library to cultivate his own mind and enlighten those of his children. Let his home be made more wholesome, pure, and fit to live in. Let the streams of mud which flow down some of our streets be swept away, and so avoid a very fruitful source of infectious disease; thus indeed we may find that the past years, with all their regrets, all their "might have beens", will have taught us all a lesson, so that it will be quite unnecessary for us to compare
"Then with Now."

12th March 1903 – KN&N UDC Baths, Parks and Cemeteries Committee

Resolved that the work necessary to be done at the Lodge be carried out, also that the tiles of the Lodge and Shelter and the Village Trees be renewed and the iron fencing to the Park be painted and that the matter be left to the Chairman acting with the Surveyor.

22nd May 1903 – KN&N UDC Baths, Parks and Cemeteries Committee

A letter was read from Mr Josiah Thos Horton the Keeper of Selly Oak Park, stating that he had nothing to report to the Committee. The Chairman reported that he had sanctioned the expenditure of 30/- in seeds for the flower beds.

6th June 1903 – Birmingham News

Notes and Jottings

Selly Oak Victoria Band will commence to give concerts in the park next Wednesday evening.

27th June 1903 – South Birmingham Chronicle

There is another long editorial in this edition dedicated to "Recreation Grounds Wanted" in relation to the proposed development of the Muntz Estate. It contains the following reference to Selly Oak Park:

"Now what provision has the Council made to obtain for the different parts of the district sites for recreation grounds? We are afraid that little has been done in this direction, and if we except the Park at Selly Oak, so generously given a few years back by Mrs. and Messrs. Gibbins, there are neither parks nor recreation grounds of any kind in our district, and it is now very doubtful whether there will be any chance of obtaining suitable sites for the purpose at anything but prohibitive and exorbitant figures. ...."

1st July 1903 – Minute of KN&N UDC

Mr. Councillor Oswald presented the following report of the Baths, Parks and & Cemeteries Committee (minuted 15th June 1903)

> Your Committee beg to report that they have made an inspection of the two Cemeteries and the Park, and now beg to recommend:-
>
> Selly Oak Park
>
> That the Pavilion roof be repaired, and the Superintendent's Lodge papered and whitewashed, and the Tree-guards and Swings varnished.
>
> That the footway along the Park frontage be widened 6in. so as to protect the base of the unclimbable iron fencing, and that the fence be painted by the Council's own men.

It was moved by Mr. Councillor Oswald, seconded Mr. Councillor Olivieri, and resolved (minute 289), that the pavilion roof at the Park, Selly Oak, be repaired, and the Superintendent's Lodge papered and whitewashed, and the tree-guards and swings varnished.
    It was moved by Mr. Councillor Oswald, seconded Mr. Councillor Olivieri, and resolved (minute 290), that the footway along the Park frontage at Selly Oak be widened 6 in. so as to protect the base of the unclimbable iron fencing, and that the fence be painted by the Council's own men.
    It was moved by Mr. Councillor Oswald, seconded Mr. Councillor Bladon, and resolved (minute 291), that the report of the Baths, Parks and Cemeteries Committee be approved and adopted.

21st July 1903 – KN&N UDC Baths, Parks and Cemeteries Committee, reported on 29th July 1903 – Minute of KN&N UDC

The Surveyor reported as follows:
    That the repairs to the tiling of the Pavilion roofs had been done, also the torching to projecting eaves in gables, and damaged ridging to the Lodge and outbuildings had been replaced with similar ridging to that used on the Pavilion.
    That it was necessary to raise the fence for a considerable distance so as to enable the asphalt to be taken underneath and that this work had now been completed.
    That tree guards and swings had been varnished.
    That tenders had been invited for painting papering and whitewashing of the Lodge and that the tender of Mr Alfred Flavell of Woodgate in the sum of £7. 14. 6 had been accepted by the Chairman.
    Resolved that the Chairman's action be approved.

Application for use of Park for Children's Fete A letter was read from Mr Fred Allen applying for permission to use Selly Oak Park for the purposes of the Selly Oak and Bournbrook Children's Fete of the 27th July and also asking for permission to make a small charge to the general public for admission to the Park on that date.

Resolved that the permission asked for be granted but that the Committee do not give any sanction to a charge being made to the Public, such permission being granted subject to the usual rules and regulations being observed.

Gas Fittings to Lodge The Surveyor reported he had instructed the Gas Department to give an estimate for the pipes and fittings necessary for lighting the Lodge with gas.

25th July 1903 – South Birmingham Chronicle

Selly Oak and Bournbrook Children's Fete

As already announced[48] the Selly Oak and Bournbrook children's fete will be held on Monday next, the 27th inst., in Selly Oak Park. The programme is now out, and among other items contains the following list of prizes, which have been offered by the committee:- For the best decorated vehicle: First prize 10s., second 6s 6d., third 3s. 6d.; to assemble in Heeley Road near Station Gates at 12 o'clock. Best decorated mailcart: First prize 7s. 6d., second 5s., third 3s. 6d.; to assemble in Exeter Road, near Heeley Road, at 12 o'clock. Best decorated bicycle: First prize 7s. 6d., second 5s, third 3s. 6d.; to assemble in Hubert Road, between Dartmouth Road and Exeter Road, at 12 o'clock. Best novelty of any description: First prize 10s., second 6s. 6d., third 3s. 6d.; to assembly in Dartmouth Road, near Heeley Road, at 12 o'clock. A singing competition: All children of school age are invited to compete. Medals will be given for the best rendering of "Home, Sweet Home" for girls; the best rendering of "The National Anthem" for boys; the best rendering of any duet, for girls; the best rendering of any duet, for boys; the best recitation of poetry, for boys; the best recitation of poetry, for girls; musical adjudicators, Messrs. Fred Allen, and J, Mills; recitation adjudicator, Mr. W. Haddon. Councillors W. Holmes and E.A. Olivieri will present the prizes. A prize of 7s. 6d. for decorated shop; a prize of 7s. 6d. for best decorated house on the route. A special prize of one guinea will be given to the best group of not less than six children, mounted on either horses, ponies, or donkeys. The committee appeal to the inhabitants to do all they can by way of decorations. The procession will start from Dawlish Road Schools at 1.0 prompt, and will proceed by way of High Street, Bournbrook, and High Street and Church Road, Selly Oak, to the Park. Stalls will be let to villagers only at a charge of 2s., and if over 2 yards frontage 1s. per yard extra. General public will be admitted after 5 o'clock. It will be noticed that a charge for

---

[48] In the "What We Hear" bullet points printed earlier in this edition of the paper.

admission of twopence is being made this year for adults. We understand the committee in doing this had two objects in view – helping to raise funds to defray the expenses of the fete, and to keep out any outside element which in years past appears to have furnished a strong contingent to the adult section attending the fete.

1st August 1903 – South Birmingham Chronicle

Selly Oak and Bournbrook Children's Fete

Monday, July 27th, was the date that had been fixed for the annual children's fete. The day opened with some slight promise of fair weather, which promise was, however, very soon broken, for the rain commenced to fall about 9 o'clock, and practically continued the whole day through. Disappointment on every side was keen. Committee men who had arranged for time to attend to the children's wants were looking glum. The children themselves were standing in small groups, talking and wondering whether the fete would be held that day or not. A crowd of them gathered round the Friends' Institute, where the committee were holding a final meeting to decide what should be done. Eventually a wise decision (as it turned out) was arrived at. Postponement till the next day did not seem a very long way off, but the faces of the children waiting round the Institute reflected the great amount of disappointment which they undoubtedly felt. Tuesday arrived, and one could scarcely hope for a brighter-looking morning or a day that could be better fitted for the work that had to be done. "What time will the procession start?" was the question being asked by the children on all hands. "Will it keep fine?" was another query. Anxious eyes turned towards the chimney stacks, watching the way the smoke went. The procession had been timed to start from Dawlish Road schools at two o'clock, and start it did exactly to time, with a glorious sun shining, and the band in front playing, the children's procession wended its way towards the park. Councillor William Holmes, who has for so many years marshalled the procession, was again seen on his charger at the head of affairs. Although the number of children taking part was not so large as last year it was certainly made up in the quality of the children's dresses, which were spoken of by all as the prettiest that had ever been seen.

The prizes given by the Procession Committee were allocated as follows:-

Best decorated vehicle: Wm. Hughes.

Best decorated mailcart: Mrs. Silvester, 1st prize; Mrs. Kimberley, 2nd prize; Mrs. Valance, 3rd prize.

Best novelty: Mrs. Taylor, 1st prize; Mrs. Monk, 2nd prize; Master J. Compton, 3rd prize. Special prizes, Mr. Clark and Mr. Stead.

Arriving at the park, the smaller children were lifted from their conveyances, and all entered in high spirits. A rush was made for the steam horses, and that commodity was very soon busily engaged. It would be just as well here to speak of the handling of the procession, and the great assistance that was rendered by Inspector Griffin and his staff of police. The great feast was being prepared by willing helpers, of which there was a goodly staff of local ladies and gentlemen, and when the bell rang, announcing that all was in readiness, the children speedily made their way to their allotted positions. Mr. Humphries, the schoolmaster, who had arranged these matters, than whom there is no one more capable, simply electrified everyone by the simplicity and perfect order in which the children stood to order awaiting the good things. Grace having been said, they sat down, and great steaming cans and churns of tea were soon being ladled out; tremendous baskets of festal cake and golden lemon cake were being emptied very fast. Bread and butter of the very best was quickly disappearing from sight. It was a very busy time, each child seeming to vie with his or her next door neighbour to see which could eat or drink the most. What made the affair such a grand success from every point of view was the fact that no child left that field without he or she had had their fill. When children refuse to have more it is time to give up, and once more a rush was made for different parts of the park where sports were about to be held. Races for boys, gambolling races with tied legs, which caused an endless amount of fun, and thread needle races for girls. All combined to make one whole happy afternoon. Mr. H. White's Selly Oak Band was in attendance, and they must be complimented in the highest possible way for the beautiful music they discoursed during the day. One of the features of the fete was the may-pole dance, under the able direction of Mr. Humphries. The children were attired in fancy dress of the most charming description, and large crowds witnessed each of the three performances, which were accompanied by the Selly Oak Band. Great credit is due to Mr. Humphries and the teachers for the admirable way in which this was organised.

There was one competition which was being looked forward to with a great amount of excitement. It was a musical competition that had been arranged by several gentlemen of the committee. There were eight gold centre silver medals for the successful competitors, and a programme had been issued, so that the affair was watched with an extraordinary amount of enthusiasm. The appointed adjudicators were Messrs. Fred Allen and J. Mills for the musical portions, and the Rev. F.H. Roach and Mr. W. Haddon for the recitations. The successful children were as follows:

Solo for girls. Two prizes. Thirteen competitors.
Myra Barton and Marion Edith Clark
Duet for girls. One prize. Eight competitors.
"Life's dream is o'er"
Elisabeth Mills and Katie Green
Boys' solo. One prize. Three competitors.
The National Anthem.
H. Smallridge.
Recitation for girls. Two prizes. Twenty-one competitors.
"Home coming of the Eurydice"
Mary Lockington.
"Wolsey's Farewell".
Nellie Newman.
Recitation for boys. One prize. One competitor.
"The Alarm"
Fred Steele.

The whole of the competition was finely carried out, and augurs well for anything of the same description that may be inaugurated in the future. The singing competitions were very close, the competitors being almost on a level, and certainly made the task of the judges something more than a sinecure. The recitations showed a surprising amount of intelligence and power of elocution in children of such tender years. It should be mentioned that two of the girls were highly commended for their recitations – Marion Clark, who recited "Curfew shall not ring to-night", and Myra Barton, "The Spanish Armada". The judges were only sorry that they had not more prizes at their disposal. A further extension of these competitions in the future is very desirable; they arouse interest and enthusiasm, and are also educational as far as the children are concerned.

As the light began to wane and the children were passing out of the gates to fetch their buns the fun was relaxed a little, everyone was getting tired, and who shall say they were not entitled to be tired after such a glorious time. Children wending their way homewards loaded inside with cake and tea, and arms full of presents and prizes won in the different competitions. Happiness on everyone's face. Delighted mothers and fathers. Committee men all satisfied with themselves. Thus ended the Selly Oak and Bournbrook children's fete for 1903.

1st August 1903 – The Birmingham News

Selly Oak and Bournbrook

Children's Fete. – The fete for the children resident in Selly Oak and Bournbrook was to have been held on Monday, but owing to the unfavourable weather had to be postponed until the following day. Tuesday dawned bright and clear, and when the children assembled at the Dawlish Road School at two o'clock, the sun was shining brilliantly, auguring well for the success of the gathering. In former years prizes were offered for the best decorated house and shop, but on this occasion they were withdrawn, in consequence of which the rivalry formerly existing among the inhabitants regarding the decoration of their houses and places of business was not so keen, but nevertheless many of the residences along the line of the route were gaily decked with bunting and other draperies. The procession, headed by Mr. W. Holmes on horseback, and the Selly Oak Brass Band, proceeded to Selly Oak Park, where the fete was held. Following directly after the band was a number of maypole girls, dressed in white, and at various points in the procession were traps, wagonettes, and vans, containing the younger children, the majority of which were prettily decorated, as were also several mailcarts. In addition to the prizes offered for the above there were three prizes offered for the best novelty of any description, of which there were several, and the novel "get up" of some afforded much amusement to the spectators on the line of the route. On arrival at the park the children were provided with tea and cake, and afterwards entertained with sports, games, and other amusements. The prize for the best decorated vehicle was won by Mr. W. Hughes. The following were the winners in the other

Thomas Gibbins (1796–1863) & Emma Joel Gibbins (nee Cadbury). Photograph kindly provided by Haverford College Library, Haverford, Pennsylvania: Quaker Collection, Jones-Cadbury Collection, folder 2, box 127.

Emma Joel Gibbins (1811–1903). Photograph kindly provided by Haverford College Library, Haverford, Pennsylvania: Quaker Collection, Jones-Cadbury Collection, album, box 118.

The sons of Mrs Emma Joel Gibbins who, with her, donated Selly Oak Park. Top left[1]: Thomas Gibbins (1842–1908) Chairman of KN&N UDC. Top right[1]: William Gibbins (1840–1933). Bottom left[1] John Gibbins (1848–1931). Below Right[2] Benjamin Gibbins. Photograph credits: 1. The Birmingham Battery and Metal Company (1936). 2. Haverford College Library, Haverford, Pennsylvania: Quaker Collection, Jones-Cadbury Collection, folder 4, box 127.

Emma Joel Gibbins and her family. Photograph kindly provided by Haverford College Library, Haverford, Pennsylvania: Quaker Collection, Jones-Cadbury Collection, folder 4, box 127. There are also portrait photographs of Thomas (Snr) and Emma Joel Gibbins in a collection of "Family Letters and Portraits" held in the Archive Section of Birmingham Central Library (Cat. No. 491779).

Members of the next generation of the Gibbins Family: R. Lloyd Gibbins (1877–) Park extension donor. W. Waterhouse Gibbins (1869–) Park extension donor Henry C. Gibbins (1877–) Photographs copied from The Birmingham Battery and Metal Company (1936).

The Park Keeper, Josiah Thomas Horton (1863–1940) (reproduced from our family archive).

Edith Grove, the Park Keeper's Wife (reproduced from our family archive).

The Park Keeper – On Duty (reproduced from our family archive).

The Park Keeper – Off Duty (reproduced from our family archive).

competitions: Best decorated mailcart: Misses Silvister, 1; Mrs. Kimberley, 2; Mrs. Valance, 3. Best novelty of any description: Mrs. Taylor, 1; Mrs. Monk, 2; Master Compton, 3; Mr. Clark, 4. Much interest was manifested in the singing and reciting competitions for children, for which silver medals, with gold centre, were offered as prizes. Messrs. Fred Allen and J. Mills acted as adjudicators in the singing competition, and their awards were as follows: – Solo for girls, "Home sweet home", Miss M. Barton, 1; Miss M.E. Clark, 2. Duet for girls, "Life's dream is o'er", Miss E. Mills and Miss K.E. Green. On the competition for songs Master Smallridge secured the prize for the best rendition of the National Anthem. The keenest rivalry took place for the prize offered for the best recitation by girls, and Mr. W. Hadden, who acted as the judge, awarded the first prize to Miss Mary Lockington, and the second to Miss Nelly Newman, whilst Miss M. Clark and Miss M. Barton were highly commended. Master Fred Allen was the successful competitor in the recitation for boys.

5th September 1903 – South Birmingham Chronicle

Selly Oak Victoria Brass Band
(This was a front page photograph feature, but the quality of the photograph does not permit reproduction here.)

The above band held their annual sports in the Selly Oak Park on Saturday last, when between 700 and 800 people attended. The weather was splendid, and the efforts of Mr. H. White, the conductor of the band, were attended with success. The band is an old institution, and have (sic) always been ready to offer their services for any local function.

A capital sports programme had been arranged, a most interesting item being a football match between the Sweeps and the Bakers. The first item was a lads' race, which was very keenly contested. In the two mile walking handicap Mr. Hobbis was the winner, Mr. Hewitt, however, who had won the mile handicap, running him close. One of the features of the afternoon was the entertainment given by the Silver Stream Minstrels, under the direction of Mr. Alf. Baker. Negro choruses and melodies were given, and songs were capitally rendered by Miss Harper and Miss Dovey, and Messrs. Baxter, Hutchinson, Harding, Meeks, Ebourne and Gurney. Some finely-played banjo solos were rendered by Mr. Miller, and the accompanist was Miss Nash. During the afternoon and evening the band, under the conductorship of Mr. H. White, rendered selections, and in the evening dancing was indulged in. In addition to the sports there were roundabouts, cocoanut booths, and all the paraphernalia of a fair. We understand that the affair proved highly successful. The following are the prize winners in the various events:-
Lads' race, 100 yards: 1 (brushes and rack), J. Davidson; 2 (album), W. Smith; 3 (inkstand), W. Stoney. One mile walking handicap: 1 (set of carvers), J. Hewitt; 2 (iced cake), J. Hobbis; 3 (silver-mounted walking stick), A. Slatter. 120 yards scratch

race (open): 1 (time-piece), W. Wilkes; 2 (umbrella), A. Copestick. Two mile walking handicap: 1 (time-piece), J. Hobbis; 2 (writing desk), J. Hewitt; 3 (set of salts), W. Nicholls. Potato race: 1 (silver albert and medal), J. Hobbis; 2 (time-piece), J. Lakin; 3 (briar pipe), J. Pallett. In the six-a-side football contest seven teams entered, Bournbrook Rovers Reserves being the winners. In the Sweeps and Bakers match the Bakers were the winners.

5th September 1903 – The Birmingham News

Selly Oak and Bournbrook

Band Sports – The annual fete and sports promoted by the Selly Oak Victoria Brass Band were held in the Park, on Saturday. There was a good attendance to witness a programme of six events, which attracted a large number of entries. The following are the results:- Boy's race – 1. Davenport; 2. Smith; 3, Stoney. One mile walking match – 1, Hewitt; 2, Hobbis; 3, Slacker. 120 yards scratch race – 1, Wilkes; 2, Copestick. Potato race – 1, Hodgett; 2, Lakin; 3, Pallett. Two miles walking match – 1, Hobbis; 2, Hewitt; 3, Nicholls. There were seven entries for the football competition, which was won by Bournbrook Rovers. A programme of music was rendered by the band, under the conductorship of Mr. White, and an entertainment was provided by the Silverstream Minstrels, under the able direction of Mr. Baxter. In the evening dance music was played by the band, and a very enjoyable afternoon concluded with a display of fireworks.

9th September 1903 – KN&N UDC Baths, Parks and Cemeteries Committee (Also see the following minute)

The Superintendent's report was presented and read and approved.
Resolved that the Superintendent be supplied with a new uniform and cap.

7th October 1903 – Minute of KN&N UDC

In the absence of Mr. Councillor Oswald, Mr. Councillor Lane presented the following report of the Baths, Parks and Cemeteries Committee (minute dated 9th September 1903)

Your Committee beg to report:-

<u>Visitors to the Park</u>

That the visitors to the Selly Oak Park during the summer have been more numerous than in previous years, more especially on Wednesday evenings when the Weekly Concerts given by the Selly Oak Band took place.

8. 1903

<u>Planting of trees</u>

That instructions have been given for (a) trees to be replanted in High Street, Bournbrook, and Selly Oak to replace the old ones; (b) the trees up the centre drive of the Park, which are not flourishing, to be removed and new ones substituted of a more hardy variety.

<u>Requirements</u>

That bulbs to the value of 30s. have been ordered to be purchased, and also a new uniform and cap for the Park Keeper.

It was moved by Mr. Councillor Oswald, seconded Mr. Councillor Brown, and resolved (minute 396), that the report of the Baths, Parks and Cemeteries Committee be approved and adopted.

10th October 1903 – Birmingham News

Notes and Jottings

Selly Oak Park is becoming more popular than it was.

As the village expands there will be no dearth of visitors to the park, but at present its patronage is checked by the distance that has to be travelled to get to it.

Despite this fact, however, the weekly concerts given by the Selly Oak Band have attracted good crowds.

Chapter 9

1904

30th January 1904 – South Birmingham Chronicle

FORTHCOMING COUNTY COUNCIL ELECTIONS
Councillor Thomas Gibbins
(The front page feature includes a photograph which is not suitable for reproduction here.)

The County Council elections are to take place on Wednesday, March 2nd, and the old Northfield division, which has hitherto returned one member only, has been divided into three parts – Selly Oak West, Selly Oak East, and Northfield (including Bartley Green) – each of which will choose its own. For Selly Oak West district Councillor Thomas Gibbins was adopted as candidate some time ago, and up to the present time appears likely to be returned unopposed.

Councillor Gibbins is a valued member of the King's Norton and Northfield Urban District Council. He was the first chairman of that body, and presided over it until 1901. By his impartial conduct and courtesy of manner he won the esteem of every member of the Board, and he is well known and respected by a large circle of friends. He is one of the proprietors of the Birmingham Battery Company, of which his father was one of the founders, and with which he himself has been associated ever since he left school. He comes from an old and well-known family. His mother was a Miss Cadbury, and a prominent member of the Society of Friends.

Councillor Gibbins, in conjunction with his family made the splendid gift of Selly Oak Park to our district. Not only was the land given, but the grounds were laid out at the donor's expense. He has taken a great interest in Poor Law administration, and was for some years a member of the Birmingham Board of Guardians, and he is a Guardian of the poor for our own district. In Councillor Gibbins our local institutions have found a generous supporter, and the needy a sympathetic benefactor.

9th March – 1904 KN&N UDC Baths, Parks and Cemeteries Committee

The Surveyor reported that the painting of the Lodge had now been carried out according to the instructions of the Committee.

No report was received from the Park Keeper.

13th July 1904 – KN&N UDC Baths, Parks and Cemeteries Committee

The Superintendent reported that the iron fencing fronting the Park required painting badly (sic), also the seats, band-shade (sic) shelter, and also the ironwork belonging to the swings, and that sand was required to fill up the holes under the swings in various places. Resolved that the Chairman of the Committee with Mr Councillor Bednall be requested to visit and inspect the Park and to give such instructions to the Surveyor with regard to the work required to be done as they may deem advisable.

<u>Band in Selly Oak Park</u> The Clerk reported that an application had been received from Mr H White for the band to play in the Selly Oak Park as usual during the months of June July and August and that he had laid the same before the Chairman of the Committee who had given his permission thereto.

Resolved that the action of the Chairman and Clerk be approved.

16th July 1904 – South Birmingham Chronicle

THE CHILDREN'S FETE

Adjourned meeting

(From a long report of a meeting of a new committee membership to consider the arrangements for the annual Children's Fete:)

The first business engaging attention was the report of the sub-committee appointed last week to enquire into the value of the assets belonging to the old committee. Mr. W.C. Clarke stated that these assets had been examined, and had been valued as follows:- ………… Mr. Mills explained that the valuation was very low, most of the things being valued at much less than they were worth. The tea urns, etc., were in good condition, and credit was due to Mr. Horton, the Park Keeper, for the manner in which they had been kept. ………… The sub-committee also recommended the appointment of five trustees to hold all the property of the committee, consisting of Messrs. E.A. Olivieri, T.A. Cole, A. Gittins, Lawrence and Horton. On a motion by Mr. Baldwin, however, consideration of this matter was deferred for a fortnight. …………

16th July 1904 – The Birmingham News

Selly Oak and Bournbrook Children's Fete Committee

A meeting of the Selly Oak and Bournbrook Children's Fete Committee was held at the Institute on Thursday night. – Mr. T.A. Cole, who was appointed chairman of the committee last week, owing to pressure of business, wished to be relieved of the post, and Mr. J. Kesterton was elected as chairman. – Mr. Cole, however, consented to act as vice-chairman of the committee. The committee, which was formed last week, agreed to pay £13 for the assets of the old committee, but refused to take any further liability. After some discussion it was decided to hold a fete in the Park at Selly Oak on August 31st, and Finance, Catering, Procession, and Sports and Fields Sub-committees were appointed to carry out the arrangements. – Mr. Lawrence was appointed to act as treasurer to the new committee.

28th July 1904 – KN&N UDC Baths, Parks and Cemeteries Committee

The Clerk reported that he had received an application from Mr T G Skinner for the use of the Selly Oak Park on August 31st for the purpose of the Selly Oak and Bournbrook Children's Fete and that the Chairman of the Committee had given his permission thereto.
Resolved that the action of the Chairman and Clerk be approved.

30th July 1904 – The Birmingham News

Bournbrook Children's Festival Committee

At a meeting of the above committee, under the presidency of Mr. J. Kesterton, on Thursday evening, several collectors paid in amounts which indicate that the local public are according their support to the festival in no half-hearted manner. Such an augury of success was felt to be very encouraging by those present. It was decided to engage the Selly Oak Band, and to invite the local ambulance corps to be represented in the procession. A Procession Committee was formed, with Mr. C.A. Lucas as chairman and Mr. J.H. Dowler as secretary; Messrs. T.A. Coley, A. Gittins, T.W. Lawrence, and Horton were appointed trustees of the committee's property. The secretary read a letter from the clerk to the District Council, intimating that the Baths and Parks Committee had acceded to their request to grant the use of Selly Oak Park for the festival on August 31.

10th August 1904 – Minute of KN&N UDC, and reported on
12th August 1904 – South Birmingham Chronicle

Mr. Councillor Holmes presented the following report of the Baths, Parks and Cemeteries Committee.

Your Committee beg to report:-

3 <u>Selly Oak Park</u>

That they have authorised the Chairman of the Committee (Mr. Councillor Holmes) and Mr. Councillor Bednall to give instructions to the Surveyor with regard to the execution of the painting and other work required at the Selly Oak Park.

That they have granted permission to the Church Lads' Brigade to drill once or twice a week in the Selly Oak Park, such permission to continue only during the pleasure of the Council. That they have also granted permission (as in previous years) for the Selly Oak Brass Band to play in the Park during the months of June, July, and August.

It was moved by Mr. Councillor Holmes, seconded Mr. Councillor Lane, and resolved (minute 228), that the report of the Baths, Parks and Cemeteries Committee be approved and adopted.

3rd September 1904 – South Birmingham Chronicle

Selly Oak and Bournbrook Children's Fete

The date for the Selly Oak children's festival was fixed for Wednesday last, but owing to the inclement weather it had to be postponed. The children all assembled, and in fact the procession started on its way to the Park, headed by Mr. Mr. J. Kesterton, the president. When Heeley Road was reached, however, the conditions were such that it became quite patent to everyone that the function could not be proceeded with, and the children were accordingly dispersed. The workers also turned up in force, and in about an hour had had all the eatables ready for the children. Their efforts, however, as far as the day was concerned, were vain. They were thanked for their services by Mr. Kesterton, who acknowledged the admirable manner in which they had performed their duties, and had to ask them to meet again in the afternoon if the weather was fit to have the fete. A committee meeting was immediately afterwards held, the outcome of which was a message to the children via a bell-ringer that the festival would be held on the morrow.

The weather on Thursday opened favourably. Bright sunshine brought happiness to the children in its wake. No move was made until afternoon, but at three o'clock the children assembled, and formed into processional order. This time there was no hitch, and the park was soon reached, tea being served very shortly after. What with flags, bunting, gay costumes, and Japanese parasols the field presented a very animated appearance. The children quickly disposed of tea, served up to them by a large band of lady and gentleman helpers. Moves were then made in various directions. There were heaps of attractions. Roundabouts, swings, donkey carts, a "Punch and Judy" entertainment, and many other things to delight the juvenile mind. The Selly Oak Victoria Brass Band were present, under the conductorship of Mr. H. White, and they enlivened the proceedings considerably. But one attraction outdid all the others for a time. A gentleman appeared among the children dispensing sweets, and the simultaneous rush made in his direction was astonishing. The children went on enjoying themselves in various ways until towards dusk, when the time came for their dispersal. Mr. Kesterton, as president of the movement, addressed a few words to those assembled. He explained the reason the fete had to be held on Thursday, and spoke in terms of high praise of the workers. He was pleased to see that everyone in the village had cooperated to make the affair a success. The sports that were to be held in conjunction with the festival had been postponed until Saturday. This was on account of the time the children had already had from school. The president was of the opinion that the children were well pleased with their fete, a thought in the minds of all, and evidenced by the children's demeanour. There were altogether 3,400 children to look after, and 200 lady and gentlemen helpers to do it. The affair had been a great success, a fact which gave them cause for mutual congratulations.

3rd September 1904 – The Birmingham News

Selly Oak and Bournbrook Children's Festival

Wednesday, the day fixed for the Selly Oak and Bournbrook Children's Festival, broke bright and clear, and soon the main street of the village presented a very pleasing appearance, flags and decorations of various kinds being put out in honour of the occasion, but before noon the sky was overcast, and a fine drizzling rain commenced to fall. In spite of this the committee decided to go on with the festival, hoping that the weather would clear. The children, numbering about 3,600, were marshalled in procession and headed by the Selly Oak Victoria Band and three Crimean veterans, proceeded on the way to the park, but before they reached the railway station the rain was falling so heavily that it was decided to postpone the event, and the children wet and disconsolate, dispersed. Later in the afternoon it was announced that the children would have their tea in the park on the following afternoon. On Thursday the weather was more favourable, and at 3.30 the children left their respective schools for the park, the younger children being conveyed in vehicles lent for the occasion by a number of local tradesmen. Amongst those in charge of the procession were Messrs. J. Kesterton (chairman of the committee), J.A. Cole (vice-chairman), T.W. Lawrence (treasurer), F. Skinner (general secretary), A Gittins and Councillor B.C. Bednall (chairman and secretary respectively of the Catering Committee), together with the headmasters, mistresses, and teachers of the schools. After tea the children were entertained with rides on the hobbyhorses, which were in charge of Mr. W. Clarke and Mr. C.A. Lucas; Punch and Judy shows, and other amusements. An exhibition was given by the maypole children, under the direction of Mrs. Barton and the Misses Connop. The Selly Oak Victoria Brass Band played selections of music in the evening. The committee are indebted to the following who kindly lent utensils:- Master of the Workhouse, urns; Mr. Cadbury, urns, tea pots and jugs; Mr. Cook (on behalf of the Bournville Trust), urns; and Mr. A. Gittins, tables, cups, tablecloths, jugs, baskets, &c. The programme of sports, together with the singing and reciting competition, will be completed on Saturday, and another performance will be given by the Maypole dancers.

9. 1904

10th September 1904 – The Birmingham News

Selly Oak and Bournbrook

<u>Children's Festival</u> – The postponed programme of sports in connection with the Selly Oak and Bournbrook Children's Festival took place on Saturday afternoon, in the Park, and included flat, egg and spoon, skipping rope (girls), obstacle, and three-legged races, and long jump for the boys. There were a very large number of entries for the events, and over 300 prizes were distributed, including a number of caps given by Messrs. Fosters Bros., High Street, a pendant from Mr. Randle, High Street, and chocolate from Messrs. Cadbury Bros. Messrs. S. McIntosh, J. Dowler, C.A. Lucas, H.A. Nunn and other helpers were responsible for the arrangements. The competitions for recitation and singing were well patronised, there having been over 40 entrants. As far as one could tell they appeared to be a great attraction, for a large and appreciative audience was gathered round the platform for over two hours. The method adopted in the judging was the one usually obtaining in singing competitions. If after the singing of one verse the adjudicators considered the singing good the child was allowed to sing again, and at the second time the children were classed according to age. Nine prizes of equal value were awarded for singing, and seven for recitations, the following being the judges, Councillor B.C. Bednall and Mr. J. Mills:- Singing: Daisy Barton, A. Dowler, M. Grimsby, E. Hemus, A. Watton, W. Newman, W. Smallbridge; duet, W. Knight and H. Knight. Recitations: E. Harris, N. Nooman, E. Clarke, J. Howes, M. Mills, M. Barton, E. Grimsby. The maypole children were also in attendance and gave a pleasing display under the direction of Mrs. Barton and the Misses Connop.

14th September 1904 – KN&N UDC Baths, Parks and Cemeteries Committee, and reported on
5th October 1904 – Minute of KN&N UDC

The Park Keeper reported that the engine attached to the roundabout at the Children's Festival had slightly damaged the asphalt drive in the Park.
    Resolved that the same be repaired.
    Resolved also that the Chairman and Park Keeper be authorised to expend the sum of £2 in purchasing bulbs for the Selly Oak Park.
    The Committee considered the report of the Sub-Committee appointed on the 13th July to inspect the Selly Oak Park. In accordance with the recommendations therein contained it was resolved:-
    That tenders be obtained for the painting of the iron fencing along the road frontage, the ironwork of the swings and gymnastic apparatus, the park seats, and the woodwork of the shelter where formerly painted, and that the Park staff be instructed to paint the tree guards.
    That the Surveyor be instructed to obtain tenders for providing and fixing three double back seats for the shelter, and also for strengthening the overhanging eaves of the shelter roof.

That the Park Keeper be instructed to thin out and replant the shrubs in the borders, and to send to Lodge Hill Cemetery any spare shrubs which the Cemetery Superintendent may be able to make use of.

That the Surveyor be authorised to purchase three truck loads of sea sand for the floor of the swings and gymnastic apparatus.

Resolved also that the report of the Sub-Committee be approved and adopted.

12th October 1904 – KN&N UDC Baths, Parks and Cemeteries Committee, and reported on
2nd November 1904 – Minute of KN&N UDC

The Park Keeper reported that the work of removing the shrubs should be commenced as soon as possible and he asked if the Committee would authorise the employment of additional labour to assist in the work.

Resolved that two men be engaged to carry out the removal of the shrubs as ordered by the Committee and that the matter be left in the hands of the Chairman and Surveyor to employ such men for such time and for such wages as they may consider advisable.

A letter was also read from the Park Keeper applying for an increase in his wages which were at the present time 24/- per week.

Resolved to recommend: that the wages of Mr J T Horton, the Keeper of the park be increased from 24/- to 27/- per week.

A letter was also read from the Park Keeper with regard to his man, James Finch and requesting the Committee to consider the advisability of placing this man upon a permanent wage. It appeared that Finch's wages at the time were 24/7d per week when at full time and 20/- to 21/- per week when on short time.

Resolved that the Chairman be requested to make inquiries into the matter and report thereon to the next meeting.

<u>Cricket Pitch and Bowling Green at the Park</u> The Committee considered the proposal to lay out a cricket pitch and bowling green in the Selly Oak park and after some discussion it was resolved that a Sub-Committee consisting of the Chairman, and Councillors Bednall, Coley and Shepherd be requested to visit the Park and submit a plan showing the position of the proposed cricket pitch and bowling green.

9th November 1904 – KN&N UDC Baths, Parks and Cemeteries Committee, and reported on
7th December 1904 – Minute of KN&N UDC, and on
10th December 1904 – The Birmingham News

The Superintendent stated that he had no report to present at this meeting.

The Surveyor reported that in accordance with the instructions of the Committee he had prepared a plan and details of three double seats back to back (with section between) for the shelter at the Park; also plan showing proposed purlins and brackets to shelter, and that he had received tenders for this work from Messrs T A Cole and Son (£26. 15s) and from T Halward and Sons (£33). Resolved that the plan and details submitted by the Surveyor be approved and that the tender of Messrs T A Cole & Son in the sum of £26. 15s be accepted.

The Surveyor also reported that he had prepared a specification of the work to be done in painting the iron fence along the road fronting to the Park, the ironwork of the swings and gymnastic apparatus, the park seats and the woodwork of the shelter and that he had obtained the following tenders:-

Alfred Flavell	£34.. 0..0
J. Farrow	29..17..6
J.C. Smith	31..12..0
W. Jones	34..10..0

Resolved that the tender of Mr J. Farrow in the sum of £29.17s.6d be accepted.

14th December 1904 – KN&N UDC Baths, Parks and Cemeteries Committee, and reported on
5th January 1905 – Minute of KN&N UDC, and on
7th January 1905 – South Birmingham Chronicle

The Superintendent reported that he had received from the order of Mr William Gibbins, 3 doz forest trees (18 limes and 18 elms) and had planted the same in place of the horse chestnuts up the centre drive of the park.

Resolved that the best thanks of the Council be accorded to Mr William Gibbins for his generous gift.

The Chairman reported that he had authorised the Superintendent of the Park to commence the work of planting out these new trees, and it was resolved that his action be approved.

The Surveyor reported that as instructed by the Committee orders had been given to the contractors for the painting of the Park, and the alterations to the shelter, etc.

Chapter 10

1905

11th January 1905 – KN&N UDC Baths, Parks and Cemeteries Committee

The Surveyor reported that the work in connection with the painting of the Lodge was well in hand and that the alterations to the shelter and the construction of the seats was being proceeded with.

8th February 1905 – KN&N UDC Baths, Parks and Cemeteries Committee

The Park Superintendent reported that he had forwarded 270 shrubs to Lodge Hill Cemetery, that the cricket pitch would shortly be completed, and that the trees given by Mr W. Gibbins had been planted along the central drive.

Resolved that the report be approved.

8th March 1905 – KN&N UDC Baths, Parks and Cemeteries Committee

The Park Keeper reported that he had planted five plane trees provided for High Street Selly Oak and had attended to the trees from Griffins Hill to Bournbrook. He also reported that he had selected and utilised the most suitable of the tree guards lying at the Selly Oak Depot.

Resolved that the Surveyor be authorised to continue the assistance at present being rendered to the Park Keeper for such period as he may consider necessary.

29th April 1905 – South Birmingham Chronicle

Death of Mrs. Thomas Gibbins[49]

Members of the Society of Friends in Birmingham have, through the death of Mrs. Thomas Gibbins, of Carpenter Road, Edgbaston, lost one of the oldest and most noteworthy persons belonging to their number. Mrs. Gibbins, who was in her ninety-fifth year, was the last survivor of the elder generation of the Cadbury family. Richard Tapper Cadbury, from whom the Birmingham and Philadelphia families of this name have sprung, came to Birmingham from Torquay over a hundred years ago, and set up in business as a draper in Bull Street. By his wife, Elizabeth Head, of Ipswich, he had four sons and four daughters. The sons were Benjamin Head

---

[49] There is further on this in Appendix I.

Cadbury (father of the present Mr. Joel Cadbury and the late Miss Hannah Cadbury), John Cadbury (father of the late Richard Cadbury and the present George Cadbury), Joel Cadbury (who went to the United States and founded the family of Philadelphia Cadburys), and James Cadbury. The daughters were Mrs. Sarah Barrow, of Lancaster (mother of the late Alderman R.C. Barrow); Maria and Ann Cadbury, who died unmarried; and Emma Joel Cadbury, who married the late Mr. Thomas Gibbins, the founder of the Birmingham Battery Company, and whose death we now record as having taken place at her residence, 10, Carpenter Road on Wednesday.

Mrs. Gibbins took a deep interest in the various organisations connected with the Society of Friends, and was a liberal supporter of charitable undertakings. A few years ago Mrs. Gibbins and her four sons, of whom three are connected with the Birmingham Battery Company, gave to the King's Norton District Council a recreation ground at Lodge Hill, for the benefit of the inhabitants of Selly Oak. Having lived in five reigns, and retained her memory for a remarkable long period, Mrs. Gibbins was able to relate many interesting reminiscences. She was born in Bull Street, when Birmingham was comparatively a small town. When she was only a year old her parents went to live out in the country – where Islington Row now stands. At that time Broad Street was fronted by gentlemen's houses standing in their own grounds, of which the Children's Hospital is the last relic. Mrs. Gibbins remembered hearing of the death of King George III, and seeing some illuminations in celebration of the battle of Waterloo. Throughout her life she dressed in the quaint style of a Quaker lady, and up to a few years ago she was a familiar figure in Edgbaston, being often seen in her carriage. Only a year ago she was able to go out in a Bath chair, and it was not till October last year that the infirmities of age compelled her to take to her bed. Her kindly disposition won her a large circle of friends. Of her seven children, four sons and one daughter survive her. The funeral will take place at Witton Cemetery today (Saturday), at 2.30.

10th May 1905 – KN&N UDC Baths, Parks and Cemeteries Committee

The Park Superintendent reported that the cricket ground would be ready for use about June 1st.
Resolved that the Park Superintendent be instructed that the cricket pitch in the Park is in future to be used only by children of school age and that a notice board to this effect be placed in the Park.

14th June 1905 – KN&N UDC Baths, Parks and Cemeteries Committee, and reported on
5th July 1905 – Minute of KN&N UDC

<u>Selly Oak Brass Band</u> The Clerk read a letter from Mr. H. White of 78 Lottie Road, Selly Oak asking for permission to play in the Selly Oak Park as in previous years and asking whether the Committee could see their way to help the band financially.

Resolved that permission be given to play in the Park as heretofore and that the Clerk be instructed to report to this Committee as to the legality of their providing music for the use of the band.

Selly Oak and Bournbrook Children's Festival The Chairman reported that after consultation with the Clerk he had granted permission for the Committee of the Selly Oak and Bournbrook Children's Festival to have the use of the Selly Oak Park on Wednesday 26th July the occasion of their annual festival.
Resolved that the action of the Chairman be approved.

14th July 1905 – KN&N UDC Baths, Parks and Cemeteries Committee

The Clerk reported that he had considered the point raised at the last meeting and was of opinion that the Council had no power to make any contribution towards the expenses of the Selly Oak Brass Band or to purchase music for their use. After some discussion it was resolved that the Band be allowed to place a sheet at the entrance to the Park to receive voluntary contributions in a similar way to that prevailing in certain of the Parks belonging to the Birmingham Corporation.

22nd July 1905 – Birmingham News

Notes and Jottings

Arrangements for the Selly Oak Children's festival, which takes place next Wednesday, are now practically complete, and given good weather the children should have a very joyous time of it.
There is, however, still need for further financial support.
Everybody ought to contribute to so worthy an object. The financial problem always acute in connection with this old hardy annual would never exist if the townspeople would act on the "every penny helps" principle.
It is hoped that the tradesmen and residents will show their interest in the event by decorating their premises with flags, flowers, etc., and the loan of vehicles to convey the younger children to the park in is desired and specially invited.

29th July 1905 – Birmingham News

Selly Oak and Bournbrook Children's Fete
A Great Success

The Selly Oak and Bournbrook children's red letter day of the year was reached on Wednesday, when the fete organised for their pleasure was held. The institution is not one which in recent years has altogether found favour with the weather clerk – perhaps he weeps in sorrow at the bad feeling which some who do no work on behalf of the festival exhibit towards those who give their days and nights to it. Last

10. 1905

The Fire Brigade may have been a normal part of the procession of the annual Selly Oak and Bournbrook Children's Festival. It definitely led the procession to the Park in 1906. (Photograph kindly supplied by Wendy Pearson - Reproduced from a Christmas card she had received from local councillors).

Whilst this is not of a Park event, it does show how the Children's Festival Maypole may have looked. Taken from Dowling, G., Giles, B.A. and Hayfield, C. (1987), "Selly Oak Past and Present: a photographic survey of a Birmingham suburb". University of Birmingham.

year the fete had to be postponed because of Nature's watery displeasure, and on Wednesday all was not sunshine. Days of brilliant weather had preceded it, but gloomy leaden skies where there to chill the hopes of all on the festival morning. Happily, however, fears were not realised, and after the deity of the weather had in one heavy shower early in the afternoon spent his vexation at the churlishness of those who took up an attitude of passive resistance towards the children's high holiday, he closed the sluices of nature until after the little ones were snugly abed experiencing anew the day's pleasures in their dreams; and beamed his kindliest approval upon the work of those who forgot themselves and laboured only for the happiness of others. These gentlemen are amongst those who have learned life's great lesson that to be happy is to make others happy, and not for a moment would they at the end of a long tiring day have changed places with those who sourly held aloof from this joyous festivity, when the contact with blithesome innocent childhood made the old ones more young in spirit.

The family that had to be entertained this year numbered 3,600, and they came from their respective schools in squadrons, brave in their holiday attire, and singing, laughing and flag-flaunting in the tumultuousness of their gaiety, to the appointed tryst in Dawlish Road, where the festival procession was organised. As the factory bulls hoarsely proclaimed the arrival of the dinner hour, the drum commenced to beat, the Selly Oak Brass Band struck up and as pretty a procession of youngsters as ever challenged the judgment of a misanthrope, moved off. No attempt had been made to produce a spectacular show by the offer of part of the children's money in prizes for decorative exhibitions, but there was nevertheless no suggestion of sombreness in the procession. Bright, gay colours abounded in the children's dresses, and a charmingly chaste effect was produced by the uniform white attire of the Maypole dancers, set off in the case of the girls with garlanded hair. There were two sets of dancers, the one from Raddle Barn Lane Council School – and here it may be mentioned that the boys were dressed in imitation Pierrot costumes – and the other from St. Edward's Catholic School. The latter were in miniature in every respect. The whole, Maypole as well, was small enough to be comfortably ensconced in a vehicle, with the tiny tots of dancers gathered around in the midst of an opulence of decorative colour. Her Majesty, the baby May queen, seated in the lap of the instructress, won everybody's heart. The procession was three-quarters of a mile long, and took an hour to reach Selly Oak Park, where, as in former years the fete was held. Sports, Maypole dances, riding the hobby horses, shooting for goal with the captive football, and watching cruel Punch punish Judy and Toby, and eventually suffer for his misdeeds, brought tea time quickly enough. Here it was that the services so freely rendered this year by the school teachers were most valuably exercised. The children were ranged together according to their schools, and the presence of the teachers secured perfect orderliness. Tea was a splendid illustration of a "disappearing industry", but it would form no fit subject for the tariff reformer's melancholy muse. In his grotesque mythology the people starve; at Selly Oak Park the children fattened upon what they fed, and there were some cases in which we would be prepared to swear an affidavit that the process was visible to the naked eye. Seven hundred and twenty pounds of bread, 168lbs. of butter, and over 800lbs. of cake, all went one way, swilled thereto by a river of tea, brewed with 40lbs. of best black leaves, and made "scrumptious" to the young hopefuls' discriminating palates with the aid of 224 lbs of sugar and 216 pints of milk – from the cow and not from Switzerland. At the finish there was not amongst the whole of that great family so much as a solitary Oliver Twist; nay, one could not be created, even by coercion. They had exorcised even his ghost. Need it be said also that the committee's provision store was like Old Mother Hubbard's cupboard – bare! After tea came a repetition of the relaxations previously indulged in, with the addition of cake walk competitions (for a parasol, given by Councillor Harbun), and singing and recitation competitions. Mr. B.C. Bednall, Mr. A. Wood, Mrs. Darling and Mrs. Appleton had these latter in hand, and in the words of the song "they did have a lively time". But so, for the matter of that, did those who supervised the races, and amongst whom were Messrs. G. Shann and F. Darling. Figure balloons were sent up, and a noticeable feature of the elephants was that they would persist on rising rear tail first – to the great glee of the youngsters. Chocolates, the gift of Messrs. Cadbury Bros., were amongst the other comestibles appreciatively committed to the interior. The fete closed as evening began to blacken out the light with a pleasing little function, in which the arduous work of the maypole dance trainers was acknowledged. Miss Pritchett (who trained the Raddle Barn School dancers) received a gold brooch, the gift of Councillor Harbun, and her assistant, Mrs. Quinton, received a silver brooch, the gift of Mr. W.C. Clarke. Miss Beasley, who instructed the St. Edward's School dancers, received a silver brooch with gold centre, the gift of Mr. C.A. Lucas. The fete was a financial as well as social success, and in addition a deficit from last year had been cleared off. Amongst the large number of workers to whom thanks are due omission can hardly be made of Messrs. Nunn (chairman of the committee), Councillor Harbun (vice-chairman), F. Wilson (treasurer), C.A. Lucas (general secretary), A. Wood (assistant secretary), I. Underwood and W.C. Clarke (chairman and secretary respectively of the Finance sub-committee), C.H. Harbun and J. Kesterton (Procession Sub-committee), W.C. Clarke and S. Mackintosh (Fields and Sports Sub-Committee), Councillor Thomas, A. Gittins, W.C. Clarke, I. Underwood, W. Humphreys, T.A. Cole and J. Roberts (Catering Sub-Committee). The prizes won by the scholars at Raddlebarn School were presented on Friday morning by Councillor Thomas, who reminded the scholars that they would soon be able to engage in a new sport, as the baths would be open, he hoped, before next year. Amid cheers he promised a prize for the boy or girl who swam three lengths of the bath in quickest time within six months of their opening, and also with the aid of friends would offer a shield or cup for competition annually by a team representative of each school in Selly Oak and Bournbrook.

13th September 1905 – KN&N UDC Baths, Parks and Cemeteries Committee

The Superintendent reported that on the occasion of the Selly Oak and Bournbrook Children's Festival no damage whatever had been done to the Park. Upon his report it was resolved:

That children under the age of 14 years be allowed to play football in the Park

That any surplus shrubs and trees be removed to the other Recreation Grounds as occasion may require

That the previous minute of the Committee as to the laying out of a Bowling Green at the Park be discharged.

11th October 1905 – KN&N UDC Baths, Parks and Cemeteries Committee

The Park Superintendent reported that he required a new uniform and requested that he might be allowed to purchase a coat, vest and two pairs of trousers: he also asked that an allowance of £2 might be made for the purchase of bulbs for planting in the Park.

Resolved that these requests be granted subject to the things purchased being to the satisfaction of the Chairman.

18th November 1905 – KN&N UDC Baths, Parks and Cemeteries Committee

Resolved that the boys of the Selly Oak School be allowed to play football in the Selly Oak Park on Saturday mornings subject to the supervision of the Superintendent.

Chapter 11

1906

10th January 1906 – KN&N UDC Baths, Parks and Cemeteries Committee

<u>Selly Oak Park – Trees in Streets</u> The Supt of the Selly Oak Park reported that he had given the whole of the trees in Selly Oak Village very careful attention and that with the exception of a few old limes that required replacing with planes, all were doing well; he also called attention to the old oak in Oak Tree Lane which he stated should have all the dead wood taken from it, and remarked that if the Committee intended planting new trees this year, operations should be commenced as soon as possible. He also reported that the Park was in very good order at the present time. Resolved that the Surveyor be authorised to give the Superintendent instructions to do such work in such streets as he should consider advisable.

Resolved also that the report of the Superintendent be approved.

14th February 1906 – KN&N UDC Baths, Parks and Cemeteries Committee

The Superintendent drew the attention of the Committee to the desirability of having gas laid on to the lodge and fittings supplied in order that he might have use of the same.

Resolved that the Surveyor be instructed to carry out the necessary work, the fittings in connection therewith to be simple in character.

<u>Trees in Streets</u> The Clerk reported that the Public Works Committee had agreed to the recommendation of this Committee that the control and management of trees in streets for the maintenance of which the Public Works Committee were responsible should be vested in this Committee subject in the case of new streets to the Public Works Committee approving of the planting of trees therein and that a resolution to this effect had been passed by the Council.

A letter was read from Mr W.B. Parker of Forest Road, Moseley with regard to the lopping of trees in Forest Road, which was referred to the Superintendent of the Brandwood End Cemetery.

Resolved that Mr Grimwood be requested to report as to the condition of trees in highways in the parish of Kings Norton and that the Superintendent of the Selly Oak Park be requested to report in a similar manner as to the trees in the parish of Northfield.

Application for increase of salary An application from Mr Finch the Park Keeper's assistant at Selly Oak for an increase of his wages was referred to the Surveyor for him to report thereon to the next meeting.

7th March 1906 – Minute of KN&N UDC

Mr. Councillor Oswald presented the following report of the Baths, Parks and Cemeteries Committee.

>Your Committee beg to report:-

>4 Selly Oak Park

>That they have given instructions for a supply of gas to be laid on to the Lodge at Selly Oak park, and for the necessary pipes and fittings to be fixed.

It was moved by Mr. Councillor Oswald, seconded Mr. Councillor Olivieri, and resolved (minute 232), that the report of the Baths, Parks and Cemeteries Committee be approved and adopted.

11th April 1906 – KN&N UDC Baths, Parks and Cemeteries Committee

The Superintendent presented a list of seeds required for the ensuing season and it was resolved that the same be approved and that the Superintendent be authorised to purchase the seeds accordingly.

9th May 1906 – KN&N UDC Baths, Parks and Cemeteries Committee

The Superintendent of the Park reported in reference to wire fencing and protections required at the Park and it was resolved that the Surveyor be directed to submit an estimate of the cost to the next meeting.
   Resolved also that the Surveyor be authorised to purchase twenty loads of sand for use in the Park at the price of 6d per load plus the cartage.

7th July 1906 – Birmingham News

Letters to the Editor
Selly Oak Park Band Performances

To the Editor
Dear Sir, – I have received a letter from Mr. William Gibbins kindly offering to give £1 10s. towards each of three performances by special bands in Selly Oak Park in July, August and September. As I think this is a very commendable suggestion I should be very pleased to acknowledge the receipt of any further donations for the same

purpose which anyone interested in this matter cares to send. I need not say how great a boon such performances would be to the working people in Selly Oak and district. Unfortunately the Council cannot provide the funds for this purpose from the rates, and therefore we must depend on voluntary subscriptions. Yours truly;

George Shann
Chairman of the Baths and Parks Committee

34, Linden Road, Bournville,
July 3rd, 1906.

14th July 1906 – Birmingham News

Letters to the Editor
Selly Oak Park Band Performances

To the Editor
Dear Sir, – I was very pleased to see the letter from Councillor Shann in last Saturday's "News", and hope his appeal will meet with a generous response.

Any scheme which can bring variety, more sunshine, and more happiness into the grey, monotonous lives of the majority of Selly Oak and Bournbrook people should be welcomed with open arms.

I shall be pleased to assist Councillor Shann in arranging the concerts, and feel sure he will find plenty of willing workers in such a cause.

I hope a concert will be given at the Bournbrook end of the district. No doubt a field for the purpose can be readily secured. – Yours faithfully,

Frank B. Darling.

39, Maple Road, Bournville, July 11, 1906

Children's Festival Selly Oak, July 18, 1906. Copy of a postcard held in Archive & Heritage Section, Birmingham Central Library Ref: MS 1074/60.

21st July 1906 – Birmingham News

Notes of the Week

The committee and all concerned are to be heartily congratulated on the unequivocal success which attended the Selly Oak and Bournbrook Children's Festival on Wednesday. The festival has become in very deed and truth one of the great local events of the year. All sections of the community readily co-operate in the effort to make the day one of undivided pleasure to the little ones, and it is easy to imagine that in such congenial work the greater the success achieved the greater the feeling of satisfaction alike among the workers and subscribers. It is an altogether excellent thing for the district that for once a year at any rate all classes should be brought into friendly association by a movement of this kind, and in the interests of the children we trust that the enthusiasm manifested in the festival will not be allowed to wane.

Selly Oak and Bournbrook Children's Festival

Without doubt the most interesting and successful event of the season was that of the children's festival which was celebrated in glorious weather on Wednesday last at Selly Oak Park. The treat – one of the oldest local institutions – is always looked forward to with great expectation both on the part of children and parents, but never on any former occasion has the whole thing passed off with so much satisfaction to all concerned as the event on Wednesday.

The scholars of the various schools in the district assembled at 12.30, and were marshalled into processional order in Dawlish Road. The procession, headed by the Selly Oak Fire Brigade, under the command of Captain Crump, started soon after one o'clock, and paraded the main street to the park. The procession was well regulated, and was made up as follows:- Fire Brigade, Representatives from Committee, Boys of the Bournville Gymnastic Troupe, under the direction of Mr. Hackett (instructor), the Selly Oak Brass Band (Bandmaster, Mr. H. White), the Junior Maypole Dancers of St. Edward's Schools, under the care of Miss D'Arcy (head teacher), the Hubert Road School Boys, under the Headmaster, Mr. Humphreys, Dawlish Road Infants, St. Stephen's, Fasoda Road, Dawlish Road Boys, St. Mary's Church School (Miss Peck), Raddle Barn Lane Schools, under direction of Mr. J. Poppiette, Mrs. Quinton and Miss Clulee. In connection with the school was the senior troupe of Maypole Dancers in full regalia. Non-scholars. Mr. Bull, Bournville, under Mr. Fielden. The local Ambulance Corps was in attendance. The younger scholars were conveyed in vehicles kindly lent by Messrs. Brickwood, G.R. Hinton, C.W. Pember, Chillingsworth, Wilson and Sons, C.A. Lucas, — Hyde, Greenwood and Page, Cook, Monk Bros., E.F. Smith, Jos. Hinde, and others.

Altogether the procession, which was composed of nearly 4,000 scholars and teachers, formed a most imposing spectacle, reaching the whole length of the village. On reaching the Park gates every scholar upon entering was presented with a bar of milk chocolate, the gift of Messrs. Cadbury Bros., Ltd., of Bournville, which was much appreciated by the youngsters. A large and varied programme of amusements was arranged by the committee, consisting of maypole dances, sports, Punch and Judy, roundabouts, etc. Tea was commenced at 4.30. The committee adopted the plan of putting up each scholar's supply of bread and butter and cake in paper bags, so as to ensure each scholar getting his and her full allowance, and tea was handed round by a large staff of willing workers. During the tea a telegram was received from Councillor J.A. Thomas, who is just recovering from a serious illness, "Congratulating the committee on having a fine day, and hoping everyone will thoroughly enjoy themselves, with kind remembrances." The following reply was sent to Mr. Thomas: "Committee reciprocate kind remembrances for today's festival. All going well. – H.J. Nunn, chairman." At 5.30 the Park gates were thrown open to the general public, when the large concourse of people who had patiently awaited admission passed into the grounds. By this time the various attractions were in full swing. The performances of the maypole dancers, junior and senior, came in for special attention by the crowd of appreciative admirers who frequently applauded the various moves. The junior (St. Edward's Schools) troupe, being quite little dots, presented a remarkable spectacle in their various dances, the boys being dressed as little Jack Tars in full dress, while the little maidens were in various coloured dresses, they acquitted themselves well, and much credit is due to Miss D'Arcy and Miss Beasley, their trainers.

The senior troupe of maypole dancers, consisting of upwards of 70 performers, also gave a perfect display; their beautiful dresses in most cases were made by or under the direction of Mrs. Quinton, their trainer, to whom great praise was due for the very efficient manner in which they performed their various set pieces. Councillor Harbun and Mr. Frank Wilson presented a gold brooch to Mrs. Quinton and Miss D'Arcy respectively, as a slight appreciation of the labours involved. Mr. Hackett's troupe of 50 boys gave a very pleasing gymnastic display, which was well done and much admired. The trial heats of the races were run off at the various schools previous to the day of the festival, the finals only being run at the park. The prizes gained will be distributed at the respective schools on Friday morning, July 27th. Each scholar was provided with a ticket for a free ride on the roundabouts. The various entertainments were kept up until dusk, and dancing was indulged in to the strains of the Selly Oak Band. After the scholars had finished tea they resumed the sports while the teachers, committee, and helpers partook of tea provided in the committee's marquee. By the kindness of Mr. Frank Wilson a good supply of strawberries and cream was provided at the tables: – Mr. H.J. Nunn, chairman, moved a vote of thanks to teachers for their kind assistance in cutting up and arranging the supplies for their various contingents, this being seconded by Councillor Spencer, who delivered some well chosen remarks on the work and success of the day. The thanks of the committee were also given to Mr. T. Fernihough and Mr. F.W. Bickle for their generous gifts of new milk. At 9.15 the band played off the park, and thus ended the most enjoyable day of the year. We understand that the Raddle Barn Lane Maypole Troupe have kindly consented to repeat their performance at Selly Oak Park on Wednesday evening next.

Letters to the Editor
Selly Oak and Bournbrook Children's Festival

To the Editor

Sir, – The officers and committee of the Selly Oak and Bournbrook Children's Festival beg to tender their sincere thanks to all who have so generously given of their time, services and money, to bring about such a happy and enjoyable day to the many festival children on Wednesday last.

H.J. Nunn (Chairman)
C. Harbun (Vice-Chairman)
F. Wilson (Hon. Treasurer)
C.A. Lucas (Hon. Secretary)

Weoley Park Road, Selly Oak
July 19th, 1906

28th July 1906 – Birmingham news

Notes and Jottings

At a concert given by the Selly Oak band at the Park on Wednesday evening a performance was given by the Raddle Barn maypole dancers who appeared at the children's festival on the previous Wednesday, and for whose charming performance Mrs. Quinton (their trainer) is chiefly to be thanked.

11th August 1906 – Birmingham News

Selly Oak and Bournbrook
Selly Oak Park Band Performances

As a result of Councillor Shann's appeal and the subscriptions of Mr. Gibbins and others a fund sufficient to provide a first class band performance in Selly Oak Park has been raised. The famous band of the Royal Staffordshire Blues has been engaged for two concerts on Saturday, September 1st. The band will play in the afternoon and again in the evening. The Educational Committee of the Progressive Association have the arrangements in hand, and rely on all parties co-operating in such an excellent movement. The concerts will be free, but collecting sheets will be fixed in the park.

18th August 1906 – Birmingham News

Notes and Jottings

The Royal Staffordshire Blues band will give first-class concerts in Selly Oak Park on Saturday, Sept. 1st, in the afternoon at 3.15, and in the evening at 6 o'clock.

Admission is free. The sheets will be spread for voluntary contributions to clear expenses. The concerts are experimental, and if properly supported will be continued. They are given under the auspices of the Progressive Association.

Letters to the Editor
The Selly Oak Band

To the Editor

Sir, – I have been talking to Mr. White, our head bandmaster, about the concert on September 1st. He told me he had talked the matter over with Mr. Shann. Mr. White told me the Selly Oak band had played in the park about seven years free. Councillor Shann and committee have not done their business very courteously. They knew the Selly Oak band were in the Park weekly. I think it would have been more respectful if they had gone up to the Park and explained. I think it is a great insult to our band which comes out at all times for a good cause. In conclusion, I hope the Selly Oak people will show they don't approve of the way in which they have done their work for September 1st. – Yours truly, GS

8th September 1906 – Birmingham News

Selly Oak and Bournbrook
Music in the Parks

On Saturday last two performances were given at Selly Oak Park by the Royal Staffordshire Blues Band, under the direction of Mr. A. Roberts, bandmaster. The sultry weather affected the attendance at the afternoon performance, it being but meagre, but in the evening when the temperature had fallen a little and when also more people were free from other calls upon their time, the attendance was gratifyingly large, and showed that the enterprise of the promoters of the performances was well conceived. We sincerely hope that the Progressive Association Education Committee, under whose auspices the band appeared, will be able to arrange other similar concerts. Mr. Shann and his friends, with whom the idea of providing such attractions for the benefit of the local public originated, will assuredly have the thanks of all who had the pleasure of listening to the excellent music given in the park last Saturday. The Midlands is rich in good bands, the engagement of many of which would not involve so heavy a financial obligation as did the initial venture, and we doubt not that the local music-loving public could have the pleasure of hearing them by showing the appreciation of the committee's efforts, by doing their best to make the concerts self-supporting. The programmes given by the Staffordshire band on Saturday are worthy of reproducing to those who were not present and give an idea of the kind of music performed, and we have only to add that the technique was excellent. In the afternoon the items were:- March, "Royal Staffordshire Blues"; overture, "Il Barbiere de Seville"; musical farce; waltz, "Rossini"; selection on popular songs and dances; suite (a) "Buds" (b) "Zephyr" (c) "Centifolie"; humorous sketch, "Alabama"; "L'Cordiale Entente", "A Dream Picture"; descriptive, "A Hunting Scene". In the evening the programme was: – Overture, "Rosamunde"; cotillion, "Princess Charming"; "Souvenir di Richard Wagner" (including movements from Rienzi, Tannhauser, Flying Dutchman, Lohengrin, etc.); piccolo solo, "Little Robin", W. Barnes; musical comedy, "The Messenger Boy"; descriptive, "Motor ride"; waltz, "Claribel"; excursion, "To Blackpool"; serenade, "In the Woods"; gallop, "Express".

Notes and Jottings

The flower beds in Selly Oak Park are looking exceedingly well just now.

10th October 1906 – KN&N UDC Baths, Parks and Cemeteries Committee

The Superintendent in his report drew the attention of the Committee to the following requirements:
a) Greenhouse 25 feet by 12 feet to provide for 4000-5000 plants with potting shed attached
b) Standards and wire for protection of beds
c) Bulbs for planting – estimated cost £2 to £2.10s
d) The planting of trees for the protection of the shelter from wind and rain.

Resolved that requirements b) and c) be approved; that the question of planting trees for the protection of the shelter be referred to a Sub-committee consisting of Councillors Shann, Fryer, Harbun and Shephard; and that the consideration of the advisability of erecting a greenhouse be also referred to such Sub-committee with power to instruct the Surveyor to obtain estimates for carrying out the work for consideration by this Committee.

13th October 1906 – Birmingham News

Selly Oak and Bournbrook
Selly Oak and Bournbrook Children's Festival Committee

The winding up meeting of the committee that arranged this year's Selly Oak and Bournbrook Children's festival was held at the Institute on Wednesday night, Councillor C.H. Harbun presiding in the absence of Mr. H.J. Nunn. ....

(Further on in a long report:)

They recommended that £1 6s. 0d. be paid to the Park Keeper and his assistants for the work they rendered. ....

29th October 1906 – KN&N UDC Baths, Parks and Cemeteries Committee

Upon the report of the Sub-Committee it was resolved that the Surveyor be authorised to submit to the next meeting an estimate of the cost of erecting a greenhouse and potting shed in the Park.
    Also a similar estimate in respect of erecting a shelter.
    The Sub-Committee also recommended that as regards the cost of this shelter Mr. Thomas Gibbins be approached and asked if he would be willing to defray the same.

14th November 1906 – KN&N UDC Baths, Parks and Cemeteries Committee

The Superintendent reported as to the condition of certain rooms in the lodge and the necessity for whitewashing and papering the same.
    Resolved that the Surveyor be authorised to carry out any cleaning or repairs at the lodge that he may consider necessary.
    Resolved also that the question of enlarging the pantry at the lodge and enclosing a rubbish heap in the Park be referred to Councillors Shann and Shephard and the Surveyor.

12th December 1906 – KN&N UDC Baths, Parks and Cemeteries Committee

Resolved that the Surveyor report to the next meeting as to the condition of the Lodge.

Chapter 12

1907

6th February 1907

Mr. Councillor Shann presented the following report of the Baths, Parks and Cemeteries Committee (minute dated 22nd January 1907)

Your Committee beg to report:-

4 Selly Oak Park

That they have considered the following tenders for erecting a pantry at the Superintendent's lodge at the Selly Oak Park:

T. Loud & Son, Selly Oak	£17 0 0
T. A. Cole & Son, Selly Oak	17 15 0
G.T. Stopher, Kings Heath	19 3 9

and they have accepted the estimate of T. Loud & Son.

It was moved by Mr. Councillor Shann, seconded Mr. Councillor W.H. Davison, and resolved (minute 59), that the report of the Baths, Parks and Cemeteries Committee as amended (nb amendment was nothing to do with the Park) be approved and adopted.

13th March 1907 – KN&N UDC Baths, Parks and Cemeteries Committee

Planting of Shrubs at Libraries The Clerk read a report from the Superintendent of the Selly Oak Park as to the planting which he had carried out at the various libraries in the district and at the Bournbrook and Muntz[50] recreation grounds.

Resolved that the Superintendent be instructed to plant a golden privet hedge at the Northfield Library.

---

[50] This was a recreation ground in Stirchley named after the donor of the land. Mr J. E. Muntz opened the Recreation Ground on Friday, 7 June 1907 at 5pm.

13th April 1907 – Birmingham News

Selly Oak and Bournbrook

Selly Oak Horticultural Society – This year's exhibition of the Selly Oak, Bournbrook, and District Horticultural Association takes place on Saturday, July 27, at Selly Oak Park, and the prize schedule has just been issued to the members and others interested. Ninety-nine classes are scheduled, for gentlemen's gardeners, amateurs, cottagers, ladies interested in artistic table decoration with flowers and foliage, beekeepers, and the children (for whom the usual wild flower classes are provided), and in nearly all at least three prizes are offered. In some classes there are four, and in others five awards to be gained. The officers for the year are as follows: – President, Councillor J.S. Nettlefold, J.P.; ex-president, Mr. R.E. Bull; hon. treasurer, Mr. C.A. Lucas, Selly Oak; hon. auditors, Messrs. W.H. Goodwin, A.C.A., and L.P. Appleton; hon. secretary, Mr. S. McIntosh; committee, Messrs. E. Fuller (chairman), J. Butt, C.G. Compton, J.T. Clark, J. Dudley, F.B. Darling, R.E. Fowler, jun., A.T. Gittins, C. Green, C.B. Greenwood, J. Hardy, J. Hartwell, G. Kirk, C. Lock, J. Mansfield, H.J. Nunn, J. Pickett, S. Pickstone, W. Rice, R. Stone, W. Shayler, J. Thomas and Councillor F. Wilson. With good weather this year's show should be a successful function from all points of view.

15th May 1907 – KN&N UDC Baths, Parks and Cemeteries Committee

The Committee considered two applications for the use of the Selly Oak Park, one from the Selly Oak, Bournbrook and District Horticultural Society to hold their annual exhibition on Saturday the 27th July 1907, and one from the Secretary of the Selly Oak and Bournbrook Children's Festival to hold the Festival on Wednesday the 17th July 1907.

Resolved that the applications be granted subject to the applicants undertaking to make good any damage which may be thereby occasioned.

<u>Cricket Pitches</u> The Chairman read a letter from the Secretary to the Selly Oak Wesleyan Sunday School as to the allocation of cricket pitches in the Selly Oak Park to different schools.

Resolved that the matter be referred to the Baths Sub-Committee.

18th May 1907 – Birmingham News

Village Gossip

Parkless Kings Heath – With the advent of summer the lack of a park for Kings Heath again becomes painfully prominent. Selly Oak has its park, Stirchley has this week come into the possession of twelve and a half acres of public ground, but Kings Heath, as usual, is all forlorn. Meanwhile the children play in the bye-roads, and the youths disport themselves at cricket on the waste ground near Kings Heath Institute. The matter was on the agenda of Wednesday's meeting of the Ratepayers' Association, but no definite information was forthcoming, and it was resolved to postpone the question till a meeting in June, when it is hoped Councillor Coley, who has taken some interest in the proposal, will be able to attend and explain what has and what can be done to achieve the desired end.

Selly Oak and Bournbrook

Children's Festival Arrangements – On Tuesday night a well attended meeting was held at the Selly Oak Institute to receive the report and balance-sheet of the annual children's festival, to consider the advisability of holding a festival this year, and to make all necessary arrangements.

(At the end of a long report:)

The date fixed for the festival, which is to be held at Selly Oak Park, was Wednesday, July 27, and a resolution was passed that the clergy and teachers of the district should be placed on the committee.

28th May 1907 – KN&N UDC Baths, Parks and Cemeteries Committee

<u>Allocation of Cricket Pitches</u> Resolved that the matter be left in the hands of Councillors Harbun and Shann with power to act in the meantime.

12th June 1907 – KN&N UDC Baths, Parks and Cemeteries Committee

The Superintendent submitted a report setting out the suggestions as to the times of opening the various recreation grounds and as to the staff at the recreation grounds.
    Resolved that the matters contained in the report be referred to the Baths Sub-Committee.

19th June 1907 – KN&N UDC Baths, Parks and Cemeteries Committee

The Superintendent of the Selly Oak Park submitted a report suggesting certain alterations in the staff for the various parks and recreation grounds belonging to the Council. After some discussion it was resolved that the Chairman be requested to formulate a scheme in conjunction with the Superintendent of the Selly Oak Park and to submit the same to the next meeting of the Baths, Parks and Cemeteries Committee.
    The Superintendent also made certain suggestions as to the wages of the present staff and it was resolved that the consideration of these matters be left to the Baths, Parks and Cemeteries Committee.

Resolved also that this Committee cannot see their way to recommend an increase in Mr J.T. Horton's salary.

Resolved also to recommend that in the event of the Baths, Parks and Cemeteries Committee approving of a fixed wage being paid to the employees at the parks and recreation grounds, the wages of each employee be 23/- per week.

Applications for use of Selly Oak Park The Chairman submitted several applications for the use of Selly Oak Park for entertainments by Pierrot troupes.

Resolved to recommend that Pierrot troupes be permitted to give entertainments in the Selly Oak Park, subject to the entertainments being entirely at their own expense.

10th July 1907 – KN&N UDC Baths, Parks and Cemeteries Committee

Staff at Selly Oak Park and Recreation Grounds The Chairman reported that in conjunction with the Superintendent of the Selly Oak Park he had prepared a scheme for the re-arrangement of the staff at the Selly Oak Park and the recreation grounds. After some discussion it was resolved that the consideration of the matter be deferred and that the Chairman be requested to make further enquiries and to report fully to the next meeting of the Committee.

Allocation of Cricket Pitches The Chairman reported that with Mr Councillor Harbun he had visited the Selly Oak Park with a view to ascertaining if it would be possible to allocate cricket pitches to the various schools and they were of the opinion that it would be possible to allocate these pitches and still leave sufficient room for the recreation of other children. Resolved that three pitches be allocated subject to regulations to be drawn up by the Clerk and that the Clerk be instructed to write to the Corporation of Birmingham requesting them to forward a copy of the regulations made by them in respect to cricket pitches in their parks.

Applications for use of Selly Oak Park and Recreation Grounds for entertainments Resolved that the Clerk be instructed to write to all applicants desiring to give entertainments in the Selly Oak Park and Recreation Grounds granting them permission to do so, but informing them that the entertainments must be entirely at their own expense.

The Heydays Of Selly Oak Park

20th July 1907 – Birmingham News

Public Announcements
SELLY OAK AND BOURNBROOK FLOWER SHOW,
SATURDAY NEXT, JULY 27th, 1907,
IN SELLY OAK PARK.
(Two minutes from Tram Terminus)
ROYAL STAFFORDSHIRE BLUES BAND,
BOURNBROOK CONCERT PARTY
ROYAL ENSIGN CADETS
and other attractions, to be Opened at 2 p.m.,
by J.W. Wilson, Esq., M.P.
Admission 6d. all day. Tickets, if purchased
before the 26th, 4d. Children under 12, 2d.
DANCING after 6.30 p.m.

CHILDREN'S FESTIVALS
Charming Functions at Bournville and Selly Oak

The children's festival season is upon us, and Saturday and Wednesday last witnessed two spectacles, one at Bournville and one at Selly Oak, as charming from every point of view as one could wish to look upon. Few outside those engaged in the organisation of these events have any idea of the labour and self-sacrifice they involve. In each of the two festivals held since our last issue £100 would hardly have honoured the labour bill, if the work done by the committee and helpers had had to be paid for instead of given voluntarily and counted as a pleasure, as it was. One of the most pleasing features in the life of the community is the way in which men and women of all views and callings set aside all personal considerations when such occasions of ministering to the pleasure of children arise. Of the Bournville festival we give a photo of the maypole dancers, as well as the chairman and secretary of the Village Council, and of the Selly Oak event in addition to the two executive officials, we give a group of principals in the maypole dances.

SELLY OAK

Wednesday was the red letter day of the year for some 4,000 children living within the area of the two wards of Selly Oak. On that day they were entertained at the Park, on the occasion of the 20th annual Selly Oak and Bournbrook Children's Festival. There was a wealth of sunshine all day long, with a refreshing breeze to temper the heat, and this, together with the sense of success, must have been gratifying to every man and woman who took part, and even helped the children to a greater enjoyment of this one event in the year at which their happiness is the only thing that matters. From an early hour a host of willing workers were busy making preparation for the event. The work included the erection of marquees,

12. 1907

This is the picture of the Bournville maypole dancers, referred to in the introduction to this article – reproduced here to give an impression of the Selly Oak event.

The principals of the Selly Oak maypole dancing.

setting up trestle tables, cutting bread and butter, etc., and the hundred and one other things which an event of this sort entails. A pleasant spirit prevailed all round. The village itself, apart from the decorations, had a different appearance; the cheerfulness of the inner thoughts was reflected on faces, and hopefulness showed itself in the garments. At twelve o'clock the procession formed at the bottom of the village, the children having come in contingents from their respective schools, and headed by the Selly Oak Brass and Harborne Industrial School Bands, paraded along High Street, some being in gaily decorated vehicles and others on foot, the greater part going by Chapel Lane to their destination. The procession was most successful from the point of view of the easy and spontaneous management which Inspector Pass and his men, and the marshals, rendered, in the face of that bugbear to those in charge of such an affair, the crowd. On arrival each child was presented with a bar of chocolate (kindly given by Messrs. Cadbury Bros. Ltd.). The proceedings commenced with the running off of the non-scholars' races, those of the others having been got off the day before, under the direction of Mr. Wood and the members of the Sports Committee. This over, the event of the afternoon, the maypole dancing, was given. About 90 daintily dressed juniors, under the direction of Mrs. Barton and Miss Barton, took part. At one time it was thought that this part of the programme, which had always been one of the most attractive features, would have to be abandoned, because some of the schools were unprepared to again bear the onus of getting it up. Mrs. Barton, however, magnanimously succumbed to requests from the committee, that she would take it up, and the pitch of perfection to which the children had been brought in three weeks was truly remarkable. All the more so when one remembers the bad weather, which made rehearsals almost impossible. Amongst the children who took part, besides the "Queen", Miss Mabel Guest, were a number who attracted special notice by their fancy dresses, the vari-hued (sic) colours of which greatly added to the gorgeous colouring in the scheme generally. They were Master Alec Johnson and Miss Dorothy Evans ("Chinese Pagoda"), Miss Minnie Harper ("Spider's Web"), and Misses Ethel Webb, Lily Jones, Annie Dowler, May Lees, Lily Sheasby, Edith Harris, Grace Evans, Lizzie Brooks ("Gipsies"). The provision of tea for the huge crowd was in itself a herculean task, but this, like everything else during the day, was speedily and successfully accomplished with the aid of the committee, the teachers, and other workers. So smooth working were the arrangements, in fact, that within five minutes' time of the ringing of the bell to announce that it was tea time, every child was provided for. The sight of 4,000 children, whose bright, happy faces, showed them to be entirely contented, was one that would have brought joy to the heart of a veritable gorgon. After tea further sports were indulged in, and other diversions were provided in the form of roundabouts, swings, etc.

After the helpers had had their tea, there was a little speech-making, initiated by Councillor Harbun, who made a personal present to Mrs. Barton of a wrist bag, as a token of appreciation of her work in training the children for the maypole dances. He alluded to the fear that the committee at one time entertained of there being no such item in the programme of this year's event, and bespoke their gratefulness to Mrs. Barton for the generous way in which, singlehanded, she stepped into the breach. He had heard more than one say that they would not have done the work in value for £20. Mr. Harbun proceeded to thank the company, as chairman of the committee, for the way in which they had worked together to bring the festival to the successful issue that it had undoubtedly achieved. If it was a right thing to single out from the rest there was one name that he must mention. It was hardly necessary, however, to utter the name – they all knew whose it was – (applause) – that of their secretary, Mr. Lucas. (Renewed applause.) Any society that wished to prosper must have a good secretary; he was the axle of the wheel, and upon him the weight of the work rested. He got all the bumps, and oftentimes but very little of the praise. He felt that he must publicly thank Mr. Lucas for the way in which he had worked on behalf of the institution, which as they knew was a year or two ago in a dilapidated condition. He thanked one and all for the service they had rendered, and all would unite with him in thanking the clerk of the weather for the beautiful day he had sent them. (Laughter and applause.) – Mrs. Barton neatly expressed her thanks for the gift made to her, and Mr. Lucas acknowledged the kind words spoken to him by Mr. Harbun. Both said that the success of what they had undertaken had been the sweetest and amplest reward they could have had. The speech-making over, the bands, conducted by Mr. R.W. Kirby and Mr. H. Grainger respectively, discoursed

Councillor Harbun, chairman.　　　　　　　*Mr Lucas, secretary.*

selections of music. The public were now admitted, and the maypole dancing was repeated for their benefit. Judging by the applause they evidently appreciated it. At nine o'clock the bell, indicating that the time for closing the park had come, rang, and the children, tired with their various exertions beneath a blazing sun, but nevertheless contented, wended their way homewards. It would be impossible, even if space permitted, to give anything like all the names of those who assisted to make the event such a signal success, because there were over 130 teachers alone assisting, in addition to large numbers co-opted on the various committees. The following, however, were some of the principals: – Teachers: Mr. J.A. Poppiette and Miss Clulee (Raddle Barn Lane); Mr. W. Humphries (Hubert Road); Mr. J. Fielden (Bournville); Mr. F. Pownell (Tiverton Road); Miss Saddler (Dawlish Road); Miss Peck (St. Mary's); Miss Ward (Tiverton Road Infants); Miss D'Arcy (St. Edward's). The following ladies gave exceedingly useful service in the tea tent: – Mrs. H. Roberts, Mrs. C.H. Harbun, Mrs. Cotterell, Mrs. Usherwood, Miss Watson, Miss Harris, and Miss Russell, and others. The following members of the committee all worked hard in various ways: – Field and Sports: Messrs. W.C. Clarke, Wood, Huskisson, H. Bates and F. West. – Finance: Messrs. Wilson, Harper, Usherwood, Elwell and Gittins. – Catering: Messrs. Usherwood, Roberts, Wilson, Weekes, and Timerick. – Procession: Messrs. Greenwood, Widdup, Mansfield, Wright, West, H.J. Wride, Weekes, Knowles, Timerick and Harper. Any report of the festival would be incomplete without making special mention of Mr. C.A. Lucas, who, in his position of hon. secretary, had to cope with more work, and that at considerable personal expense, than a lot of people, even on the committee, have any idea of, and the fact the festival was a triumph of perfect organisation, is in no small way due to his capable and energetic superintendence of details. Councillor Harbum, as chairman of the committee, also contributed a big share to the work of organisation. Two other names must not be omitted – those of Mr. H. Roberts and Mr. I. Usherwood, who worked like Trojans all day long. Amongst the visitors to the festival were the Rev. L.B. Sladen (vicar of Selly Oak) and Rev. W.M. Smith.

27th July 1907 – Birmingham News

Selly Oak and Bournbrook

Festival Notes – In our report of the Selly Oak Children's Festival, in last week's issue, we should have stated that a drill display was given by a number of children from Bournville School, under the direction of the headmaster, Mr. Fielden. In the list of workers supplied to us the names of Mr. R.E. Bull (treasurer), Mr. Sewell (vice-chairman) were missed.

To-day's Flower Show – As will be seen from our advertising columns the greatest of local summer events takes place today (Saturday) in the flower show to be held at the park. In addition to the attractions, practically guaranteed by a record number of entries for nearly all classes of the exhibits, the committee have arranged a programme which, given the weather, will do much to make the affair a genuine success. The Royal Staffordshire Blues Band has been specially engaged for the occasion, as well as the Bournbrook Concert Party and the Royal Ensign Cadets. There are also to be ever interesting demonstrations of the art of bee-keeping by the County Council expert (the Rev. Ellis Davenport).

Letters to the Editor
Selly Oak and Bournbrook Children's Festival

Sir, – On behalf of the Selly Oak and Bournbrook Children's Festival Committee, we desire to tender our thanks to the school teachers, to the owners of vehicles, the subscribers, and all who helped to make the children's Festival such a happy and successful one. – We are, yours sincerely,

C.H. Harbun (Chairman)
R.E. Bull (Treasurer)
C.A. Lucas (Hon. Secretary)

Selly Oak
July 25th, 1907

3rd August 1907 – Birmingham News

Selly Oak Flower Show
Effect of the Bad Weather on Garden Produce[51]

The seventeenth annual horticultural exhibition at Selly Oak took place last Saturday in Selly Oak Park. The show suffered greatly, as was to have been expected, from the bad season, and a further stroke of ill-luck was experienced in the heavy rain which fell in the evening preceding it, when in many cases the produce intended for the exhibition had to be lifted. The entries were 200 fewer than those of last year, and, further than this, a more than usually heavy proportion of the produce intended for staging was not actually shown. The result was that the tables showed many gaps, and the gentlemen's gardeners and amateurs' sections were in the unusual position of overshadowing in number the cottagers' department. On the other hand, it has to be stated that what was shown was, generally speaking, of very good quality, especially among the root crops. Honorary exhibits were shown by Mr. George Cadbury, who sent a grand collection of greenhouse plants, and Messrs. W.H. Simpson and Son, who staged some exceptionally fine sweet peas and herbaceous flowers. There was but one

---

[51] The bad weather at this show, and the recent apathy surrounding the Selly Oak, Bournbrook and District Horticultural Association led to its winding up and dissolution at a meeting on 31st December 1907 – reported in the Birmingham News of 4th January 1908. Just three weeks later, on 20th January 1908, another association, under the same heading, had been convened! – reported in the Birmingham News of 25th January 1908.

group of plants entered for competition, but this was of really good quality, and deservedly won first prize for Mrs. Normansell, whose gardener is Mr. S. Gibbs. This lady was a very successful exhibitor in other departments, by the way, and took the R.E. Bull silver cup for the exhibitor in that division gaining the greatest number of points. Mrs. Normansell gained 33 points, while the runner-up, Mr. A.E. Forty, gained 29. In the cottagers' division the silver cup hitherto competed for was won outright last year, and Mr. Edward Cadbury this year gave a handsome cup for competition. This was won by Mr. B. Jones with 27 points, Mr. C. Bragg and Mr. R. Hall tieing (sic) for second place with 25 points each. The Toogood silver shield was won by Mrs. Normansell; their bronze shield by Mr. Forty, and their certificate of excellence by Mr. R. Jones. The attendance at the show was fair, but would no doubt have been larger than it was but for the other local fixtures having been arranged for the same day. Compared with previous years the gate receipts were decidedly "down", but still it is hoped to be able to meet the expenses of the exhibition, which are not small, despite the most economical management. The committee are to be commended upon the excellence and thoroughness of the show arrangements, and an especial word of approbation is due to the secretary, Mr. McIntosh, upon whom, for the third year in succession, fell the brunt of the work. The attractions, apart from the exhibitions, were very good. The music for the occasion was largely supplied by that excellent combination, the Royal Staffordshire Blues band, which had been engaged at considerable expense. The Bournbrook Concert Party, under the direction of Mrs. Norman, gave most interesting programmes, which shows them to be an asset of value to any committee having to provide entertainments to the public. The Royal Ensign Cadets also added to the gaieties of the afternoon and evening, and finally there was dance music towards the close for those whose inclinations lay in that direction. The Rev. E. Davenport, the Worcestershire County Council's expert, and his assistant were the centre of a great deal of interest with their bee-keeping demonstration and manipulations with the bees – all apparently "as tame as flies", as if they were a special stingless brand of apis mellifica.

The association was again favoured with the presence of the Member of Parliament for the division (Mr. J.W. Wilson), who had gladly accepted the invitation to formally open the show, and with him were Mr. And Mrs. Alan Tangye. Councillor J.S. Nettlefold (the president of the society) took the chair, and with him and those just mentioned on the platform were the Rev. L.B. Sladen, Miss Baker, Councillors Frank Wilson and H. Spencer, Mr. and Mrs. Joseph James, Messrs. C.A. Lucas, S. McIntosh, J. Dudley, R.E. Bull, and E. Fuller, while Mr. Hy. Lloyd Wilson was amongst the crowd gathered around. Mr. Wilson in discharging his duty in the matter, commended the following of the pursuit of horticulture, and spoke of his own love of the garden. He regretted that there were not more exhibitors, and hoped that interest in the show would not be allowed to wane. He also voiced the indebtedness which all concerned must feel to the committee for the work they had done in connection with the exhibition. Mr. Wilson was heartily thanked for his services on the proposition of Councillor Wilson, and seconded by

Councillor Spencer, and Councillor Nettlefold was similarly rewarded for presiding, Mr. C.A. Lucas and Mr. E. Fuller proposing and seconding the vote.

The Prize Winners

(There then follows a very long list of prize-winners in all the categories, but it was interesting to note the following:
Vegetables: Collection (five varieties). – 1, T. Horton
Eschalots – 1, C. Bragg; 2, R. Hall; 3, T. Horton
Lettuce – 1, A.T. Rainbow; 2, R. Jones; 3, T. Horton)

11th September 1907 – KN&N UDC Baths, Parks and Cemeteries Committee

Staff at Selly Oak Park and Recreation Grounds The Chairman reported that as requested by the committee he had made further enquiries with a view to the rearrangement of the staff at the Selly Oak Park and the recreation grounds of the Council and he was of opinion that the present staff would be sufficient for the winter months but the matter would need to be considered next summer.

9th October 1907 – KN&N UDC Baths, Parks and Cemeteries Committee

a) Selly Oak Park b) Muntz Park
Upon the request of the Superintendent of the Selly Oak Park it was resolved that he be authorised to expend the sum of £3 in the purchase of bulbs to be planted in the Selly Oak and Muntz Parks.

13th November 1907 – KN&N UDC Baths, Parks and Cemeteries Committee

Report of Superintendent The Superintendent presented his report as to the condition of this Park and the report was approved.

Provision of tennis courts Resolved that a Sub-Committee consisting of the Chairman and Mr Councillor Harbun with the Surveyor be approved to visit this park and to report as to the necessity of providing tennis courts there and that the Surveyor be instructed to obtain estimates for laying out such courts.

Chapter 13

1908

12th February 1908 – KN&N UDC Baths, Parks and Cemeteries Committee

<u>Lawn Mower</u> The superintendent of Selly Oak Park requested that a 22" mowing machine be purchased for use at that Park and it was resolved that the Clerk be instructed to obtain estimates from Ransomes Ltd of Ipswich and Parker Winder Achurch Ltd of Birmingham for supplying a 22" lawnmower and that the purchase of such machine be left in the hands of the Chairman, Mr Councillor Harbun and the Clerk.

<u>Tennis Courts</u> Resolved that the Surveyor be instructed to submit estimates to the Committee for laying out two tennis courts at the Selly Oak Park.

15th February 1908 – Birmingham News

Letters to the Editor
Selly Oak Horticultural Association Revival[52]

Sir, – The joint letter of your correspondents, Messrs. A.H. Beard and James Beacham, appears to indicate that those who were the officers at the time of the dissolution of the Selly Oak and Bournbrook Horticultural Association are to blame for the apathy shown by exhibitors and the public. As I was the last hon. treasurer, I beg to inform your correspondents that every officer and member of the committee worked solely in the interests of horticulture. If one of these gentlemen who were invited in the early part of 1906 had accepted the office of treasurer, I probably should not have had the honour of occupying this important position; although I had been a subscriber to the funds for nine years. I presume these gentlemen (some of whom have now joined the newly-formed association), did not relish the idea of the heavy debt with which the association was saddled. To find out the beginning of the trouble of the association I think we must go back to the year 1904, when the show was held in the Bournbrook Road, on August Bank Holiday Monday and Tuesday, which were two ideal days for a floral exhibition. The gate was a record with £223 9s. 5d., and the total income of the year was no less a sum than £445 7s. 8d., but the extravagant expenditure of £476. 4s. 2d., left a debt for others to pay off of £30 16s. 6d. This, I am pleased to say, has been done, the last cheque

---

[52] This is just one letter of many about the dissolution and resurrection of the Horticultural Association, but this one does contain specific mention of the Park.

of £25 towards this 1904 expenditure being paid as recently as November 1906. On the occasion of the 1905 show in Oak Tree Lane, the first day being wet it caused the association's debt to increase to £75. This fairly frightened the committee, resignations coming in wholesale, leaving only about six or seven members of the committee to do the best they could, and, to their credit, they manfully and courageously commenced to find ways and means to wipe off the debt. A sum of £11 was got together by means of a prize distribution, the late Councillor Olivieri kindly giving a hamper of wine and champagne[53]. I gave a sucking pig[54], other friends giving smaller articles. The Progressive Association organised two concerts in the autumn of 1905, the artistes kindly giving their services, which resulted in £14 10s. being handed over to the Horticultural Association. In February, 1906, I accepted the office of hon. treasurer, and I impressed on the committee the desirability of becoming solvent, and we decided to have the exhibition in the Selly Oak Institute, and so saved much of the attendant expenses of an outside show, and with much energy on the part of the committee in collecting subscriptions we were able to finish up 1906 with a balance in hand of £1 7s. 4d. The 1906[55] show was held in Selly Oak Park. The weather on the day of the show was beautiful, but the cold, wet summer caused a check to the exhibits, and the committee were not supported by the public as they deserved to be, and at the annual meeting a resolution, of which every subscriber received notice, was unanimously carried: "That in the interests of the subscribers of the association it is essential that the association be now dissolved". It was also resolved that the balance in hand of 12s. 6d. be handed to the Selly Oak and Bournbrook Poor Children's Christmas Tree Fund.

I beg to thank the subscribers and all who helped the committee to leave the association clear of debt. There would have been no need to have dissolved the association if your correspondents and their friends had given the association a helping hand. – Yours sincerely,

Charles A. Lucas

Selly Oak, February 12, 1908

11th March 1908 – KN&N UDC Baths, Parks and Cemeteries Committee

(i) <u>Mowing Machine</u> The Clerk submitted the following estimates for the provision of a 22" mowing machine for use in the Selly Oak Park viz:-
Parker, Winder and Achurch Ltd, Birmingham £7:17:3
Hiller & Harwood, 152 Milcote Road, Bearwood, Smethwick £7:17:3
Ransomes, Sims & Jefferies, Orwell Works, Ipswich £7:17:3

Resolved that the estimate of Parker, Winder and Achurch, Ltd in the sum of £7:17:3 for supplying a Green's 22" mowing machine be purchased accordingly.

---

[53] Councillor Olivieri was a wine merchant.
[54] Mr. Lucas was a farmer.
[55] The 1906 show was actually held in the Friends Institute, Bournbrook on Tuesday, 7th August – see the Birmingham News, 11th August 1906. Presumably 1907 was meant.

The Committee also considered the report of the Superintendent dated 11th February 1908 suggesting certain repairs to the mowing machine at present in use and it was resolved that the Superintendent be instructed to have such mowing machine repaired in accordance with his report.

(ii) <u>Tennis Courts</u> The Surveyor submitted an estimate in the sum of £55 for laying out two tennis courts at the Selly Oak Park and it was resolved that this matter be placed on the agenda for the July meeting of the Committee.

1st April 1908 – KN&N UDC Baths, Parks and Cemeteries Committee

<u>Bandstands</u> The Surveyor submitted estimates for supplying bandstands to the King's Heath, Selly Oak, Cotteridge and Muntz Parks and after some discussion it was resolved that the Surveyor be instructed to obtain further estimates for submission to the next meeting of the Committee.

9th April 1908 – KN&N UDC Baths, Parks and Cemeteries Committee, and approved on
9th April 1908 – Minute of KN&N UDC

<u>Bandstands</u> The Surveyor submitted drawings of bandstands and the following estimates for supplying the same to the parks of the Council:-

The St Pancras Iron Works Co Ltd. London, £94:6:8 each
W. Macfarlane & Co. Glasgow, £115 each
Hill & Smith, Brierley Hill, Birmingham, £160, £168, and £187 each.

It was moved and seconded that it be a recommendation to the Council that the estimates of W. Macfarlane & Co. of Glasgow for supplying bandstands to the Selly Oak, Cotteridge and King's Heath Parks, in the sum of £115 each be accepted subject to their entering into a contract and bond (with approved sureties) for the due performance of the work and that the common seal of the Council be affixed to such contract and bond.

As an amendment it was moved and seconded that it be a recommendation to the Council that the estimate of the St Pancras Iron Work Company Ltd of London in the sum of £94:6:8 each be accepted.

Upon a vote being taken there appeared:

For the amendment	3
Against the amendment	2

The Chairman thereupon declared the amendment carried and it was resolved to recommend that the estimate of the St Pancras Iron Work Company Ltd of London for supplying bandstands at Selly Oak, Cotteridge and King's Heath Parks in the sum of £94:6:8 each be accepted subject to the Company entering into a Contract and Bond (with approved sureties), to be prepared by the Clerk, for the due performance of the work and that the common seal of the Council be affixed to such Contract and Bond.

It was also resolved to recommend that the concrete bases be constructed for the purpose of erecting thereon such bandstands at an estimated cost of £20 each and that the work be carried out departmentally.

Resolved also to recommend that concrete bases be constructed at the Muntz Park and Bournbrook recreation ground at an estimated cost of £20 each and that the work be carried out departmentally.

Resolved also to recommend that application be made to the Local Government Board for their sanction to the borrowing of the sum of £450 towards the cost of purchasing and fixing the above mentioned bandstands and of constructing the above mentioned concrete bases.

Resolved also that the question as to the positions in which such bandstands and concrete bases shall be fixed be left in the hands as regards Selly Oak Park, Muntz Park and Bournbrook Recreation Ground of the Chairman and Mr Councillor Harbun, as regards Cotteridge Park, of the Chairman and Mr Councillor Fryer and as regards King's Heath Park, of the Chairman and Mr Councillor Brown.

<u>Chairs</u> Resolved that the question of providing chairs in the parks and recreation grounds be referred to a Sub-Committee consisting of Councillors Shann, Coley, Fryer, Harbun and Shephard.

11th April 1908 – Birmingham News

Public Announcement
Kings Norton and Northfield Urban District Council
Entertainments in Parks

The above-named Council invite OFFERS from Bands and Concert Parties to give entertainments in the various parks in their district during the months of June to September, both inclusive.

The Council are prepared to make a payment of £1 to Bands of 20 performers or more, but no other payment will be made.

They will, however, have no objection to a collection being taken and a charge being made for the use of chairs within an enclosed space, where such chairs are provided.

Applications, expressing the nature and particulars of the entertainments it is proposed to give should be sent to the undersigned, from whom any further particulars may be obtained.

By order,
Edwin Docker

Clerk to the Council
10 Newhall Street,
Birmingham.
11th April, 1908

7th May 1908 – KN&N UDC Baths, Parks and Cemeteries Committee

<u>Bandstands</u> The Clerk reported that the Contract and Bond with the St Pancras Iron Work Company Limited for supplying bandstands to the Selly Oak, Cotteridge and King's Heath Parks had been executed by them. He also presented letters from the Company stating that if it was necessary to make a second journey from London to fix either of the bandstands after the other two had been fixed an estimated extra expenditure of £9:12:6 would thereby be incurred.

Resolved that if it becomes necessary for the representatives of the St Pancras Iron Work Company, Limited to make a second journey from London to fix either of the bandstands after the other two have been fixed, the sum of £9:12:6 be paid to the Company for the extra cost thereby incurred.

16th May 1908 – Birmingham News

Selly Oak and Bournbrook Children's Festival

In connection with the Selly Oak and Bournbrook Children's Festival a public meeting was held on Thursday in the Selly Oak Institute to receive report and balance sheet for 1907 and to consider the advisability of holding a festival for 1908.

.... The secretary's report was read by Mr. E.A. Lucas, hon. secretary. It stated that although the year 1907 would long be remembered for its very wet summer, happily it was fine on the day of the festival, which was undoubtedly a great success. The number of parents and friends who visited the park in the evening constituted a record attendance. Special thanks were due to the teachers for their kindly interest, and all those who helped to make the festival a success. They regretted that a little boy was hurt with tents while out on hire. ....

The festival will take place on July 15th, provided the Baths and Parks and Education Committees agree.

30th May 1908 – Birmingham News

Death of Mr. Thos. Gibbins, J.P.

.... Mr. Gibbins took a keen interest in the public affairs of Selly Oak for very many years. One of the earliest outstanding evidences of this was afforded in the part he played along with other members of his family in the presentation to the district of Selly Oak Park. He also gave the site upon which the Free Library stands. .... [56]

---

[56] There is a full transcript of this newspaper report in Appendix I dealing with the Gibbins Family.

13. 1908

3rd June 1908 – Minute of KN&N UDC

<u>Death of Mr. County Councillor Gibbins</u>

It was moved by Mr. Councillor Moffat, seconded by Mr. Councillor Brown, and resolved: -

264 That this Council desire to place on record the deep regret with which they have learned of the death of County Councillor Thomas Gibbins, and their appreciation of the public services he rendered to the district as Chairman of this Council from 1898 to 1901, and as a member of the Council from 1898 to 1905, and to convey to the relatives of the late Mr. Gibbins an expression of their most sincere sympathy with them in the bereavement which they have sustained.

6th June 1908 – Birmingham News

Kings Norton and Northfield Urban District Council
Tribute to the Late Mr. T. Gibbins

Prior to the commencement of the business of the meeting the Chairman referred in terms of deep sympathy to the death of the late Mr. T. Gibbins, and paid an eloquent tribute to his public services and private worth. He moved a resolution placing upon record the Council's appreciation of his services, and offering its condolences to the relatives in their bereavement. Mr. Gibbins, he said, was not only a magistrate of the county, a county councillor, a poor law guardian, and a member of the Higher Education Committee set up in the district by the County Council, but his public activities entered also into various philanthropic and other movements especially in that immediate neighbourhood. They, of course, knew best his work as a member in the past of the Council. He was the first chairman, after it became an urban authority, and was twice afterwards re-elected to that position, and in addition he was for several years chairman of one of its hardest working committees (the Public Works Committee). He was one of the donors of Selly Oak Park, and gave also the site upon which Selly Oak library stood. A record of public service such as that was one of which any man might be proud. He did his work, too, with unfailing tact and courtesy, and lent dignity to every office he assumed. All his public service was rendered without any desire or effort at self-seeking, and personal interest was ever subordinated to the public weal. He had left an ideal worth striving after both in his public and his business life.

Councillor Brown seconded the proposition, to which Councillors A.J. Kelly and J.C. Lane also spoke, and it was carried by the members rising in their places.

10th June 1908 – KN&N UDC Baths, Parks and Cemeteries Committee, and reported on
1st July 1908 – Minute of KN&N UDC

<u>Entertainments in parks and recreation grounds</u> The Committee considered a timetable prepared by the Clerk allocating dates to the various bands and concert parties who had offered to give entertainments in the parks and recreation grounds.
   Resolved that the timetable be approved.
   Resolved also that the Clerk be instructed to prepare a poster and have the same printed and posted in the district advertising the entertainments as set out in the above mentioned timetable.
   Resolved also that an advertisement be issued in the "Birmingham News" and the "Birmingham Daily Mail" advertising the entertainments.

20th June 1908 – Birmingham News

Selly Oak and Bournbrook

Children's Festival – The Selly Oak and Bournbrook Children's Festival will be held on Wednesday, July 15, in Selly Oak Park. All children attending school and resident in Selly Oak, Bournbrook, and that part of Bournville in Selly Oak Ward, are eligible to attend. The committee has engaged the Selly Oak Victoria Brass Band, The Harborne Industrial Boys' Band, Punch and Judy show, and maypole dances, and each child will receive a ticket for free ride on the roundabouts.

27th June 1908 – Birmingham News

Letters to the Editor
Selly Oak and Bournbrook Children's Festival

Dear Sir, – As I am not at present taking my usual prominent part in the work of the Selly Oak and Bournbrook Children's Festival, which is to take place on July 15th at the Selly Oak Park, an impression has got abroad that I have severed my connection with this good work.
   I shall be glad of an opportunity in the columns of the "News" to say that I am still a member of the Festival Committee, and have acceded to the request to undertake the management of the hiring of the festival marquees; and I hope, after I have finished hay-making, to take a more active share in the work of preparing for this great annual treat. The school teachers, all denominations, as well as all parties sharing in the work, care, the feeding, and entertaining of our 4,000 children, and I trust the public will again give generous support so that the festival may again be a success. – Yours sincerely,
C.A. Lucas

Selly Oak, June 25, 1908

11th July 1908 – Birmingham News

Public Announcements
Kings Norton and Northfield Urban District Council
Entertainments in Parks

ENTERTAINMENTS will be given on the evening of SATURDAY, JULY 11th, 1908 at 6.30, in the Parks of the Council, as follows:-
SELLY OAK PARK – Royal Ensign Cadets Concert Party.
COTTERIDGE PARK – Northfield Institute Prize Band.
VICTORIA COMMON – Royal Islington Entertainers.
An entertainment will also be given on the evening of SUNDAY, JULY 12th, 1908, at 7.45, in the VICTORIA COMMON, NORTHFIELD, by the Northfield Prize Band.
By Order,
EDWIN DOCKER
Clerk to the above-named Council.
10, Newhall Street, Birmingham.
11th July, 1908

16th July 1908 – Birmingham City Council, Parks Department

Mr. John Bowen commenced work in the park as a labourer – and would remain there until his retirement through ill health in 1925.

REGISTER OF PARKS EMPLOYEES AND OFFICIALS[57]

Register no.: 169
Name: Bowen, John
Date of Birth: 6.4.1866
Date of entering service of Parks Department: 16.7.1908
Park or Cemetery at which employed: Selly Oak
Grade (under Committee Minute No. 4634): Park Labourer
Rate of Pay: [£]2 – 09[s] – 7[d] [per week]
Date of leaving service of the Parks Department: 16.7.1925
Remarks: Superannuated 4/- per week plus 50% war allowance.

18th July 1908 – Birmingham News

Selly Oak Children's Festival
4,000 Children Spend a Delightful Afternoon

The children's festival at Selly Oak and Bournbrook took place on Wednesday. The first festival in the district was held at Woodbrooke in 1865, when 45 children took

---

[57] Birmingham Library, Archive & Heritage Section – reference BCC Acc 1998/083.

part. Since then the district has developed enormously, and on Wednesday no fewer than 4,000 children participated in this great annual event. Tradesmen and residents in the district showed their interest in the gathering by decorating their premises with flags, flowers, mottoes, etc., and so assisted to make the festival a red letter day as it always is in the year's history of the little ones. All children attending school and resident in Selly Oak and that part of Bournville in Selly Oak Ward were eligible to attend. The children assembled at their various schools and marched in procession to Corporation Road, where they all joined together in one big procession. Headed by the Selly Oak Victoria Brass Band the children processed by way of Harrow Road and High Street to Gibbins Park. Following the band came a group of children on a vehicle representing a Queen with her ladies in waiting, Britannia and the four colonies (Canada, Australia, South Africa and New Zealand). After them came the senior Maypole dancers, who looked very pretty, dressed in white and wearing wreaths of flowers on their heads. The latter half of the procession was enlivened with music by the Harborne Industrial School Band, after which came the St. Edward's Infant School Maypole Dancers. The younger children were carried on 96 vehicles kindly lent by tradesmen in the district. An ambulance corps was also in attendance, but fortunately their services were not required. During the passing of the procession along High Street, which occupied about an hour, the trams were stopped. This proved of much advantage to the children, and also to the large number of spectators who were anxious to see the procession. Thanks to the police, in charge of Inspector Pass, the children arrived at the park safely and with a minimum of inconvenience. On arrival each child was presented with a stick of milk chocolate, Messrs. Cadbury Bros. giving 15 gross of sticks, and Mr. W. Nash, of High Street, Selly Oak, supplying the committee with 10 gross at wholesale price. In the park numerous entertainments

Group of Maypole Dancers.

13. 1908

The Maypole.

had been provided for the benefit of the children. One of the most interesting of these was the display by the St. Edward's Infant Schools dancers, under the direction of Miss D'Arcy. The way in which they danced the Lancers brought forth rounds of applause. The Bournville School Boys' went through a number of marching and dumb-bell exercises creditably, under the direction of Mr. F. Earp. Punch and Judy entertainments were given by Professor Alexander and the first half of the programme was brought to a conclusion with the Senior Maypole Dance. Mrs Barton, who again trained the children, must be congratulated on the efficiency with which the various dances were executed. After this came an interval, during which tea was served by many willing workers. The figures representing the bulk of the provisions used in the feeding of so great a family are worth stating. They are as follows: Cake, 1,250 lbs; bread, 1,000 lbs; butter, 1½ cwt.; sugar, 2 cwt.; milk, 30 gallons; tea, 40 lbs. Before the commencement of tea the band played the old hundredth, and all the schools joined in the singing of grace. At the conclusion of the meal the festivities recommenced and continued until 8 p.m. At 5.30 the gates were opened, and parents were permitted to enjoy the entertainments which had been making the children so happy all the afternoon. Unfortunately, at about 7.30 rain commenced to fall, and although it did not cause any curtailment of the programme, it somewhat marred the conclusion of one of the most successful festivals held at Selly Oak. A popular feature was the roundabout, upon which earlier in the afternoon each child had been given a ticket for a free ride. Lit up at dusk with electricity it presented a very pretty appearance. Everything passed off without a hitch, and the officers and their helpers must be congratulated on the success that has crowned their efforts.

The Heydays Of Selly Oak Park

Never have they worked together with more unanimity, and never was the outcome of their labours more gratifying. In addition to the school teachers the following are the principal list of workers – Councillor C.H. Harbun (chairman), Mr. I. Usherwood (vice-chairman), Mr. R.E. Bull (hon. treasurer), Mr. T. Harper (hon. secretary), Mr. G.W. Harris (assistant hon. secretary); procession committee, Messrs. E. Fuller (chairman), J.H. Widdup (secretary), J. Mansfield, H. Wright, C.S. Weeks, E.D. Smith, J.W. Knowles, E. West and F. Hunter; catering committee, Councillor F. Wilson (chairman), Messrs. H. Roberts (secretary), I. Usherwood, C.S. Weeks, Moore, A.F. Looker, C.A. Lucas; field and sports committee, Messrs. W.C. Clarke (chairman), A. Wood (secretary), F. Horton, F. Hunter, W. Geddes, A. Birbeck, J. Mansfield, G. Bishop, H. Bates, J. Hart, E.D. Smith, W, Wright, W. Cousins, A. Price, and R. Fowler. The members of the ladies committee also worked well. A meeting of workers was held after the conclusion of the festival in the Selly Oak Institute. Councillor Harbun, who presided, congratulated the committee on the successful issue of their efforts, and thanked the members of the various sub-committees for their services, and for the way in which they had worked together. He also specially thanked Mr. T. Harper for the way in which he had acted as secretary, and regretted that owing to business

A Children's Festival in Selly Oak Park, July 1908. Taken from Dowling, G., Giles, B.A. and Hayfield, C. (1987), "Selly Oak Past and Present: a photographic survey of a Birmingham suburb". University of Birmingham. [Note: This picture has remarkable similarities to that appearing in the Birmingham News on 18th July, 1908 (see earlier), suggesting that they were taken at the same event, though by different photographers. The mention in both commentaries of Mr. Bull and Miss / Mrs Barton is further evidence of this.]

reasons Mr. Harper would shortly have to leave the district. The secretaries of the sub-committees thanked Mr. Harper. The cost of the festival is expected to amount to £110, and towards this sum Mr. R.E. Bull, the energetic hon. secretary (sic), has received about £96. A large part of this has been raised by house to house collections. On Saturday last the Bournville Prize Band paraded Selly Oak and Bournbrook for the benefit of the festival funds, collections being made along the route taken.

25th July 1908 – Birmingham News

Public Announcements
Kings Norton and Northfield Urban District Council
Entertainments in Parks
ENTERTAINMENTS will be given on the evening of SATURDAY, JULY 25th, 1908 at 6.30, in the Parks of the Council, as follows:-
MUNTZ PARK – Northfield Institute Prize Band.
SELLY OAK PARK – Royal Islington Entertainers.
Entertainments will also be given in the SELLY OAK PARK on SUNDAY, JULY 26th, 1908, at 3.30 p.m. and 7.30 p.m., by the Royal Staffordshire Blues Band.
By Order,
EDWIN DOCKER
Clerk to the above-named Council.
10, Newhall Street, Birmingham.
24th July, 1908

Kings Heath Park
Opposition at the Local Government Board Inquiry

Never has there been a Local Government Board enquiry held in the district which excited so deep an interest as the one which took place on Wednesday morning at Kings Heath Institute, to enquire into the application made by the Urban District Council of Kings Norton and Northfield, for sanction to borrow the sum of £11,000 for the purchase of Kings Heath House, for the purposes of a public park. ....

(from a long report:)

The council had always been keenly desirous of providing parks and open spaces, either by gift if possible or by purchase, because they held that they were greatly conducive to the good government of the district, to the better preservation and maintenance of the public health, especially of young children, and generally beneficial to the community. The first park was acquired by gift in February 1899, consisting of a site in Old Lane, Selly Oak, of 11a. 2r. 5p., which was given through the good offices of the late respected Mr. Thomas Gibbins and his family, and was known as the Gibbins Park; then on 20th May, 1905, the Council acquired by gift a second park in Umberslade Road, Selly Oak, of three acres, from Mr. F.E. Muntz. On 29th July, 1905, they acquired by gift a further park known as Victoria Common, Northfield, of four acres, given by the generosity of Mr. George Cadbury. The Council were indebted to Mr. Cadbury and other members of his family for many generous gifts. On the 8th February, 1905, the Council purchased Cotteridge Park, containing 12a. 2r. 1p., for £2,655, from the Russell and Stock's Trustees. In November 1906, Mr. W.A. Cadbury gave 1¼ acres in Stirchley Street, and on 29th September, 1906, the Council acquired 4,510 square yards in George Road, Bournbrook, so that the Council had not been unmindful of their duty in endeavouring to secure public parks and open spaces on every possible opportunity. The total area secured was now 33 acres. ....

Selly Oak and Bournbrook

<u>Charity Sports</u> – The seventh annual charity sports in aid of the Selly Oak and Bournbrook District Nurses Fund were held on Saturday, in Selly Oak Park. The proceedings opened with a procession round the village, headed by the Selly Oak Victoria Brass Band. Prizes were offered for the best novelties, best dressed clowns and best decorated vehicles. At the park the principal feature of the entertainment was the fire brigade competition, for challenge cups and medals value 25 guineas. Eight fire brigades entered, and the drill consisted of one man, two men and four men. Lieutenant Chandler, of Smethwick, acted as judge, assisted by Engineer Sherwood, of Cape Hill. The Smethwick engine and hose were used. The contest resulted as follows: 1, Selly Oak, one man 37 1.5 sec., two men 35 2.5 sec., four men 26 sec., aggregate 96 2.5 sec.; 2, Kings Heath, 41 1.5 sec., 29 sec., 31 2.5 sec., 101 3.5 sec.; 3, Stourbridge, 37 2.5 sec., 36 4.5 sec., 28 2.5 sec., 102, 4.5 sec.; Bournville, 44 1.5 sec., 33 4.5 sec., 25 1.5 sec., 103 1.5 sec.; Oldbury, 43 3.5 sec, 42 2.5 sec, 30 4.5 sec, 117; Studley, 52 4.5 sec., 42 2.5 sec., 30 4.5 sec., 117; Bromsgrove, 52 4.5 sec., 43 4.5 sec., 34 1.5 sec., 130 3.5 sec.; Yardley, 58 sec., 39 3.5 sec., 34 sec., 131 3.5 sec. The first prize was a challenge cup, presented by the Charity Sports Committee, the second prize a challenge cup presented by Messrs. Cadbury Bros. Ltd., and the third prize four medals, given by Captain Crump. The prizes were distributed to the successful teams by County Councillor A.C. Hayes, and they were acknowledged by Captain Crump of Selly Oak, Captain Arnold, of Kings Heath, and Lieutenant Walker of Stourbridge. Votes of thanks were accorded Councillor Hayes for handing away the prizes, and also to Lieut. Chandler and Engineer Sherwood, for acting as judges. An excellent programme of sports was also carried out, including one mile flat, half mile flat, 100 yards flat, quarter mile scratch, and obstacle races. The full list of prize winners is as follows:- one mile flat race: 1, A. Merrill; 2,Turrell; 3, A. Walls – Half-mile flat race: 1, A. Merrill; 2, Turrell; 3, E. Rodin – 100 yards flat race: 1, A. Merrill; 2, A. West; 3, P. Halward – Quarter mile scratch race: 1, A. Merrill; 2, Hodgetts; 3, P. Halward. Obstacle race: 1, E. Rodin; 2, P. Halward; 3, Hancocks – Slow cycle race: 1, Holmes;

13. 1908

1. PRIZE BAND, BRISTOL ROAD, NORTHFIELD, c.1912   BIRMINGHAM PUBLIC LIBRARIES

One of the bands that played in the Parks during 1908. (Birmingham Public Libraries).

2, Turrell. – Sack race: 1, Fountain; 2, H. Yates; 3, A. Merrill. – Potato race: 1, E. Rodin; 2, Hancox; 3, A. Merrill. – Skipping rope race: 1, Miss Horton; 2, Miss M. Harrison; 3, Miss K. Patterson. – Egg and spoon race: Miss K. Hughes (only one finished). – Ham cutting competition: Mr. Lawlor. – The procession prizes were awarded as follows; – Best decorated vehicle, Mr. Shears of Wheels Ltd. Best decorated clown: 1, W. Washbrook; 2, W. Faultless, jun.; 3, W. Hughes. Novelty: 1, J.F. Round; 2, A. Rolph; 3, "Wilkie Bard".

The following tradesmen resident in the district gave prizes:- Messrs. Mitchells and Butlers, Mr. Sadler, Mrs. Priest, Mr. Daniels, Mrs. T. Halward, Mrs. Hambleton, Mr. Peel, Managers of Foster Brothers, Ltd., Mr. W, Nash, Mr. T. Monk, Mr. Knowles, Mr. Twiddy Randle, Messrs. Morton, Mr. W. Husselber, Mr. J. Smith, Mr. J. Whitehouse, Manager of Checkleys, Mr. Farrell, Mr. M.F. Harvey, Mr. W. Lewis, Mr. J. Faultless, Mr. J. Deaman, Mr. Hinton, Mr. W. Hopewood, Mr. Hughes, Mr. A. Keyte, Mr. J. Webb, Mr. J. Gough, Mr. W. Ecckles, Mr. J. Walls, Mr. Lawrence, Mr. J. Walton, Mr. C. Cartwright, Mr. Fisher, Mr. J. Draper, Mr. C. Woolley, Mr. Biabrand, Mr. H. Burford, and Mr. A. Gregory.

1st August 1908 – Birmingham News

Public Announcements
Kings Norton and Northfield Urban District Council
Entertainments in Parks

ENTERTAINMENTS will be given on the EVENING of SATURDAY, AUGUST 1st, 1908 at 6.30, in the Parks of the Council, as follows:-
   Victoria Common – Mr. R.G. Merrick's Concert Party.
   Muntz Park – Royal Islington Entertainers.
   Bournbrook Recreation Ground – Northfield Institute Prize Band.

An entertainment will also be given in the Selly Oak Park on Sunday, August 2nd, 1908, at 3.30 p.m. by the Bartley Green Brass Band.
On MONDAY NEXT, August 3rd, ENTERTAINMENTS will be given as follows at 3 p.m. and 6 p.m.:-
   Selly Oak Park – Sterling Concert Party.
   Cotteridge Park – Mr. R.G. Merrick's Concert Party.
And on TUESDAY NEXT, August 4th, ENTERTAINMENTS will be given in the Selly Oak Park by the Sterling Concert Party at 3 p.m. and 6 p.m.

By Order,
EDWIN DOCKER
Clerk to the above-named Council.

10, Newhall Street,
  Birmingham.
    1st August, 1908

8th August 1908 – Birmingham News

Public Announcements
Kings Norton and Northfield Urban District Council
Entertainments in Parks

ENTERTAINMENTS will be given on the evening of SATURDAY, AUGUST 8th, 1908 at 6.30, in the Parks of the Council, as follows:-
   Selly Oak Park – Royal Ensign Cadets.
   Muntz Park – Mr. R.G. Merrick's Concert Party.
An ENTERTAINMENT will also be given in the BOURNBROOK RECREATION GROUND on SUNDAY, AUGUST 9th, 1908, at 3.30 p.m., by the Bartley Green Brass Band.

By Order,
EDWIN DOCKER
Clerk to the above-named Council.

10, Newhall Street,
  Birmingham.
    1st August, 1908

15th August 1908 – Birmingham News

Public Announcements
Kings Norton and Northfield Urban District Council

An ENTERTAINMENT will be given in the SELLY OAK PARK by WIGLEYS' MASCOTS THIS (SATURDAY) Evening, at 6.30.

By Order,
EDWIN DOCKER
Clerk to the above-named Council.

10, Newhall Street,
   Birmingham. 15th August, 1908

29th August 1908 – Birmingham News

Public Announcements
Kings Norton and Northfield Urban District Council
Entertainments in Parks

An ENTERTAINMENT will be given THIS (SATURDAY) EVENING, August 29th, 1908, at 5.30 o'clock in the SELLY OAK PARK by Wigleys' Mascots.

The following entertainments have also been arranged:-

SUNDAY, August 30th, 1908, at 6 p.m., at the COTTERIDGE PARK, the Northfield Institute Prize Band.

SATURDAY, September 5th, 1908, at 6 p.m., at the VICTORIA COMMON, the Kings Heath Band.

SUNDAY, September 6th, 1908, at 3.30 p.m., at MUNTZ PARK, the Northfield Institute Prize Band.

By Order,
EDWIN DOCKER
Clerk to the above-named Council.

10, Newhall Street, Birmingham.
28th August, 1908

7th October 1908 – Minute of KN&NUDC

Mr. Councillor Shann presented the following report of the Baths, Parks and Cemeteries Committee.

Your Committee beg to report:-

4 <u>Entertainments</u>

That twenty three entertainments have been given by arrangement with your Committee in the various parks and recreation grounds of the Council, during the months of July, August, and September. Fourteen of the entertainments were given by bands, and your Committee have authorised the payment of £1 to the various bands in respect of each entertainment.

It was moved by Mr. Councillor Shann, seconded by Mr. Councillor Coley, and resolved (minute 422), that the report of the Baths, Parks, and Cemeteries Committee be approved and adopted.

4th November 1908 – Minute of KN&N UDC

Mr. Councillor Shann presented the following report of the Baths, Parks, and Cemeteries Committee.

Your Committee beg to report:-

4 <u>Selly Oak Park – tennis courts</u>

That they have considered as to the advisability of providing tennis courts at the Selly Oak Park, and beg to recommend that tennis courts be laid out at a cost not exceeding £50.

It was moved by Mr. Councillor Shann, seconded by Mr. Councillor Wilson, and resolved (minute 477), that tennis courts be laid out at the Selly Oak Park at a cost not exceeding £50.

Chapter 14

1909

20th March 1909 – Birmingham News

>Kings Norton and Northfield Urban District Council
>Entertainments in Parks and Recreation Grounds

The above-mentioned Council invite OFFERS from BANDS and CONCERT PARTIES to GIVE VOLUNTARY ENTERTAINMENTS in the following Parks and Recreation Grounds:-
    KINGS HEATH PARK
    SELLY OAK PARK
    COTTERIDGE PARK (FRANKLIN ROAD)
    MUNTZ PARK (UMBERSLADE ROAD)
    VICTORIA COMMON, NORTHFIELD
    BOURNBROOK RECREATION GROUND

Bands and concert parties are requested to note that the Council DO NOT ENGAGE the services of any band or concert party, neither do they guarantee the repayment of any loss sustained, or expenses incurred with the entertainments given. The Council are, however, prepared to contribute towards the expenses of entertainments given by BANDS at the rate of one shilling and sixpence for each performer and five shillings for the band master, such contribution being limited to twenty-five performers.
    All Bands and Concert Parties may, however, make a charge for the hire of seats within the band-stand enclosure, where such are provided, and the Council will have no objection to a collection being made.
Offers, giving full particulars of the Band or Concert Party and of the proposed programme should be sent to the undersigned as soon as possible.
>By Order,
>EDWIN DOCKER
>Clerk to the above-named Council.

 10, Newhall Street,
    Birmingham,
       20th March, 1909.

The Heydays Of Selly Oak Park

6th April 1909 – Minute of KN&N UDC

Mr. Councillor Shann presented the following report of the Baths, Parks and Cemeteries Committee.

Your Committee beg to report:-

4 <u>Entertainment</u>

That they have given instructions for advertisements to be issued inviting offers from Bands and Concert Parties to give entertainments in the parks and recreation grounds of the Council, and agreeing on behalf of the Council to contribute towards the cost of entertainments given by bands at the rate of one shilling and sixpence for each performer and five shillings for the conductor, the contribution being limited to 25 performers.

It was moved by Mr. Councillor Shann, seconded by Mr. Councillor Fryer, and resolved (minute 142), that the report of the Baths, Parks, and Cemeteries Committee, as amended (nb – amendment was nothing to do with the Park), be approved and adopted.

15th May 1909 – Birmingham News

Kings Norton and Northfield Urban District Council
Entertainments in Parks and Recreation Grounds

ENTERTAINMENTS will be given TODAY (SATURDAY), at 6 o'clock p.m., in the KINGS HEATH PARK, by the Kings Heath Adult School Brass Band, and in the SELLY OAK PARK, by the Handsworth Comedy Company.
ENTERTAINMENTS have also been arranged to be given at the following Parks and Recreation Grounds of the above-named Council during the summer months:-
   KINGS HEATH PARK
   SELLY OAK PARK
   COTTERIDGE PARK
   MUNTZ PARK
   VICTORIA COMMON, NORTHFIELD
   BOURNBROOK RECREATION GROUND
Notices giving particulars of such Entertainments will be posted at the entrances to the Parks where the Entertainments are to be given.
                    By Order,
                       EDWIN DOCKER
                          Clerk to the Council.

10, Newhall Street,
    Birmingham, 15th May, 1909.

14. 1909

9th June 1909 – Minute of KN&N UDC

Mr. Councillor Shann presented the following report of the Baths, Parks and Cemeteries Committee.

Your Committee beg to report:-

5 <u>Tennis courts and bowling green</u>

That tennis courts are now open for the use of the public at the King's Heath, Selly Oak, and Cotteridge Parks at a charge of eightpence per hour for each court. At the Cotteridge Park a bowling green has also been opened for use at a charge of twopence per hour for each player.

It was moved by Mr. Councillor Shann, seconded by Mr. Councillor Coley, and resolved (minute 223), that the report of the Baths, Parks, and Cemeteries Committee be approved and adopted.

17th July 1909 – Birmingham News

Children's Festivals at Bournville and Bournbrook
Successful Gatherings
A Huge Party at Bournbrook

The annual festival of the school children living in Selly Oak and Bournbrook took place on Wednesday. The festival has been in existence for many years, and has become one of the most interesting functions of the year in the district. The number of children who participate in the festival has grown year by year, and on Wednesday nearly 5,000 children were present, and enjoyed themselves to their heart's content. Fortunately the weather clerk was in one of his happiest moods, and graced the proceedings with some of the brightest sunshine that has been experienced this season.

The children assembled at their various schools, and, marshalled by the teachers, marched to Harrow and Coronation Roads, where one big procession was formed. Headed by the Bournville Prize Band, the procession moved along the main road to the park. Many of the traders displayed flags and mottoes, and the route bore quite a festive appearance. Following the band came the senior maypole dancers, who looked charming in their white dresses, red, white, and blue sashes, and wreaths of flowers. The Harborne Industrial School Band provided music for the latter half of the procession, and following them came the St. Edward's R.C. junior maypole children, whose appearance excited general admiration. The queen (Miss Agnes Parkes) was attired in a pretty pale blue dress with scarlet train, and her page (Leslie Yeomans), as little Lord Fauntleroy, wore a black velvet suit with lace collar and cuff. Both the queen and her page were only

The Heydays Of Selly Oak Park

five years old, and the former was chosen by the children themselves. The maypole girls had white needlework dresses, with pale blue trimmings, and white pearl hats, while their partners wore purple and green coats alternately, with black round hats and feathers to match their coats. The dresses were designed by Miss D'Arcy, who was in charge of the children, and credit is also due to the parents for their co-operation in making the dresses. The younger children were carried on about fifty decorated vehicles, which had been kindly placed at the committee's disposal by tradesmen. Mr. J. Mansfield acted as chief marshall. During the passing of the procession the trams were stopped, and the police, in charge of Inspector Pass, rendered every assistance possible for the safety of the children. The scholars of the Raddle Barn, Bournville, and Selly Oak Church Schools proceeded straight to the park from their respective schools.

At the park numerous entertainments were provided, and there was not a dull moment from start to finish. The senior maypole dance was in charge of Mrs. Barton, and she was assisted by Miss Morris and Miss Marion Barton. Miss Daisy Barton acted as Queen, and Britannia (Miss Edith Bayliss) was in attendance. The children executed the various dances very well, and they were heartily applauded, especially at the evening performances. The junior maypole also gained well merited applause. Miss D'Arcy, who was assisted by Miss Beasley, kept to the traditional English maypole dance, which opens with the crowning of the Queen. The flowers which formed her crown and bouquet were bought (sic) by the children themselves. The Bournville Prize Band supplied the music for the dances. At the conclusion of the evening performances Councillor Harbun, on behalf of Councillor Wilson and himself, presented Mrs. Barton and Miss D'Arcy with very handsome silk umbrellas. An innovation was the morris dances, which were given by Bournville school children, under the direction of Miss Maggie Cox, and they proved to be one of the features of the afternoon. Punch and Judy entertainments were given at intervals by Professor Alexander, and Messrs. Strickland's steam galloping horses, on which every child had a ride, were very popular.

Tea was provided at 4.15 p.m. The feeding of such a large number of children necessitated a small army of workers, and in this respect the committee were greatly helped by the teachers. The amount of food consumed was as follows:- Cake (fruit, seed and plain), 1,331 lbs.; bread, 1,000 lbs.; butter, 1½ cwts.; sugar, 2 cwts.; and tea, 40 lbs. The children were grouped in rows by their teachers on both sides of the main path, and did full justice to the good things provided.

After tea the parents and friends were allowed in the park. Four schools entered for the inter-school tug of war contest. In the first round Hubert Road beat St. Steven's, and Raddle Barn beat Tiverton Road. The final, after a great struggle, ended in a victory for Hubert Road, who were a heavier set of lads than Raddle Barn. Mr. A.H. Bellot acted as judge for this event. At 8 p.m. dancing was indulged in, the music being supplied by the Bournville Prize Band, and in another part of the field by the Harborne Industrial School Band, who also played selections during the afternoon. In view of the fine weather the park was kept open until 10 p.m., and during the last hour Bill Jones's Male Voice Choir gave selections. The roundabouts, which were lit up by electricity, did a good trade, and over £10 was taken on them. The festival was one of the most successful held, and the officers and committee are to be complimented upon the result of their earnest work. In view of the King's visit to Bournbrook to open the University[58], the committee thought it desirable that the children should be given some memento. Aluminium medals, made at the Birmingham Mint, were provided, and one was given to each child attending the festival. The cost of the festival is expected to be nearly £150, and of this about £80 has been collected, so that if the committee are to start next year with a balance in hand much more money will be required.

The head teachers and their assistants ungrudgingly supported the committee, and greatly helped towards the success of the festival. Messrs. Cadbury Bros. Ltd. gave 15 gross of sticks of milk chocolate, and these were given to the infants and the children in standard one of the schools. At the conclusion of the festival a meeting of the committee was held in the Institute, and congratulatory speeches were made.

Amongst those to whom acknowledgement is due for service rendered in the organisation of the festival, in addition to the names already mentioned, are the following:- Councillor Harbun (chairman of the general committee), Councillor F. Wilson (vice-chairman), Mr. H. Roberts (hon. treasurer), Mr. R. Fowler (hon. secretary), Mr. H. Moore (assistant hon. secretary), Messrs. J. Mansfield, J.H. Widdup, H. Bates, J. Hunter, A.E. Looker, J.H. Peppiette, E. West, F.J. Walton, H.

---

[58] This had occurred during the previous month.

Wright, F. Williamson, E.D. Smith, F. Duffy, A.H. Bellot, W.C. Clarke, A. Wood, T. Horton, A.M. Hedge, G. House, G.B. Bishop, F. Williamson (sic), S. Bayliss, A. Birbeck, J. Hart, T.G. Pinson, A. Holland, W. Geddes, E.D. Smith (sic), H.J. White, J.G. Bland, J. Usherwood, J.W. Knowles, C.A. Lucas. To these gentlemen, and possibly to others not named, the grateful thanks of the people of Selly Oak and Bournbrook and their children are due for Wednesday's "day of delight".

24th July 1909 – Birmingham News

Selly Oak and Bournbrook

Co-operative Children's Party. – The children's party held each summer by the Selly Oak and Bournbrook branches of the Ten Acres and Stirchley Co-operative Society took place on Saturday, at Selly Oak Park. The children, who numbered over 1,000, assembled at the University Stores, and marched in procession to the park, headed by the Selly Oak Victoria Brass Band. The younger children were conveyed on gaily decorated vehicles, and many carried flags. At the park a substantial tea was provided. Entertainments were given by a pierrot troupe, and Professor Archer amused the children with a Punch and Judy show. Selections were played by the band, and in the evening fire balloon ascents were made. The children each received a packet of sweets.

21st August 1909 – Birmingham News

Extension of Cotteridge Park
Local Government Board Inquiry
Interesting Statistics

An enquiry was held by Mr. Edgar Dudley, F.S.I., on behalf of the Local Government Board, at Stirchley Institute, on Thursday morning, into an application by the Kings Norton and Northfield District Council for sanction to borrow £2,530 for the purchase of land for the extension of Cotteridge Park.

(further in the report:)

At present the Council owned or leased the following parks and recreation grounds:-

Name and Situation	Area a r p	Purchase Price	Cost per acre
Selly Oak Park	11 2 5	Gift	—
Cotteridge Park	3 2 0	£500	£142
" "	9 0 21	£2,155	£236
Muntz Park, Selly Oak	3 0 30	Gift	—
" "	2 2 9	£2,030	£796

Victoria Common, Northfield	4 0 0	Gift	—
Stirchley Playground	1 1 22	Gift	—
Kings Heath Park	15 2 6	£11,000	£707
Bournbrook Recreation Ground	4,510 sq. yds.	On Lease,	£5 per annum
Stirchley Bowling Green	2,400 sq. yds.	On Lease,	nominal rent.

2nd October 1909 – Birmingham News

Selly Oak and Bournbrook

Charity Sports – The annual charity sports in aid of the Selly Oak and Bournbrook District Nurses' Fund took place on Saturday at Selly Oak Park (kindly lent by the Kings Norton and Northfield Urban District Council). A street parade took place prior to the sports, and prizes were given for fancy dresses and decorated vehicles. The procession was headed by the Selly Oak Victoria Brass Band and the Selly Oak and Bournville Fire Brigades also took part. At the park the principal event was the Fire Brigade competition. The drills consisted of one man, two men and four. Only four brigades entered, and one (Oldbury) failed to turn up. By a smart performance Bournville won the first prize, and thereby hold the handsome challenge cup, value 16 guineas for the ensuing year. Kings Heath took the second prize (Messrs. Cadbury challenge cup, value 8 guineas), and Selly Oak the third (medals value £1 1s. given by Captain Crump). Lieut. Chandler (Smethwick) and Engineer Sherwood (Cape Hill) officiated as judges. The times were:- Bournville: One man, 36.3, two men 27.2, four men 21.4, total 85.4 sec. Kings Heath: One man 33.4, two men 30.4, four men 22.1, total 86.4 sec. Selly Oak: One man 43, two men, 30, four men 24.4, total 97.4 sec. At the close of the sports the prizes were presented by Dr. W. J. Garbutt, and on the proposition of Captain Hackett (Bournville), he was accorded a hearty vote of thanks. The sports were arranged by the committee, of which Mr. H. Seabourne is secretary and Mr. C.H. Woolley treasurer. The sports results were as follows:-
One Mile Flat Handicap. – 1, W. Wareham; 2, H. Bywater.
100 yards Flat Handicap. – 1, B. Fox; 2, E. Roden.
Half-mile Flat Handicap. – 1, H. Mason; 2, E. Porter
Obstacle Race. – E. Roden and E. Fox, dead-heat, 1; 3, H. Mason.
100 Yards Boys' Race. – 1, W. Hewitt; 2, I. Hadley, 3, J. Parrock.
Egg and Spoon Race (Nurses). – 1, M. Faultless; 2, K. Hughes; 3, D. Horton.
Girls' Race. – 1, M. Harrison; 2, D. Horton.
Best-dressed Clowns. – 1, W. Washbourne; 2, W. Hughes; 3, G. Thompson; 4, F. Hetherington.
Best-decorated Vehicle. – 1, Misses Woolley.
Best Novelty – 1, Mr. Hackwood.
Air Rifle Shooting. – Team competition: 1, Messrs J.T. Horton, J. Horton, H. Horton and J. Shield. Individual: 1, S. Grove.

6th October 1909 – Minute of KN&N UDC, and reported on
9th October 1909 – Birmingham News

Mr. Councillor Shann presented the following report of the Baths, Parks and Cemeteries Committee.

Your Committee beg to report:-

4 Selly Oak Park – gift of a peacock

That Mr. C. Cartwright, of Chapel Lane, Selly Oak, has presented a peacock to be placed in the Selly Oak Park, and your Committee have conveyed the best thanks of the Council to Mr. Cartwright for his gift.

It was moved by Mr. Councillor Shann, seconded by Mr. Councillor Harbun, and resolved (minute 354), that the report of the Baths, Parks, and Cemeteries Committee be approved and adopted.

9th October 1909 – Birmingham News

Village Gossip
Kings Norton's Parks

The various parks and recreation grounds which now exist in the Kings Norton district have not been acquired without a good deal of expense on the part of the community, but there is probably no public asset that the people would be less willing to surrender. I have been very much impressed with the extent of the use which the people make of them, and this of course is the measure of their appreciation. The efforts which the Council are making to add to the attractiveness of the parks entitle them to the grateful thanks of their constituents. At Selly Oak, at Cotteridge, and at Kings Heath the whole aspect of the parks as they were even a year ago has been altered. Now I see a further five or six hundred pounds is to be spent upon them, in addition to the ordinary maintenance expenses. Two birds are to be killed with one stone also, for in doing so work is to be found for the unemployed. I think no one will object to this form of municipal enterprise, and on the contrary, I imagine there are others who will feel like myself, viz., anxious to say a word of commendation in order that the Council may feel that their work is not unappreciated in this direction at least.

3rd November 1909 – Minute of KN&N UDC

Mr. Councillor Shann presented the following report of the Baths, Parks and Cemeteries Committee.

14. 1909

Your Committee beg to report:-

8 Entertainments in parks

Your Committee beg to submit the following summary showing the entertainments given in the various parks during the past summer:-

Park	No. of band performances	No. of other entertainments	Total No. of entertainments	Amounts Contributed to Bands £ s d
King's Heath Park	24	24	48	15 13 0
Selly Oak Park	11	7	18	13 10 6
Cotteridge Park	12	8	20	12 3 0
Muntz Park	5	7	12	5 17 0
Victoria Common	5	1		6 15 6
Bournbrook Recreation Ground	4	2	6	7 9 0
Totals	61	49	110	61 8 0

It was moved by Mr. Councillor Shann, seconded by Mr. Councillor Harbun, and resolved (minute 403), that the report of the Baths, Parks, and Cemeteries Committee as amended (nb – amendment was nothing to do with the Park) be approved and adopted.

193

Chapter 15

1910

26th February 1910 – Birmingham News

Kings Norton and Northfield Urban District Council
Entertainments in Parks and Recreation Grounds

The above-named Council invite OFFERS from BANDS and CONCERT PARTIES to give Voluntary Entertainments in the following Parks and Recreation Grounds:-
   KINGS HEATH PARK
   SELLY OAK PARK
   COTTERIDGE PARK (Franklin Road)
   MUNTZ PARK (Umberslade Road)
   VICTORIA COMMON, NORTHFIELD
   BOURNBROOK RECREATION GROUND

Bands and Concert Parties are requested to note that the Council DO NOT ENGAGE the services of any Band or Concert Party, neither do they guarantee the repayment of any loss sustained, or expenses incurred, with the entertainments given. The Council are, however, prepared to contribute towards the expenses of entertainments given by BANDS at the rate of one shilling and sixpence for each performer, and five shillings for the band master, such contribution being limited to twenty-five performers.

All Bands and Concert Parties may, however, make a charge for the hire of seats within the Bandstand Enclosure, where such are provided, and the Council will have no objection to a Collection being made.

Offers, giving full particulars of the Band or Concert Party, and of the Proposed Programme, should be sent to the undersigned as soon as possible.
                    By Order,
                    EDWIN DOCKER
                        Clerk to the above-named Council.

10, Newhall Street,
      Birmingham,
            26th February 1910.

6th April 1910 – Minute of KN&N UDC, and reported on
9th April 1910 – Birmingham News

Mr. Councillor Shann presented the following report of the Baths, Parks and Cemeteries Committee.

Your Committee beg to report:-

<u>7 Enclosures round band stands in parks and provision of seats for same</u>

That they have considered the following tenders for supplying and fixing iron fencing 4 feet 6 inches high for the purpose of making an enclosure round the band stand in each of the King's Heath, Selly Oak and Cotteridge parks:-

	In respect of each park
Mr. John Elwell, Birmingham	£33 7 0
Messrs. Hill and Smith, Brierley Hill	£34 2 0
Bayliss, Jones, and Bayliss, Ltd., Wolverhampton	£37 16 0
Francis Morton and Co., Ltd.	£49 19 0

Your Committee being of the opinion that an enclosure 3 feet 6 inches high would be more suitable obtained a further estimate from Mr. John Elwell in the sum of £26 1s in respect of each park for supplying and fixing fence 3 feet 6 inches high, and they beg to recommend that the tender of Mr. John Elwell, in the sum of £78 3s., for supplying and fixing iron fencing 3 feet 6 inches high for the purpose of forming enclosures round the band stands in King's Heath, Selly Oak, and Cotteridge parks be accepted, subject to his entering into a contract, to be prepared by the Clerk, for the due performance of the work, and that the Common Seal of the Council be affixed to such contract.

Your Committee have also considered the question of providing chairs to be placed in the above-mentioned enclosures, and they beg to recommend that they be authorised to purchase eight dozen chairs for each of the King's Heath, Selly Oak, and Cotteridge parks, at a cost not exceeding £2 per dozen.

It was moved by Mr. Councillor Shann, seconded by Mr. Councillor Wilson, and resolved (minute 109), that the tender of Mr. John Elwell, of Phoenix Works, Birmingham, in the sum of £78 3s., for supplying and fixing iron fencing 3 feet 6 inches high for the purpose of forming enclosures round the band stands in King's Heath, Selly Oak, and Cotteridge parks be accepted, subject to his entering into a contract, to be prepared by the Clerk, for the due performance of the work, and that the Common Seal of the Council be affixed to such contract.

It was moved by Mr. Councillor Shann, seconded by Mr. Councillor James, and resolved (minute 110), that the Baths, Parks, and Cemeteries Committee be authorised to purchase eight dozen chairs for each of the King's Heath, Selly Oak, and Cotteridge parks, at a cost not exceeding £2 per dozen.

7th May 1910 – Birmingham News

Kings Norton and Northfield District Council

On the motion for the adoption of the report of the Baths, Parks, and Cemeteries Committee, Councillor Thompson asked by whose authority demonstrations, whether political or otherwise, were allowed to be held in the parks.

Councillor Shann, in reply, said the authority was given by the committee and was afterwards sanctioned by the Council. The policy of the committee was not to allow the use of the parks for sectional demonstrations but for united gatherings or children's festivals. Every case was brought before the Council and endorsed by them. The only political demonstrations held in the parks had been two, these having been a Conservative demonstration held at Kings Heath, and a Labour Party demonstration held last Saturday in the Cotteridge Park.

Councillor Thompson said the case of the Labour Party demonstration had not been before the Council for sanction, and he intimated that he would raise the question at the next meeting of the committee.

28th May 1910 – Birmingham News

Selly Oak Children's Festival
To be or not to be?

(A long article reporting a meeting at which various opinions on the advisability of holding the event, given the general lack of support, were aired. It was eventually agreed, after several amendments to a proposal, to hold the event. The last sentence of the article reads:)

The date of the festival was fixed for July 13 at Selly Oak Park.

1st June 1910 – Minute of KN&N UDC

Mr. Councillor Shann presented the following report of the Baths, Parks and Cemeteries Committee.

Your Committee beg to report:-

3 <u>Selly Oak Park – shelter</u>
That they have considered a plan and specification, prepared by the Surveyor, for the construction of a wind screen for the shelter in the Selly Oak Park, together with an estimate of the cost thereof amounting to £65, and they beg to recommend that the work be carried out, and that your Committee be authorised to obtain tenders therefor.

It was moved by Mr. Councillor Shann, seconded by Mr. Councillor Coley, and resolved (minute 195), that a wind screen for the protection of the shelter at the Selly Oak Park be constructed at an estimated cost of £65, and that the Baths, Parks, and Cemeteries Committee be authorised to obtain tenders for the execution of the work.

4th June 1910 – Birmingham News

Public Announcements
Kings Norton and Northfield Urban District Council
To Refreshment Caterers and Others

The above-named Council are prepared to receive offers from refreshment caterers and others for the right to sell refreshments in the following parks and recreation grounds of the Council for the period ending 31st October, 1910:-

Kings Heath Park
Selly Oak Park (Gibbins Road)
Cotteridge Park (Franklin Road)
Victoria Common (Northfield)
Muntz Park (Umberslade Road)
Selly Park Recreation Ground (Selly Avenue)
Stirchley Playground and Bowling Green (Hazelwell Street)

The right to sell refreshments will be granted subject to the following conditions:-

(i) The contractor shall erect a stall for the sale of such refreshments in accordance with plans and designs and in a situation to be first approved by the Council
(ii) The charges for refreshments shall be reasonable; the Council to be the sole judges as to the reasonableness of the charges.
(iii) The contractor shall not supply intoxicating liquors.
(iv) In the event of the Council closing the parks or recreation grounds to the general public for a short period, the contractor shall not be entitled to provide refreshments during such period.
(v) No refreshments shall be sold on Sundays.
(vi) In the event of the breach on the part of the contractor of any or either of the foregoing conditions, the contractor shall immediately upon request by the Council cease to supply refreshments in the above-named parks or recreation grounds.

Offers in sealed envelopes endorsed "Sale of refreshments in Parks" must reach the undersigned not later than 12 noon on Monday, the 20th day of June, 1910.

By Order,
EDWIN DOCKER
Clerk to the above-named Council.

10, Newhall Street,
　　Birmingham.
　　　　4th June, 1910

Selly Oak and Bournbrook

Children's Festival Not to be Held – A meeting of the Selly Oak Children's Festival Committee was held on Thursday evening, at the Selly Oak Institute, Mr. C.H. Harbun presiding. It will be remembered that a long discussion took place on the preceding Thursday as to the advisability of holding a children's festival or not. It was then decided to hold a festival by a small majority. The subject was again introduced at Thursday's meeting, and similar arguments were advanced to those used at the previous meeting. Eventually a resolution that no festival be held this year was carried by 17 votes to 11. The committee will not be disbanded, but will be called together again in the spring of next year.

6th July 1910 – Minute of KN&N UDC

In the absence of the Chairman of the Committee Mr. Councillor Hayes presented the following report of the Baths, Parks and Cemeteries Committee.

Your Committee beg to report:-

5 Applications for use of the parks
That they have granted the use of portions of the following parks to the Ten Acres and Stirchley Co-operative Society, Limited, for the purposes of holding children's summer parties in connection with the society:-

2nd July, 1910, Cotteridge Park;
9th July, 1910, King's Heath Park;
16th July, 1910, Selly Oak Park.

6 Provision of swings, etc., for Selly Oak and Cotteridge Parks
That they have considered the following estimates for supplying swings, a "giant stride", and a see-saw for each of the Selly Oak and Cotteridge Parks:-

Messrs. Clapshaw & Cleave, Birmingham	£54 12 6
Mr. W. Grenville, Birmingham	£35 4 0

and they beg to recommend that the estimate of Mr. W. Grenville, in the sum of £35 4s., be accepted.

9 Chairs for band stand enclosures
Your Committee beg to recommend that a further eight dozen chairs be purchased for the band stand enclosures in each of King's Heath, Selly Oak, and Cotteridge parks, at a cost not exceeding £2 per dozen.

It was moved by Mr. Councillor Hayes, seconded by Mr. Councillor Kelley, and resolved (minute 238), that the estimate of Mr. W. Grenville, of Birmingham, in the sum of £35 4s for supplying swings, giant strides, and see-saws for the Selly Oak and Cotteridge parks be accepted.

It was moved by Mr. Councillor Hayes, seconded by Mr. Councillor Fryer, and resolved (minute 242), that a further supply of eight dozen chairs be purchased for the band stand enclosures in each of King's Heath, Selly Oak, and Cotteridge Parks at an estimated cost of £2 per dozen.

9th July 1910 – Birmingham News

[The Urban District Council of Kings Norton and Northfield placed a long Public Announcement under the Advertisements Regulations Act 1907. Part II of that act regulated "the exhibition of advertisements in such places and in such manner or by such means to affect injuriously the amenities of a public park or pleasure ground." Effectively hoarding advertisements had to be 150 yards away from a park; and then they could not exceed 20 ft in height and illuminated letters could not exceed 2 ft in height.

An associated schedule made the regulations applicable to the Council's parks, including Selly Oak Park.]

Kings Norton and Northfield District Council
The Co-op. and the Use of the Parks for Treats

The Chairman read a letter sent to him by the secretary of the Selly Oak and Bournbrook Traders' Association, complaining of the exclusive use of the parks being granted to the local Co-operative Society for children's treats on the ground that they were organised as trading advertisements. A similar letter had been sent to other councillors, including the chairman of the Baths and Parks Committee, which was responsible for giving permission for the holding of the treats. Councillor Shann, being unable to be present to answer on behalf of the committee, sent a letter to the chairman, in which he stated that the society was not allowed the exclusive use of the parks, but given permission only to rope off a small portion during the period that tea was served. Further, the treats were not a trade advertisement as they were confined to the children of the members of the society.

Councillor Lucas expressed the hope that any cause for complaint would be avoided in future by the use of the parks being refused to any trading society.

Councillor Ball said he understood that the Selly Oak Park was closed while tea was being served.

Councillor Lloyd expressed his regret at the discussion. The party was for the benefit of the children of the members of the society, and no appeal or advertisement of any sort was made in the park. The only method of making known the party was by the use of posters. He regretted that opposition to such a party should come from "the children's friends".

Councillor Whittaker asked whether the park belonged to the Council or the people. If five thousand families in the district were desirous of the use of the park for giving their children a treat he asserted that they have a right to have it.

Dr. Lilley said the troubles that had arisen in regard to the use of the parks seemed to be due to the committee having no settled policy.

The Chairman said it was difficult to frame rules to meet a question of that kind. The committee was given a discretion as to granting the use of the parks for special purposes.

The subject was then dropped.

23rd July 1910 – Birmingham News

Kings Norton and Northfield Districts

Co-operative Children's Summer Party. – About twelve hundred children participated on Saturday in the annual summer party of the Bournbrook and Selly Oak branches of the Ten Acres and Stirchley Co-operative Society, the arrangements being carried out by the local committee. The children assembled at the University Branch, Bristol Road, and headed by the Selly Oak Brass Band and May pole children, the latter looking exceedingly pretty and attractive, they marched in procession to the Selly Oak Park (a portion of which had been kindly placed at the society's disposal by the Baths and Parks Committee of the District Council). The procession was marshalled by Mr. C. Hemming, a director of the society. On reaching the park a substantial tea was provided. Two performances were given by the May pole children under the direction of Mrs. Barton, assisted by Mr. H. Bates and several friends. At the conclusion of tea parents and friends of the children were admitted, and a goodly number availed themselves of the opportunity of being present. During the evening fire balloon ascents were made, but were not very successful owing to a very strong wind. The children thoroughly enjoyed themselves, and Messrs Wood and Sodon caused much amusement to them as clowns.

27th July 1910 – Minute of KN&N UDC

Mr. Councillor Shann presented the following report of the Baths, Parks and Cemeteries Committee.

Your Committee beg to report:-

4 Selly Oak Park – provision of wind screen in shelter
That they have considered the following tenders for supplying and fixing a glazed wind screen in the shelter at the Selly Oak Park:-

	£	s	d
Mr. W.C. Jamieson, York Road, King's Heath	63	14	10
Messrs. T. Halward & Sons, Selly Oak	70	0	0
Messrs. Thos. Loud & Sons, Bournbrook	75	0	0
Mr. A.R. Waldron, King's Heath	82	11	5
Mr. John Dawson, King's Heath	88	12	0

and they beg to recommend that the tender of Mr. W.C. Jamieson, in the sum of £64 13s (sic) 10d., be accepted, subject to his entering into a contract, to be prepared by the Clerk, for the due performance of the work, and that the Common Seal of the Council be affixed to such contract.

It was moved by Mr. Councillor Shann, seconded by Mr. Councillor Coley, and resolved (minute 293), that the tender of Mr. W.C. Jamieson, of York Road, King's Heath, in the sum of £64 14s 10d., for supplying and fixing a glazed wind screen in the shelter at the Selly Oak Park, be accepted, subject to his entering into a contract, to be prepared by the Clerk, for the due performance of the work, and that the Common Seal of the Council be affixed to such contract.

30th July 1910 – Birmingham News

Kings Norton and Northfield District Council

Improvements in parks. On the recommendation of the Baths and Parks Committee it was decided to erect a new shelter in the Cotteridge Park at a cost of £275.

Councillor Shann (chairman of the committee) said the present shelter only accommodated about 12 people and was not adequate for the park which was the largest and most important in the district. The (sic) proposed to erect the shelter on the same lines as at Kings Heath park. It was also decided to erect a wind screen for the shelter in Selly Oak Park at a cost of £64; and to provide public conveniences in the Victoria Common Northfield, at a cost of £240, which would include the cost of making a sewer along the line of an intended road from the Street Farm in Banbury Road.

The Coop and the Parks. Councillor Thompson asked the chairman of the Baths and Parks Committee why the parks were closed on the occasion of the Co-operative children's festival. They were told at the last Council meeting that the parks would not be closed and that only a portion would be roped off for the children to have tea in.

Councillor Shann said he knew nothing about it as he was away from the last committee meeting, but if such was the case it was absolutely against the orders of the committee.

Councillor Lucas said the public was admitted to the Selly Oak Park most of the afternoon, but the gates were closed just for a few minutes after the children had entered. He thought it was just a mistake and one they should not take any notice of.

Councillor Coley said he noticed a letter in the press re the closing of Kings Heath Park and he was glad to find that it was not by the authority of the committee that the gate in Avenue Road was closed for some time.

Councillor Lloyd, who was a director of the Co-operative Society, said with regard to the fete at Selly Oak Park, that to get control of the children they had to close the gates for a few minutes, and he thought that the Park Keeper in doing so had acted in the right way.

The report was adopted.

5th October 1910 – Minute of KN&N UDC

Mr. Councillor Shann presented the following report of the Baths, Parks and Cemeteries Committee.

Your Committee beg to report:-

3 <u>Cycle for Mr. J.T. Horton, Superintendent of Parks</u>
That they have had under consideration the number of parks and recreation grounds under the supervision of Mr. J.T. Horton, and in order that he may be in a position to supervise the same adequately, your Committee beg to recommend that Mr. Horton be provided with a cycle at a cost not exceeding £10.

It was moved by Mr. Councillor Shann, seconded by Mr. Councillor Fryer, and resolved (minute 318), that Mr. J.T. Horton, Superintendent of Selly Oak and other parks, be provided with a cycle at a cost not exceeding £10 to facilitate the carrying out of his duties.

2nd November 1910 – Minute of KN&N UDC

Mr. Councillor Shann presented the following report of the Baths, Parks and Cemeteries Committee.

Your Committee beg to report:-

4 <u>Receipts for use of tennis courts and bowling greens in various parks</u>
That the following amounts have been received for the use of the tennis courts and bowling grounds in various parks:-

	Tennis courts	Bowling greens	Total
King's Heath Park	17 12 10	15 6 8	32 19 6
Cotteridge Park	12 19 0	23 18 8	36 17 8
Selly Oak Park	2 15 8	–	2 15 8
Stirchley Bowling Green	–	3 7 4	3 7 4
Totals	33 7 6	42 12 8	76 0 2

5 Entertainments in parks

That they have received the following statement as to the entertainments given in the various parks during the past summer:-

Park	No of band performances	No. of other entertainments	Total No. of entertainments	Amounts Contributed to Bands £ s d
King's Heath Park	18	44	62	12 11 0
Selly Oak Park	10	15	25	10 14 6
Cotteridge Park	10	26	36	9 2 6
Muntz Park	10	8	18	10 11 6
Victoria Common	5	3	8	5 9 6
Bournbrook Recreation Ground	3	0	3	3 5 6
Totals	56	96	152	51 14 6

7th December 1910 – Minute of KN&N UDC

Mr. Councillor Shann presented the following report of the Baths, Parks and Cemeteries Committee.

Your Committee beg to report:-

3 Selly Oak Park – painting of lodge, etc

That they have considered the following tenders for painting the lodge and wind screen in the shelter at the Selly Oak Park:-

	Winds screen £ s d	Lodge £ s d	Total £ s d
Mr. H. Spencer, King's Heath	19 10 0	14 0 0	33 10 0
Mr. J. Harvey	20 0 0	5 14 0	35 14 0
Messrs. Daniel and Son	24 10 0	18 0 0	42 10 0
Mr. G.H. Atkins	28 12 0	15 0 0	43 12 0
Mr. A. Humphries	29 0 0	18 0 0	47 0 0

> Your Committee beg to recommend that the tender of Mr. H. Spencer, in the sum of £33 10s, be accepted.

It was moved by Mr. Councillor Shann, seconded by Mr. Councillor Fryer, and resolved (minute 394), that the tender of Mr. H. Spencer, of King's Heath, in the sum of £33 10s, for painting the lodge and wind screen in the shelter at Selly Oak Park, be accepted.

Chapter 16

1911

1st February 1911 – Minute of KN&N UDC, and reported on
4th February 1911 – Birmingham News

Mr. Councillor Shann presented the following report of the Baths, Parks and Cemeteries Committee.

Your Committee beg to report:-

6 <u>Additional tennis courts and bowling greens in various parks</u>

Your Committee beg to recommend that additional tennis courts and bowling greens be constructed in various parks, at an estimated cost of £530, as follows:-

	No. of bowling greens	No. of tennis courts
Kings Heath	1	2
Cotteridge	1	2
Selly Oak	1	0
Selly Park Recreation Ground	1	2
Total	4	6

Your Committee also beg to recommend that application be made to the Local Government Board for their sanction to a loan in respect of the cost of carrying out the work.

7 <u>Entertainments in the Parks</u>

Your Committee beg to recommend that advertisements be issued inviting offers from bands and concert parties to give entertainments in the parks and recreation grounds of the Council, and that the Council agree to contribute towards the cost of entertainments given by the bands, at a rate of one shilling and sixpence for each performer, and five shillings for the conductor, the contribution being limited to 25 performers; also that a sum not exceeding £100 be expended in this respect during the ensuing season.

It was moved by Mr. Councillor Shann, seconded by Mr. Councillor Fryer, and resolved (minute 27), that four additional bowling greens and six tennis courts be constructed in the various parks referred to in paragraph 6 of the report of the Baths, Parks and Cemeteries Committee, at an estimated cost of £530.

It was moved by Mr. Councillor Shann, seconded by Mr. Councillor Coley, and resolved (minute 28), that application be made to the Local Government Board for their sanction to the borrowing by the Council of the sum of £530 in respect of the cost of constructing four additional bowling greens and six tennis courts in various parks.

It was moved by Mr. Councillor Shann, seconded by Mr. Councillor Valentine, and resolved (minute 29), that advertisements be issued inviting offers from bands and concert parties to give entertainments in the parks and recreation grounds of the Council, and that the Council agree to contribute towards the cost of entertainments given by the bands, at a rate of one shilling and sixpence for each performer, and five shillings for the conductor, the contribution being limited to 25 performers; also that a sum not exceeding £100 be expended in this respect during the ensuing season.

4th February 1911 – Birmingham News, and again on
11th March 1911

Kings Norton and Northfield Urban District Council
Entertainments in Parks and Recreation Grounds

The above-named Council invite OFFERS from bands and concert parties to give voluntary entertainments in the following Parks and Recreation Grounds:-

KINGS HEATH PARK
SELLY OAK PARK
COTTERIDGE PARK (Franklin Road)
MUNTZ PARK (Umberslade Road)
VICTORIA COMMON, NORTHFIELD
BOURNBROOK RECREATION GROUND

Bands and concert parties are requested to note that the Council do not engage the services of any band or concert party, neither do they guarantee the repayment of any loss sustained, or expenses incurred with the entertainments given. The Council are, however, prepared to contribute towards the expenses of entertainments given by bands at the rate of one shilling and sixpence for each performer and five shillings for the band master, such contribution being limited to twenty-five performers.

All Bands and Concert Parties may, however, make a charge for the hire of seats within the band-stand enclosure, where such are provided, and the Council will have no objection to a collection being made.

Offers, giving full particulars of the Band or Concert Party, and of the proposed programme, should be sent to the undersigned not later than 31st March, 1911.

By Order,

EDWIN DOCKER

Clerk to the above-named Council.

10, Newhall Street,
    Birmingham,
        4th February 1911.
        (11th March 1911)

1st March 1911 – Minute of KN&N UDC

Mr. Councillor Shann presented the following report of the Baths, Parks and Cemeteries Committee.

Your Committee beg to report:-

<u>5 Selly Oak Park – salary of Superintendent</u>

That they have had under consideration the wages paid to Mr. J.T. Horton, Superintendent of the Selly Oak Park, and having regard to the fact that several of the other parks and recreation grounds are also under his control, together with the grounds at several of the libraries, and trees in certain of the highways of the district, your Committee beg to recommend that his wages be increased from 28s. to 30s. per week, rising by annual increments of 1s. per week to the maximum of 32s. per week.

It was moved by Mr. Councillor Shann, seconded by Mr. Councillor Fryer, and resolved (minute 77), that the wages of Mr. J.T. Horton be increased from 28s. to 30s. per week, rising by annual increments of 1s. per week to the maximum of 32s. per week.

4th March 1911 – Birmingham News

Selly Oak and Bournbrook
Coronation[59] Festival Committee

Mr. C.H. Harbun presided over a good attendance of the Coronation Festival Committee on Thursday at the Selly Oak Institute. Among the new members present were the Revs. A.E. Haviland and F.W. Walker. – The Secretary reported that he had applied to the Baths and Parks Committee for use of Selly Oak Park. He had received a reply that no objection would be raised to the park being used for the annual festival on Coronation day, but on no account must the park be closed at any time to the

---

[59] The Coronation of King George V.

general public. The Secretary said that he had replied to the letter, saying that they wished for the park to be closed, and the matter was going to receive further consideration at the next meeting of the committee. The Secretary said he had corresponded with the Oddfellows and Foresters, Liberal and Conservative Associations, Boy Scouts, the clergy, Church Lads' Brigade, Rechabites, etc., with a view to their cooperation in the festival. The Oddfellows and Foresters had promised to do what they could, and the Boys Scouts, through Mr. Miller, promised their assistance. The C.L.B. could not give any answers yet. The question of fireworks was left to the Field and Sports Committee. It was decided to engage Mr. W. Jones's Male Voice Choir and Mr. Quinton's Choir. The conveners of the sub-committees' first meetings were appointed as follows: – Field and Sports Sub-committee, Mr. Bates; Procession Sub-committee, Mr. West; Catering Committee, Mr. A.E. Looker. With regard to the finance question, the Chairman thought that all the heads of firms in the district ought to be approached for a subscription. The richer people, in his opinion, also ought to help them. – It was decided to make an appeal for funds the first week in May, unless the Finance Committee decided otherwise. The next meeting was arranged for April 27. Further subscriptions towards the cost of the festival had been received from Councillor Lucas and Mr. C. Pember, £1 1s, each, and Councillor F.B. Darling 10s.

5th April 1911 – Minute of KN&N UDC

Mr. Councillor Shann presented the following report of the Baths, Parks and Cemeteries Committee.

> Your Committee beg to report:-
>
> 5 <u>Selly Oak Park – children's festival and shopping week festival</u>
>
> That they have given permission for the Selly Oak and Bournbrook Children's Festival to be held in the Selly Oak Park on Coronation Day, and for the Shopping Week Festival Committee to organise a band concert and sports in that park on the evening of May 17th, 1911.

It was moved by Mr. Councillor Shann, seconded by Mr. Councillor Shephard, and resolved (minute 125), that the report of the Baths, Parks and Cemeteries Committee be approved and adopted.

13th May 1911 – Birmingham News

Selly Oak Shopping Week Festival

Selly Oak and Bournbrook were "en fete" on Thursday, the occasion being the opening of the Shopping Week Festival which is being held under the auspices of the Local Traders' and Ratepayers' Association. ………………

16. 1911

The Shopping Festival will conclude next Wednesday when there will be sports in the Selly Oak Park, and a torchlight tattoo by the F Company of the 8th Battalion Worcestershire Regiment at dusk. The Bournville Prize Band has been engaged, and will discourse music during the evening.

20th May 1911 – Birmingham News

Selly Oak Shopping Week
Sports in Selly Oak Park

A successful week's shopping festival at Selly Oak was brought to a conclusion on Wednesday evening with sports in the Selly Oak Park (by permission of the Kings Norton and Northfield Urban District Council). Favoured by beautiful weather, several thousand people congregated to see the various events and spent a most enjoyable evening. The proceedings opened with tea in the Park Shelter, at which nearly 90 tradesmen and their friends sat down. County Councillor A.C. Hayes (President of the Festival), presided, and there was also present Mrs. and Miss Hayes, Mr. Douglas Timins, Councillor and Mrs. C.A. Lucas, Mr. and Mrs. A.E. Looker, Mr. and Mrs. H. Roberts, Mr. and Mrs. W. H. Roberts, Mr. and Mrs. Jarvis Jones, Mr. and Mrs. E. Jones, Mr. and Mrs. C.H. Harbun, Mr. and Mrs. Pember, Mr. and Mrs. Usherwood, Mr. T. Deaman, Dr. W.J. Garbutt, Mr. and Mrs. McKennon, Mr. Musson, Mr. Pinson, Mr. and Mrs. White, Mr. and Mrs. F.S. Williamson, Mrs. and Miss Cotterell, Mr. and Mrs. Pearce, Miss Musson, Mr. and Mrs. Hedge, Mr. and Mrs. J.C. Tustin, Mrs. Tustin, Miss Hobbs, Mr. and Mrs. Benton, Mrs. Maries, Mrs. Beach, Mrs. Bickle, Mr. and Mrs. W. Smith, Miss Russell, Miss Ellson, Miss Coton, Mr. Baugh, and others. The catering was in the able hands of Mr. J. Haynes.

At the conclusion of tea Councillor Hayes presented the diplomas for window displays as follows:-

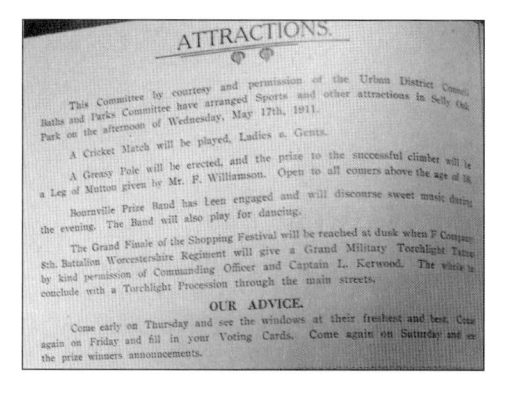

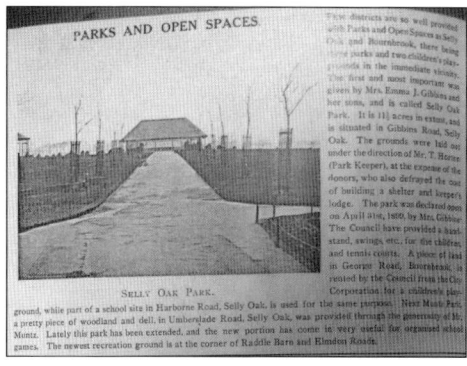

Extracts taken from the Souvenir Programme of the Selly Oak and Bournbrook Shopping Week Festival, 11-17th May 1911. Left: Page 17; Right: Page 39. Archive & Heritage Section, Birmingham Central Library, Ref: 996264 LF 92.3.

209

General Drapers. – 1, H. Roberts; 2, E. Jones; 3, E.J. Wilton.
Fancy Drapers. – 1, E. Jones; 2, H. Roberts; 3, Dixon and Co.
Milliners. – 1, H. Roberts; 2, Dixon and Co.; 3, E. Jones.
Grocers and Dairymen. – 1, C.W. Pember; 2, Maypole; 3, Moyles.
Butchers. – 1, K.S. Williamson; 2, Honeybourne; 3, Whitehouse.
Fruiterers. – 1, Steatham; 2, Tucker; 3, Musson.
Boot and Shoe Dealers. – 1, Morton and Co.; 2, Stafford and Northampton; 3, Munn.
Tailors. – 1, Jarvis Jones; 2, Bob Roberts; 3, Warr.
Clothiers. – 1, Hedge; 2, Partridge, 3, Farrell.
Bakers – 1, Deaman; 2, Looker; 3, Woodward.
Confectioners. – 1, Eckersley; 2, Sneath; 3, Nash.
Tobacconists, Toys and Jewellers. – 1, Harbun; 2, Roddis; 3, Gunning.
Florists and Corn Dealers. – 1, Peace; 2, Mills; 3, Green.
Furnishers, etc. – 1, Godleys; 2, J. Cox; 3, McKinnon.
Chemists. – 1, Mayon; 2, Colley; 3, Birt.
Outside Decorations. – 1, W.H. Roberts and Dixon and Co.; 2, E. Woodward; 3, H. Roberts and E Jones.

Mr. W.H. Roberts (Chairman of the Committee) thanked Mr. Hayes for his services, not only in distributing the prizes but in taking such a great interest in the festival. Mr. A.E. Looker supported the vote of thanks, and in reply Mr Hayes said he hoped the outcome of the festival would be success to Selly Oak.

A humorous Ladies v. Gentlemen cricket match was then started. The ladies batted first, and with the help of the scorer (Mr. W.H. Roberts) knocked up the respectable score of 170 in record time. In reply the gentlemen, who had to bat with broomstales, could only total 10, and the ladies were therefore easy winners. Scores:-

Ladies
Mrs. Ensor b Hayes	14
Mrs. Benton c Looker b Hayes	10
Miss Hobbs c Loames	11
Miss Taylor b H. Roberts	14
Mrs. Roberts b H. Roberts	12
Mrs. Harbun b Usherwood	14
Mrs. Williamson b H. Roberts	0
Miss Lilley b Hayes	14
Mrs. Hedge b H. Roberts	9
Miss Cotterell b H. Roberts	37
Mrs. Looker b Loames	6
Mrs. Haynes b Harbun	8
Mrs. E. Jones not out	10
Extras	10
Total	170

Gentlemen

C.H. Harbun b Miss Cotterell	0
A.C. Hayes b Mrs. Jarvis Jones	0
H. Loames b Mrs. Jarvis Jones	0
T. Deaman b Miss Cotterell	2
I. Usherwood not out	4
— Davies lbw b Miss Cotterell	3
A.E. Looker b Mrs E. Jones	1
— Poole b Mrs. E. Jones	0
H. Roberts b Mrs. E. Jones	0
Dr. Garbutt b Mrs Jarvis Jones	0
— Hedge b. Mrs. Harbun	0
Total	10

Sports were then indulged in. The ladies' egg and spoon race was first to be run off, and Mrs. Roberts, Mrs. Cotterell, Miss Cotterell, Miss Bishop, Mrs. Smith, and another lady succeeded in getting into the final, which was won by Miss Cotterell, Miss Bishop being second. A sack race for men provided an exciting struggle, and ended in favour of Mr. Benton, and Mr. T. Deaman was second. A gentlemen's potato and bucket race was then taken in two heats, and the finalists were Mr. Mills, Mr. Looker, Mr. Roddis, and Mr. Parry. Mr. Looker succeeded in winning easily, Mr. Mills being second. A similar event for the ladies was won by Mrs. Looker, Miss Bishop being second. A mixed blindfold race caused much amusement, and ended in favour of Mrs. Looker, Mr. Benton being second. The sports ended with a ham cutting competition, and after several good attempts by previous competitors the ham was cut down by Mr. Walter Smith. For the greater part of the evening a greasy pole defied the efforts of youths and boys to climb it, but eventually a youth named Hadley succeeded in getting the flag from the top, and thus became entitled to a leg of mutton given by Mr. F.S. Williamson. A kite flying competition for boys was also held and the prizes were awarded to:-
Kite Flying. – 1, A. Deeley; 2, Fred Elliot and W. Radford; 3, Clarence Simpkins.

The remaining competition was between six a side football teams. Eleven teams entered as follows:- Bournbrook Rovers, Bournbrook United, Dingle Rangers, Selly Oak Wesleyans, White Horse, Stepping Stone, Bournville Youths, Star F.C., Friends' Hall Juniors, and a traders' team. After keen contests Bournbrook Rovers and Star F.C. succeeded in getting into the final, but the game was abandoned owing to an accident to a player. During the evening the Bournville Prize Band, conducted by Mr. Sylvester, R.M.S.M., played selections of music, and towards dusk dancing on the green took place. The grand finale was reached about 9 o'clock when F Company of the 8th Battalion Worcestershire Regiment (Territorials), by permission of Captain L. Kerwood, gave a military torchlight tattoo. This was watched with interest by a large number of spectators. Afterwards, headed by the Bournville Band, The Territorials and members of the Selly Oak Company of the Church Lads Brigade participated in a torchlight procession through the main streets, which formed a fitting conclusion to the evening's festivities. Unfortunately there were two rather serious accidents. In the football competition one of the players, Bert Capewell, of Bournbrook Rovers, had the misfortune to break his ankle, and he was removed on the horse ambulance to the hospital. The other accident occurred earlier in the evening, a little boy breaking his arm. Dr. W.J. Garbutt rendered first aid, and the unfortunate lad was taken home.

The week's festival has been a great success, and the anticipations of the promoters have been realised. In connection with the Window Dressing Display, there was a competition for the nearest forecast to the judges' awards. About 400 entries were received, and after careful perusal of the post cards the prizes were given as follows:- 1, A. Anderson; 2, Miss Veccary and W. Hurlstone; 3, H. Cooper, W. Bell and Miss Twitty. There was also a children's essay competition, but the adjudications have not been made yet. The arrangements for the festival were in the hands of the following committee:- Messrs. W.H. Roberts (chairman), Frank Wilson (hon. treasurer), Jarvis Jones (secretary), A. Benton, W. Dufficy, R.W. Greenwood, C.H. Harbun, J. Haynes, A.M. Hedge, E. Jones, C.A. Lucas, A.E. Looker, A. Mills, W.E. Musson, W. Parry, C.W. Pember, W.J. Randall, J.E. Richardson, H. Roberts, B. Roberts, J. Roddis, A.J. Stainton, E.J. Walton, H. White, F.S. Williamson, and E. Woodward. Mr. A.E. Looker and Mr. Jarvis Jones were chairman and secretary respectively of the Finance and Advertising Committee, and Mr. Harry Roberts and Mr. J. Haynes chairman and secretary respectively of the Attraction and Competition Committee.

27th May 1911 – Birmingham News

Selly Oak and Bournbrook

Coronation Committee – A well-attended meeting of the Selly Oak and Bournbrook Coronation Committee was held on Thursday at the Selly Oak Institute, Mr. C.H. Harbun presiding. .... With regard to the proposed bonfire the secretary (Mr. R. Fowler) reported that the Battery Company had promised several loads of wood and empty tar barrels and some tar. Permission had been granted by the Parks and Baths Committee for the bonfire to be held in Selly Oak Park providing the committee take over the responsibility of accidents and damage. The secretary's action was confirmed. ....

7th June 1911 – Minute of KN&N UDC

In the absence of the Chairman, Mr. Councillor Fryer presented the following report of the Baths, Parks and Cemeteries Committee.

Your Committee beg to report:-

4 <u>Ten Acres and Stirchley Co-operative Society, Ltd – use of parks for children's parties</u>

That they have granted permission for children's parties in connection with the Ten Acres and Stirchley Co-operative Society, Ltd, to be held in Selly Oak, King's Heath, and Cotteridge parks on three Saturdays in July respectively, on the understanding that the admission of the public to the park is not restricted in any way. The society will be permitted to rope off a portion of ground in each park during a short period whilst the children partake of tea.

7 <u>Additional tennis courts and bowling greens – loan</u>

That the sanction of the Local Government Board has been received to the borrowing by the Council of the sum of £530 for the construction of tennis courts and bowling greens in various parks, such sum to be repaid within a period not exceeding 16 years from the date of borrowing the same.

8 <u>Playing of cricket and football in parks by adults in early morning</u>

That they have granted permission for adults to play cricket and football in the parks from the time of opening the same until 8.30 a.m.

It was moved by Mr. Councillor Fryer, seconded by Mr. Councillor Allen, and resolved (minute 206), that the report of the Baths, Parks and Cemeteries Committee be approved and adopted.

17th June 1911 – Birmingham News

Local Coronation Celebrations
Interesting Programmes

The preparations for the celebration of the Coronation in the various districts are now completed and some interesting programmes have been prepared. We give below summaries of the arrangements:-
Selly Oak and Bournbrook – Morning services will be held in the St. Mary's and St. Wulstan's Churches, and at one o'clock a procession, headed by the Woodgate and Cotteridge Prize Bands, will take place. All school children will participate, vehicles being provided for the infants. On the arrival at the park an excellent programme of entertainments will begin. As usual, the parents will be admitted after tea. The old people will be entertained to dinner in the Institute at three o'clock, and a concert will follow. The programme of entertainments for this park is timed to commence at two o'clock. The Woodgate Prize Band and Mr. Jones' Male Voice Choir will occupy the bandstand and give selections at intervals. The bonfire will be lit at nine p.m., and daylight fireworks will be let off at intervals.

The Heydays Of Selly Oak Park

23rd June 1911 – Birmingham Mail, and
24th June 1911 – Birmingham News

The Coronation
Selly Oak and Bournbrook

The celebrations at Selly Oak took the form of a children's festival and a dinner to the old people of 60 years of age and upwards. The streets were gaily decorated, the residents having used flags and bunting with great effect. In the morning services very similar to the Coronation service at Westminster were held at both the Parish Church and St. Wulstan's and there were large congregations. Early celebrations of Holy Communion were also held. The children assembled at their various schools at 12 p.m., and marched to Dawlish Road, where a procession was formed under the direction of Councillor R.E. Bull (chief marshall), Mr. Jarvis Jones (deputy marshall), and Mr. W.C. Clarke (secretary of procession committee). It was of an imposing character and was pronounced by many to have been the best yet seen in the district. Following the Selly Oak Fire Brigade came the Woodgate Prize band. Then passed in order the Maypole children, out-scholars, May Queen party and the children from the various schools. There was also a tableau representing a ship, manned by the members of the Selly Oak Discharged Sailors and Soldiers' Society. The concluding half of the procession was enlivened by the Cotteridge Prize Band, and the main feature was the prettily attired dancers from the St. Edward's Schools.

    The route taken was Coronation Road, Harrow Road, High Street, and Frederick Road to the Park. Upon arrival a lengthy programme of entertainments was commenced, the arrangements being in the hands of the fields and sports committee of which the Rev. F.W. Walker is chairman and Mr. H. Bates, secretary. The ex-Army and Naval men manned their "boat" and the St. Edward's Dancers marched round it singing "Rule Britannia". Action songs were prettily given by the scholars of Raddle Barn Infants' School under the direction of Miss Brady, and the St. Edward's Infant School Dancers gave a number of Maypole and other dances very effectively, Miss D'Arcy being in charge. They were followed by the Mrs. Barton's Senior Maypole Dancers, who went through their evolutions in a creditable manner. The Sunday School children of the Bournbrook Congregational Mission gave their charming May Queen Entertainment. Mr. Woodward conducting and afterwards the Boy Scouts commanded by the Rev. G.T. Miller gave an interesting display. The St. Edwards Senior School Dancers also gave a pretty display under the direction of Miss Hudson and brought the first half of the entertainment to a close. The children were then provided with tea, they being arranged in their various schools on both sides of the principal walk. A small army of workers were required for the serving of so many children, and in this connection valuable help was given by the school teachers, who also assisted in the cutting up. The fare provided included tea, bread and butter and cake. Before the commencement of the meal the children impressively rendered

16. 1911

en masse the National Anthem and Rule Brittannia. During tea enjoyable selections of music were given by the Woodgate Prize Band. Following the usual custom the parents were then admitted and for their benefit the entertainments given in the afternoon were repeated with the addition of several songs by the Hubert Road Church of England Boys' School. The band stand was occupied by the Woodgate Prize Band, and Mr. W. Jones' Male Voice Choir and their selections were very much appreciated. Successful fire balloon ascents and daylight firework displays were given at intervals by Messrs. Bland and Clarke. At dusk a huge bonfire was lit and about 15 loads of fuel consumed. The festivities were marred by an accident of a rather serious nature. As the children entered the park a salute was given by the Selly Oak C.L.B. on their muzzle loading naval gun. During reloading operations a charge prematurely exploded through a short damper and injured the right hand of a lad named Sargent, aged 13, of 27, George Road, Bournbrook, so badly that it had to be amputated. First aid was rendered by the Ambulance Corps on the ground, and the injured youth was taken on the horse ambulance to the Queen's Hospital where the operation was performed. Several other lads were badly scorched through the accident. At the meeting of the committee held in the evening after the close of the festival sympathy was expressed with the lad and it was decided to open a subscription list for him. This was started with donations of £1 1s. from Messrs. C.H. Harbun

Not the Selly Oak Coronation procession, but an impression of how it may have looked. Taken from Dowling, G., Giles, B.A. and Hayfield, C. (1987), "Selly Oak Past and Present: a photographic survey of a Birmingham suburb". University of Birmingham.

and Douglas Timins, and 10s. from Mr. H. Roberts. Collections were also made on the ground.

The old people's dinner took place in the afternoon at the Selly Oak Institute. All persons of 60 years of age and over were invited to be present, and about 400 accepted the invitations, while 70 others had their dinners sent them on Coronation Day before one o'clock. Very good fare was provided, and included roast beef and pickles, boiled ham, bread and butter, cake, strawberries, bananas, oranges and tea. The old people were heartily welcomed by Mr. C.H. Harbun who made it clear that the dinner was for rich and poor alike, and that no distinction was made. Following the dinner an entertainment was provided, Councillors Lloyd and Bull acting as chairmen. Among the artistes who gave their services were Messrs. J. Nix, E. Gregg, D. Timins, W. Keay, D. Strachan, Miss Eva Fowler, Miss Doris Taylor, Miss N. Cotterell, and the children from St. Edward's Schools, Mixed and Junior Departments. Mrs. R.E. Bull presided over the deliberations of the committee which had the arrangements in hand, and Mrs. R. Fowler acted as hon. secretary.

Mr. C.H. Harbun acted as chairman of the festival, and Messrs. F. Wilson and A.E. Looker as vice-chairman. Mr. H. Roberts discharged the onerous duties of treasurer in an able manner, and Mr. R. Fowler once more demonstrated his capabilities as a secretary. Messrs. J. Hanson and George Leonard were assistant secretaries. The officers were most loyally supported by the committee members who spared no effort to make the festival a success.

1st July 1911 – Birmingham News

The Coronation Accident at Selly Oak
Benefit Fund for the Injured Lad

We have received the following letter:-

Dear Sir, – The committee, at their meeting last evening, instructed me to write and ask you if you would be good enough to open a list in the "Birmingham News" on behalf of the lad William Sargent, a member of the Church Lads' Brigade, who was unfortunately injured while firing a Royal salute in Selly Oak Park on Coronation Day.

I regret to say his right hand has been amputated, which will very much hamper him in earning his living in the future.

Whilst my committee take no responsibility for the accident, yet they all feel it to be their bounden duty to do all that is possible to help the lad. A most generous response has already been made to the appeal issued, as the following contributions will show (see enclosure). – Yours faithfully,

ROBT. FOWLER, Secretary
8, Elm Road, Bournville,
June 28th, 1911

Enclosure

List of contributions already promised:-			
George Cadbury, Esq., J.P.	£20	0	0
R. Deykin, Esq., Captain Church Lads' Brigade	20	0	0
Rev. E.A. Haviland, M.A.	5	0	0
Councillor A.C. Hayes, Esq., J.P.			
Councillor R.E. Bull	1	1	0
Mr. C.H. Harbun	1	1	0
W. B. Bedington	1	1	0
Douglas Timins, M.A.	1	1	0
Mr. C.W. Pember	1	1	0
Doctor Cochrane	1	1	0
Canon Reader Smith	1	0	0
Mr. Harry Roberts		10	6
Mr. A.E. Looker		10	6
Mr. I. Usherwood		5	0
Mr. E. Southall		5	0
Mr. Ritchie		2	6
Mr. Spurrier		2	6
Mr. A. West		2	6
Collected in Park	7	14	9
*Mr. A.F. Nainby			
*Mr. H.A.R. Ellis			
*Mr. E.A. Alldridge			

*Amount not decided upon.

We have much pleasure in acceding to the above request, and contributing a guinea to the fund. The case is one specially deserving the generosity of our readers. – Ed. B.N.

Selly Oak and Bournbrook

The Coronation Day Accident – A special meeting of the Coronation Festivities Committee was held on Tuesday at the Selly Oak Institute to consider what steps should be taken to assist the lad who unfortunately lost his right hand as the result of a gun accident during the festivities. At the outset Mr. C.H. Harbun (president) thanked all those who had assisted in any way in making the festival a success.

On the proposition of Mr. J. Smith, seconded by Mr. H. Roberts, it was decided that the Festival Committee should undertake the work of raising a fund for the assistance of the unfortunate boy. Mr. Harbun suggested that a sub-committee should be formed to deal with the matter. Captain Deykin, who was in command of the C.L.B. of which the lad was a member, was of the opinion that it would be advisable to have only one fund to prevent overlapping. As far as the committee's fund was concerned, he (Mr. Harbun) was very pleased with the progress that had been made. He had spoken to Mr. G. Cadbury over the telephone and he promised to give £20. (Applause.) Mr. Pember who had employed the youth some years ago had given a guinea, and Dr. Cochrane had subscribed a like sum. Other small donations had been received.

Mr. Pownell suggested that a collection should be made in the schools and this was agreed to.

The Rev. E.A. Haviland (Vicar of Selly Oak) said that as the Church Lads' Brigade worked under him, he felt that he and the church should do something. Before hearing of the committee's fund they had decided on a certain course of action. He thought it would be wise to have a street collection while the matter was fresh in the people's minds. People were willing to give and the Church Lads' Brigade were anxious to work. Whatever was done ought to be done quickly.

Captain Deykin thanked the committee very much for allowing the boys to collect in the park. The sum so collected amounted to £7 14s. 9d. The lads were also anxious to carry out a house to house collection if the committee approved.

On the proposition of Mr. H. Roberts a sub-committee consisting of the President, Treasurer, Secretary, Rev. E.A. Haviland, Captain Deykin, Mr. R.E. Bull, and Mr. J. Smith was formed, with power to add to their number to draw up the appeals and make arrangements for the collection.

Mr. J. Smith trusted that the General Committee would have a voice in the spending of the money, and Mr. Fowler (secretary) said he would see to that.

8th July 1911 – Birmingham News

The Coronation Accident at Selly Oak
Benefit Fund for the Injured Lad

In response to a request from the Selly Oak Coronation Committee we have decided to receive and acknowledge subscriptions to the fund which is being raised on behalf of the lad, William Sargent, a member of the Church Lads' Brigade who was unfortunately injured while firing a Royal Salute in Selly Oak Park on Coronation Day. The injury necessitated the amputation of his right hand. The subscriptions received so far are as follows:-

Her Majesty the Queen	£5	5	0
George Cadbury, Esq., J.P.	20	0	0
R. Deykin, Esq., Captain Church Lads' Brigade	20	0	0
Rev. E.A. Haviland, M.A.	5	0	0
Stirchley and Cotteridge Coronation Committee	3	0	0
Rt. Hon. J.W. Wilson, M.P.	2	2	0

16. 1911

Councillor A.C. Hayes, Esq., J.P.	2	2	0
Birmingham News and Printing Co. Ltd.	1	1	0
Councillor R.E. Bull	1	1	0
Mr. C.H. Harbun	1	1	0
W. B. Bedington	1	1	0
Douglas Timins, M.A.	1	1	0
Mr. C.W. Pember	1	1	0
Doctor Cochrane	1	1	0
J.J. Danielson		10	6
Mrs. F.S. Danielson		10	6
Mr. W. Bright		10	6
F.B. Darling, C.C.		10	0
F.E. Boswell		10	0
A.R. Gaul		5	0
Anonymous		5	0
Mr. W. Green, High Street, Selly Oak		5	0
Mr. I. Usherwood		5	0
Mr. E. Southall		5	0
Mr. Ritchie		2	6
Mr. Spurrier		2	6
Mr. A. West		2	6
Mr. James Smith		2	6
Collected in Park	7	14	9
Collected at C.L.B. Cathedral Parade	4	2	3
*Mr. A.F. Nainby			
*Mr. H.A.R. Ellis			
*Mr. E.A. Alldridge			
Total	£85	2	6

  *Amount not decided upon.

To the Editor

Dear Sir, – Herewith I enclose cheque value £2 2s. 0d. towards the above fund which I truly hope will be subscribed to by all Selly Oak residents at least according to their means, so that the committee and yourself may be successful in raising a fund which will, in some measure go to compensate this unfortunate youth for the loss of so valuable limb. – Yours faithfully

Albert C. Hayes.

14, New Street, Birmingham,
    July 5th, 1911

To the Editor

Sir, – From the account of the accident in the "Birmingham News", I wrote a letter to King George V., asking his Majesty to recommend the boy for a pension to the Secretary of State for War, or some other Minister of the Crown. As there were so few accidents at the celebrating of the festivities on Coronation day, the granting of a small pension would be an act of grace worthy the occasion and would incur little expenditure. The terrible loss of a hand meant so much deprivation to the boy throughout his life, and as the occasion was one of expressing loyalty to the Crown, it seems one worthy of public recognition. I enclose the reply (copy) – Yours faithfully,

Francis Knight.

Copy

Privy Purse Office,
Buckingham Palace,
July 5th, 1911

The Keeper of the Privy Purse is commanded to acknowledge the receipt of Mr. Francis Knight's letter of the 30th ult, and is sorry to hear of the sad accident to the boy William Sargent. At the same time he regrets that His Majesty is unable to comply with the request proferred.
Francis Knight, Esq.
Lavell House,
Moseley, Worcestershire

The Queens Sympathy

Mr. Fowler (secretary of the Selly Oak Coronation Committee) acting upon instructions, wrote to their Majesties the King and Queen calling their attention to the sad accident. He has received the following replies:-

Sir, – In reply to your application of the 3rd instant, I much regret that it would not be consistent with rule for His Majesty to subscribe to a fund such as you are so worthily raising on behalf of William Sargent, who met with such an unfortunate and regrettable accident on Coronation Day.

Had it been in my power I should have been only too pleased to comply with your request. –

Yours faithfully, N. Carrington.
Privy Purse Office,

Buckingham Palace, July 5.

16. 1911

Dear sir, – I have laid your letter before the Queen and am commanded to forward to you a donation of £5 5s, 0d., which Her Majesty hopes will be good enough to add to the fund which has been opened with the object of assisting William Sargent, who met with such a serious accident on Coronation Day. The Queen desires me at the same time to express her sincere sympathy with the poor boy in his sad misfortune. – I am, yours faithfully,

E. W. Wallington.

Buckingham Palace, July 5.

Mr. Fowler has also received the following letters:-

Dear Sir, – I beg to acknowledge your letter of July 3, and will give the matter my further attention, although I hardly think it is a case which the Home Secretary could be expected to bring before their Majesties' notice.
Meanwhile I have pleasure in enclosing a donation of two guineas from myself, and hope that you will be able to lay out the money being collected in a way that will permanently assist the lad towards getting a living. He has my true sympathy. – Yours sincerely,
John W. Wilson.
4, Whitehall Court, S.W., July 4.

Dear Sir, – Mr. Alfred R. Gaul encloses an order for 5s. on behalf of the youth, William Sargent, for whom you have appealed. Mr. Gaul would be glad if you tell the lad how greatly he feels for him in his trouble, for as a fact Mr. Gaul is not able to write to you in consequence of an accident which has deprived him of the use of his right hand. – Yours truly H. L. Hopkins for A.R. Gaul.
Gillott Lodge, 473 Gillott Road, Edgbaston, July 5.

15th July 1911 – Birmingham News

The Coronation Day Accident at Selly Oak
(Editorial Leader)

We feel we need make no apology for specifically directing the attention of our readers to the fund which is being raised on behalf of the lad, William Sargent, a member of the Church Lads' Brigade, who was unfortunately injured whilst a Royal salute was being fired in Selly Oak Park on Coronation day. The injury necessitated the amputation of his right hand. In spite of the enormous crowds which assembled in every town and village throughout the country, and the elaborate nature of the local schemes of festivity, in the majority of cases ending with displays of fireworks, there were happily few accidents on Coronation Day. This general immunity only serves to accentuate the deplorable character of the accident at Selly Oak. The Coronation will be indelibly impressed upon the public memory as a felicitous occasion of Empire rejoicing. But to this lad it will be associated throughout life with the knowledge that on this day he was permanently maimed. The loss of the limb imposes a handicap upon him from which there is no possible escape, and for this reason we should like to see a sufficient amount subscribed to enable an investment to be made capable of yielding him a fixed income when he comes to be dependent upon his own exertions for his livelihood. The case is one in which every donation, however small, will be helpful. Her Majesty the Queen, with the ready womanly sympathy with misfortune for which she is distinguished, has graciously sent a contribution of five guineas, and her example ought to be, and we hope it will be, an inspiration and stimulus to the local public. The reputation of Birmingham people stands high for the readiness and generosity of their response to the appeals of deserving charity, and we trust the people of Selly Oak and district will in this respect show that they are in every way worthy of the proud traditions which they will shortly be called upon to share[60]. We shall be pleased to receive and acknowledge all contributions to the fund.

The Coronation Accident at Selly Oak
Benefit Fund for the Injured Lad

In response to a request from the Selly Oak Coronation Committee we have decided to receive and acknowledge subscriptions to the fund which is being raised on behalf of the lad, William Sargent, a member of the Church Lads' brigade who was unfortunately injured while firing a Royal Salute in Selly Oak Park on Coronation Day. The injury necessitated the amputation of his right hand. The amount already acknowledged is £85 2s. 6d.

During the past week the following further subscriptions have been received:-

	£	s.	d.
Miss M.F. Haviland	1	0	0
Selly Oak Ambulance Corps		10	6
"Lance"		5	0
J. Bland		5	0
F.S. Williamson		5	0
A.M. Hedge		2	6
Mr. Longdon		2	6
W.H. Hart and Son		2	6
Priory Tea Co.		2	6
W. Ayre		2	0
S. Wileman		2	0
Total	88	1	0

---

60   This is a reference to the impending Birmingham extension which would occur in November 1911.

In aid of the fund a benefit performance was given at the Selly Oak Picturedrome on Wednesday. There was only one house and a large audience watched with an interest an attractive programme of pictures. The Queen's letter was shown on the screen during the evening and evoked hearty applause. The pictures were interspersed with enjoyable musical selections by Mr. Harry Smith and Miss L. Banner both of whom contributed three songs. Mr. Smith was an excellent voice and the clear renderings of his songs was much appreciated. Councillor Bull proposed a hearty vote of thanks to Mr. Brueton the manager of the picturedrome for the services he had rendered. The Rev. M.W. Smith seconded the resolution, which was carried with applause.

22nd July 1911 – The Birmingham News

The Coronation Accident at Selly Oak
Benefit Fund for the Injured Lad

In response to a request from the Selly Oak Coronation Committee we have decided to receive and acknowledge subscriptions to the fund which is being raised on behalf of the lad, William Sargent, a member of the Church Lads' Brigade who was unfortunately injured while firing a Royal Salute in Selly Oak Park on Coronation Day. The injury necessitated the amputation of his right hand.

Mr. George Davis writes that the amount given to the fund by the Stirchley Coronation Committee is £3 3s. and not £3 as recorded in these columns. Those having collecting boxes are asked to return them to Mr. Fowler, 8. Elm Road, Bournville, not later than July 31. Amount previously acknowledged £88 4s. The donations received this week are as follows:-

	£	s.	d.
Teachers and scholars of Tiverton Road Council Schools	1	5	0
George Cadbury, jun.	1	1	0
Edward Cadbury, Esq., J.P.	1	1	0
Performance at Selly Oak Picturedrome	1	0	0
Teachers and scholars Moseley Girls' National School per Miss E. Johnson		10	0
Collected by Mrs. Pearce, Book No.		12	3
Teachers and scholars Dawlish Road School Infants Dept., per Miss Field		8	11
Mr. John Morgan		5	0
Mr. Frank Wilson (Banbury)		2	6
Total	£95	19	8

29th July 1911 – The Birmingham News

The Coronation Accident at Selly Oak
Benefit Fund for the Injured Lad

In response to a request from the Selly Oak Coronation Committee we have decided to receive and acknowledge subscriptions to the fund which is being raised on behalf of the lad, William Sargent, a member of the Church Lads' Brigade who was unfortunately injured while firing a Royal Salute in Selly Oak Park on Coronation Day. The injury necessitated the amputation of his right hand.

In our last week's list we gave the amount received from the Moseley Girls' National School as 10s. instead of 16s., and the balance has been added to last week's total which now stands at £96 5s. 8d. Considerable progress has been made by the fund this week. The Earl of Plymouth has contributed £5, while Mr. Henry Lloyd Wilson has sent £3 3s. 0d. Those having collecting boxes are asked to return them by July 31 either to the treasurer, Mr. R. Roberts or the secretary Mr. R. Fowler.

We have received a handsome donation of £5 from Mr. Francis Knight, of Lavell House, Moseley, which he, however, desires shall not be applied to the fund, but be handed over to the parents of the boy Sargent, to assist the family in their trouble. Mr. Knight's reason for asking us to present the money to the parents is because he is away from home, on a visit to Southampton.

	£	s.	d.
Earl of Plymouth	5	0	0
Mr. Henry Lloyd Wilson	3	3	0
Collection C.L.B. Parade at Harborne	1	6	6
Mr. H.A.R. Ellis	1	1	0
Mr. Chas. Winn	1	1	0
Miss Nettlefold	1	0	0
Moseley Boys' National School per Mr. Greenhill		14	6
Rev. G.T. Miller		10	0
Mr. R.O. Sanders		10	0
Mr. E.J. Harrison		10	0
Mr. William Gibbins		10	0
Mr. Laurence		10	0
Harborne Lane Boys' School per Mr. C.W. Harris		6	0
Mr. A.J. Collings		5	0
Mr. C.J. Howson		5	0
Raddle Barn Boys' School per Mr. J.A. Poppiette		3	6
Total	£113	1	2

5th August 1911 – The Birmingham News

The Coronation Accident at Selly Oak
Benefit Fund for the Injured Lad

In response to a request from the Selly Oak Coronation Committee we have decided to receive and acknowledge subscriptions to the fund which is being raised on behalf of the lad, William Sargent, a member of the Church Lads' Brigade who was unfortunately injured while firing a Royal Salute in Selly Oak Park on Coronation Day. The injury necessitated the amputation of his right hand.

Among the amounts received this week is a sum of £10 which has been sent from the headquarters of the Church Lads' Brigade, at London. Collectors who have not returned their books are asked to do so at once, either to the secretary, Mr. R. Fowler, 8, Elm Road, or the treasurer, Mr. H. Roberts, Bournbrook. The amounts previously acknowledged total £113 1s. 2d.

C.L.B. Headquarters, London	£10	0	0
Collected by Mr. Maybury	1	1	0
" " Miss E.K. Fowler		14	0
" " Mrs. Haste		10	0
" " Mr. Johnson		8	7
" " Mr. Harrington		7	1
" " Mrs. Grazeley		4	2
Mrs. A. Halward		1	6
Total	£126	7	6

12th August 1911 – The Birmingham News

The Coronation Accident at Selly Oak
Benefit Fund for the Injured Lad

In response to a request from the Selly Oak Coronation Committee we have decided to receive and acknowledge subscriptions to the fund which is being raised on behalf of the lad, William Sargent, a member of the Church Lads' Brigade who was unfortunately injured while firing a Royal Salute in Selly Oak Park on Coronation Day. The injury necessitated the amputation of his right hand. The total amount received up to date is £125 7s. 6d.

The Heydays Of Selly Oak Park

26th August 1911 – The Birmingham News

The Coronation Accident at Selly Oak
Benefit Fund for the Injured Lad

In response to a request from the Selly Oak Coronation Committee we have decided to receive and acknowledge subscriptions to the fund which is being raised on behalf of the lad, William Sargent, a member of the Church Lads' Brigade who was unfortunately injured while firing a Royal Salute in Selly Oak Park on Coronation Day. The injury necessitated the amputation of his right hand.

The chief amount received since the publication of the last list of subscriptions is a contribution of £2 from Sir Henry Wiggin, Bart. A large number of collectors have not yet returned their collecting books and they are asked to do so at once. The amount previously acknowledged was £126 7s. 6d.

	£	s.	d.
Sir Henry Wiggin	2	0	0
W.H. Dunkley		2	6
A.E. Priest		2	0
Total	£128	12	0

2nd September 1911 – The Birmingham News

The Coronation Accident at Selly Oak
Benefit Fund for the Injured Lad

In response to a request from the Selly Oak Coronation Committee we have decided to receive and acknowledge subscriptions to the fund which is being raised on behalf of the lad, William Sargent, a member of the Church Lads' Brigade who was unfortunately injured while firing a Royal Salute in Selly Oak Park on Coronation Day. The injury necessitated the amputation of his right hand.

The following amounts have been received by the secretary (Mr. R. Fowler) during the past week. Last week's total was £128 12s.

	£	s.	d.
Anonymous per R. Deykin	5	0	0
Rubery Coronation Committee per Mr. H. Moore	1	0	0
Miss Baker (Kidderminster)		18	0
Collected at the Austin Motor Works per R. Potter		17	4
Per Mr. George Watson – Mr. and Mrs. Pimm 5s, Mr. and Mrs. Chinnery 1s. 6d., Mr T. Clift 2s. 6d.; amounts			

less than 1s 6d. 4s. 8d.	13	8
Rubery Council School		
per Mr. H. Moore	11	6
Rev. M. Smith, M.A.	10	6
Rev. J.M. Cunningham	5	0
Total	£138 18	0

9th September 1911 – The Birmingham News

The Coronation Accident at Selly Oak
Benefit Fund for the Injured Lad

In response to a request from the Selly Oak Coronation Committee we have decided to receive and acknowledge subscriptions to the fund which is being raised on behalf of the lad, William Sargent, a member of the Church Lads' Brigade who was unfortunately injured while firing a Royal Salute in Selly Oak Park on Coronation Day. The injury necessitated the amputation of his right hand.

The house to house collection made by the members of the Selly Oak C.L.B. has resulted in a sum of £35 6s. 7d. being collected for the fund, which added to last week's total brings the total amount collected to £174 4s. 7d. All the amounts collected by the lads with the exception of which was collected at the parks and for which an official receipt was given are included in the £35. The committee would esteem it a favour if those friends who intend to contribute to the fund and have not done so, would send their donation along as early as possible, so that the fund can be brought to a close. Any amounts however small will be thankfully received.

7th October 1911 – The Birmingham News

The Coronation Accident at Selly Oak
Benefit Fund for the Injured Lad

In response to a request from the Selly Oak Coronation Committee we have decided to receive and acknowledge subscriptions to the fund which is being raised on behalf of the lad, William Sargent, a member of the Church Lads' Brigade who was unfortunately injured while firing a Royal Salute in Selly Oak Park on Coronation Day. The injury necessitated the amputation of his right hand.

The following amounts have been received since the last list of donations to the fund was published:-

	£	s.	d.
Previously acknowledged	178	15	0
Mr. Pember's Book	4	13	0
Mr. A. Bedford		5	0
Total	£183	13	0

14th October 1911 – The Birmingham News

The Coronation Accident at Selly Oak
Benefit Fund for the Injured Lad

In response to a request from the Selly Oak Coronation Committee we have decided to receive and acknowledge subscriptions to the fund which is being raised on behalf of the lad, William Sargent, a member of the Church Lads' Brigade who was unfortunately injured while firing a Royal Salute in Selly Oak Park on Coronation Day. The injury necessitated the amputation of his right hand.

A donation of 7s. 6d. for the fund has been received from the Northfield Unionist Club, and this makes the total £184 0s. 6d.

21st October 1911 – The Birmingham News

The Coronation Accident at Selly Oak
Benefit Fund for the Injured Lad

In response to a request from the Selly Oak Coronation Committee we have decided to receive and acknowledge subscriptions to the fund which is being raised on behalf of the lad, William Sargent, a member of the Church Lads' Brigade who was unfortunately injured while firing a Royal Salute in Selly Oak Park on Coronation Day. The injury necessitated the amputation of his right hand.

There are still several collecting books which have not been returned, and those having them are asked to send them to the secretary, Mr. R. Fowler, 13, Elm Road, Bournville, or to the treasurer, Mr. H. Roberts, High Street, Bournbrook. Intending subscribers also are asked to send in their amounts as soon as possible, as the committee are anxious to bring the fund to a close.

A contribution of £4 18s. 0d. has been received from the Moseley and Kings Heath Coronation Committee, per Councillor G. Bullock, and this brings the total amount received to £188 19s. 4d.

Mr. G. Cadbury has written to the secretary of the fund as follows:- Dear Mr. Fowler, – Thanks for your letter. As you are closing the William Sargent Fund probably it will be a convenience if I were to remit the £20 promised, and I am therefore doing so. – Yours truly, G. Cadbury. October 19.

It will be remembered that Mr. Cadbury first promised to give £5 a year for 4 years.

11th November 1911 – Birmingham News

The Passing of the Districts
Kings Norton

The urban district of Kings Norton and Northfield, which ceased to exist at midnight on Wednesday, has a worthy record in the sphere of local government activities. ………

16. 1911

The provision of parks, baths and washhouses next became a burning question, but this took far longer to settle. A magnificent impulse was given to the movement, however, by private generosity, the Gibbins family making a gift to the community of a fine park at Selly Park (sic). ....

So far as the District Council was concerned a period of remarkable activity was ushered in about seven ago and since then parks and open spaces and allotments have been provided in all directions, until today there is no district around Birmingham and probably few in the country better furnished in this respect than Kings Norton and Northfield. ....

18th November 1911 – The Birmingham News

> The Coronation Accident at Selly Oak
> Benefit Fund for the Injured Lad

Contributions received since the last list was published are as follows: The Coronation Committee Kings Norton, per Mr. J.F. Moore, £1 1s.; collected by Mr. H. Brinkworth, 1s. 9d., making a total of £196 1s. 1d.

24th November 1911 – Birmingham City Council, Parks Committee[61]

The following table is extracted from the first report to the new administration and confirms the situation of Selly Oak Park at the time of the handover:

The following are the particulars of the added areas, which will now be controlled by the Parks Department

District	Description and Situation	Area	Particulars of Staff	Remarks
Kings Norton and Northfield	Selly Oak Park, Gibbins Road	A R P 11 2 5	1 Superintendent at 30s. week, with house, coal and gas 4 men at 24s. week	

---

[61] The Archive & Heritage Section of Birmingham Central Library.

Chapter 17

OTHER COMMENTARIES & REFERENCES

There are a number of other sources of information / commentaries about the park.

City of Birmingham (1892) – Public Parks and Pleasure Grounds; Their costs, areas, and maintenance; Bye-laws and regulations[62].

Whilst this book pre-dates Selly Oak Park, it is a valuable reference for anyone wanting a history of Birmingham's first parks and the circumstance which lead to their establishment.

Dent R K (1916) – City of Birmingham – History and Description of the Public Parks, Gardens and Recreation Grounds.[63]

Page 36 – "Selly Oak Park (18 acres, 1 rood). A small park at Selly Oak, with an area of 11a. 2r. 5p., was presented to the late King's Norton Urban District Council by Mrs. Gibbins and her sons in February, 1989. After this park was taken over by the City Council a further gift was made by Messrs. W. and J. Gibbins, on February 15th, 1913, bringing up the total area of this park to 18a. 1r."

There is a multi-volume History of the Corporation of Birmingham which gives details of the administration of Birmingham's Parks and the Department, based on first-hand analysis of Council minutes, reports and the like. These give a very interesting general overview of activities. It is possible to pick out specific references to Selly Oak Park.

Vince C A (1923) – History of the Corporation of Birmingham (1900-1915), Vol IV.[64]

Page 231 – Part of a classified list of all the Parks, Recreation Grounds (R.G.) and Gardens that were under the control of the Parks Committee in 1914:

---

[62] Birmingham Central Library Ref: B Col 27.3.
[63] Birmingham Central Library Ref: B Col 27.3. Also – Amongst the minutes of the Administrative Sub-Committee of the Birmingham City Council Parks Committee, there is a minute of the Record Sub Committee held at the Council House on the 11th January 1916 at which it was resolved "That Mr. R. K. Dent be paid an additional fee of £5 in recognition of the extra services rendered by him in the preparation of the history of the Parks".
[64] Birmingham Central Library Ref: B Col 30 HIS.

(c) Transferred from Councils of Added Areas, 1911.	Area Ac	r	p	Cost of Maintenance £
Kings Norton & Northfield				
Bournbrook R.G.	2	0	2	173
Cotteridge Park	22	3	17	540
King's Heath Park	30	1	16	624
Muntz Park, Selly Oak	5	3	3	187
Selly Oak Park	**18**	**1**	**0**	**342**
Selly Park R.G.	20	3	32	118
Stirchley Playground	1	1	22	74
Victoria Common, Northfield	9	2	33	81
Village Green, King's Norton		3	16	–
Village Green, Moseley			20	–

Page 242 – "Throughout the history of the Public Parks it is observable that the liberality, or the restraint, of the Council stimulates or checks private generosity. Accordingly the year 1913 was signalized by many gifts to the Parks in addition to that already mentioned. Mr. William Gibbins gave six acres and three roods of land for the extension of Selly Oak Park in Gibbins Road, which had been given to the public by members of his family, and also paid the cost of conveyance and fencing."

Rowntree A (ed) (1936) – The Birmingham Battery and Metal Company. One Hundred Years, 1836-1936.[65]

This publication traces the history of the development of the Birmingham Battery and Metal Company during the years 1836 to 1936. The company's owners were members of the Gibbins family, and there are occasional references in the publication to their involvement with Selly Oak Park. More on this connection can be found in Appendix I at the end of this volume.

Jones J T (1940) – History of the Corporation of Birmingham (1915-1935), Vol V, Part 2[66] – has a chapter (24) devoted to the "Parks and Recreation Grounds" of the City. In particular it reports:

Page 432 – "Additions were made to Canon Hill Park (seven acres), Perry Park (fifteen acres), and Selly Oak Park (thirteen acres). The last-named property was presented (in 1919) to the Corporation by Messrs. W. Gibbins, J. Gibbins, W.W. Gibbins and R.L. Gibbins."

---

[65] Birmingham Central Library Ref: L65.642 BIR.
[66] Birmingham Central Library Ref: B Col 30 HIS.

Black H J (1957) – History of the Corporation of Birmingham (1935-1950), Vol VI, Part 2[67] – has a chapter (22) devoted to the "Parks and Recreation Grounds" of the City. In particular it reports:

Page 458 – "There was an addition of 0.07 acres to the Selly Oak Park, Gibbins Road, gifted in 1935 by Mr. D.D. James; bringing the total area of the park to 31.15 acres."

---

[67] Birmingham Central Library Ref: B Col 30 HIS.

Chapter 18

THE OAK TREE OF SELLY OAK MEMORIALISED IN SELLY OAK PARK

The late James Hyland, History schoolteacher and local historian, has written an account of the history of Selly Oak (http://www.virtualbrum.co.uk/history/sellyoak.htm). In it he describes how in 1909 the oak tree that used to be in the centre of the village was removed, and a stump of the tree was relocated to Selly Oak Park and marked with a memorial plaque. He wrote:

> *It is known that the oak tree was located on the corner of Oak Tree Lane and Bristol Road at a site called Oak Tree Place, a blue Victorian sign (1880) is still attached to a shop on the North side of Oak Tree Lane.*
>
> *The tree was damaged by the construction of houses nearby, now used as shops, which damaged the roots resulting in changing the tree into a stag oak. It is possible to exactly locate the missing tree by the difference in roof levels on contemporary photographs.*
>
> *By May 1909, the state of the tree, fears about its safety, its lopped branches and the demands of road traffic and pedestrians led to its removal around the 21st of May. The stump was then saved and removed to Selly Oak Park. A brass plaque recorded that it had been put there by Kings Norton and Northfield Urban District Council.*
>
> *The plaque read 'Butt of Old Oak Tree from which the name of Selly Oak was derived. Removed from Oak Tree Lane, Selly Oak 1909'. By 1976 it was reported that the stump was mostly rotten, but in 2001 the remains of stump and plaque can still be found, covered in ivy.*
>
> *A new oak tree was planted in 2000 outside Blockbuster on the Bristol Road and Oak Tree Lane junction. A plaque notes that it is a replacement for the old oak but does not repeat the canard that the area is named after its predecessors.*

There are comments in issues of the Birmingham News around May 1909 – one in particular, in the issue of 1st May 1909, is entitled "Selly Oak Oakians at Dinner – Mourning the Felling of the Old Oak", and it contains some interesting history of Selly Oak generally. The report indicates that a Mr. T. Horton attended the dinner.

THE HEYDAYS OF SELLY OAK PARK

The Oak of Selly Oak memorialised in Selly Oak Park

Above: taken from Butler, J., Baker A. & Southworth P. (2005). "Images of England: Selly Oak and Selly Park"; Tempus Publishing Ltd.
Left: from Archive Section, Birmingham Central Library.
Top and bottom left: supplied by James Hyland: http://www.virtualbrum.co.uk/history/sellyoak.htm
Bottom right: supplied by Lepidus Magnus http://www.wikimedia.org.

Appendix I

THE GIBBINS FAMILY, DONORS OF SELLY OAK PARK

Some of the information in this appendix is taken from The Birmingham Battery and Metal Company (1936)[68] – a company publication celebrating its centenary.

The Company, owned by the the Gibbins family, commenced operations in Digbeth (on the site subsequently occupied by the Digbeth Institute) before eventually settling and expanding in Selly Oak. Several senior members of the family were bankers and influential in the city of Birmingham during the eighteenth and early nineteenth centuries.

The following table shows that part of the Gibbins family involved in the company. It is clear from what follows, and other parts of this research, that not all members were involved directly in the company – i) Benjamin was one of the brothers associated with the gift of the Park, but is not shown in this family tree; ii) Emma, sister of William, Thomas, Richard Cadbury and John, wrote on behalf of the surviving family when the death of their father, Thomas Gibbins, in 1908 was acknowledged by Birmingham City Council.

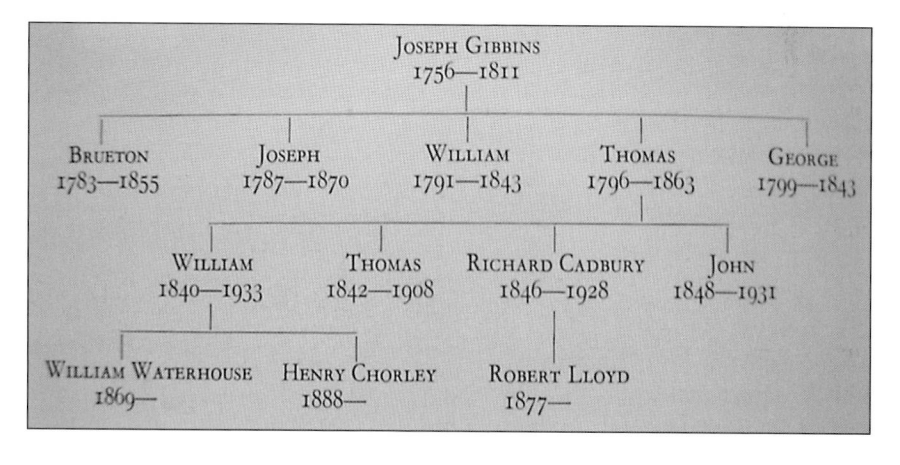

```
                    JOSEPH GIBBINS
                      1756—1811
    ┌───────────┬─────────┼─────────┬───────────┐
  BRUETON     JOSEPH    WILLIAM   THOMAS      GEORGE
 1783—1855  1787—1870 1791—1843 1796—1863   1799—1843
                                    │
              ┌─────────┬───────────┼───────────┐
           WILLIAM    THOMAS   RICHARD CADBURY  JOHN
          1840—1933 1842—1908    1846—1928   1848—1931
              │         │            │
      WILLIAM WATERHOUSE HENRY CHORLEY  ROBERT LLOYD
           1869—          1888—           1877—
```

Reproduced from The Birmingham Battery and Metal Company (1936).

---

[68] A limited edition private publication. A copy is available in the Archive & Heritage section of Birmingham Library – Ref: L65.642 BIR.

The publication (p64) records:

Selly Oak Park

"It may be of interest to put on record, although not directly associated with the activities of the Company, that shortly after the final transfer from Digbeth, and when the works were firmly established in their new home at Selly Oak, a desire to do something for the social amenities of the district took shape in the minds of some of the senior members of the family. This was finally crystallised in the gift made by Mrs. Emma J. Gibbins and her sons William, Thomas, John and Benjamin, to the Kings Norton and Northfield Urban District Council of 11½ acres of the Weoley Park Estate, with entrance lodge, pavilion and general lay-out, to form a park and playground for the district, under the name of Selly Oak Park (February, 1899)."

"In February, 1913, William and John Gibbins gave a further 6½ acres to the Corporation of Birmingham (the district in the interval having been absorbed within the City boundaries), to be used mainly as playing fields. A final additional gift was made in December, 1919, by William, John, W. Waterhouse and R. Lloyd Gibbins, of 12¾ acres, with a lodge and second entrance from Harborne Lane."

Mrs Emma Joel Gibbins (nee Cadbury) (1811-1903), who with her sons gifted Selly Oak Park, was the wife of Thomas Gibbins (1796-1863). She obviously gave her Cadbury name to one of her sons.

Further detail about the 1919 gift is contained in the publication:

Battery Sports Club

"In 1919 the Weoley Park farm estate of about 100 acres, on the high land above Gibbins Road, and adjoining the Selly Oak Park, was purchased from Mr. Ledsam of Northfield. Possession was obtained on the expiration of the lease in 1922. Part of this land was privately presented to the Corporation as an extension of the Park. Out of the balance, about nine acres were set aside as a Sports Ground for the Works. This has been laid out with cricket pitch, two football grounds, bowling green and tennis courts, and is one of the best works sports grounds in the district. The new pavilion was provided by the shareholders of the Company and John Gibbins in 1930; it was officially opened on April 25th 1931, by Mrs. John Gibbins."

"In 1934 most of the balance of the land was sold for building purposes, the Company retaining a total of about eleven acres, including the sports ground."

Appendix I. The Gibbins Family, Donors of Selly Oak Park

THE PAVILION, SPORTS GROUND.

Reproduced from The Birmingham Battery and Metal Company (1936).

There is also a commentary on Thomas Gibbins:

Thomas Gibbins, 1842-1908

"The Report of 1909 notes the death of Thomas Gibbins in the previous year. He had been in the Glass Works, and was known as a man of great will power before entering this business in 1864, when he joined his brother William in the management. The Report states that "his care, energy and good judgment largely contributed to the success of the business." By his will a gift was made to the Directors for the provision of a superannuation, or sick, or nursing fund, for the benefit of the workpeople and clerks employed by the Company. His gift formed the foundation of the pension scheme which came into operation in 1910, taking over some privately administered responsibilities. Other members of the firm also made gifts to this fund."

"The Selly Oak Library was largely due to the initiative of Thomas Gibbins, as he presented the ground for the building, which was erected in High Street. He opened the library on June 23rd 1906, and was presented with a key by the Architect, for the unlocking of the door. The library was a Carnegie foundation."

"Thomas Gibbins had been a member of the Kings Norton Board of Guardians, representing the Edgbaston ward, for a number of years; he also served from 1898 to 1902 on the Kings Norton and Northfield District Council. After serving for a year as Chairman of this body he retired, and was elected for Selly Oak West on the Worcester County Council in 1904. Two years later he was appointed Justice of the Peace for Worcestershire, and sat on the Northfield Bench."

Notable items in the Press about the Donors of Selly Oak Park:

10th November 1900 – The South Birmingham Chronicle

COUNCILLOR THOMAS GIBBINS, J.P.
(An image was reproduced in the paper; but it
is not suitable for copying from the microfilm)

It is with no small degree of pleasure that we give our readers this week the portrait of the much-respected and highly-esteemed Chairman of the Kings Norton and Northfield Urban District Council. We take the opportunity of doing so in view of the ceremony he performed on Tuesday at Lifford in connection with the extension of the drainage area, a report of which will be found in another column. As we have remarked before, the inclusion of the outer districts of Kings Norton and Northfield in the sewerage system of the Birmingham Tame and Rea Joint Drainage Board is undoubtedly one of the greatest improvements which has ever taken place in our district.

The subject of our sketch has been Chairman of our Urban Council since it came into existence, about two years ago, and has, during this time, won the esteem and respect, not only of every member of it, but of everyone connected with it, by his strict impartiality, absolute fairness, genial manner, and marked courtesy. As our readers are well aware, Mr. Gibbins is one of the proprietors of the Birmingham Battery Co., of which his father was one of the original founders, and with which he has been himself associated ever since he left school. He comes from an old and well-known family. His mother was a Miss Cadbury, and a prominent member of the Society of Friends, in which, although now something like 87 years of age, she still takes a keen interest. Mr. Gibbins was for some years a member of the Birmingham Board of Guardians, and is at the present moment a Guardian of the Poor for our district. Selly Oak owes to Mr. Gibbins's family its Park, which was presented to the inhabitants only a short time since. Not only was the land given, but the grounds laid out at their own expense. Mr. Gibbins is well known for his generosity towards our local public institutions, and for his charity to those in need of it. No one, we feel sure, ever appealed to him in vain for help, if the case had been a deserving one.

6th July 1901 – The South Birmingham Chronicle:

Mr. John Gibbins
(A photograph is printed – but its quality renders it unsuitable for copying)

Mr. John Gibbins has many titles to the gratitude and admiration of the people of Selly Oak and district. He is a member, and a prominent one, of a family which is looked upon, with reason, by everyone as one of those which has done more than most others to make Selly Oak what it is today. He has always taken a keen interest

Appendix I. The Gibbins Family, Donors of Selly Oak Park

in the working-classes, and has generously subscribed to charitable objects, and has ever evinced a keen interest in the welfare of the employees of the firm of which he is a director, and which affords employment to so many of our people.

Mr. John Gibbins has also done a great deal for beneficial instruction in our district, and has been the treasurer of the Technical Board for a number of years, discharging the onerous duties of his office with considerable ability in very difficult times. To his efforts is, in a great measure, due the recent special interest taken by the County Council and local manufacturers in our Technical Institute, and it is not too much to say that to him principally belongs the credit of having obtained an additional building grant from Worcester this year. We might also add that he has been connected with the Early Morning School at Severn Street and Selly Oak for men for many years. The subject of our sketch was born in Birmingham in 1848, and is therefore 53 years of age. He resides with his family at Barnt Green, where he is well-known and highly respected.

30th January 1904 – South Birmingham Chronicle

FORTHCOMING COUNTY COUNCIL ELECTIONS
Councillor Thomas Gibbins
(The front page feature includes a photograph which is not suitable for reproduction here.)

The County Council elections are to take place on Wednesday, March 2nd, and the old Northfield division, which has hitherto returned one member only, has been divided into three parts – Selly Oak West, Selly Oak East, and Northfield (including Bartley Green) – each of which will choose its own. For Selly Oak West district Councillor Thomas Gibbins was adopted as candidate some time ago, and up to the present time appears likely to be returned unopposed.

Councillor Gibbins is a valued member of the King's Norton and Northfield Urban District Council. He was the first chairman of that body, and presided over it until 1901. By his impartial conduct and courtesy of manner he won the esteem of every member of the Board, and he is well known and respected by a large circle of friends. He is one of the proprietors of the Birmingham Battery Company, of which his father was one of the founders, and with which he himself has been associated ever since he left school. He comes from an old and well-known family. His mother was a Miss Cadbury, and a prominent member of the Society of Friends.

Councillor Gibbins, in conjunction with his family made the splendid gift of Selly Oak Park to our district. Not only was the land given, but the grounds were laid out at the donor's expense. He has taken a great interest in Poor Law administration, and was for some years a member of the Birmingham Board of Guardians, and he is a Guardian of the poor for our own district. In Councillor Gibbins our local institutions have found a generous supporter, and the needy a sympathetic benefactor.

14th January 1905 – The South Birmingham Chronicle

Mr. Thomas Gibbins
(A photograph unsuitable for reproduction accompanies this front page article)

Many rumours have been flying lately round the district concerning Mr. Thomas Gibbins and his intentions in regard to the forthcoming elections. Mr. Gibbins, it has been said, is to come out under the "progressive" banner to stand as an independent, as a working man's representative, and to retire altogether. We have been unable to obtain any definite statement at first hand, and we believe that Mr. Gibbins is himself uncertain, but it must be hoped that the last-mentioned story is incorrect, for Mr. Gibbins is of the stamp of man which the Council can ill-afford to lose – of trained judgment and ability, energetic, and independent in his views. It is just this characteristic of independence which seems to be generally looked upon as the cause of his retirement – that is, if he should actually determine to retire – for it will be remembered that when the tramway negotiations with Birmingham and Mr. Underhill's conduct of them were engaging the attention of the Council Mr. Gibbins voted as his conscience directed him, and not as his "progressive" friends would have liked him to. The prompt result was a warning at a Progressive indignation meeting that even so good a friend of the working classes as Mr. Gibbins must not consider his seat safe if he should venture to incur the ire of that domineering association. In the circumstances some indication of Mr. Gibbin's intention is awaited with unusual interest. Everyone who wishes for the real well-being of the district must hope that his services may be retained. But he would naturally look for a good deal of his support from the members of the "progressive" association, and if the leaders of that body find him too independent for their purpose, and prefer to desert him in favour of a walking delegate prepared to take his voting orders from themselves, then Mr. Gibbins will presumably retire into private life without seeking the suffrages of the ratepayers. In the circumstances a definite announcement of Mr. Gibbins's intentions is awaited at the present moment with unusual interest.

29th April 1905 – South Birmingham Chronicle

Death of Mrs. Thomas Gibbins

Members of the Society of Friends in Birmingham have, through the death of Mrs. Thomas Gibbins, of Carpenter Road, Edgbaston, lost one of the oldest and most noteworthy persons belonging to their number. Mrs. Gibbins, who was in her ninety-fifth year, was the last survivor of the elder generation of the Cadbury family. Richard Tapper Cadbury, from whom the Birmingham and Philadelphia families of this name have sprung, came to Birmingham from Torquay over a hundred years ago, and set up in business as a draper in Bull Street. By his wife, Elizabeth Head, of Ipswich, he had four sons and four daughters. The sons were

Appendix I. The Gibbins Family, Donors of Selly Oak Park

Benjamin Head Cadbury (father of the present Mr. Joel Cadbury and the late Miss Hannah Cadbury), John Cadbury (father of the late Richard Cadbury and the present George Cadbury), Joel Cadbury (who went to the United States and founded the family of Philadelphia Cadburys), and James Cadbury. The daughters were Mrs. Sarah Barrow, of Lancaster (mother of the late Alderman R.C. Barrow); Maria and Ann Cadbury, who died unmarried; and Emma Joel Cadbury, who married the late Mr. Thomas Gibbins, the founder of the Birmingham Battery Company, and whose death we now record as having taken place at her residence, 10, Carpenter Road on Wednesday.

Mrs. Gibbins took a deep interest in the various organisations connected with the Society of Friends, and was a liberal supporter of charitable undertakings. A few years ago Mrs. Gibbins and her four sons, of whom three are connected with the Birmingham Battery Company, gave to the King's Norton District Council a recreation ground at Lodge Hill, for the benefit of the inhabitants of Selly Oak. Having lived in five reigns, and retained her memory for a remarkable long period, Mrs. Gibbins was able to relate many interesting reminiscences. She was born in Bull Street, when Birmingham was comparatively a small town. When she was only a year old her parents went to live out in the country – where Islington Row now stands. At that time Broad Street was fronted by gentlemen's houses standing in their own grounds, of which the Children's Hospital is the last relic. Mrs. Gibbins remembered hearing of the death of King George III, and seeing some illuminations in celebration of the battle of Waterloo. Throughout her life she dressed in the quaint style of a Quaker lady, and up to a few years ago she was a familiar figure in Edgbaston, being often seen in her carriage. Only a year ago she was able to go out in a Bath chair, and it was not till October last year that the infirmities of age compelled her to take to her bed. Her kindly disposition won her a large circle of friends. Of her seven children, four sons and one daughter survive her. The funeral will take place at Witton Cemetery today (Saturday), at 2.30.

6th May 1905 – South Birmingham Chronicle

Funeral of the late Mrs. Gibbins

On Saturday afternoon, at the Witton Cemetery, the funeral took place of the late Mrs. Emma Joel Gibbins, of 10, Carpenter Road, Edgbaston. There was a large attendance, the Society of Friends in the city being strongly represented. Members of the City Council were present in the persons of Alderman J.H. Lloyd, Alderman Clayton, Alderman Baker, and Councillor Harrison Barrow. The assembly further included Mr. and Mrs. George Cadbury, Mr. Barrow Cadbury, Mrs. Richard Cadbury, Mr. W. Cadbury, Mr. R. Cadbury, Mr. George Cadbury, jun., Mr. Walter Barrow, Dr. Barrow, Messrs. Joseph Smith, Barclay, Smithson, Henry Lloyd Wilson, Dr. Huxley, Mr. and Mrs. Alfred Southall, etc. On the arrival of the carriages at the Quakers' ground at the cemetery, which is situated near the chapel, the coffin was borne to a grave 18 ft. deep by the six grandsons of the deceased. The mourners followed – the four sons, Messrs. William, R.C., John and Thomas Gibbins and Miss Gibbins. A short prayer was offered at the graveside by Mr. George Cadbury, and the coffin was lowered by the bearers. Afterwards a meeting took place in the chapel, when Mr. George Cadbury and Mr. W.C. Braithwaite spoke, and prayer was offered by Mr. J. Wilson of Kendal. The depth of the grave was unusual. Worked in flowers on the coffin lid were the two simple words "at rest".

In our last issue it was stated that Mrs. Gibbins' father, Richard Tapper Cadbury (the founder of the local Cadbury family), came to Birmingham from Torquay. We are informed that he came from Exeter, not Torquay.

10th June 1905 – Birmingham News

Mrs. Emma J. Gibbins's Legacies

Mrs. Emma Joel Gibbins, of Milton House, Carpenter Road, Edgbaston, who died on the 26th April last, aged 94 years, widow of Mr. Thomas Gibbins, founder of the Birmingham Battery Company, and daughter of Mr. Richard Tapper Cadbury (and great aunt of the present Mr. George Cadbury and Mr. Joel Cadbury), left estate of £100,203 including personalty of the net value of £99,988. Probate of her will, dated 15th October, 1900, has been granted to her sons, Mr. William Gibbins, of Beech Hill, Sir Harry's Road, Edgbaston, Mr. Thomas Gibbins, of Milton House, and Mr. Richard Cadbury Gibbins, of Faymstowe, Wellington Road, Edgbaston, manufacturers. By her will of the 15th October, 1900, she bequeathed £50 each to the Society for the Relief of the Aged and Poor Women, the Society for Nurses for Poor Lying-in Women, and the Women's Temperance Society. She bequeathed £2,000 to her daughter Emma; £200 to her cousin, Elizabeth Bevington Clibborn; £20 to her Bible woman, Mary Parnbram; and the ultimate residue of her estate to her six children, Benjamin, John, William, Thomas, Richard Cadbury and Emma Gibbins, in equal shares; and she directed that her share in the Birmingham Battery and Metal Company should, if possible, be retained and taken as part of their share by her children.

30th May 1908 – Birmingham News

Death of Mr. Thos. Gibbins, J.P.
THE FUNERAL
Public References

The public life of Kings Norton district is the poorer by the death on Saturday last of County Councillor Thomas Gibbins, J.P., of 10, Carpenter Road, Edgbaston. Mr. Gibbins had been slightly indisposed for a week, and had deemed it wise to keep to the house, but there was nothing in his condition to give any cause for anxiety until suddenly pneumonia developed, and the outlook at once of course became critical. He succumbed early on Saturday to heart failure. The deceased gentleman was

Appendix I. The Gibbins Family, Donors of Selly Oak Park

born in 1843, in a house in Digbeth, which occupied a site upon which Digbeth Institute now stands. He was the second son of the late Mr. Thomas Gibbins, who founded the metal works, which has now developed into the business at Selly Oak, known as the Birmingham Battery and Metal Co. The business was commenced in the '30's, at premises having a frontage to Digbeth, and an old manor house adjoining was made use of both as a place of residence and as business offices. It was a large building consisting of a set of central rooms and two wings. The one wing was used for the purposes of the works offices, the family occupied the centre, and the other wing was used by someone else as a shop. It was in this house that Mr. Gibbins was born nearly 66 years ago. The works were transferred to Selly Oak some thirty five years ago, and were converted into a private limited company, of which the deceased was a

Thomas Gibbins.

director. Mr. Gibbins took a keen interest in the public affairs of Selly Oak for very many years. One of the earliest outstanding evidences of this was afforded in the part he played along with other members of his family in the presentation to the district of Selly Oak Park. He also gave the site upon which the Free Library stands. When the local authority was invested with urban powers Mr. Gibbins was returned as a representative of Selly Oak and was at once elected chairman, a position which he occupied for three years. He was also returned as a representative of Selly Oak upon the Kings Norton Board of Guardians, but when his term of office expired he retired and was re-elected to the Board as a representative of Edgbaston. Upon the break-up of the old Northfield County Council division Mr. Gibbins was returned as the representative of one of the three new ones as formed, and was again returned to the Council two years after a contested election. His name was added to the County Commission of the Peace in 1902.

The Funeral

The funeral took place at Witton Cemetery on Wednesday afternoon, when a large and representative attendance bore testimony to the esteem in which the deceased gentleman was held. Mr. Gibbins was a member of the Society of Friends, and a large number of members of the denomination attended the funeral. The simple

Quaker service at the graveside consisted of a prayer by Mr. Barrow Cadbury, and short addresses by Mrs. George Cadbury, Mr. W.C. Braithwaite, and Mr. Barrow Cadbury. The mourners were Miss Gibbins (sister), Mr. R.C. Gibbins (brother) and Mrs. Gibbins, Mr. and Mrs. Clibborn, Mrs. Clark, Mr. W. Waterhouse Gibbins, Mr. W.B. Gibbins, Mr. R. Lloyd Gibbins, Mr. Hugh Gibbins, Mr. David Gibbins, Mr. Rowland B. Gibbins, Miss Ada Gibbins, Miss Dora Gibbins, Mrs. Cotterell, and Mr. and Mrs. Sturge. Messrs. Walter Barrow, Barrow Cadbury, Walter Southall, G. Sykes, J.E. Southall and G.E. Wilson acted as bearers. The Kings Norton Board of Guardians were represented by Messrs. T.A. Bayliss (chairman). F. Barlow (vice-chairman), J. Walter, F.J. Gibbs, T.P. Garrett, A. Jones, A. Blackwell, R. Waite, A. Gittins, T. Hall and R.J. Curtis (clerk). The Worcestershire County Council was represented by Messrs. F. Smith, J. Heaven and L.C. Tipper, while Mr. J.J. Moffat (chairman), Dr. Lilley, Messrs. W. Bishop and A.J. Kelly attended on behalf of the Kings Norton and Northfield Urban District Council. Amongst others present were Alderman and Mrs. J.H. Lloyd, Alderman Clayton, Alderman Baker, Councillor A. Godlee, Mr. and Mrs. Joel Cadbury, Mrs. George Cadbury and the Misses Cadbury, Mrs. Barrow Cadbury, Mr. Edward Cadbury, the Misses Cadbury (Bristol Road), Councillor and Mrs. Harrison Barrow, Mr. and Mrs. W.A. Cadbury, Mr. Richard Cadbury (Worcester), Miss Constance Barrow (Lancaster), Mr. L. Barrow, Mr. George Tangye, Mr. R.H. Kirton, Mr. C. Robinson (Brighton) and Miss Robinson, Mr. Southall, Mr. L. Southall, Mrs. W. Barrow, Mrs. Bigland, Mr. Joseph Sturge, Mr. Walter Priestman, Mr. C. Butler, Mr. J.E. Gillett (Banbury), Mr. L. Braithwaite, Mr. Foster, E. Brady, Mr. W.C. Braithwaite, Mr. T.J. O'Brien, Mr. A. Butler, Mr. John Earle, Dr. Hollinshead, Dr. Huxley, Mr. W. Humphries, Mr. Henry Brown, Mr. W. Doubleday, Mr. E.M. Everett, Mr. W. Kentish, Mr. W. Noble, Mr. T. Walker, Mr. J. Smithson, Mr. J. Gladsyer, Mr. J.T. Wilson (representing the Police Institute), Mr. J. Boston (representing the Northfield Bench), Major Deykin and Mr. Salt (representing the Warwick and Birmingham Canal Company), Mr. J.G. Perser and Mr. J. Whitehouse (representing the Northfield Overseers), and Mr. H. Whitewell (Birmingham Y.M.C.A.). The various departments of the Birmingham Battery Company's Works, of which the deceased was a director, were represented by the following employees: T. Evans, T. Stokes, J. Bryan, H. Smith, D. Smith, S.W. Hopkins, H. Connoy, T. Jones, W. Perry, W. Partridge, W.H. Stephens, W. Brearley, W. Travis, E.H. Baker, R.S. Ormond, E. Sanders, F.G. Ganders, A. Morris, E.F. Barlow, J. Usher, and J. Overton.

Public References

Before the commencement of the business at Kings Heath Police Court on Wednesday, Mr. G.F. Lyndon, the presiding justice, referred to the loss sustained by the death of Mr. Thomas Gibbins. The deceased gentlemen, Mr. Lyndon remarked, was widely known in the Selly Oak district, especially on account of the good work he had done for that part of the county. Some years ago Mr. Gibbins was chairman of the District Council, and as such occupied a seat on the Bench for

Appendix I. The Gibbins Family, Donors of Selly Oak Park

his year of office, after which he was appointed permanently to the bench of magistrates. He did not attend very often, but he was a most conscientious man in the way he carried out his duties. He (Mr Lyndon) was sure he expressed the feeling of the Court when he said that the Bench and the officials condoled and sympathised sincerely with the relatives in the great loss they had sustained.

Mr. J.J. Tomson said he should like to associate himself with the expressions of sympathy of the chairman and regret at the death of Mr. Gibbins.

At a meeting on Tuesday of the Kings Norton Education Committee the Chairman (Councillor T. Quinney) said they had heard with deep regret of the painfully sudden death of a gentleman who not long ago was a colleague of theirs – Mr. Thomas Gibbins. Many of them had known him for a number of years with an intimate personal relationship, while to others he had been known better as a public man, but whether they had known him in his private life or his public capacity he was sure they would all feel that the community had suffered a heavy loss in his death. His conscientiousness and high-mindedness were conspicuous in all that he did. The speaker concluded by moving a vote of condolence with the family and an expression of the committee's appreciation of the services which he rendered in his public capacity – Canon Barnard seconded and Mr. J.W.B. Brown supported the resolution, which was carried in silence.

The Vacant Offices.

Two places become vacant by the death of Mr. Gibbins, one on the Board of Guardians and the other on the County Council., and upon formal notice being given on the prescribed form steps have to be taken by the responsible official in each case for filling the posts. No definite step, as far as we know, has been taken in regard to the Edgbaston vacancy on the Board of Guardians, but at Selly Oak the subject of who is to succeed to the County Council vacancy has been busily engaging the attention of a number of gentlemen interested in the public affairs of the locality. Mr. W.W. Gibbins (nephew of the deceased) has been asked to allow himself to be nominated, but business considerations render him unable to accede to the request.

Appendix II

THE PARK KEEPER, JOSIAH THOMAS HORTON (1863-1940)

Josiah Thomas Horton was born in Harborne, Staffordshire, on 10th July 1863, the second son of John Horton, age 25 years, and his wife, Maria Thompson, age 28 years. At the time he had one brother, John William, who was about three years old. They were an established Harborne family. He was christened at St Peter's Church[69], Harborne (Church Register No. 318) on 3 September 1863; his father was a silversmith.

There were soon another two sisters and two brothers:

- Susannah M Horton, born about 1865, in Harborne;
- Annie Horton, born about 1867, in Harborne;
- Charles Henry Horton, born about 1869, in Harborne; and
- Ernest Horton, born about 1870, in Harborne.

So by the time of the 1871 census, Josiah Horton was 7 years old and living with his parents and five siblings, in Harborne.

1871 census Civil Parish of Harborne, Eccl. Parish of St John's – RG 10/3085 No street or house number given.					
John Horton	Head	M	32	Silversmith	Staffordshire Harborne,
Maria Horton	Wife	M	35		Birmingham,
John W. Horton	Son		9	Scholar	Staffordshire Harborne,
Josiah T. Horton	Son		7	Scholar	Staffordshire Harborne,
Susannah M. Horton	Dau		6	Scholar	Staffordshire Harborne,
Annie Horton	Dau		4	Scholar	Staffordshire Harborne,
Charles H. Horton	Son		2		Staffordshire Harborne,
Ernest Horton	Son		7mo		Staffordshire Harborne.

---

69 Data from the microfilm records from St Peter's Parish Church, Harborne in the Archive & Heritage Section, Central Library, Birmingham.

APPENDIX II. THE PARK KEEPER, JOSIAH THOMAS HORTON (1863-1940)

Another two sisters and a brother arrived:

- Lilian Horton, born about 1873, in Harborne,
- Bertram Horton, born about 1877, in Harborne; and
- May Horton, born about 1879, in Harborne.

The family had experienced tragedy. There had been another brother, Alfred Horton, born in January 1875 but sadly he died on 24 September in the same year.

So at the 1881 census, Josiah, listed as Thomas, was 17 years old. He was still living with his parents at High Street, Harborne, and now eight siblings. He was working as a Grocer's Assistant, as were his next two sisters – I assume in their father's business, since John Horton senior was by this time a Grocer.

1881 census
Harborne, Staffordshire – RG 11/2959
High street – but no house number given.

John Horton	Head	M	42	Grocer	Staffordshire Harborne,
Maria Horton	Wife	M	45		Birmingham,
John W. Horton	Son	U	19	Stone Mason	Staffordshire Harborne,
Thomas Horton	Son	U	17	Grocers Assistant	Staffordshire Harborne,
Susannah M. Horton	Dau	U	16	Grocers Assistant	Staffordshire Harborne,
Ann Horton	Dau	U	14	Grocers Assistant	Staffordshire Harborne,
Charles Horton	Son		12	Scholar	Staffordshire Harborne,
Earnest Horton	Son		10	Scholar	Staffordshire Harborne,
Lilian Horton	Dau		8	Scholar	Staffordshire Harborne,
Bertram Horton	Son		4	Scholar	Staffordshire Harborne,
May Horton	Dau		2	Scholar	Staffordshire Harborne.

In 1883 Josiah's oldest brother, John William, emigrated with his new wife, Isabella Jane Tooth, to Brisbane in Australia, as a stonemason working on the railway – only to be met with a tragic series of events – the loss of his first child, and then shortly afterwards his wife. He remained in Brisbane and married the Australia born daughter of Prussian immigrants a little while later. They had two children before John died within six years of being married and when he was still only 32 years old.

Sometime between 1881 (the last census) and 1885 (when he was married), Josiah changed his work from being an assistant grocer to a gardener.

Josiah Thomas Horton married Edith Grove on 15 February 1885 at St Peter's Parish Church, Harborne. They were 21 and 20 years old respectively. Josiah was a gardener at the time of their marriage.

The detail copied from their marriage certificate is:

1885 – Marriage solemnized at Harborne in the Parish of Harborne in the County Borough of Staffordshire.
Entry No 393. Feb 15, 1885

Josiah Thomas Horton, 21, Bachelor, Gardener, Harborne. Father's name – John Horton, Jeweller.

Edith Grove, 20, Spinster, Harborne. Father's name – Samuel Grove, Joiner. Married in the Parish Church according to the Rites and Ceremonies of the Established Church after Banns by Frederick Roberts, Curate.

This marriage was solemnised between us – Josiah Thomas Horton; Edith Grove – in the presence of – Samuel Grove (i.e. Edith's father), Susannah Maria Horton (i.e. Josiah's sister).

This marriage is recorded in the District of Kings Norton in the 2nd Quarter of 1885 (Edith Grove is listed in the record though Josiah Horton is not). (Volume 6c, p [56]47. See: England and Wales, Civil Registration Index: 1837-1900, via – www.ancestry.com/.)

It looks as though Edith was a pregnant bride for their first child was born by the middle of 1885:

- Edith May Horton, born about 1885, in Harborne; christened at St Peter's Parish Church Harborne, on 5 Jul 1885 (Church Register No. 219); perhaps named after her mother; her father was a Gardener.

More children followed:

- John (aka Jack) Horton, born about 1886, in Harborne; christened at St Peter's Parish Church, Harborne, on 3 Jul 1886 (Church Register No. 475); perhaps named after his grandfather; his father was a Gardener;
- **Herbert Horton (my grandfather)**, born on 28 February 1889, in Harborne; christened at St Peter's Parish Church, Harborne, on 13 May 1891 (at the same time as his sister Ethel – see following) (Church Register No. 157); his father was a Gardener; and
- Ethel Ann(i)e Horton, born 1891, just 3 weeks before the census, in Harborne; christened at St Peter's Parish Church, Harborne, on 13 May 1891 (at the same time as her brother Herbert – see foregoing) (Church Register No. 159); her father was a Gardener;

By the time of the 1891 census, Josiah (listed as Thomas) Horton, age 27 years was living with his wife, Edith, in Tennal Road, Harborne. Susannah, Josiah's sister, and her husband, recently married, were visiting – perhaps to see the new baby or to help with her care. The census only records two of the children – the younger ones, Herbert and Ethel. 5 year old Edith May was staying with her Grandparents Horton and appears in the census with them. 3 year old John was staying with his Grandparents Grove and appears in the census with them. Had these older two been farmed out to make way for the visiting aunt and uncle, or just to allow time for the new arrival and younger family to settle?

Appendix II. The Park Keeper, Josiah Thomas Horton (1863-1940)

1891 census image:
Civil Parish of Harborne; Eccl. Parish of St Peter's – RG12/2361
Tennal Road.

Thomas Horton	Head	M	27	Gardener, Employed	Staffs Harborne,
Edith Horton	Wife	M	26		Worcs Selly Oak,
Herbert Horton	Son		2		Staffs Harborne,
Ethel Horton	Daur		3 wks		Staffs Harborne,
George Morris	Brother in law	M	23	Railway Servant, Employed	Warks, Coventry
Maria Morris	Sister	M	26		Staffs Harborne.

Josiah's occupation at this time was Gardener. I know that he worked for some time at Queen's Park, Harborne, just around the corner from Tennal Road. There is an entry in the Birmingham City Council records that he was employed at Queen's Park Harborne on 2 January 1898, but left on 4 March 1898 to lay out Selly Oak Park for the separate Kings Norton & Northfield authority which did not join the City until its enlargement in November 1911

PARKS DEPARTMENT,
REGISTER OF PARKS EMPLOYEES AND OFFICIALS[70]

Register no.: 167
Name: Horton, Josiah Thomas
Date of Birth: 10.7.1863
Date of entering service of Parks Department: 1.11.1911
Park or Cemetery at which employed: Selly Oak
Grade (under Committee Minute No. 4634): Park Keeper
Rate of Pay: [£]2 – 19[s] – 7[d] [per week]
Nature of Emoluments (if any): House Fuel Light & Uniform
Remarks: Started Queens Park Harborne 2/1/1898 left 4/3/1898 to lay out Selly Oak Park for K[ings] N[orton] & N[orthfield] transferred on extension of City 1/11/1911

This is consistent with my research that indicates that Queen's Park Harborne was not purchased and developed until the late 1890's and was not officially opened until 5 October 1898. So prior to his service in the Park(s), where was Josiah a gardener?

Three more children – all girls – arrived during the next ten years:

- Dorothy (aka Dolly) Horton, born about 1897, in Harborne; christened at St Peter's Parish Church, Harborne, on 23 March 1898 (Church Register No. 54)

---

[70] Birmingham Library, Archive & Heritage Section – reference BCC Acc 1998/083.

at the same time as her sister Ina Gladys (see following); their father was a Gardener and they lived at 7 Tennal Road:
- Ina Gladys (aka Gladys) Horton, born about 1898, in Harborne; christened at St Peter's Parish Church, Harborne, on 23 March 1898 (Church Register No. 55) at the same time as her sister Dorothy (see foregoing); their father was a Gardener and they lived at 7 Tennal Road; and
- Marjorie Horton, born 1 January 1900, in Selly Oak (so far I have been unable to find her christening details).

There was also a house move, judging by the birthplaces of Gladys and Marjorie, sometime between 1898 and 1900. There was also a change of job for Josiah around this time. He was one of 33 applicants who were interviewed for the post of Park Keeper at the newly gifted Selly Oak Park in Gibbins Road (formerly Old Lane), Selly Oak. It was reported in the minute of the King's Norton and Northfield Urban District Council dated 29th March 1899 that Josiah had been successful and had been appointed the first Park Keeper at 24/- per week, on a month's notice, with residence at the Lodge, coat and cap provided. He was about 36 years of age. The Park would be formally opened on Easter Monday, 3rd April 1899.

At the 1901 census, he and his wife and six of their children were living at Gibbins Road, Selly Oak, Birmingham, and Josiah's occupation was a Park Keeper, "working at home". They were living in the newly constructed Park Lodge at Selly Oak Park; it still has the date 1899 clearly engraved in the stonework on the side of the house. Once again, as at the time of the previous census, their eldest daughter, Edith May, was residing with her grandparents Horton at 253 High Street, Harborne. I have not been able to discover whether this was a coincidence, or whether she lived there as a permanent arrangement.

1901 census image:
Village of Selly Oak (part of); Eccl. Parish of St Mary's – RG13/2809
Gibbins Road

Thomas Horton	Head	M	37	Park Keeper, Working at Home	Harborne Staffs,
Edith Horton	Wife	M	36		Selly Oak Worcs,
John Horton	Son	S	16	Chocolate Moulder,	Harborne Staffs,
Herbert Horton	Son		12		Harborne Staffs,
Ethel Horton	Dau		10		Harborne Staffs,
Dorothy Horton	Dau		4		Harborne Staffs,
Gladys Horton	Dau		3		Harborne Staffs,
Marjorie Horton	Dau		1		Selly Oak Worcs.

More girls were born:

- Freda Agatha Horton (aka Freda), born 18 November 1902, in Selly Oak; christened at St Mary's Church, Selly Oak, on 12 July 1905 (Church Register

Appendix II. The Park Keeper, Josiah Thomas Horton (1863-1940)

No. 4306)[71] at the same time as her sisters Phyllis and Clarice Irene (see following); their father was a Park Keeper and they lived at The Lodge, Selly Oak Park;

- Jesse Horton, born about 1903, in Selly Oak (- so far I have been unable to find her christening details);
- Phyllis Horton, born 11 February 1904, in Selly Oak; christened at St Mary's Church, Selly Oak, on 12 July 1905 (Church Register No. 4307) at the same time as her sisters Freda Agatha (see foregoing) and Clarice Irene (see following); their father was a Park Keeper and they lived at The Lodge, Selly Oak Park;
- Clarice Irene Horton, born about 30 April 1905, in Selly Oak; christened at St Mary's Church, Selly Oak, on 12 July 1905 (Church Register No. 4308) at the same time as her sisters Freda Agatha and Phyllis (see foregoing); their father was a Park Keeper and they lived at The Lodge, Selly Oak Park. Clarice died in March 1906, aged only 11 months, and was buried on 2 April 1906 in what would become her parent's grave at Lodge Hill Cemetery, Selly Oak.
- Kathleen Horton, born on 13 March 1907, in Selly Oak; christened at St Mary's Church, Selly Oak, on 8 April 1907 (Church Register No. 4585); her father was a Park Keeper and they lived at The Lodge, Selly Oak Park; and
- Twins Madge and Mary Horton, born 20 May 1910, in Selly Oak; christened at St Mary's Church, Selly Oak, on 2 July 1910 (Church Register, no reference number); their father was a Park Keeper and they lived at Park Lodge, Gibbins Road, Selly Oak. Madge would be the fourth person buried (on 26 March 1956) in the family grave after she died on 22 March 1956 (i.e. Clarice Irene first, father second, mother third and Madge fourth).

By the 1911 census Josiah and Edith were well established at the Park Lodge in Gibbins Road, and there were 9 daughters, ranging in age from 20 years to 10 months, living with them in a house with a kitchen and 5 rooms in total. The census records that 17 children had been born to them during their 26 years of marriage; 13 were still living, 4 had died (clearly I still have to find the record for two more!). Josiah was listed as the Park Superintendent in the employ of the Urban District Council.

1911 census image:
Park Lodge, Gibbins Road, Selly Oak

Josiah Thomas Horton	Head	47	Park Superintend. Urban Dist. Council	Staffs, Harborne
Edith Horton	Wife	46		Worcs, Selly Oak
Ethel Horton	Dau	20	French Polisher Chad Valley Works	Staffs, Harborne
Dorothy Horton	Dau	14	Chocolate Worker Bournville Works	Staffs, Harborne

---

[71] Archive Section of the Birmingham Central Library, Microfilm 220.

Gladys Horton	Dau	13	School	Staffs, Harborne
Marjorie Horton	Dau	11	School	Worcs. Selly Oak
Jessie Horton	Dau	9	School	Worcs. Selly Oak
Freda Horton	Dau	8	School	Worcs. Selly Oak
Phyllis Horton	Dau	7	School	Worcs. Selly Oak
Kathleen Horton	Dau	4		Worcs. Selly Oak
Madge Horton	Dau	10 months		Worcs. Selly Oak
Mary Horton	Dau	10 months		Worcs. Selly Oak

Clearly this was a large family – 2 sons and 11 daughters still living – not too dissimilar from the large clutch that Josiah had himself grown up in, and indeed Edith's family of origin was not small. However there would be a strange twist of history. Despite the great fecundity, the Horton name through Josiah, would end – for whilst both his sons, Jack and Herbert, had children, they would all be females. Of course when any of Josiah's daughters or granddaughters married they would take their new husband's name; there was no continuation in this line of the Horton name – despite so many offspring!

Josiah was the Park Keeper at Selly Oak Park for about 30 years. The marriage certificate for his son, Herbert, on 24 December 1919, includes the detail that Josiah was a Corporation Park Keeper.

A Mr. T. Horton is mentioned in a number of reports. I don't know whether this is Josiah Thomas Horton, or another. I am inclined to believe it was my great grandfather – he was listed as Thomas Horton in the 1881, 1891 and 1901 census – see foregoing.

Mr. T. Horton is found in connection with:

- the Selly Oak Gymnastic Club (South Birmingham Chronicle, 1st November 1902) – "assistant secretary, Mr. T. Horton";
- the annual Selly Oak and Bournbrook Children's Festival held in the park (see earlier main text) – various reports in the weekly Birmingham News over the years;
- the Horticultural Show, 1904 – prize winner in two classes of potatoes (see Birmingham News, August 16th, 1904);
- the Flower Show on behalf of the Relief Society, 1904 – prize winner for cucumbers (see Birmingham News, October 1st, 1904);
- the Horticultural Show held in the park in 1907 (again see earlier main text) – a prize winner;
- an attendee at a dinner given in mourning of the felling of the Oak Tree in May 1909 (see earlier text);
- a committee member of the Selly Oak and Bournbrook Horticultural Society during 1909 (see the report of that year's show in the Birmingham News, 7th August 1909);
- the Horticultural Show held in the Station Hotel, Bournbrook (Birmingham News, 18th September 1909) – prize winner for potatoes and parsnips;

Appendix II. The Park Keeper, Josiah Thomas Horton (1863-1940)

- the Boot Fund Ball, in each of 1909, 1910 and 1911 – i) "The hall was tastefully decorated by Mr. T. Horton, with evergreens, shrubs, etc." (Birmingham News, 6th November 1909); ii) "The hall was very tastefully decorated by Mr. Horton and Mr. Dunn." (Birmingham News, 31st December 1910); iii) "The stewards were: ..... Mr. and Mrs. T. Horton, ..." – (Birmingham News, 25th February, 1911) – "The committee to whom every credit is due for the satisfactory arrangements, was constituted as follows: – .... and T.J. Horton.";
- a committee member of the Selly Oak and Bournbrook Poor Children's Christmas Tree Fund (Birmingham News, 31st December, 1910; and 2nd April, 1911);
- the Nurses Ball, 1910 and 1911 – i) ".... and the following ladies assisted with the refreshments and in other ways:- Mesdames ...., T. Horton, ..."; "The committee who had charge of the arrangements, were:- Messrs ...., T. Horton, ..." (Birmingham News, 19th February 1910); ii) "They also heartily thank ...., Mr. Horton, and the others who helped to decorate the hall: also to .... Mrs Horton, ..., who so kindly assisted at the refreshment stall" (Birmingham News, 2nd April, 1910); iii) "Considerably over 200 persons were present, and these included .... Mrs. Horton ...."; "Great credit for the success of the function is due to the committee, which is constituted as follows: – Messrs. ...., T. Horton, ..." (Birmingham News, 18th February, 1911);
- attended the second annual Old Residents' Dinner on Tuesday, 31st May, 1910 at the Bournbrook Hotel. Amongst the entertainments were "Messrs S. Grove, H. Short and H. Withers (handbell ringers), ... (Birmingham News, 4th June 1910) (Nb. Samuel Grove was Thomas Horton's brother in law.);
- a steward at a swimming gala at the Selly Oak baths on 4th July 1910 – his son John Horton was also a steward. (Birmingham News, 9th July 1910);
- the Horticultural Show held in a field in Gibbins Road (owned by Mr. A.P. Marsh, of Weoley Park Farm) in 1911 – Prizewinner i) 2nd prize in "Five varieties vegetables"; ii) 3rd prize in "Cabbage" (Birmingham News, 19th August 1911);
- at a complimentary dinner given to "Mr. Walter Barnes of Frederick Road, Selly Oak, who is leaving for Australia, was entertained to dinner at the Oak Hotel on Friday last" (Birmingham News, 18th November, 1911).
- with his wife, assisted at a function at the Selly Oak Baths when 400 old people were entertained to dinner (Birmingham News, 30th December 1911).

Family and community life was obviously busy. There are also reports of their children's activities:

- Birmingham News, 9th April, 1910 – Under the section "Selly Oak and Bournbrook" there is a report – "Excelsior Band of Hope Annual Meeting – .... Afterwards an operetta entitled "Jack Frost" was very well rendered by the children. .... The principal parts were well taken by the following:- .... "Fairy Sunshine", **Dorothy Horton**; .... "Peggy Summer", **Ina Horton**; ....". "The children taking part in the chorus were – **Marjory, Jessie and Dorothy Horton**, ...";

- Birmingham News, 8th April 1911 – Under the section "Selly Oak and Bournbrook" there is a report of a meeting of the "Excelsior Band of Hope". Towards the end of the report: "Afterwards an operetta by A.L. Cowley, entitled "A merry party" was very successfully performed by the children, the choruses being given with fine effect by a well trained choir. The skipping rope chorus, display of fancy skipping, and "My own dear home", were especially well rendered and well merited the applause given. The chief parts were sustained by the following;- "Sister Flora", Kathleen Davis; "Mistress Mary", **Dorothy Horton**; "Old Woman", Kate Bayliss; "Miss Muffett", **Gladys Horton**; ……………. The dresses of the children were very effective and credit is due to the parents for the trouble taken in providing them. ……………."

Up until 1911 Josiah was not only the Park Keeper at Selly Oak Park, but he also gradually had more and more supervision of the other parks and recreation grounds administered by the Kings Norton and Northfield District Council to whose Baths, Parks, and Cemeteries Committee he reported regularly. He also had oversight of trees in the streets in Selly Oak. At the end of 1911, Kings Norton and Northfield was subsumed into the City of Birmingham, under the terms of the Birmingham Extension Order 1911, and Josiah found himself responsible just for Selly Oak Park, and in a longer reporting line to the City Council's Parks Committee, through its Superintendent, Mr Morter.

Kelly's Directory of Birmingham lists "Horton, Josiah T., Park Keeper, Selly Oak Park, Gibbins Road, Selly Oak" in all the volumes it produced from 1901 until 1928. The Lodge was eventually numbered 26 Gibbins Road. By the 1929 directory there was another Park Keeper at the Lodge; Josiah had retired from that post; he would have been 65 years old by this time. On 6th May 1929, and on behalf of the Parks Committee, the Lord Mayor presented illuminated copies of resolutions in respect of long service to four ex-employees of the Parks Department; one of them went to Josiah who had given 30 years service.

After Josiah retired from the park in 1928, he and Edith must have lodged somewhere (I have not yet discovered where) before they moved to 133 Hay Green Lane, Bournville, Birmingham at sometime between 1933 and 1934. From the Street Directory of 1933 it might be assumed that No 133 was a newly built house; it and its neighbours were listed in 1934 (when it was occupied by Josiah Horton), but not in 1933.

During their lifetime they would have seen their children married; and enjoyed the company of many grandchildren:

- Edith May (aka May) Horton, married John Skett
  - John Skett
- John (aka Jack) Horton, married Gertrude "Unknown",
  - Edith Horton
    and later married Winnifred "Unknown"
- Herbert Horton, married Florence Horton, on 24 December 1919 at the Kings Norton Register Office.

Appendix II. The Park Keeper, Josiah Thomas Horton (1863-1940)

- - Josephine Irene Horton (4 October 1920, at Station Road, Kings Norton, Birmingham)
  - Ruth Mary Horton (12 May 1929 at 40 Vimy Road, Billesley, Birmingham)
- Ethel Horton, married James Stone
  - Robert Thomas Stone
- Dorothy Horton, married Victor H Davies
  - Dorothy Davies
- Ina Gladys Horton, remained a spinster
- Marjorie Horton, married William Chapman
  - John Chapman
- Freda Horton, married Stanley Lester
  - Morris Lester
- Jesse Horton, married Henry E. Skinner
  - Valerie Margaret Skinner
  - John Skinner
- Phyllis Horton, remained a spinster
- Kathleen Horton, married Ernest Venn
  - Terence Venn
  - June Venn
- Madge Horton, remained a spinster
- Mary Horton, married Harry Nash in 1936 at St Francis Church, Bournville
  - Anthony Nash
  - Neal Nash
  - Ian Nash

Josiah died on 24 February 1940, age 76 years, at Hay Green Lane – from the effect of an anthrax carbuncle on his neck – the anthrax was contracted through woollen socks rubbing and causing a sore on his foot. Josiah died before I was born. He was buried at Lodge Hill Cemetery in the grave[72] that had been opened for their daughter Clarice Irene in 1906.

Edith continued another ten years. I can just remember being taken as a small boy to see Great Grandma Edith Horton at Hay Green Lane. There was a parrot[73] chained to a stand in the living room; it would sing and chatter away from time to time. I knew my great grandmother as "Nanny with the Polly Parrot". She died on 16 February 1950, age 85 years, at Hay Green Lane and was buried in the family grave at Lodge Hill Cemetery on 21 February 1950. A memorial card was printed:

---

[72] Grave No. 196 in Section C9 of the Cemetery – information obtained in writing from the Cemetery Office. I have searched the area but have not been able to find a grave marked 196, despite being told there are posts and a kerbset on the grave. (I found Grave No. 192.)

[73] Terry Venn told me that the parrot's name was Pardoe.

In Loving Memory

of

Edith Horton,

Who fell asleep Feb 16th, 1950,
Aged 85 years.

Laid to rest in Family Grave at Lodge Hill Cemetery.